THE FALL OF

PARIS

ALSO BY HERBERT R. LOTTMAN

Albert Camus: A Biography

*The Left Bank: Writers, Artists and Politics from the Popular
Front to the Cold War*

Pétain, Hero or Traitor

The Purge

Flaubert: A Biography

Colette: A Life

THE FALL OF
PARIS

JUNE 1940

HERBERT R. LOTTMAN

HarperCollins*Publishers*

HarperCollins books may be purchased for educational, business, or sales promotional use. For information, please write: Special Markets Department, HarperCollins Publishers, Inc., 10 East 53rd Street, New York, NY 10022.

FIRST EDITION

Designed by Jessica Shatan

LIBRARY OF CONGRESS CATALOGING-IN-PUBLICATION DATA

Lottman, Herbert R.
  The fall of Paris:June 1940/by Herbert R. Lottman.
    p. cm.
  Includes index.
  ISBN 0-06-016520-0 (cloth)
  1. World War, 1939–1945—Campaigns—France—Paris. 2. Paris
(France)—History—1940–1944. 3. World War, 1939–1945—Campaigns—
Western. I. Title.
D762.P3L68 1992
940.54'21436—dc20   92-52608

92 93 94 95 96 AC/RRD 10 9 8 7 6 5 4 3 2 1

France played its part. It consisted in offering itself to be crushed, since the world decided to arbitrate rather than to help or fight, and to see itself buried for a time in silence. When you attack, some men have to be in the front line. They almost always die. But for the attack to succeed, the front line must die.

—ANTOINE DE SAINT-EXUPÉRY, *Flight to Arras*

It was the end of a world in which Paris was supreme, in which France was alive, in which there was a breath of freedom. There was oil in the blackened air, and soot in the rain, and the wretched city was pressed upon by the lowering sky.

—ELLIOT PAUL, *The Last Time I Saw Paris*

The end of Paris is the end of the world; for all our lucidity, can we accept that?

—VICTOR SERGE, *Mémoires d'un révolutionnaire*

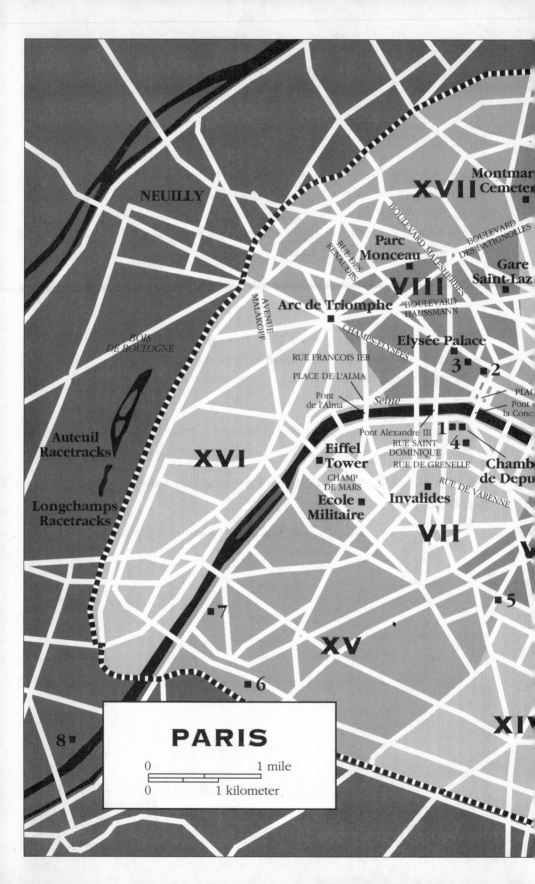

■ Porte de la Villette

1. Ministry of Foreign Affairs
2. American Embassy
3. British Embassy
4. Ministry of Defense and War
5. Gare Montparnasse
6. Air Ministry
7. Citroën Plant
8. Renault Plant
9. Gare d'Austerlitz

XVIII

Gare du Nord ■

DE CHÂTEAUDUN

Gare de l'Est ■

XIX

X

X

BELLEVILLE

II

ONCORDE

PLACE DE LA
RÉPUBLIQUE

I

III

lais de Justice

RUE DES ROSIERS

XI

XX

Hôtel-de-Ville ■

IV

OULEVARD
T-GERMAIN

RUE
UFLOT

■ 9

Gare de Lyon ■

MICHEL

Panthéon ■

Seine

XII

V

■ Santé Prison

XIII

BOIS
DE VINCENNES

Contents

Illustrations follow page 370

MAPS

THE FALL OF

PARIS

PROLOGUE

Eight months of declared war without serious fighting ended for France on the short night of May 9–10, 1940, as German armies violated the frontiers of three neutral neighbors, the Netherlands, Belgium, and Luxembourg. Ignoring border defenses, German aircraft released paratroops over the industrial Dutch heartland, while other airborne units dispatched to Belgium took fortifications and bridges from their unprotected rear. At first light, Hermann Goering's Luftwaffe sent waves of planes over the surprised neutrals, creating confusion and panic.

Awakened shortly after midnight by his aide-de-camp, French commander-in-chief General Maurice Gamelin studied first reports from French military attachés of "unusual movements" in the northeast. Soon information began arriving from closer in, of Luftwaffe attacks on French military airfields below the war zone. No doubt about it: the offensive was under way. The Second World War had come to France.

French prime minister Paul Reynaud was roused from sleep at four that morning to take a call from Belgium's ambassador to Paris. The Germans were justifying the invasion of Belgium with the allegation that French and British troops were themselves ready to march into that neutral nation; tiny Belgium, under fire and in shock, formally requested French assistance. The request was expected. General Gamelin made that clear in his order of the day: "The attack that we had foreseen since last October was launched this morning. Germany has undertaken a struggle to death against us. The watchwords for France and its allies are courage, energy, confidence."

Parisians heard that on the first radio news of the day. They also heard Premier Reynaud:

> Three free nations, the Netherlands, Belgium, Luxembourg, were invaded during the night by the German army. They have called to the Allied armies for help. This morning . . . our soldiers, the soldiers of freedom, crossed the frontier. . . .

Just a month earlier, on April 10, General Gamelin had confided to Maxime Weygand, commander of French forces in the eastern Mediterranean, that he ardently desired such an enemy offensive, for this would make it possible for him to carry out his own strategy. He planned to rush French and British troops north into Belgium to take up positions on the river Dyle, from which defense line the French could then mount a vigorous counterattack.

At the daily newspaper *Paris-Soir,* a military specialist shared General Gamelin's satisfaction. "That's it," he told his colleagues. "Hitler has made his mistake."

"Three mistakes like that and he's in Paris," replied playwright Henry Bernstein, who had been visiting the newspaper to get the latest news.

1

PRELUDE TO THE FIRST DAY

Could this be war? It was a question often asked in the winter and spring of 1940, especially if one was French or British. To Hitler's aggression against Poland at the beginning of September 1939, France and Britain had responded with an immediate declaration of hostilities; then very little happened. True, in a gesture of solidarity with embattled Poland so far away, French forces advanced during the first month of war toward the German front in the Saar basin. But then they drew back again, to more secure positions behind the Maginot Line, that barrier of imposing fortifications along the frontier with Germany, which, then and forever, was to symbolize immobility.

After that, nothing. It was as if the French were waiting for the Germans to move, as they had moved in 1914. Less than a generation earlier, Kaiser Wilhelm's Germany had invaded neutral Belgium the day after declaring war on France, advancing rapidly south and west to be stopped at the threshold of the Paris region—the Marne. Then followed four years of offensives and counteroffensives over tortured French soil at the cost of the best young men on both sides, and that included the best young men of Britain until the best young men of the United States of America added their strength to break the stalemate and end the war.

But the time is May 1940, and the French and British are again pitted against the Germans (watched by a benevolent neutral across the seas, the United States). Even the Russians, who began the first War as allies of the west, are now neutral and worse—bedfellows of the Germans, thanks to Stalin's nonaggression pact with Hitler. Troops sent across the English Channel by the United Kingdom camp alongside French troops in France, British planes park on French airfields, the Allies share patrols on the high seas. It seems that a delicate balance of power makes it unwise for either side to move from its positions. On the French side this is called strategy; the Germans use the time to consolidate their victory over Poland in preparation for other victories in the west.

These long months of immobility became known in France as the *drôle de guerre,* the odd or funny war; in English, one preferred the harsher "phony war." Bored soldiers and parked tanks, big guns usually silent (except for symbolic barrages). Habits became ingrained, and the character of the war hardly seemed to change in April 1940 when Hitler's forces executed a long-planned Scandinavian campaign, beginning with Denmark, an easy border crossing for the assailants; the one-day invasion is barely a footnote in history books. Then a crossing to Norway, to prove that the Nazis could outdo the British on their own ground (the sea). The surprised, overconfident Allies could soon offer Norway nothing but hospitality for the king and exile government.

And still all was quiet on the eastern front.

For Pierre Mendès France, a young member of Parliament representing a rural constituency in Normandy, then serving with the French air force in the Mediterranean theater, the return to Paris early in May, after nearly eight months in a state of permanent alert in Beirut, came as a shock. Parisians seemed to be settled into their phony war as if in a state of peace. That signified relative comfort, few restrictions. The best opinion was that time was on France's side, that the war would be won without the shedding of blood. One did what one could to make the waiting comfortable.

Someone told Mendès France about a Rosebush Fund for the Maginot Line, a good work of kindhearted Frenchwomen hoping to bring a touch of poetry to the frontier forts. One could, if one was a Very Important Person, visit the forts with a retinue of photographers. A salvo was fired for the Duke of Windsor; American correspondent Dorothy Thompson was allowed to set off a 75-millimeter cannon, pride of France.

Rank-and-file Parisians began the war obeying air raid sirens and carrying gas masks (and occasionally putting them on) as they filed down to the nearest shelters. Patriots answered newspaper appeals for the donation of scrap metal and watchdogs for military patrols. Maurice Chevalier's gift of an old motorcar was a perfect story for the illustrated press. An advertisement for hair oil suggested that it be sent to soldiers at the front because wearing a helmet or a kepi could cause hair to fall out.

On the declaration of war in September 1939, the theaters of Paris were closed down. Then, when the nature of the war became apparent, they opened again. "Paris must remain Paris," explained, Maurice Chevalier, "so that soldiers on leave can find a bit of Parisian charm despite all." Theater programs contained maps pinpointing the location of the nearest shelters, and the number of spectators was limited to the number of places available in nearby cellars. But the variety of offerings remained impressive. Take the listing for the fatal day, May 10 (obviously prepared before anyone knew what would happen). The repertory troupe of the Comédie Française announced a regular performance, its sister theater on the Left Bank, the Odéon, a preview of a new play. The press listed twenty-six scheduled events for that evening, including the famous actor Louis Jouvet in Jean Giraudoux's play *Ondine*. Among twenty-two cabaret or music hall shows, one was called "Drôle de Revue," an obvious allusion to the warless war. Not to forget forty-three advertised movies, including two that would last as long as free Paris did, *Ninotchka* and *The Hunchback of Notre Dame*— starring vehicles, respectively, for Greta Garbo and Charles Laughton.

A writer who studied the drôle side of the *drôle de guerre*, Philippe Richer, found that soldiers at the front took this life-as-usual attitude of Parisians badly. They knew about the crowded restaurants and the queues outside cinemas. Those who should have felt guilty but clearly did not sometimes thought of men in uniform as the idlers. One soldier at the front, Jean-Paul Sartre, recorded a neat example of this attitude. A shopkeeper in uniform gets a letter from his wife asking him to deal with some paperwork. "You write to the customer," she says, "since you don't have anything to do. I've got my hands full."

Of course one missed loved ones posted to distant forts and garrisons, and at times women flouted the rules to travel to the front to visit their men. Some stayed. Officers occasionally found ways to drive to Paris in their own automobiles for a spot of leave, authorized or not. What tension there was derived from real or imagined enemies on the home front.

Thus the government waged a relentless crusade against France's Communists, in reaction to the entente between the Soviet Union and Nazi Germany, an entente that allowed Stalin to follow Hitler into Poland to divide the spoils. The Communist Party and affiliated organizations were banned on September 26, 1939, a month after the closing down of the ubiquitous Communist press. Violations of the ban were punishable with one to five years of prison. Leading Communist personalities went underground. Party chief Maurice Thorez was called up for military service but managed to slip away, to sit out the war in Moscow. In Paris a clandestine cell published an underground edition of the banned official Party daily, *L'Humanité,* beginning on October 26, 1939. In that and later issues the Communists argued that France's war against Germany was not the workers' war. The French government expelled the Soviet ambassador on March 28, 1940. In a telegram congratulating Stalin for the Soviet-German peace agreement, he had called the French and British "warmongers."

This is not to say that the *drôle de guerre* was only talk. On February 26, after dark, enemy reconnaissance planes flew over the Paris region, and French antiaircraft batteries opened fire. One of the French shells fell in Paris's Fifth District, near the Censier subway station on Rue de Mirbel. The shell dug a hole a foot and a half wide, damaging the elementary school on Rue Monge and a café. Two women were killed, a man suffered an amputated leg, and they were not the only victims. There had been no warning, no siren. That night there were sirens— but no planes.

PARISIANS, DON'T REMAIN
IN THE STREET
WHEN YOU HEAR ANTIAIRCRAFT GUNS

was the obvious conclusion drawn by a headline.

Art was getting better protection than bodies. Ever since the Other War, with its memories of Boche vandals, museum curators had resolved not to allow France's artistic treasures to fall into enemy hands, or to be damaged or destroyed. There was detailed planning of which works of art would go where, who was to watch over them. Often a historical monument far from Paris was chosen as shelter for a more portable work.

The first alert came nearly a year before the declaration of war, at the time of Hitler's threat to Czechoslovakia in September 1938. Two days before the meeting in Munich of the British and French prime ministers with Hitler and Mussolini, the Louvre Museum dispatched a first convoy of trucks to the Renaissance castle of Chambord near the Loire River. The announcement of the signature of the Munich pact between the democracies and the dictators allowed the keepers of Paris art treasures to breathe more easily; the evacuation was canceled, although crates were left open, ready for packing, in exhibition galleries. Then the declaration of war on September 3, 1939, was the signal for a serious exodus. In the next four months between 150 and 200 truckloads of works of art went to Chambord, sometimes as a halfway house en route to more distant and thus surer refuge in one of fifteen castles-become-warehouses in southwest France. Rose Valland, then attached to the Jeu de Paume, the Paris home of the Impressionists, remembered that it was on October 3 that the twenty-ninth convoy drove off with the Louvre's most precious marbles, the Venus de Milo, Victoire de Samothrace, and Michelangelo's *Slaves*. Sculpture too heavy to move was left in place, protected by sandbags. Crates waiting to be loaded in the courtyard of the Louvre bore meaningless numbers so that bystanders couldn't guess which art treasure was being loaded. But some Parisians couldn't help thinking that art was flying off to safety, and they remained behind.

*   *   *

When the government thought about bodies, it was about feeding them. Although food was still plentiful, the likelihood of shortage was debated as early as February 1940. To prepare for rationing, a new census was undertaken. Bread, then a more basic food than it has since become, was the chief preoccupation of the planners. Henceforth, only a standard loaf was to be sold, none of the fancy twists some families preferred. Croissants were *not* banned. Restaurants could serve only 150 grams of bread per person with expensive meals; diners in bistros ordering cheaper meals had a right to 300 grams. Butter was not to be put on the table (a lesson many restaurants remembered long after the war). Shops specializing in pastry, chocolate, and candy were to remain closed on Tuesdays, Wednesdays, and Fridays, on which days pastry was also absent from restaurant menus. Alcoholic beverages couldn't be purchased or consumed in public on Tuesdays, Thursdays, and Saturdays.

Newspapers made it a point to remind readers of what their week would be like:

MONDAY Closing of butcher and cold-cut shops, including tripe and horsemeat shops.

TUESDAY Closing of butcher and cold-cut shops. No aperitifs or other alcoholic drinks served. Closing of pastry and candy shops.

WEDNESDAY No butcher or candy shops.

THURSDAY No alcohol.

FRIDAY No pastry or candy.

SATURDAY No alcohol.

SUNDAY No restrictions.

The problem was that nothing during the seemingly interminable phony war seemed urgent. When war did come at last, and the French reacted to it so slowly, a junior government officer, Max Brusset (chief assistant to Minister of Colonies Georges Mandel) was convinced that the inertia had its roots in the long months of waiting. As he put it, the phony war had served its purpose.

2

Thursday, May 9

The influential senator Jacques Bardoux, a staunch conservative hostile to the Popular Front governments of the 1930s but unshakably patriotic, kept a war diary. His entry for May 9 begins: "A peaceful prewar morning, a Paris green, calm, bustling, sunny." It was hard not to talk about the weather at that privileged moment. The month of May was to be one of the warmest observed by the national weather bureau since 1874, and one of the sunniest. Only four times in those sixty-six years of recorded weather reports had May produced more sunshine.

At the age of sixty-six, Jacques Bardoux was a retired professor of diplomatic history at the War College; on election to the Senate he got an immediate assignment to the Foreign Affairs Committee. He asked questions and he listened. That morning he heard about the cabinet crisis. Paul Reynaud, fed up with the way the war was being waged by Defense Minister Daladier and his protégé, General Gamelin, had threatened to resign as head of government.

Across the channel, Neville Chamberlain—the man of Munich who thought his pact with the dictators guaranteed peace in our time—was still his country's prime minister, ignoring the eloquent appeal of a fellow Conservative member of Parliament: "In the name of God, go!"

*   *   *

In the opinion of Dominique Leca, director of Paul Reynaud's office staff, the French parliamentary system failed to allow for decisive leadership by the prime minister (whose actual title was Chairman of the Council of Ministers). Even a pugnacious leader like Reynaud was not quite master of his ship. He could not simply decide to change his defense minister or the commander-in-chief and then do it. Yet few heads of government of the Third Republic had been as *determined* as he was to shake things up.

A man who knew the Premier well and who had dealt with him when Reynaud was finance minister couldn't help thinking of the caricatures by a wicked cartoonist who called himself Sennep, portraying Paul Reynaud as Mickey Mouse, for he did indeed look like Mickey. "Yet he doesn't lose an inch of his height, and his extraordinary vitality hasn't diminished despite the daily strains," noted diarist Robert de Saint Jean, author and civil servant. "The same mocking tone, the same vivacity in the way he looks at you, the same quick thinking; he looks ten years younger than his 61 years."

Like most politicians who made a name in Paris, Reynaud had provincial roots. He was born in Barcelonnette, a village in the southeast mountains, and attended one of Paris's most prestigious business schools. As early as 1930, this centrist politician had been finance minister, a post he held again in 1938. Reynaud had long been what Americans would later call a hawk on defense matters, and Charles de Gaulle, advocate of a striking force equipped with tanks, had won his ear as early as 1934. Reynaud was one of the rare political leaders to call for sanctions against Italy following Mussolini's attack on Ethiopia. He had opposed appeasement of Hitler at Munich (an act for which Edouard Daladier was in part responsible, if reluctantly). In a word, Paul Reynaud was a Cassandra of the prewar decade. He had seen the Second World War looming and sought to hasten preparations for it, breaking with more conservative political friends who favored appeasement of Hitler up to the day war broke out. When it came, France could not have had a better man at the helm. But now, on May 9, he was about to abandon his high charge.

He had followed developments in the Norway campaign with increasing dismay; he and not the passive, good-natured Daladier should have been minister of defense and war. Reynaud's conviction had been reinforced just a few days earlier by a letter from the front sent by Colonel de Gaulle, in which the outspoken officer had made a plea for a conversion of French armed forces to a tank strategy. That required a change in leadership, de Gaulle made clear. "Once again I say that the military corps, by a conformity inherent in its nature, will not reform itself alone. It's a question of state—the first of all questions." De Gaulle had already chosen his man. "You alone," he told Reynaud, "because of your position, your personality, the stand you have taken on the subject—taken alone, and for the past six years—can and should achieve this task."

But on the morning of May 9, Reynaud had marched into the office of the President of the Republic as early as he decently could to announce that he was about to create a cabinet crisis. Did he really have to? a worried Albert Lebrun asked him. After all, Daladier—a grassroots politician who was a village mayor and legislator representing France's deepest south, president of his party, and twice prime minister—remained a most popular figure, while General Gamelin was a favorite of the British ally. Yes, insisted Reynaud, he had to. He had the responsibility, and now he intended to obtain the power to make the decisions that cried out to be made.

Under the constitution of the Third Republic, which had governed France ever since the fall of Napoleon III, the French enjoyed the ultimate in parliamentary democracy, with a prime minister and cabinet answering to the lower chamber; the figurehead President of the Republic, elected by both houses, could only bow to prevailing winds. The multiplicity of political parties enhanced democracy but played havoc with stability, leading to frequent cabinet crises and changes of prime ministers. The elections of spring 1936—the last before the war—brought a left-oriented Popular Front to power (led by Socialists and Radical Socialists—who, despite their name, upheld traditional lay republican values; the Communists were not part of the government, but supported it). But between May 1936 and Paul Reynaud's accession to the premiership in March 1940, there had been four cabinets, two run by Socialist Léon Blum, two more by Radical Socialists. Only crisis and war would keep the present government from falling.

On return to his own office, Reynaud dispatched messengers with a call for an emergency session of the cabinet, to be held at his office in the Foreign Ministry on the Quai d'Orsay. One of his ministers, closet anarchist Anatole de Monzie, would tell his private diary that he couldn't guess why they were meeting just then. "The little prime minister wears his smile at once victorious and reticent," Monzie noted.

"Gentlemen," Reynaud began, "I must talk to you about the command situation." He spoke of errors committed in Norway, concluding with his feeling that General Gamelin had to be replaced as general-in-chief of French forces.

Daladier protested. There was no reason to blame Gamelin for what was happening in Norway, for the British were running that war. Reynaud, who was delighted to have an excuse to get rid of a politician who represented everything he detested about the Third Republic's obliging and ineffectual leadership, declared that their disagreement put an end to the cabinet; they should all consider themselves as having resigned. But because of the war emergency, ministers were asked to keep their resignations secret until a new government was formed and he could announce it.

That evening, William Christian Bullitt, the American ambassador just back from consultations in Washington, threw a dinner party at his residence on Place d'Iéna for Premier Reynaud—still premier despite his secret resignation. The guest list included Minister of Armament Raoul Dautry, Governor of the Bank of France Pierre Fournier, senior British officers including Air Marshal Arthur S. Barratt, and two of Bullitt's countrymen, war correspondents Vincent Sheean and Dorothy Thompson. Table talk turned on whether the Germans would attack during the course of the year. Minister Dautry thought not, and indeed the French arms production program was based on that assumption. Banker Fournier broke in: "If that is your theory then we are in greater danger than I suspected. The German attack could happen at any minute now and might well come in a matter of days."

One witness to the discussion, U.S. Counselor of Embassy Robert Murphy, listened in awe to these high-ranking officials who could entertain viewpoints so far apart. After dinner a small group, including one of the British officers, went on to the Hotel Meurice to continue their discussion in Dorothy Thompson's suite. The talk went on long past midnight; the British officer, thought Murphy the next morning, would have gotten back to his headquarters at Compiègne barely in time to discover that the German offensive was under way.

3

Friday, May 10

Adolf Hitler, who considered himself above all commander-in-chief of German military forces, personally approved the spring offensive against France and Belgium, the precise date depending on the outcome of German operations in Norway, and of course on meteorological conditions. Beginning on May 4, German units were advised that they would receive twenty-four hours' notice of the attack. The weather hadn't been favorable for the air offensive that was to decide the battle; then at last it improved. At 5:00 P.M on May 9, Hitler boarded the train that would take him to field headquarters near Münstereifel, on a height facing Belgium (and to which he gave the code name Felsennest: "Eyrie"). At nine the forecast continued to be satisfactory, so Hitler ordered the attack, transmitted down the line by the code word "Danzig."

By then, Joachim von Ribbentrop's Foreign Ministry had given final form to the white paper that was to justify the violation of Belgian and Dutch neutrality.

For the use of Paul Reynaud and his staff, his cabinet aide Maurice Dejean kept track of events at that dramatic moment. Dejean was now camping at Reynaud's office at the Foreign Ministry (for Reynaud was then both foreign minister and prime minister), but he'd get little sleep that night.

The first call came in just half an hour after midnight, this from the French minister to the Duchy of Luxembourg, Charles Tripier, who reported "unusual incidents" on Luxembourg's border with Germany. "Tourists" had been causing trouble.

At 1:00 A.M. the French ambassador to Brussels, Paul Bargeton, telephoned to announce that he was sending an urgent coded message, but then proceeded to give its substance on the phone. Both the Belgian and Dutch armies had reported "unusual activity" on their frontiers.

After that, silence. Until four, when Minister Tripier phoned again from Luxembourg to ask if he should burn secret files. (He should.) Fifteen minutes later the Brussels embassy phoned with the news that the Luxembourg frontier had indeed been crossed, with the loss of several local gendarmes. At 6:00 A.M., Jacques de Blesson, secretary at the French Legation in the Hague, telephoned from the Dutch Foreign Ministry there to report that German airborne troops had been dropped on Dutch territory; forts and airfields had been bombed. The Dutch immediately blew up bridges over the Meuse River, separating them from Germany, but the enemy was attempting a crossing in small rubber dinghies.

Fifteen minutes after that, Ambassador Bargeton called Emile Charvériat, political affairs director at the Foreign Ministry. He had been trying to get through for forty-five minutes, a delay that seemed suspicious to him. . . . In any case, the Germans had indeed launched an offensive against Belgium, whose government was now requesting French support under the terms of the Franco-Belgian mutual assistance pact.

At 6:17 A.M., Charvériat passed that news on to the War Ministry, and then told Premier Reynaud. The Belgian ambassador to France drove up to the Quai d'Orsay to confirm reports of the invasion of his country, handing over a formal Belgian request for assistance. At 6:25 the Dutch minister in Paris asked to speak to Reynaud; he too requested French aid. Five minutes later Tripier called again from Luxembourg. He had started driving to Paris but found the road blocked

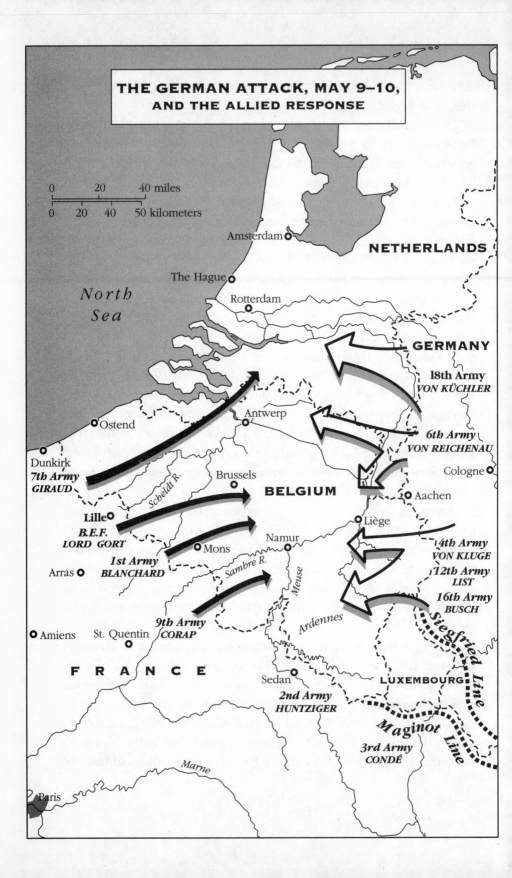

THE GERMAN ATTACK, MAY 9–10,
AND THE ALLIED RESPONSE

0   20   40 miles
0 20 40 50 kilometers

North Sea

NETHERLANDS

Amsterdam

The Hague

Rotterdam

GERMANY

18th Army
VON KÜCHLER

Ostend

Scheldt R.

Antwerp

6th Army
VON REICHENAU

Dunkirk

7th Army
GIRAUD

Brussels

BELGIUM

Cologne

Lille

B.E.F.
LORD GORT

Mons

Namur

Liège

Aachen

4th Army
VON KLUGE

Arras

1st Army
BLANCHARD

Sambre R.

Meuse

12th Army
LIST

16th Army
BUSCH

Amiens   St. Quentin

9th Army
CORAP

Ardennes

Siegfried Line

F R A N C E

Sedan

2nd Army
HUNTZIGER

LUXEMBOURG

Maginot Line

3rd Army
CONDÉ

Marne

Paris

by German parachutists, so he was back in his office; his American counterpart was with him. At Charvériat's instructions, Tripier raised an American flag over the French Legation, giving it the protection of a neutral state.

Officials at the Foreign Ministry heard the first German radio announcement of the attack at seven-thirty that morning, in the form of a communiqué proclaiming that because the French and British planned to invade Germany through Belgium and the Netherlands, with the encouragement of those neutral nations, the Germans had sent troops into the Netherlands, Belgium, and neighboring Luxembourg to thwart the Allied move. Listening to the German statement with Reynaud, Foreign Ministry officer Roland de Margerie suggested to the premier that Pope Pius XII be asked to issue a public condemnation of Germany's invasion of neutral nations, whose populations were largely Catholic. Reynaud agreed, adding that Belgium's King Léopold could also appeal to the Pope. Such religious and dynastic considerations might keep Mussolini from allying himself with the German Führer.

Standing beside his telephone as day broke in the sky of Paris, Reynaud realized that Adolf Hitler had forced his hand. Now he would have to remain in office, and he was obliged to hold on to do-nothing Maurice Gamelin as well; one could hardly replace "the clockmaker who had wound up the Belgian operation."

Later nearly everyone, even the usually noncommittal President Lebrun, would attribute the defeat at least in part to the "strategic error" perpetrated that morning, an error that had been carefully planned—the French march into Belgium. (General Gamelin was the "clockmaker" of that.) It was the first step in what military historian Colonel Adolphe Goutard called "the most lamentable campaign" in French history. Let it be said that Britain's official war historian, J. R. M. Butler, shows that the British High Command favored an Allied push into Belgium, and for Gamelin's reasons.

Colonel Paul de Villelume, who was then Premier Reynaud's chief military aide, was alerted by a telephone call from Reynaud's companion Hélène de Portes, who sometimes appeared to be as much a

political adviser as a hostess. After stopping off at the Quai to see
Reynaud, Villelume drove on to Gamelin's headquarters at Vincennes,
on Paris's eastern edge. There he discovered a general staff effusive in
its delight at the German attack. Privately, Villelume was surprised,
and concerned, because German planes were not attacking French
troops as they moved north into Belgium; the Germans were *allowing*
them in. He was convinced (or so he said later) that the enemy had
baited a trap.

Reynaud seemed to share his conviction. "Doesn't it trouble you,"
he asked Gamelin, "that the Allied armies are entering Belgium without being hit by the German air force?" Gamelin replied that he
wasn't worried at all—but Reynaud remarked that his face had red-
dened. If military men wondered why a poorly equipped and insufficiently trained French army was being moved out of easily defensible
positions to meet advancing enemy forces on territory that had been
neutral as recently as the day before, they didn't say so at the time.

That members of the government might learn of the German offensive
from a woman who was neither part of the political nor the military
chain of command surprised no one. They were used to the omnipres-
ence and omniscience, not to say omnipotence, of Countess Hélène de
Portes, who was already a legend by the tenth of May, although all but
invisible to the general public. In the minds of many who knew about
the countess but could only mention her in whispers, her influence on
the chief of government was pernicious. It's hard to know what to
believe, for Reynaud was to show himself to be France's most determined war leader. Yet in the legend Hélène de Portes was a defeatist.

She was born Hélène Rebuffet, daughter of a successful contractor
in Marseille. She had been friendly with Reynaud and his wife before
their marriage in 1930. Then her interest in Paul led to scenes in the
Reynaud household, until, in 1938, he moved out of his residence on
Rue du Faubourg Saint-Honoré to bachelor quarters on Place du Palais-
Bourbon, just across the way from the Chamber of Deputies. There
were murmurs of a stormy private life leaving little time or energy for
anything else. And yet there is the frenzied public life, the vigorous
conduct of the war, to belie these murmurs.

*   *   *

It was only coincidence, but on the day Reynaud withdrew his resignation, determined to continue as France's war leader, a new war leader came to power across the Channel. As first lord of the admiralty, Winston S. Churchill was already a familiar face to the British, thanks to the Norwegian campaign; in fact, an argument could be made that he shared the blame for the Allied failure. Instead, he was welcomed by the public and by parliament as a desirable replacement for tired Neville Chamberlain, the man of Munich and appeasement.

Fernande Alphandery, then twenty-eight years old and unmarried, worked as business manager in a pharmaceutical manufacturing company, a job largely unaffected by the phony war. Indeed, although born to Jewish parents—a Sephardic family established in France since the beginning of the sixteenth century—the war barely entered her consciousness. She had even been a Communist, resigning from the Party not because of ideological qualms but simply because she didn't have time to attend cell meetings. The Spanish Civil War had preoccupied her more than the present French war; she saw that as a reaction typical of left-wing intellectuals.

But events moved her to keep a diary. There was something to report on May 10, an air-raid alert at five in the morning. She didn't go down to the cellar of her apartment house on Rue Victorien-Sardou (just off the Avenue de Versailles); obeying civil defense rules had begun to seem silly.

Still, since she was now wide awake, she could admire the sunrise from her window. "It's a fine, pink and cool day," she noted poetically. The birdsong was "deafening," and she could hear it over the sirens, over the opening and closing of windows and doors, over the drone of airplanes. She reassured herself with the thought that the planes were "ours." But were they? For she could also hear antiaircraft fire now.

Slowly, familiar street sounds returned—of milk trucks, for example, on their morning rounds. Downstairs, early risers had gathered around a helmeted civil defense warden to ask if the raid was over. Fernande Alphandery knew that the warden would learn the answer to the question in the same way they'd all find out, by the second round of sirens signaling the all-clear. By nine that morning she and everybody she talked to had decided it had all been a joke. And then they began switching on radios to learn that the alert had been part of a bigger picture. Soon neighbors would begin to talk about "the other one," the First World War, which had ended twenty-two years ago.

A. J. Liebling, correspondent for *The New Yorker* magazine, whose reports from the battlefields of Europe were essays, stood at the window of his favorite hotel at dawn as the sirens sounded. It was the first daytime alert, he realized, since the early weeks of the war. The view from his room on Square Louvois was "an Elizabethan theater, with tiers of spectators framed in the opened windows of every building. Instead of looking down at a stage, however, they all looked up." The people at the windows were still in nightdress, which garments appeared dingier on the higher floors, noted Liebling, "since the prosperity of tenants in a walkup is in inverse ratio to their altitude." Antiaircraft fire had startled the birds in the trees below; tracer shells lit up the early-morning sky. The reporter couldn't tell whether the planes he heard were German or French. When one of them flew high over the city, the guns went silent. Liebling guessed that the French defenders didn't want an enemy plane descending in flames over the rooftops of Paris.

Airman Pierre Mendès France, who had just obtained a commission as flight observer, was anxious to begin flying combat missions. Thanks to his status as a member of Parliament, he could make his request to the top man. On the previous day he had put in a phone call to Air Minister André Laurent-Eynac to ask for an appointment; the minister had invited him to drop in to his office next morning at nine.

Mendès's day began with the sirens. If the Germans were flying daylight raids over Paris it was a new development, he decided. The morning papers provided no enlightenment: the front-page war was taking place far off in Norway. That was where he would like to be flying. The Air Ministry building on Boulevard Victor appeared calm and businesslike. No one could tell him why the sirens had gone off at dawn. Minister Laurent-Eynac received him at the appointed time. Mendès spoke of his experience in Syria, then got around to Norway and the assignment he desired.

"Willingly," the minister told him. "But with what's happening right now, I don't see how we can send any planes there."

"What exactly is happening?"

"Do you mean that you don't know?" Soon Pierre Mendès France did know, and quickly made a change in his request; he asked to be sent to Belgium.

When Lieutenant Mendès France left the Air Ministry, he could see by the expressions on people's faces that they had heard the morning news. Those he talked to were in good humor, pleased rather than angered that their long wait was over at last. At lunch with his wife, he ran into Henri de Kérillis, a fellow member of Parliament, arch-conservative and patriot. "In a month," said Kérillis, "the Germans will be in Paris or we'll be in Berlin. For France it's not just one of the battles of the war; it's the decisive battle."

Robert de Saint Jean, one of the writers recruited by the hastily improvised Ministry of Information, which had taken over the Hotel Continental for its offices, kept a diary for observations not necessarily suitable for wider dissemination just then. " 'Finally!' That's all you hear in Paris this morning," he noted on May 10.

High school teacher Simone de Beauvoir, whose companion, Jean-Paul Sartre, was a soldier posted to eastern France, bought a newspaper out of habit at the stand near the Café du Dôme, glancing at it as she walked along Boulevard Raspail. She stopped at a curbside bench, sat down to cry. In the days that followed she became an avid newspaper reader—something new for her.

To hear entertainer Maurice Chevalier tell it, the surprise attack actually raised spirits. "It's about time for a good fight," was the collective sigh. Chevalier, already an international celebrity with nearly thirty years on French stages and seven years of Hollywood behind him, was then performing at the Casino de Paris, one of the best music halls in town. It was as if an electrical charge had set the theater to vibrating. "They'll see what we can do, the Jerries. The time for speeches is over. The bigger the battle, the faster the war will be over."

* * *

So the cabinet would not be decimated; Hitler's surprise attack had seen to that. But there were things Paul Reynaud could do, all the same, to make it a war cabinet. He brought in two prominent members of the parliamentary right, Louis Marin and Jean Ybarnégaray, the latter an ally of controversial anti-Communist crusader Colonel François de La Rocque. It was enough to make a genuine Fascist tremble with rage. "Naturally these men of the right leap to Reynaud's call like dogs on a bone," growled Alain Laubreaux of the extremist weekly *Je Suis Partout*—in his private diary.

Senator Jacques Bardoux got the news early—a friend's phone call. "The decisive hour has sounded, sooner than I thought it would," he told his diary. "God save us." After signing his mail, he went out of doors to a "Paris of great days, silent and calm. Everyone knows it would be indecorous to chatter, since our children are to die." Clearly Senator Bardoux didn't meet the people who went to hear Chevalier sing.

After seeing to family affairs, above all to getting his children and grandchildren away to safer latitudes, Bardoux stopped by at the British Embassy to talk to Ambassador Sir Ronald Campbell, finding him "solemn, weary, very sad." That told the senator something about the true state of affairs. The ambassador agreed with Bardoux that Hitler had been encouraged to attack the Low Countries by the Allied retreat in Norway, as well as by cabinet crises in London and Paris. What they needed, said Bardoux, was American aircraft. Couldn't the Dutch queen and the Belgian king appeal for help to the United States?

Before the day was over, Paul Reynaud would sit down to a frank discussion with the American ambassador—not the first such talk, not the last. Reynaud gave William Bullitt the good news with the bad. Ominous sign: the Dutch had flushed out and captured no fewer than 150 German parachutists who had landed on Dutch soil wearing Dutch army uniforms. Of course they had been shot.

Yet, as Bullitt was to report to the U.S. Department of State immediately following this meeting, Reynaud appeared in excellent spirits. He revealed that French troops had already gone as far north as Brussels, Antwerp, Namur. "The battle which is now engaged," Bullitt quoted him, "is after all a fight for liberty in the world, and on the outcome of it will depend whether we in France and you in America as well can hold our heads a little higher or must hold them much lower." For his part, Reynaud had agreed to bury personal differences with Defense Minister Daladier. Bullitt could report to Washington that the German attack was making it possible for the plucky premier to weather the political crisis. "His resignation has not been announced in the French press and is known to a surprisingly small circle."

Bullitt was of course part of the circle. Wise Frenchmen, if they were also members of the ruling elite, knew that they had a friend in Ambassador Bullitt, representative of a neutral nation whose resources and industrial potential were regularly acclaimed in the French press to comfort morale. Bullitt was also a singular personality, the most interventionist of diplomats, a man who truly felt that France was worth the trouble. That day, and on succeeding days, the ambassador would be available for whatever support or solace the envoy of a great but dormant nation could offer. From the French point of view, no one was doing more. This diplomat knew and loved France, knew its language. He was also an intimate of President Franklin D. Roosevelt, and could get his ear at any time.

Bullitt was born on January 15, 1891, of a singular combination of progenitors. On his father's side he descended from seventeenth-century Protestant émigrés from France (whose name was actually Boulet). Through marriages he was related not only to George Washington and Patrick Henry but apparently even to the Indian princess Pocahontas. On his mother's side there were German and Jewish ancestors including the surgeon Samuel Gross, honored by a statue at the Smithsonian Institution for contributions to American medicine. The Bullitts had status and money. Young William learned his German in Munich; at home his mother spoke to him in French. He was the first American ambassador to France in his time who could speak the local tongue.

His college was Yale; he was studying law at Harvard when his father died. The young man began the First World War as a reporter, ending it at the State Department, where he quickly became a specialist on Europe and postrevolutionary Russia. President Woodrow Wilson took him along to Versailles for the peace talks, during which Bullitt was responsible for the American delegation's intelligence reports. From there he was sent to Moscow on a mission to size up the new Soviet regime. Before long he had found a way to irritate President Wilson, to hurt the campaign for American participation in the League of Nations. At the age of twenty-six he was already a disgruntled ex-government official.

Flair and connections kept him in the limelight. He divorced a Philadelphia socialite beauty to marry the widow of John Reed, the American Communist who wrote *Ten Days That Shook the World* and was buried in the Kremlin wall. Bullitt continued to move about, got his name in the papers, as when he wrote a roman à clef satirizing the Philadelphia upper class. He seemed just right for Franklin Roosevelt, another iconoclastic aristocrat. After working in Roosevelt's presidential campaign in 1932 he became the new president's informal adviser on foreign affairs, ripe for another nonconformist job handling negotiations for recognition of the Soviet Union. And then he was the obvious choice for ambassador to Moscow. While he admired the October Revolution, he found himself speaking out against Stalin's unsubtle repression, and left the embassy no longer a friend of the USSR. As an anti-Fascist he won new friends in France on his arrival in 1936 as American ambassador. Some thought of him as "the champagne ambassador" because of his lavish receptions, paid for in part with his own money. When he was the subject of a profile in *The New Yorker* by Janet Flanner, its resident Paris correspondent, she quoted a tribute to Bullitt by one of his old friends: He *rose* from the rich.

"His energy drives people either to admiring or detesting him," wrote Flanner. "He is refractory, partisan, and always a fighter, an unembarrassed patriot, and an explosive romantic." He was, she said, "adrenal"; his emotions could be read on his face. "Headstrong, spoiled, spectacular, something of a nabob, and a good showman, he has complicated ambitions which are a compound of his devotion to his own notions of idealism, his interest in his career, and his faith in the ultimate fate of the human race."

In Paris, Bullitt handled the embassy's social side all by himself, with no wife to assist him. He rented a country house near Chantilly castle and kept horses. Writing at the end of 1938, less than a year before the outbreak of war, the *New Yorker* correspondent had found him prematurely bald, "blue-eyed, pink-skinned. . . . The daily dark-red carnation he wears in his buttonhole tickles the French."

One could call him a dabbler in diplomacy, and at least one observer did, describing his record as one of a few minor successes and many failures, mocking him as Roosevelt's apparatchik. As for the effects of his advocacy, historians differ in their assessments. Had he been a warmonger who incited Hitler to attack the West? A modern Paul Revere, warning the world of present danger? Or just a "bright phony," as an American reporter in Paris privately thought, a superficial member of the establishment who had been caught up in events beyond his competence? Critics recalled that before the Czechoslovak crisis in 1938, far from being a warmonger, Bullitt had been ready to appease the Nazis. In June of that year he told Secretary of the Interior Harold Ickes that the United States had a duty to remain out of the war in order to save what could be saved of Western civilization.

Whatever the final verdict, this "F. Scott Fitzgerald character" was the booster France needed just then. At times he seemed to be France's ambassador to the United States rather than the contrary, but in context that wasn't so bad. Robert Murphy later revealed that Bullitt's intimacy with French leaders was deliberately played up to convince the Germans that the United States was more committed to France than it really was.

4

SATURDAY, MAY 11

All of the power of the new Germany was unleashed now, even if small and neutral nations were getting the brunt of it. The Germans were introducing a new kind of warfare, symbolized by the dive-bombing Stuka planes, feared nearly as much for their blood-chilling wail as they plunged to their targets as for their bomb loads. Parachuting behind the lines—the parachutists often disguised as friendly soldiers or even civilians—was a more devious tactic, but no less effective. And then the tanks. Tanks employed not (as the French used them) to support foot soldiers, but grouped in massive formations to smash front lines and force the decision.

One man to watch on the ground was German General Georg von Küchler, who would celebrate his fifty-ninth birthday as he approached the northern gates of Paris later that month. An artillery officer by training, he commanded the Eighteenth Army, striking force of the offensive against the Netherlands. Respected as a soldier in the earlier war, he had become one of Hitler's favorites. His May offensive against the Netherlands would be so one-sided it was as if the Dutch had never fought the war. Later von Küchler would distinguish himself on the eastern front, his brutal tactics winning him promotion to field marshal. Between the two campaigns he would have the honor of commanding the army that took Paris, but this would be the least bloody of his charges.

The Dutch continued to resist valiantly. There were combats in village streets, defense of the countryside canal by canal. Von Küchler's command included the Ninth Panzer Division, meaning speed; the Germans crossed key waterways before bridges could be blown up. French units moving north to assist their new allies were pinned down by enemy air attack (and never reached Dutch soil). In Belgium, French and British forces were not attaining positions assigned to them in the Gamelin plan. Troops unprepared for attack from the air, unequipped to defend themselves against concentrated armored vehicles, were easily routed. Military communications proved inadequate either to coordinate front-line action or to keep headquarters aware of the location of enemy forces.

The French had grown used to the "Sitzkrieg," as pugnacious Premier Reynaud called it. They were unprepared for Blitzkrieg, lightning war.

And then Hitler's style of warfare made it possible to attain Paris in another way, and almost from the first day, thanks to radio broadcasts masterminded from Berlin by Nazi Propaganda Minister Joseph Goebbels. Already the French were familiar with the voice of their compatriots who spoke unsubtle untruths over Nazi Radio Stuttgart. Now Goebbels introduced ostensibly French programs beamed into France from positions even closer to Paris. Speakers pretended to be French patriots unhappy with their government. It was easy to utilize such clandestine broadcasts to spread confusion. Speakers would not deny rumors of German secret weapons or the German practice of disguising paratroopers as friendly soldiers or innocent civilians—on the contrary. Soon Goebbels had launched Radio Humanité, borrowing the title of the banned Communist Party daily. "A Communist France would be safe from attack by Hitler thanks to his alliance with the USSR," a speaker on so-called Radio Humanité declared. "There is no German danger, as our capitalists exclaim noisily, only to send the proletariat to death." Naturally the ersatz Communist radio called for civil disobedience. "Don't subscribe for war bonds, don't pay your taxes, slow down your work, carry out sabotage, do only what you have to to survive."

Perhaps the greatest achievement of German radio propaganda was to convince French listeners of the invincibility of German military intelligence, of the omniscience of German spies, of the existence of the "fifth column" everybody talked about. The phrase was born of the Spanish Civil War, when one of Francisco Franco's generals boasted that the insurgents had four columns advancing against Madrid, and a fifth column of supporters already inside the city. During the phony war, Frenchmen told each other that the German radio was reporting details of French military movements as soon as they happened. When a new unit moved to the front, so people said, Radio Stuttgart would send it greetings.

This is what everybody said. But French intelligence monitors who listened in on enemy broadcasts discovered that the Germans had no such capability. France was not swarming with spies. By April 26, 1940, when the Defense Ministry circulated a directive on the subject to counterespionage officers, there had not been a single proved case of a successful mission of enemy paratroops over French territory. No clandestine transmitters on French territory were broadcasting secrets to the enemy. No spies were signaling to enemy aircraft by rocket. All of these assertions had been the subject of rumor. The military establishment wondered whether such rumormongering wasn't itself the work of a fifth column, and intelligence officers were ordered to track down false reports so that they could be exposed.

No republic is armed against such tactics. One of the few defenses available in wartime was censorship, and that weapon was wielded. Military censors were assigned to all the Parisian daily newspapers, staying with the editors and printers until the wee hours when papers went to press. What these censors did to the war news everybody could see, for the lines they chopped out of an article were left as blocks of white space in the published newspapers.

It was Saturday, and in peacetime it would have been the beginning of a three-day Whitsun holiday. But this year, by government decision, Monday was to be a working day.

While passenger traffic was heavy in trains leaving from Paris stations for the provinces [so a daily newspaper reported], there was no crush or panic, and everyone was able to get on a train. All this in an atmosphere of total calm.

It was not clear how much of the outgoing traffic was holiday weekending, how much escaping.

War correspondent A. J. Liebling expected to join a French army captain that afternoon at the Auteuil racetrack in the park on Paris's western edge. The officer phoned to announce that all leaves had been canceled. "It's good that it's starting at last," the captain added. "We can beat the Boches and have it over with by autumn." So Liebling went to Auteuil by himself, to observe that the grandstand was crowded with Parisians whose chief preoccupations seemed to be the new three-year-olds and the clothes women wore. No one seemed concerned by the German capture of Arnhem and Maastricht, or the parachutists over Rotterdam.

Indeed, Parisians Liebling talked to seemed as confident as his army friend. "The Boches have business with somebody their own size now!" was the cocky refrain. "They will see we are not Poles or Norwegians!" Of course the Germans would gain ground at first, but the war would last a long time, like the earlier one. People seemed "hypnotized" by 1918, thought the *New Yorker* correspondent.

American reporter Quentin Reynolds had arrived in Paris the previous day, just in time, thought he, to cover the offensive. But it was hard to convince French officials in charge of war correspondents that there was something urgent about the war. He was given forms to fill out, asked for photographs, but even with a letter of recommendation from Ambassador Bullitt, he wasn't about to get the permission he needed. "These things take time," Pierre Comert, the Foreign Ministry press liaison, told him. "It may take three weeks or a month."

Reynolds didn't have the patience to sit around waiting in Paris, where there wasn't a story worth writing. So he concocted a bit of subterfuge. He returned to Comert ostensibly for advice. He was sending a telegram to his "uncle," the president of the United States, asking him to request that Premier Reynaud expedite his accreditation. He wanted Comert to handle the telegram personally. The Frenchman's expression changed as he read Reynolds's total fabulation, addressed to Franklin Delano Roosevelt. "It was grand of you to phone me last night. Please give my love to Aunt Eleanor. . . ." Comert got Reynolds his papers right away.

5

SUNDAY, MAY 12

The official French war communiqué should not have upset Parisians listening to the radio at breakfast. "In the region of the Albert Canal and Meuse River, where German attacks continue with extreme intensity," it began, "our aviation is supporting Belgian troops in a massive and effective manner." On the ground, Gamelin's march into Belgium was proceeding according to plan. The evening communiqué even reported an improvement of the Dutch position, thanks in part to British air attacks.

There was considerable enemy activity in the skies over the Ardennes Forest region south of French lines, as well as in the Saar basin, and over northeastern France. The French claimed that thirty enemy planes had been downed. Surprisingly, the German High Command admitted to the loss of 31 planes that day, but claimed 320 Allied aircraft, 58 of them in aerial combat, 72 by antiaircraft fire, the remainder destroyed on the ground. Yet if one accepted the French communiqués, listened to the radio, read the editorials, one could feel quite confident that day. Havas, the official French news agency, summed it up: "The French High Command in Belgium has built a wall which will stop the German steamroller."

What was actually happening was less reassuring to those in a position to know. True, the Dutch were still able to hold on to their largest cities—Amsterdam, Rotterdam, the Hague—and virtually without assistance, for the enemy had effectively prevented General Henri Giraud's Seventh French Army from reaching them. Farther south the Germans advanced into Belgium where and when they wished to, making a shambles of French planning.

Paris was still far out of it, and perhaps for that reason readier to cope. Clare Boothe, the wife of *Time* and *Life* founder Henry Luce, was covering the war as a correspondent that spring. She had been as far as the Belgian border; driving into Paris, she decided, was like visiting a summer resort after that.

> It was not that people were happy—how could they be?—but they, too, were glad it had begun, because when a thing's begun, it's that much nearer being finished. Everybody felt that at last the *real* front had been found, and that this real front was much farther from Paris than in their most optimistic dreams they had thought it would be.

Clare Boothe Luce's Paris was the ritzy Hotel Ritz on Place Vendôme, now virtually a dormitory for war correspondents from affluent nations.

That night, friends drove her out to Versailles for a dinner party. On the return trip they were caught by the air-raid sirens. In the automobile she could hear the thunder of antiaircraft guns, could see the shell bursts, searchlights seeking out targets. A policeman whistled them to a stop, and they were invited to descend into the cellar of a nearby apartment house. There Clare Boothe found herself surrounded by grumblers and sleepy children. A woman said, "This is not a life for *ordinary* people to lead. Why can't the Germans let our soldiers fight this war? *C'est tout de même insupportable.*" Clare Boothe had to wonder, "Has it become unbearable so soon?"

Their northern neighbors had an answer to that. Belgian civilians in the path of the Nazi invasion had begun their exodus through northeastern France immediately after the launching of the German offensive. From now on and until Belgium was sealed off, there would be no end to the procession of refugees from the Low Countries, by motorcar or horse-drawn wagon, on bicycles or walking alongside carts—for many had only their feet for transportation. Then and later the French highway system took Paris as its hub. To reach safer regions, refugees from the north set their sights on Paris. They would enter the city through its northern gates, and cross on main thoroughfares, leaving through one of the city's southern gates. In passing they gave sedentary Parisians their first close-up view of a war no longer *drôle*. Refugees were escaping feared atrocities, the brutality of a German soldiery remembered from that earlier war. What Parisians now saw was this fear on the faces of people much like themselves— "weeping, frightened, weighed down with baskets and bundles," as Russian writer Ilya Ehrenburg observed them.

6

MONDAY, MAY 13

While the French and British continued to send their best fighting men north into Belgium to confront the invading Germans, the impossible occurred. Farther south, on a segment of the French border considered impenetrable, the Germans penetrated. During the night of May 12–13 Hitler's elite striking force, the armored divisions called Panzers, roared through the Ardennes hill and forest region of southern Belgium to the Meuse River, and then found ways to cross it, surprising and routing the French defenders, most of them second-line troops, reservists older and less prepared for combat than the French divisions now bottled up farther north in Belgium. In all, seven *Panzerdivisionen* participated in the attack, led in the crucial Sedan sector by one of Germany's leading proponents of tank warfare, General Heinz Guderian.

Between world wars the French had conceived the Maginot Line as a network of permanent fortifications linked by underground tunnels to seal the eastern frontier. But this defense line was intentionally limited: it did not run as far north as Belgium, a friendly country. The accepted wisdom, shared by the men who forged France's military doctrine, was that the Ardennes Forest was a natural barrier to invasion.

The German surprise sweep, part of a carefully orchestrated strategy to strike below Allied positions in northern France and Belgium, and so to entrap the best French and British fighting divisions, was appropriately known as *Sichelschnitt,* "sickle cut." Later a British historian called it one of the most inspired blueprints for victory the military mind had ever conceived, and it was of course attributed to Hitler's genius. Yet until ninety days before the launching of the German offensive, the High Command, with Hitler's blessing, had been preparing to wage the same battle it had fought a generation earlier.

Lieutenant General Erich von Manstein, who conceived and then lobbied for *Sichelschnitt,* wasn't even a member of Hitler's headquarters staff; in a sense he had no business butting in, and the High Command never forgave him for that. He had fought at Verdun in the First War, and by 1935 was a colonel and chief of operations. Although not implicated in opposition plots against the Führer, he had a reputation for plain speaking, and during a purge of the military by hard-line Nazis a year before the war he was sent off to command a division. He was fifty-two, and a newly promoted general, when war broke out. At the time of German preparations for the western offensive he served as chief of staff to General Gerd von Rundstedt, in charge of Army Group A, positioned along the Rhine River opposite southern Belgium and Luxembourg.

In offering his alternative, Erich von Manstein pointed out that the headquarters plan, which provided for an attack through neutral Belgium to attain northern France, was a repeat of the strategy of 1914 without the advantage of surprise. What he proposed was that the attack on the Netherlands and Belgium be a feint, with the *main* thrust to follow farther south. He won an ally in Heinz Guderian, who was sure that his armored units could push through the supposedly impenetrable Ardennes. At first Manstein wasn't allowed to make his case to higher echelons. In fact, a historian speculated that Hitler thought Manstein (whose father was of Polish-German origin and bore the name Lewinski) might have Jewish blood. (He had been raised by a family friend and took this second family's name.)

On February 17, 1940, Manstein—recently promoted to lead an army corps—was summoned to a lunch at which new commanding generals were introduced to Hitler. There an aide who knew Manstein arranged a private meeting with the Führer, who apparently liked what Manstein told him.

On March 10, French intelligence officer Major Henri Navarre slipped into the bar of the Hotel Eden in Lugano, Switzerland, to keep an appointment with France's best secret agent of the Hitler era, Hans Thilo Schmidt, known by the code name "H. E." or "Asche." The agent told Navarre that his brother Rudolf, one of Hitler's favorite generals, had been at the lunch during which Erich von Manstein persuaded Hitler to shift the main thrust of the coming offensive to the south in order to trap the Allies inside Belgium. French intelligence put that together with other information—for example, reports that the enemy was carrying out a study of the Ardennes terrain. But when the top echelon of military intelligence went to General Gamelin with their conclusions on March 19, the commander-in-chief's staff officers refused to believe that the Germans could pull it off.

Responsibility for the Ardennes thrust was given to the Panzer group of General Paul von Kleist; Guderian's Nineteenth Panzer Corps was only one of three put into play that day. On May 12 an unquiet Hitler actually asked von Kleist if he preferred to wait for infantry support and he said no. The attack was ordered for 4:00 P.M. German time (an hour ahead of French summer time) on May 13.

Guderian had not only surprise on his side, but also French skepticism. He was sending powerful steel against second-string foot soldiers, and even the French pursuit planes that might have compensated for the deficiencies of the infantry had been withdrawn from the sector. When French gunners actually had German tanks in their sights they remembered orders to spare ammunition, and thus failed to slow down the enemy tanks. Even when the Germans launched the artillery barrages and air raids that had to be the beginning of an offensive, the French didn't believe in it, although one would have had to be deaf or blind (so a French general later remarked) not to realize an attack was coming.

An aide to General Gamelin was to remember how the news was received at Vincennes headquarters. The source was General Joseph Georges, commanding the northeastern front, relaying a message from the Ninth Army of General André Corap that announced the crossing of the Meuse. Consternation. The river was known as a "deep pit." Doctrine had it that rivers were reliable barriers (and never mind that the doctrine had been disproved a war earlier). Minutes after the first report, General Georges's headquarters at La Ferté-sous-Jouarre announced that the French were counterattacking with tanks. So everybody held his breath.

Gamelin's aide noted that the suspense was so disquieting that Gamelin twice leapfrogged General Georges to phone directly to Corap's headquarters, something he had never done before and would not do again.

At the end of the day no Panzers had actually crossed the Meuse, although German infantrymen were already climbing up its bank and into France. Had the French attacked instead of retreating, they could probably have wiped out the small invading force (a Gaullist officer, Colonel Adolphe Goutard, said that). But General Georges would have had to order an attack, and General Georges did not know much about what was happening on the Meuse. The distance Gamelin placed between himself and the front might have given *him* the leisure to see the May 10 attack as the opening of a trap, but obviously it did not. And the French defeat (Colonel Goutard speaking) was caused not by Gamelin's advance into Belgium, but by his insistence on keeping the French army bottled up in the north, "paralyzed and useless."

Churchill made his first speech to the House of Commons as prime minister that day. "I would say to the House, as I said to those who have joined this Government: 'I have nothing to offer but blood, toil, tears, and sweat.' " His government, he said, had only one policy, to wage war. One aim: victory.

As he spoke, the land battle in Belgium seemed to be proceeding according to plan; he would not yet have heard of the Ardennes breakthrough. In its own sector, the British expeditionary force was moving up to prearranged positions on the Dyle River.

7

TUESDAY, MAY 14

The rapidity of the German assault on the Meuse frontier, the density of tank penetration allowing no riposte, the panic of an unprepared and quickly exhausted soldiery, combined with an unimaginable failure of communication, rendered German victory at once certain and confidential. Not only was Churchill unaware of battlefield developments, but neither the French commander-in-chief nor the combative premier could follow events as they occurred.

But even the public had to be told something now. The morning communiqué contained a real revelation: "The enemy has attained the Meuse from Liège to Namur and at Sedan." That afternoon the curtain was raised a little higher: "On the Meuse, south of Namur, the Germans have tried to cross the river at several points. We have launched counterattacks and the fight continues. . . ." At the daily press conference for foreign correspondents held at the War Ministry on Rue Saint-Dominique, as observer Robert de Saint Jean remarked, "they attenuate as much as possible a truth exceeding all the fears one might have had."

The truth would indeed have reflected poorly on French battlefield planning, based on the conviction that the Ardennes frontier was impenetrable, the Meuse River unbridgeable; that stretch of the line had been assigned to insufficiently trained reserve troops, older men not meant for battle. That they did fight, often with considerable courage and in the face of cruel losses, is one of the war's untold stories (if only because the lack of air and artillery support reduced the ranks of the men of the Fifty-fifth Infantry who might have been able to tell the good with the bad).

American correspondent Virginia Cowles, who had become an expert on European wars from her London base, arrived in Paris on that glorious spring day; it made it harder to believe that the city was under a threat. Paris was calm, indeed too calm, for every day seemed to be Sunday, when the city was always deserted by weekenders. Traffic was light, restaurants and shops half empty. The charm of it all was interrupted only by the occasional air-raid sirens, but there weren't any enemy planes, and no one rushed to shelter. Indeed, every Parisian did the opposite of what he was expected to do, Cowles thought. During air alerts everybody stood at a window to look up at the sky.

But this serenity was superficial, as Cowles was to discover. Each Parisian seemed to have a parachute story to tell. Enemy paratroopers supposedly dropped out of the skies disguised as priests and nuns, even as an entire ballet troupe. While she was visiting a French woman friend that Tuesday, someone rushed in to say that a German para-trooper had just landed nearby on the Avenue des Champs-Elysées. The two women went out to the balcony and saw clusters of people all along the street gazing up at the sky.

"Suddenly, at an intersection, people begin shouting because some-one, nobody knew who, had seen a parachutist landing," remembered diplomat Jean Chauvel. "The police were called and rushed over, followed by firemen and everybody else you can imagine. Whistles blew. The agitation lasted a quarter of an hour, suddenly evaporated. Thus a people which had been sheltered from the tragedy of war was ready to move, without any transition at all, from quietude to panic."

PARIS HASN'T BEEN VISITED
BY PARACHUTISTS

So *Le Figaro* reassured readers next morning. It attributed the rumor to the fall of an observation balloon.

Leaving her hostess, Virginia Cowles dropped in at the British Embassy on Rue du Faubourg Saint-Honoré to request permission to visit the front. Her contact there confided that he was more concerned about French morale than about German guns and planes. If morale held, so would everything else.

Cowles was to learn that the French remained unperturbed; the parachute incident was only an incident. The French War Ministry carried on as if it welcomed the German offensive, for that signified the dispersion of the enemy's army, making it easier to cut it off from its bases in a counterattack. The correspondent went to bed reassured.

"In a crisis as horrifying as this one," editorialist Germaine Beaumont told her readers in the morning's *Le Matin,* "the duty of French women is simple and clear. No disorderly movements, no impulsiveness, no panic, no gossip, no superfluous questions." Women were to do their duty as in peacetime, said the placid columnist. That meant "the worker in her factory, the farmer in her field, the employee in her office." Her conclusion might have disarmed the less militant of feminists: "Saint Genevieve, who stopped the barbarian hordes, had no arms besides her shepherd's crook and her spindle."

A decree signed by General Pierre Héring, military governor of Paris, called for rounding up German nationals—men aged seventeen to fifty-five—at the Buffalo Stadium, just half a mile south of the city at Montrouge. "A wise measure," agreed *Le Figaro.* Reporter Louis Gabriel-Robinet described the scene, as a line of gendarmes in khaki uniforms, armed with carbines, surrounded the huge arena faced in gray concrete, watching as German nationals arrived in taxis and private cars. Usually several persons piled out of the same vehicle, carrying personal belongings, blankets, bottles, bread. They'd sleep on straw that night.

The internees proved to be an orderly lot. The main job of the gendarmes was to turn away women—wives and sisters of the men who were surrendering to French authorities—as well as friends who had accompanied the hapless aliens to their place of detention. There were rich and poor in the crowd; there were enemies of France (said *Le Figaro*'s reporter) as well as unfortunate souls without a country. Those who failed to turn themselves in were picked up by the police. "Until late in the evening," wrote Gabriel-Robinet, "the same farewell scenes were played, the same tears flowed, the same gestures were repeated."

Next day it would be the turn of women, who were invited to report to a stadium closer to the center of Paris. On both days the catch took in resolute anti-Nazis who had fled the Hitler regime, German Jews who were the particular targets of the Nazis. Many of the innocent would spend time in notorious detention camps in central and southern France, at the mercy of their persecutors when the Germans arrived.

It was also the day that Paris began serious evacuation of children, grouped in convoys escorted by teachers. Parents were advised through the press not to bring back children who had gone away for the Whitsun school holidays.

Marshaling his best English, Premier Paul Reynaud wrote out a statement he would read over the telephone to his new colleague Winston Churchill. "I am just coming back from the War Committee," explained Reynaud, "and I would like you to take down the following statement from the French government." Doubtless Churchill put a secretary on the line:

> The situation is very serious indeed. Germany attempt to deliver a fatal blow towards Paris. The german army has broken through our fortified lines South of Sedan. The reason is that we cannot resist to a combined attack of heavy tanks and bomber squadrons. To stop the german drive while it is still time and to allow our counterattack to succeed, it is necessary to cut off the german tanks from the bombers supporting them.
>
> It can only be done by a considerable force of fighters.
>
> You were kind enough to send already 4 squadrons which is more than you promised.
>
> If we are to win this battle which might well be decisive for the whole war, it is necessary that you send at once 10 more squadrons.
>
> Without such support we cannot be sure to stop the german advance.

Between Sedan and Paris there are no fortifications left that can be compared with the line we must re-establish at almost any cost.

I am confident that in this decisive moment, England's help will not fail us.

It was not to be an easy reply. For one thing, Churchill had to reckon with his chiefs of staff. And in the opinion of Sir Hugh Dowding, head of the Fighter Command, Britain needed every Hurricane fighter plane it had, for if France was defeated, Hitler would turn against the British Isles. So Churchill had to explain to Reynaud (in what may be considered an unfortunate metaphor for this master of language) that Hurricane fighters were Britain's Maginot Line.

Soon, however, when Air Marshal Arthur Barratt, commander of British forces in France, pointed out what was being asked of RAF pilots in France—each to carry out four or five missions a day—the British cabinet agreed to dispatch four squadrons. . . . Four squadrons and not the ten Reynaud hoped for.

Ambassador Bullitt had some urgent business to take up with Reynaud that morning. The American Embassy in Rome had forwarded alarming information about Mussolini's designs on France. With the telegram in hand, Bullitt leaped into an embassy car for the short drive across the Seine to the Foreign Ministry. Reynaud happened to be conferring with his war cabinet, but at Bullitt's request he came out of the meeting.

The premier agreed with the assessment that an Italian move was impending, especially now that the Germans had racked up an "appalling success" at Sedan on the Meuse. Reynaud explained that the Germans had employed "colossal tanks" and "a totally overwhelming mass" of planes. In a coded telegram to Washington marked "Personal and Secret for the President," Bullitt summed up Reynaud's story, with more appalling news still: "The German tanks had crossed the River Meuse as if it did not exist. They had run through the French anti-tank defenses which consisted of railroad rails sunk deep in concrete and protruding from the ground as if the rails were straw."

Reynaud had summed it up grimly, in language similar to that which he used with Churchill: "At this moment there is nothing between those German tanks and Paris."

Relaying this to Roosevelt, the American ambassador found another way to put across the urgency. Even without the entry of Italy into the war, said Bullitt, "France faced one of the gravest and most terrible moments in her history. With the participation of Italy the result would be tragic not only for France and England but for every country in the world including the United States."

It was Bullitt's unsubtle warning to a president he knew well. He made Reynaud's case for more American aircraft, although Bullitt himself didn't think there were any to be had. He also hoped to persuade Roosevelt to sell some of America's older destroyers to the French and British navies for use against the pernicious German submarines.

Clearly this American ambassador saw his role as comprising more than simply observing and reporting. He passed on appeals for help, but he also endorsed the appeals. Thus, on May 13, he had relayed a French request for the training of French pilots in the United States, even if he wondered whether such a procedure would "embarrass" Roosevelt. For the President faced a reluctant Congress and a decidedly uncommitted electorate. "In my own opinion," ventured Bullitt, "it would be greatly to the advantage of our country to have more trained pilots: in defending France they would defend us." In another message he begged that steps be taken to hasten the delivery of American planes, fighters and bombers both, even if this required that American reserve pilots resign their commissions so as to be able to fly the aircraft to Europe as private citizens.

He was to be disappointed on the pilot training issue. Roosevelt explained that any such arrangement would compromise U.S. neutrality. "It is believed to be better for all concerned and much more advisable for them to go to Canada, where there are fine fields and good summer weather." Not to be put off, Bullitt directed his next cable to Secretary of State Cordell Hull, pointing out the desperate need for planes. "The wastage in the present battle at Sedan is so enormous that a time is foreseen about a month hence when any kind of plane that can take to the air will be better than none."

Then more alarming news came in from Rome, this time via the French Embassy. Italy's foreign minister, Count Galeazzo Ciano, had advised French ambassador André François-Poncet that there was a "90% chance" that Italy would enter the war on Germany's side. French intelligence put another report on Reynaud's desk: The court-yard of the Italian Embassy on Rue de Varenne was covered with crates ready to be filled.

It was time to step up attempts to keep Italy out of the war. The French and British would try it, for obvious reasons; the Americans would contribute their support as a neutral third party. In France itself, the effort to dissuade Mussolini received help from politicians whose motives Reynaud did not necessarily appreciate. Some were frank admirers of Italian Fascism, others more dreamy Italophiles who simply couldn't see that neighbor as an enemy. Both groups got help from the Italian ambassador to France, Raffaele Guariglia, who although a faithful servitor of Benito Mussolini and of Mussolini's son-in-law, Count Ciano, still thought of himself as a friend of France. The son of a law professor from Naples, Guariglia liked to recall that his own law professor was Francesco Nitti, a prominent statesman of pre-Mussolini days, now a voluntary exile from Fascism. Later Guariglia would even remember himself as a career diplomat who had no part in the Fascist hierarchy. The best thing that could be said for him was that he was kept in the dark. He was not a party to discussions between Mussolini and Hitler, hadn't been briefed on Mussolini's war plan.

Before the day was done, Paris received more ominous news of what might come, of what a war unleashed by superbly equipped fanatics could be. The Dutch were yielding to overwhelming force; their queen and her government had fled. On the ground, the German field commander, General von Küchler, stood before the vast harbor and industrial complex of Rotterdam to demand its surrender. The Dutch ceded.

Despite this—some attribute it to a failure of coordination on the German side—the core of Rotterdam was cruelly bombed, the destruction completed by inextinguishable fire. War in the Netherlands was all but over.

But the lesson wasn't forgotten by the German commander who would stand before Paris a month later—the same General Georg von Küchler. A major city could be razed in an hour.

8

WEDNESDAY, MAY 15

Just after 6:00 A.M., Defense Minister Edouard Daladier put in a call to Premier Reynaud, still home on the Place du Palais-Bourbon. "All is lost," he began. "The road to Paris is open. There is nothing to prevent the Germans from reaching the capital." An echo of what Reynaud himself had told Churchill and Bullitt the previous day. But during the night General Corap's army had withdrawn from outposts along the Meuse River, the hope being that a regrouping out of enemy range might allow the French to impose some order on what could otherwise become a rout. The withdrawal opened a breach nearly fifty miles wide in French lines.

Minutes later Daladier was back on the phone. "The situation is a little better. The Germans have evacuated some villages south of Sedan."

Despite the contradictory reports, Reynaud knew what he had to do. He asked to be connected to London, got the prime minister's residence at 10 Downing Street, roused Churchill from bed. He had again written out the little speech he was to make; the text survives thanks to Reynaud's attentive cabinet aide Maurice Dejean.

We have lost the battle last night. The road of Paris is opened.
Send us all the planes and all the troops you can.

Lost the battle? "Impossible!" said Churchill. Experience showed that every offensive runs out of steam; remember the German offensive of March 1918. . . . Churchill was sure that in a matter of days the enemy would be obliged to halt to wait for supplies, and then there would be time for the Allies to counterattack. Marshal Foch had taught him that lesson.

But they were not fighting the First World War, Reynaud argued. "Everything is different. There's a flood of Panzers charging against us."

At nine, Daladier was back on the phone to Reynaud. Now that he had had time to wash and shave, he was able to look at the situation more coolly. So the "breach," as Reynaud's Dominique Leca noted with irony, had become a "pocket." On May 15 it still seemed possible to reassure parliament and the people.

If reports from the front seemed contradictory, it could well be because of contradictory behavior on the enemy's side. The problem was the High Command, Hitler himself—Hitler, who wasn't prepared to let the Panzers go as far and as fast as they could. Twice General Guderian was ordered to stop his advance. Gerd von Rundstedt, commanding the army group, specifically ordered the tank general not to push beyond the bridgehead on the French side of the Meuse. The tactical reason was that they had to wait for supplies and infantry support. Remembering this prudence later on, the architect of the Ardennes sickle cut, Erich von Manstein, wondered whether Hitler had been trying to spare his armored divisions for future battle, or was bowing to Goering's conviction that only his air force could cut off the British escape across the Channel. A third possibility was that Hitler wished to treat the British gently in the hope of obtaining an agreement to end the war. Guderian, for his part, was to boast that he had simply ignored orders to halt.

It was at the decidedly undiplomatic hour of a quarter to nine that William Bullitt burst in on Valerio Valeri, the papal nuncio, the Vatican's man in Paris, who in his own way was a diplomat of the activist breed. Bullitt wished Valeri to know that France's military situation had reached the critical point. And he knew from an unimpeachable source that Italy's declaration of war would come in a matter of days, if not hours. The future of Christian civilization was in jeopardy, and the American ambassador suggested to the emissary of Pope Pius nothing less than a papal threat to excommunicate Mussolini, should he go to war.

Valeri used his own diplomacy to convince his visitor that the Holy Father was doing what he could to keep Italy out of the war. Indeed, the pope was largely responsible for the fact that Italy still remained neutral. He felt that what Bullitt was asking was impossible, and certain to prove unproductive, for excommunication had no significance in the modern world.

The exchange became more heated, to the point that Valerio Valeri allowed himself to remind Bullitt that the American ambassador had not always been so ardent an anti-Fascist. The nuncio kept files, or had a good memory.

The gibe hit home. Bullitt rose abruptly, as if to leave, then declared, "I have a more exalted opinion of the pope's authority." Delivering that statement seemed to calm him down, and the two diplomats concluded with expressions of hope for the final victory of the forces of good over the forces of evil.

Shortly after leaving the nuncio, Bullitt turned up at the Quai d'Orsay, at Reynaud's request. The Frenchman explained that he wanted Bullitt, and Roosevelt through Bullitt, to know just how grave the situation was. "The greatest battle in history is in progress in the region of Sedan," he blurted out. He told of the dawn call from Daladier, and explained that he had then called Churchill to make it clear that the war could be lost in a matter of days, and in Reynaud's view *would* be lost, unless the British sent planes. Churchill had "screamed" at him, said Reynaud, to insist that the war could not be lost. So Reynaud had to assure the British prime minister that as long as he was premier, France would fight on. But he had to be frank.

To Bullitt, Reynaud revealed that French aircraft were outnumbered ten to one. Could the United States help? Bullitt replied that Roosevelt was well aware of the problem, but the planes simply did not exist. Still, the French purchasing mission in the United States ought to be able to find other planes.

Reynaud renewed his request for American destroyers. Bullitt was to pass that on to Washington, with his own caveat: "The situation could not be more grave." Later that day Bullitt returned to the matter in another "Personal for the President." He had just talked to César Campinchi, naval minister, who was only asking for a dozen overaged American destroyers. Since the need was immediate, couldn't the U.S. Navy send twelve of its old but still active vessels to France, for sale or loan? As well as fifty-four old patrol bombers for antisubmarine use? "Please cable me at the earliest possible moment an affirmative answer," he pleaded. These were personal requests, and would not be presented in official form unless Roosevelt so desired.

Bullitt and his French friends were going to be disappointed. The veto came from the State Department, which explained that the request would have to be submitted to Congress, and that, "for a variety of reasons," was not opportune. There really weren't any extra destroyers to give away, so State informed Bullitt, given American obligations both in the Western Hemisphere and in the Pacific.

Today it was the turn of enemy nationals of the female sex to turn themselves in. They were to report to the Vélodrome d'Hiver just off the Quai de Grenelle, the famous Vél' d'Hiv' of the Six-Day Bicycle Race, now (in the admirative prose of *Le Matin*) "a vast concentration camp."

Erna Friedlander, for example, was a Berliner by birth. Her husband, Rodolphe, had been born in Paris of German parents. He was a Jew, she was not, although in Germany she had been politically engaged against the Nazis. When called in as an enemy national, Rodolphe was given a choice: a labor camp or the Foreign Legion. He chose the latter and was sent to Morocco. (The absorption by the Foreign Legion of relatively large numbers of alien Jews, like the Spanish Republican refugees before them, into a corps normally far removed from ideology, was not without its frictions.) The Friedlanders' daughter, then nine and a pupil in the Paris school system, had been evacuated with her class to the more tranquil countryside—exactly where, no one bothered to tell the parents.

So this morning Erna stood outside the gates of the Vél' d'Hiv', at the tail end of a long line. Germans do what they're told, thought she. If they are ordered to surrender themselves for internment, they line up to obey. Still, when her turn came at the counter, she was told to go home. Having a child in France exempted her.

But Erna Friedlander did not want to go home. She hated the idea of being alone in Paris, thought she'd be safer in a group. All her friends were being interned, women whose husbands had earlier been taken away. Why should she have to stay behind?

A woman who had come to the stadium to accompany her daughter, although she herself was exempt because ill, overheard the argument at the registration counter. She persuaded Erna to come home with her; there was plenty of room in her apartment now.

A reporter for *Le Matin* stood watch at the stadium. Well-wishers arrived with gift packages for internees (gifts but not visits were authorized). "We can't guarantee that the package will be delivered," a guard explained. "We can't say whether the person it's meant for is still there." Once inside the arena, a woman could not communicate with the outside world. "They have nothing to complain about," a neighborhood shopkeeper told the reporter. "They're well fed and treated decently."

Austrian anti-Nazi Lisa Fittko didn't enjoy the experience. "I decide who is and who isn't German!" a police interrogator snapped. She was also to discover that women who were not interned (because they had children, for example) often felt more ill at ease than she, who was. Once inside the velodrome, a place she hadn't seen since she attended a meeting in support of the Spanish Republican cause, she found the cement floor covered with straw. Some said the straw had been donated by "the Americans," others specified Quakers. She guessed that it came from a Jewish organization. Fittko was to end up near the Spanish border in the notorious "Gurs Inferno," a concentration camp built by the French to hold fugitives from Franco's Spain, and which already had its prison guards, its barracks and barbed wire.

Once again, that evening, the American ambassador was a privileged observer. He "happened" to be with Edouard Daladier, as he would tell Roosevelt, at 8:40 P.M., just when General Gamelin telephoned with the news that the Belgian army had collapsed at the crucial defense line along the Meuse south of Namur. The Germans were now pouring through. Daladier, who appeared stunned, kept saying, "It cannot be true." Gamelin also told his minister that German armored vehicles had been spotted not far from Laon—this a bare seventy miles from Paris—and outside Reims, ninety miles east of the capital. The bewildered minister begged Gamelin to order an immediate counter-attack. The general-in-chief replied that he simply did not have the men for it.

After a quarter of an hour of this incredible conversation, Daladier drew Bullitt over to a wall on which a large general staff map was hung. He pointed to a village a few miles north and east of Laon; it was where the Germans had gone after venturing as far as Laon itself. The weary politician seemed to have nothing to say after that, except that the army he had done so much to build up was about to disappear.

Bullitt's reaction was unexpected. Knowing that he was the only civilian besides the defense minister to have this information—and of course the only foreigner—he decided to remain silent. He didn't think he had the right to transmit the bad news to his own president, although he hoped that Roosevelt would be able to read between the lines of what he did report.

Men of destiny thrive, at least in part, on coincidence. Colonel Charles de Gaulle received his assignment this day. He was going to be allowed to apply the military doctrine he had been advocating all these years—tanks as an offensive weapon in their own right. Assigned to command the Fourth Armored Division, he was ordered, as it happened, to the region of Laon, with the mission to hold the line until a new French army could be moved up to close the breach exposing Paris. "For you who have always advocated the conceptions the enemy is applying, here's a chance to act," General Georges told him.

De Gaulle, who would celebrate his fiftieth birthday before the end of the year, had spent all of his adult life in the army. He had been a junior officer, wounded more than once, in the First World War, and a teacher—one of the army's rare intellectuals—as well as a staff officer. He had made a well-argued case for his offensive doctrine in articles and books in the prewar decade, despite the fact that it clashed head-on with the views of his superiors.

Not that he was being asked to carry the whole war on his shoulders even now. The point was to create his own kind of tank army—not to play a decisive role as he would have wished it, but to gain time until conventional forces could be moved into position. As he drove north to join a hopeless battle, catching glimpses of "this lost people and . . . this military rout," he resolved to continue the struggle until the final defeat of the enemy, the washing out of the stain on the nation's honor.

Roger Langeron, prefect of police of the city of Paris, made a notation in his diary about a call he received that night. The High Command at Vincennes was asking how many motorized policemen and trucks the prefect had at his disposal—to throw them into the breach. Langeron replied that because of the troop call-up, only a few hundred motorized policemen were still on duty. Of course they were at the army's disposal, but could they really stop tanks?

Before the night was over the tension subsided—or was the army looking elsewhere for reinforcements? But henceforth Prefect Langeron knew that the defense of Paris was also his concern.

A postmortem analysis of the French collapse makes sobering reading. It contains one surprise after another. France began with at least as many tanks as the Germans had, and perhaps more; the problem was that French doctrine prescribed their use only as an auxiliary to infantry, and in small groupings. The Germans applied tactics understood and publicized by de Gaulle, concentrating their armor in a striking force. Even in airpower the problem was not numbers but tactics. In 1939, at the beginning of the war, the German air force was largely bluff. French artillery was actually superior to what the Germans could muster; it was simply not adapted to a war of movement. The French had as many soldiers in uniform, and more reservists. Each side, as Colonel Adolphe Goutard summed it up in a somber review of this Battle of France—a review endorsed by his mentor de Gaulle— had sufficient weaponry for the military strategy it believed in. It was only that French strategy was a whole war too late.

A historian would point out that France lost more than 2 million men—1.4 million killed, 740,000 crippled—in the earlier war, at a time when the country's total population was 40 million. Not only arms and legs but energy and enthusiasm lacked in the between-the-wars years; there seemed to be a universal failure of nerve. Then the recession of the 1930s hit hard in this nation that was missing a generation. Disarmament was tempting, even for military men. Thus Marshal Pétain accepted appointment as minister of war in February 1934 after winning a promise that the military budget—already at a low—would not be touched. Yet when the cabinet went ahead and cut it, and that in the face of a Germany that, under its new chancellor, Adolf Hitler, had already rejected the League of Nations and the Disarmament Conference, War Minister Pétain held his tongue. The army was not given what it needed; the Maginot Line would not be extended northward to protect France's frontier with Belgium. Even when France took the initiative and declared war on Germany in September 1939, the accepted wisdom was to sit tight and wait for the enemy to move. It was as if France's army were meant only to defend.

For Germany could have been invaded and beaten in September 1939. Its best troops had been sent to Poland; the French and British could have fielded 110 divisions to Germany's twenty-three. Colonel Goutard points out what many German generals' memoirs reveal, that even after the Polish campaign the German High Command did not consider itself ready to meet the western allies in combat. But the Germans used their time well. Gamelin's tactics were defensive, and even when enemy troops were observed, they weren't fired on. During the phony war, the French had lost the very idea of movement.

On this day when Paris seemed lost, for example, the inactivity at Vincennes headquarters would have surprised the people of Paris. Gamelin's staff was not really involved in a war; that remained the responsibility of General Georges at La Ferté-sous-Jouarre, forty miles north of Paris, theoretically closer to the front. General Georges wasn't saying much to General Gamelin, not asking for help or advice. Gamelin's staff was quite simply underemployed.

Those not privy to military secrets couldn't know just how bad things were on May 15. But nothing could stop rumor. Thus *Life* correspondent Clare Boothe was getting an earful about the Meuse crossing in the drawing rooms she visited, in the cafés and bars favored by the foreign press. The rumors were pointing to the guilty, above all to General Corap and his army. Stories were making the rounds to the effect that his batallions were filled with Communists who had thrown away their arms. Deserters were being picked up in the streets, even in Paris, to be shot. Corap himself (so went the rumors) would be court-martialed and executed. Or he had already committed suicide. More charitably for the French army, the defeat was attributed to German soldiers disguised as priests or farmers, who had prevented the French from blowing up the bridges over the Meuse.

One could also blame the whole thing on the Communists, and some did. The Communist Party gave plenty of cause for concern; its leaders still believed that the war was an error, and said so. "While the German people struggle against its bourgeoisie," the underground edition of *L'Humanité* argued, "we in France must struggle against ours, which can be weakened and vanquished by our action in the factories and inside the army."

9

THURSDAY, MAY 16

Seldom had there been so much talk of Laon, capital of the Aisne district, built on a rise over rich agricultural country, dominated by a splendid Gothic cathedral. It had been occupied by the Germans for all four years of the First World War, and was one of the few towns of its region to come out of that war undamaged. Just after midnight, on the night of May 15–16, Interior Minister Henri Roy reached Premier Reynaud at home with the news. For the prefect of Aisne had just phoned to report that the situation at Laon was "confused." The place was jammed with retreating French troops, and motorized German units patrolled a short distance away.

In the absence of reporting from the front, and with its persistent inability to comprehend the enemy's intentions, the French command could well believe that the presence of German soldiers in the region of Laon was an indication that they were now training their sights on Paris (when in fact the French were seeing nothing more than the dull edge of the sickle cut, for the Germans continued to advance not southward but westward toward the Channel, a move that would seal off Allied forces in northern France and Belgium).

Dominique Leca remembered that brief night. He got his call at two, and was invited to the Interior Ministry on Place Beauvau. There he found his prime minister with Interior Minister Roy, Military

Governor Héring, Defense Minister Daladier, and a group of senior officers back from the front. The stories the military men told were terrifying: deserters flooding into Compiègne (forty-five miles north of Paris), French tanks at the front sabotaged by Communist mechanics. Indeed, recruits from the Paris region, where the French working class was concentrated, were so disruptive that loyal soldiers were turning their guns on them. By the time the officers had finished telling their stories, the mood in the conference room was close to panic.

Some of these stories stuck in the premier's mind. Years later he'd remember that French officers abandoned their men on the pretext that, in a hopeless situation, it was better to let the enemy take as few prisoners as possible. Reynaud heard of a well-to-do Parisian who found his son, a reserve officer in the Corap army, taking a bath in his Paris apartment. "The war is over," the young officer explained.

Back at his own office in the Foreign Ministry, Reynaud was handed a letter from the military governor:

> In present circumstances I deem it prudent, to avoid disorder, to suggest that you order the evacuation of the government, with the exception of the ministries concerned with defense, or at least their top echelon, together with the members of the Chamber of Deputies and Senate, to sites already earmarked for them.

Reynaud lost no time before advising his cabinet of the Héring letter, and the leaders of the two houses of Parliament, Jules Jeanneney for the Senate, Edouard Herriot for the Chamber. But he also remembered a foreign friend. The premier slipped out of his office to talk to Ambassador Bullitt on his arrival at the Quai. Reynaud confirmed what Bullitt knew from Daladier: the Germans couldn't be stopped. "I am sorry for the democracies," was Reynaud's concluding word. Bullitt made sure that it was reported within the hour, by rush cable, Personal and Secret for the President.

Maurice Gamelin, roused from sleep during the night and told to join the meeting at the Interior Ministry, stayed on and on. Until his return, nobody at Vincennes headquarters knew much about what was happening. Only when he did come back did the atmosphere liven up;

Vincennes seemed "almost" at war, as staff officer Colonel Jacques Minart observed it. The military government was henceforth in the war zone, and forty platoons of gendarmes were being detached to serve under General Héring to preserve order in Paris. They were henceforth to stop and inspect civilian vehicles coming into the city, to remove any soldiers found riding in them—to send them back to the front.

The first cabinet officer to arrive for the morning's war conference was Georges Mandel, who, a whole war earlier, had been chief adviser to that other hawk, Premier Georges Clemenceau. Mandel was now minister of colonies, a seemingly secondary assignment when war was being waged on the mainland, but the fifty-five-year-old politician exercised considerable influence beyond his sphere of activity. He symbolized fighting spirit, and made little attempt to hide his conviction that Maurice Gamelin and some of Reynaud's closest advisers lacked this spirit.

Next to arrive was Senator Jeanneney, a senior statesman with even more years behind him; in fact he had been undersecretary of war in Clemenceau's cabinet. "There must be some ninety miles between the Germans and Paris," he concluded when informed of the military situation. "They'll bridge the distance in a day!" It was a matter of hours, replied Reynaud. "In other words, tonight."

Pierre Héring walked in, patently exhausted by his sleepless night. Aloud, the Senate president expressed his astonishment that Paris could be so helpless before the enemy. Where were the fortified barriers? At the very least, wouldn't they slow down the enemy advance? Where were the troops who should be somewhere between the ruptured front and Paris? Had bridges been mined?

"I am subordinate to the commander-in-chief," the hapless general responded. "Paris is now in the war zone. I don't know what the High Command has decided." Héring couldn't even tell the war meeting whether explosives were available for the demolitions that would be required; military governors hadn't been concerned with such things until now.

At last Edouard Daladier walked in; so did Raoul Dautry, a minister of armament who seemed the right man in the right job. Then curious Anatole de Monzie, minister of public works, whose responsibilities included transport, the essential consideration in moving people and equipment out of Paris. When Reynaud asked him to make trucks available to move government departments and the two houses of the legislature, their files included, Monzie's first reaction had been to protest: they just didn't have the wheels. He also believed that to evacuate Paris was to abandon the fight, as well as to paralyze all the rest of France.

Radical Party leader Edouard Herriot, in his youth a literary scholar and since 1905 mayor of Lyon, and who himself had been premier of France on three occasions before his election as president of the Chamber of Deputies in 1936, felt that he could speak for the people: They should at least be informed of the imminence of the danger. That remark upset Anatole de Monzie, for if Parisians were alerted they would try to get out of the city, and the means to move them were simply not available.

It was agreed that, at the very least, essential facilities should be sent away from danger, and the nation's gold reserves. And then that matter of archives. Someone raised the question of the identities of secret agents contained in records held right here at the Quai d'Orsay, reminding the meeting that at least once, in Beirut, sensitive information of that kind had been captured, after which French agents were rounded up and hanged.

Although Herriot leaned toward evacuation of Parliament and thought he should make an announcement at that afternoon's session, Senator Jeanneney held back. And when Monzie announced that he could have trucks ready for the Chamber and Senate by three that day, Jeanneney snapped, "Let someone first tell us what's being done to save Paris. . . . It's more important to hold on than to flee!" Would it really require a week to draw up a defense plan for the city, as Daladier's military aide had said? "And hasn't the work begun? What are they waiting for?"

Daladier promised that the defense ministers—himself for war, plus the navy and air ministers—would be the last to go. Armament Minister Dautry patiently described the situation with respect to explosives, explaining how bridges and roads would be blown up.

Then it was Reynaud's turn. The place for the government, he concluded, was Paris, even under violent bombing. The cabinet could abandon the capital only at the very last minute, to avoid capture.

Immediately after he said this, he was called to the phone for what sounded like an answer to his statement. It was Gamelin on the line. Reynaud's aide, Maurice Dejean, listened in to take down his words. "I can no longer guarantee the security of the French government in Paris after midnight tonight." Much depended on whether the Panzers turned west toward Normandy and the Channel coast, or south for a direct assault on the capital of France.

While the ministers deliberated in the spacious ground-floor conference room, they heard odd noises out doors, dull thuds just beyond the casement windows. Bombs? Anatole de Monzie was staring up at the sky when the first green objects hurtled down from higher floors. File boxes! From the windows the ministers and their aides watched as the heap of boxes and loose papers grew on the lawn. Then someone poured gasoline over the pile, lit a match. A bonfire that would go down in history had been touched off, as the Foreign Ministry burned its most sensitive records.

Of course a bonfire in the large inner court of the Foreign Ministry, a few hundred yards from the Chamber of Deputies, could not escape notice. Members of Parliament could see it; it did nothing to calm anxiety. It was also visible to foreign diplomats friendly or otherwise, to journalists from France and abroad, to simple Parisians. (The flames couldn't be seen from the street, but the column of smoke could.) The burning of archives wasn't going to be mentioned in the censored press, but it was on everybody's tongue. Some papers weren't entirely destroyed before they floated up over the roofs of Paris, and back down to the streets.

Young civil servant François Seydoux remembered that morning for the rest of his diplomatic career and beyond. His superior, Emile Charvériat, had summoned him at dawn for an emergency meeting. The Foreign Ministry then expected the Germans to reach Paris by four that afternoon. Seydoux noticed the waxen complexion of Alexis Léger, who, as secretary-general was the Quai's senior civil servant. Gently Seydoux asked him, "What do you think?" "It's all over," replied Léger—and Seydoux detected the sob. It was the end of an era for Léger, embattled republican among diplomats—in fact the end of a career. He was to be blamed for losing his nerve, giving the order to burn the archives. Reynaud tried to soften the blow by offering him the job of French ambassador to Washington, but he turned it down; how could he undertake a mission that implied having the confidence of his superiors at the very moment he was being fired from the ministry's top administrative position?

He'd find solace, all the same, in the United States. There he could also give free rein to his other career, as the poet who signed his work Saint-John Perse; for that he would receive the Nobel Prize for literature.

That afternoon diplomats did manual labor. They lined up in their offices in shirtsleeves, to pass green boxes containing precious diplomatic papers—reports from embassies, Foreign Ministry orders, information from secret sources—from hand to hand and out the windows. François Seydoux, for one, felt that he was participating in the collapse of his country. He and his colleagues were burying a heritage.

Another junior diplomat, Jean Chauvel, who had been on the job since five that morning, remembered that Charvériat had first thought of tossing the precious files into the Seine, but then decided that they might not be totally destroyed by water; hence the fire. "If it becomes necessary," Charvériat told his colleagues, "I won't hesitate to burn the house down." Soon foreign diplomats and journalists, drawn by the smoke, swarmed over the building as sweating civil servants tossed secrets out the windows. It was a lesson in panic one of those employees regretted having to give. "We'll be the laughingstock of Europe," somebody said. Night fell before they stopped feeding the flames.

Then the order to destroy archives was canceled. The Germans were not pursuing their advance toward Paris; apparently they were giving priority to Normandy and the Channel. Foreign Ministry personnel who had begun to leave Paris for a redoubt on the Loire River were called home.

During the burning, the American Embassy's Robert Murphy showed up, sorry to see what he was seeing. By then the French had advised both the American and British embassies to burn their own archives, and they were complying.

Then it was time for the joint session of Senate and Chamber, to be held at the Palais-Bourbon, seat of the lower house. Paul Reynaud's address was brief, "very noble and very firm," decided Senator Jacques Bardoux. "When the day comes that everything seems lost the world will see what France is capable of doing," he promised. "Weakness will be punished by death."

Grumpy Anatole de Monzie, in a memoir published in Paris during the German occupation, noted that while Reynaud was addressing the chambers he overheard an argument between Edouard Herriot and members of Parliament who wanted to know why Herriot had decided to send them away from Paris. Because Reynaud wanted it that way, replied Herriot. So much for the premier's cock-a-doodle-do on the speaker's rostrum, humphed Monzie.

Of course William Bullitt also turned up at the Quai before the afternoon was over. His comment on the bonfire was "Bad job!" That was not the only bad job, Dominique Leca wanted to tell him. Leca saw the ambassador as a man of good intentions, the kind with which hell is paved. He was too much of a gadfly for Leca's taste. Of course he was anti-Nazi, unlike the American ambassador in London, Joseph Kennedy. As a gadfly, Bullitt went around stinging everybody, the British because they weren't doing enough to help, the French because they weren't winning the war, even Roosevelt because he didn't realize that Paris and London were ready to negotiate with Hitler.

On returning to the embassy, Bullitt dashed off another Personal and Secret for the President. But before giving it to his code clerk, he drafted a shorter message for David Salmon, head of State Department communications. He asked Salmon to do his own decoding, and to keep the contents of the dispatch to himself, handing it personally to Margaret LeHand, President Roosevelt's secretary. "I should like to speak what follows into your most private ear at the White House and to have no record of it," Bullitt began. "It is the sort of hypothesis that we often discuss but never put on paper. However, I cannot talk with you, so here goes."

There could not have been many diplomatic dispatches to a chief of state beginning the way this one did, but then Bullitt wasn't a traditional diplomat, and Roosevelt wasn't very tradition-minded himself. "It seems obvious," pursued Bullitt, "that unless God grants a miracle as at the time of the battle of the Marne, the French army will be crushed utterly." The British were no help at all; they kept their planes home in England while being "critical and contemptuous" of their French ally. This not very Anglophile American ambassador thought that in order to escape the consequences of defeat, the British would go so far as to install a Fascist regime in their own country, which would have the effect of turning the British navy against the United States. He advised Roosevelt to discuss with Canada's prime minister, Mackenzie King, and even with some British naval officers, the possibility of bringing the British navy across the Atlantic to Canada before anything like that happened.

Although Armament Minister Raoul Dautry wasn't panicking, he had more than his share of rescuing to attend to. Dautry, sixty years old that year, was an engineer by training. His present ministry was responsible, among other things, for scientific research, and one of the projects which came under his jurisdiction was the development of atomic energy. He had been paying close attention to the work of Frédéric Joliot-Curie, who, with his wife Irène, daughter of the discoverers of radium, had built up a research department at the Radium Institute. After Frédéric and Irène shared a Nobel Prize in chemistry in 1935 for their work on artificial radioactivity, Frédéric Joliot was appointed to the prestigious Collège de France, taking his associates with him. One of them was Hans Heinrich von Halban, born in Austria, trained in Germany, ingenious and ambitious, a disciple of the Danish nuclear physicist Niels Bohr. Another was Russian-born Lew Kowarski. Each was thirty-two years old; Joliot-Curie himself had just celebrated his fortieth birthday.

In 1939, and shortly before Enrico Fermi and Leo Szilard discovered a similar phenomenon in the United States, the Joliot team revealed the possibility of a chain reaction to create a new source of energy. Theirs became the first published report of neutron emission in the fission process; they even looked into the possibility of making use of this energy in explosives. The Collège de France scientists assured themselves of a supply of uranium from the Belgian Congo.

On the declaration of war in September 1939, Joliot-Curie was commissioned a captain, assigned back to his laboratory; his colleagues

Hans Halban (as he was now known) and Lew Kowarski were naturalized French in haste. It was then that Joliot-Curie went to see Raoul Dautry with a report on what they were up to—what the stakes were. In the United States, meanwhile, scientist Leo Szilard had gotten Albert Einstein to sign a letter to President Roosevelt that said more or less what Joliot had told Dautry:

> In the course of the last four months it has been made probable—through the work of Joliot in France as well as Fermi and Szilard in America—that it may become possible to set up nuclear chain reactions in a large mass of radium, by which vast amounts of power and large quantities of new radium-like elements would be generated. . . . This new phenomenon would also lead to the construction of bombs, and it is conceivable—though much less certain—that extremely powerful bombs of a new type may thus be constructed.

The atomic bomb project, with its unprecedented mobilization of scientific talent, unheard-of expenditures, and deepest secrecy, would soon be under way.

By then the Collège de France laboratory was observing wartime secrecy. Applications for patents had been filed, not to be published until after the war. The secrecy was relaxed for Frédéric Joliot's birthday, so Hans Halban's wife discovered. She was asked to bake a Sacher torte for the occasion, and Hans decorated it with an inscription in vanilla cream; it was a scientific formula. "Don't repeat it to anybody," he pleaded. It was lost on the wives present, except of course for Irène Curie. Halban's wife was aware only that the men had discovered a new source of energy. With her second husband, the theoretical physicist George Placzek, she would actually travel to New Mexico in July 1945 for the first explosion of an atom bomb.

Thanks to Halban's earlier work with Niels Bohr, the team believed that heavy water, a substance that had an extra dose of hydrogen, provided an ideal medium for a uranium chain reaction. The only source of heavy water was a factory in Norway. It happened to have a French owner, but the Germans were also after the precious supply. In February 1940, Dautry sent a secret emissary to Norway, assisted by agents already in place, to bring back the total available supply, which amounted to 185.5 kilograms. During the emissary's mission to Norway, a French bureaucrat clearly out of touch with reality insisted that Halban and Kowarski, former nationals of hostile nations (both were also part Jews), be sent out of Paris momentarily. In deference to their status, they were allowed to choose their places of exile. (Kowarski chose Belle Ile, off the Atlantic coast, Halban the island of Porquerolles in the Mediterranean, facing Hyères.) Then, when the drums of heavy water were safely installed at the Collège de France, the two suspects were welcomed back from exile, to plunge into work in their ultra-secret laboratory. And Hitler launched his invasion of Norway.

Now, on May 16, before the Joliot team had quite obtained a chain reaction with the recently acquired heavy water, they were asked to evacuate Paris, to keep both their materials and their secrets out of reach of the Germans. The uranium was shipped to Morocco for safekeeping. With a laboratory assistant, Halban, his wife, and their infant daughter were the first to go. He had known post–World War I Austria and its devastated economy, and had learned one lesson there. So he and his wife Els had been stocking gasoline for many months (he would fill the tank of the family Peugeot at a service station, then go off into the woods to siphon off the gas by sucking it up through a rubber tube). Gas drums were stored in the family garage. Thanks to Halban's hoarding there was enough fuel to get him, and the 185.5 kilograms of hard water, safely away from Paris.

It was a lovely day as they drove off. With the sun bright in the sky and the misery surrounding them on the highway, Els Halban couldn't help thinking of the American Civil War and Scarlett O'Hara, for she had just recently read *Gone With the Wind*.

William Bullitt hadn't been the only distinguished foreigner at the Quai d'Orsay funeral pyre that day. Winston Churchill flew in, on a first visit to France as prime minister, his first meeting with Paul Reynaud as premier. There was to be a war conference—a Supreme War Council—with Reynaud and Daladier, General Gamelin and Admiral François Darlan on the French side, Churchill's military advisers Sir John Dill and General Hastings Ismay backing up their prime minister. "Utter dejection was written on every face," noted

Churchill. For of course the French were trying to explain what had actually happened on the Meuse River at Sedan, while outside the window of the Quai d'Orsay meeting room, Churchill watched "clouds of smoke . . . from large bonfires," while "venerable officials [were] pushing wheel-barrows of archives on to them." This could only mean that the evacuation of Paris was a real possibility.

It was Gamelin's *triste* duty to explain the French plight, the breach at Sedan, the demoralization of troops caused by enemy aircraft. Reynaud's aide, Maurice Dejean, heard the general-in-chief say, "The Germans want to seize Paris." Gamelin estimated enemy strength at eighty divisions, of which fifty were engaged in the battle. After a silence Churchill asked where France's strategic reserves were positioned. "There aren't any," Gamelin replied. The French were convinced that their visitor didn't realize just how badly France had been trounced. The Englishman saw an opportunity for counterattack, while the French saw only the need for hasty retreat from the Allies' northernmost positions.

The burning question remained. Would the British send the fighters and bombers France so desperately needed? Churchill replied that he could not deprive his country of planes required for the defense of factories producing for the war. Yet he would see what could be done. That night Churchill called on Reynaud at home to announce that his government had agreed to send ten squadrons of fighters in addition to the four already pledged. That would leave twenty-five squadrons to protect Britain: an absolute minimum.

The Briton showed Reynaud the message he had sent to London to convince his cabinet and the Royal Air Force of the need for more planes. In fact it had been read over the phone, uncoded, but in Hindustani, to make certain that the Germans could make no sense of it. This was the brainchild of Churchill's aide Hastings Ismay, who was born in India and once served as military adviser to the Viceroy. Churchill had asked that the reply be telephoned to Ismay, in Hindustani of course.

The British PM slept at his own embassy on Rue du Faubourg Saint-Honoré. Next morning he summoned an embassy attaché to his bedroom facing the large formal garden; pointing to scorched patches of lawn, he asked, "What is going on here?" The embassy aide sheepishly confessed that they had been burning archives; clearly he feared Churchill's reaction to the news that precious documents had been destroyed. All Churchill said was, "Was it necessary to mutilate this magnificent lawn?"

By six that afternoon, calm had returned to the top echelon of government—outwardly at least. The cabinet would not have to abandon its capital, and Dominique Leca said as much in the radio address he drafted for Reynaud's eight-o'clock broadcast. Thinking it over, Leca decided that the scare had been salutary. It had forced the government, as well as institutions such as the Bank of France, to consider how they would move people and plant out of the city, should the time come for that. The day of the Big Scare, as it would be called, also helped Premier Reynaud sort out his own thoughts. What kind of defense minister was this Edouard Daladier, who began the war overconfident and now had to admit that he had no fighting units left to protect Paris? And Daladier was not the only one who would have to go.

That day Daladier drew up a memorandum for his generalissimo, requesting an evaluation of military operations to date, a look into the future. The document arrived at Vincennes headquarters on a day described by staff officer Colonel Minart as one of disarray, with one army after another sending in reports of failure at the front. Defense positions weren't holding, troops behaved badly. All the cafés and bistros of the region surrounding Paris were filled with customers in uniform.

At Vincennes itself, a 75-millimeter gun was wheeled to the center of the yard, aimed at the unfortified southern gate. Secretaries were given rapid instructions on its use, and gun emplacements were chosen at the entrances to headquarters buildings. In a word—Minart's word—everybody had lost his head. This was the context in which Gamelin's staff prepared a reply to the Daladier request; it took them two days to do it. In the report the commander-in-chief was to confess that the French had been guilty of serious errors. He had already removed one army commander, two corps commanders, several division commanders. There had not been any dishonorable behavior, only a lack of dynamism. When the report was signed on May 18, the enemy's intentions still weren't clear. Would the main German thrust be toward the Channel, cutting off Allied forces and preparing for the invasion of Britain? Or would it be toward Paris, striking at the heartland? The commander-in-chief was still convinced that he had been right to throw his best troops into Belgium, although he had to admit that the Germans were better prepared for war. He described the typical French soldier as unimaginative, critical of authority, seeking an easy way of life; in the period between the wars he had received no moral or patriotic education. This failure of morale took the form of looting at the front, and of an every-man-for-himself attitude at crucial moments of battle.

Paul Reynaud didn't wait two days for the report from Gamelin. At 9:50 P.M. on May 16, the day of the Big Scare, a cable went out to General Maxime Weygand, wizened veteran of the earlier war, when he had been the right-hand man of hero Marshal Ferdinand Foch. Weygand had been French high commissioner in the Orient, chief of staff of the French army, commander-in-chief of all French forces in the first half of the 1930s, at which time he opposed disarmament and fought against a reduction of the period of obligatory military service. Long past retirement age, Weygand did at last retire from active duty in 1935; his hostility to left-oriented cabinets kept him far from the seat of power until duty called in August 1939. Now, at the age of seventy-three and as commander of French forces in the Mediterranean theater, he was the best-known military man on active duty.

The premier's telegram was stamped Personal, and Weygand was asked to decode it himself.

GIVEN THE GRAVITY OF THE MILITARY SITUATION ON THE WESTERN
FRONT, I SHOULD APPRECIATE IT IF YOU WOULD TRAVEL TO PARIS
URGENTLY AFTER HAVING TAKEN STEPS TO TRANSFER YOUR COMMAND
TO AN OFFICER OF YOUR CHOICE. PLEASE, TO THE EXTENT POSSIBLE,
KEEP YOUR DEPARTURE SECRET.

To believe the perceptive correspondent of *The New Yorker*, A. J. Liebling, war panic had not really affected rank-and-file Parisians before that day. Only the most "sensitized" layers of the population—journalists, war relief workers, politicians of course—were aware of the seriousness of the situation. On the previous evening, for example, "even the neurotic clientele of the Ritz and Crillon bars had been calm." But now rumors began to circulate—say of sightings of Germans near Paris, in places far from the front line, weeks away from capture. American depositors lined up to withdraw funds from a branch of a New York bank.

Fear of the fifth column, which could either mean German spies or pro-German Frenchmen disguised as ordinary citizens as they went about their mischief-making missions, was sufficiently widespread to call for reinforced surveillance. The police began random checking of identity papers. Later the Dutch historian Louis De Jong collected some of the stories then circulating, stories that gave the enemy credit for uncanny deceptive tactics and devices, including mysterious signal lights and Morse messages flickering over the rooftops of Paris.

"Paris is well protected against the interior enemy," a front-page story assured readers of Le Figaro. "Defeatist propaganda has no place in Paris." The same issue reported the creation of an anti-parachutist militia for the suburbs surrounding the city.

Of course Parisians couldn't help noticing the disappearance of their buses. The official reason was that they were needed to transport refugees. Nothing was said about the evacuation of government personnel. To facilitate the movement of military units and of refugees both, motorists would no longer be allowed to drive out of Paris toward the north or east. Newspapers played up the reports of trials of Communist Party activists, who were drawing sentences of one to five years in prison.

But of course no one counted the number of alarmist phone calls made that day, often by members of the government or the military, persons who supposedly had reliable information, to friends not in government or in the military whose lives or liberties might be endangered by the arrival of the Nazis. Pierre Mendès France remembered one cabinet member who went down the list of his friends that day, warning them all to flee. He told his Jewish friends that they were in particular danger. Mendès was Jewish, but decided that evacuation was not on his agenda. Senator Bardoux heard of a general attached to headquarters who telephoned a Polish woman friend, telling her, "We're lost. Get out of Paris." Snapped this senator, "Another general who ought to be hanged."

The author Pierre Drieu La Rochelle, although an avowed Fascist, didn't quite know what to feel as the Nazis he admired invaded his country. "One is always astonished when something one has expected actually occurs," he confided to his diary. "I still didn't think it could happen so quickly." He attributed the success of the Germans to the fact that they represented the future. "I feel Hitler's movements as if I were he," he had noted two days before that. "I am at the center of his momentum."

Each week the forty members of the French Academy, that rusty, dusty institution founded by Cardinal Richelieu, whose members were chosen for their renown in the arts, sciences, politics, or whatever, assembled to revise the official dictionary of the French language. This day, as fear seized so many Parisians, the unperturbed academicians sat around the table discussing the verb *aimer,* to love. Before the afternoon was over they had finished defining that word, and went on to the next one, *aine,* groin.

Robert de Saint Jean left his desk at the Information Ministry late that day to pick up some news at the Foreign Ministry. It was 7:15 P.M. when he arrived at the hall porter's desk to ask for help in finding his way. "I finish work at seven," the porter told him. Nothing had changed, decided Saint Jean. "The ground is shaking under our feet, and some people continue to wind their clocks."

It's a pity that we can't talk to more survivors of those troubled days. When we do, it is often to find that later, still more traumatic events have all but obliterated memories of those waiting weeks of May and June. Most of the protagonists of the drama have long since disappeared, but some left diaries. Editor and critic Paul Léautaud, who was then sixty-eight years old—a very old sixty-eight, if one believes his complaints—lived modestly in a plain suburb, riding the suburban railway to the center of Paris nearly every day. He was a keen observer, a frank if opinionated reporter, a bit credulous, or he painted himself that way—inclined to arbitrary judgments that went into his diary once for all time.

Léautaud lived alone with his pets, most of them cats, one a monkey.

He would have preferred the company of women, but it seemed too late for that; he would not have been able to do what had to be done. That reflection in his diary is dated May 10, followed by: "This morning, at about 4, beginning of the real war for France." Then days went by with nothing more than literary jottings, by-products of his work at the literary magazine *Mercure de France,* work that brought him to the Left Bank publishing quarter. On May 15 he told his diary: "I write, I work, I forget completely that there is a war. I rest my pen, I get up, I prepare for bed, I look at the night sky outside. Reality comes back to me, like a sudden fall, a threat, a question mark." Having been informed by a friend about the German breakthrough at Sedan, he wrote, "The poor horses, the poor mules, the poor army dogs!"

At two that afternoon he heard a worker on Rue Saint-André-des-Arts telling his wife, "You can see that they're putting the Boches in jail. There are definitely fewer people on the streets." That to sum up the exodus of Parisians as seen by the working class—also by Léautaud. "There's truth in that," he comments. Now, on May 16, he discusses with a friend the advisability of sending his literary papers to safety. He is offered the hospitality of a remote castle in which the Jacques Doucet Library is storing its precious holdings. He is slow to react, for he hates to be rushed.

10

After the feverish night of May 15, the joyless bonfires of the sixteenth, the morning after seemed relaxed to Dominique Leca; one could think, or at least try to assemble one's thoughts. General Héring, who was credited or blamed for kindling panic by signing the recommendation that the government evacuate Paris, now changed his mind. But the rumors continued. While Leca breathed more easily because a reported strike of Belgian railway workers proved untrue, Ambassador Bullitt was telling Roosevelt a different story. There *had* been a strike, he said; it was broken when the Belgians shot the Communist ringleaders. In strict confidence—Bullitt wished this news to go no further than the president's "most private ear"—the ambassador remarked that most of France's heavy tanks "were manned by Communist workmen from the Renault works in the outskirts of Paris." Ordered to advance against German tanks at a crucial moment of the battle, they refused to budge. Bullitt supplied figures: In one case when sixty-three French tanks were ordered to attack, only five went forward. Tankmen reportedly smashed vital machinery. The guilty would be shot.

Still more serious, in Bullitt's view, was a Soviet-inspired mutiny on behalf of Germany. A regiment of French infantry made up of Communists from Paris's industrial suburbs revolted and seized Compiègne, a city that stood between Paris and the German front lines. Some eighty thousand dissident French soldiers still held the town, and would be attacked by French tanks and aviation that evening. Then, after telling Roosevelt all this, Bullitt added that he did not think the matter was as grave as it seemed. "As soon as Reynaud has the nerve to act on Napoleon's excellent principle 'from time to time it is necessary to shoot a general in order to encourage the others,' the 'fifth column' will disappear." Bullitt hoped, for the sake of America's future, that Roosevelt would "nail every Communist or Communist sympathizer in our Army, Navy and Air Force."

Napoleon had not said that about generals; Voltaire had, about admirals. An example of Bullitt's ardent conviction rather than of his skill in parsing rumor, the ambassador often made Communist conspiracy out of what had actually been panic.

It happened that in his daily meeting with key propaganda aides, Joseph Goebbels addressed himself that morning to the matter of dissidence in French ranks, for he knew a good theme when he saw one. Goebbels's men were told to make use of rumors that were actually circulating in France, with stress on the government's plan to flee Paris. Reynaud had denied it and should be called a liar. More, the propaganda experts were to encourage fear and suspicion of the fifth column, pinpointing German émigrés in France, Jews included. They were to spread the story that when the Germans occupied a town they confiscated bank accounts (in this way, thought Goebbels, the French would rush to withdraw savings, disrupting the banking system). And of course the French were to be told in clandestine broadcasts pretending to be French that while France was defending its territory, the British were only interested in saving themselves.

Coincidentally, the day's edition of the underground Communist Party organ *L'Humanité* denounced "the fifth column of agents of capitalism and Fascism," warning that fifth columnists disguised their sympathy for Hitler by attacking Communists. Agents of Fascism, said *L'Humanité,* could be found at all echelons of government.

Paul Reynaud needed no further proof that he was managing a losing team. His commander-in-chief had to go, but that would not be enough. The cabinet needed symbols—symbols who would also be

tough men. Georges Mandel, for instance, was being wasted as minister of colonies. Reynaud saw this obstinate personality, still remembered as the right-hand man of obstinate Georges Clemenceau, as a
forceful interior minister who could deal with the home front, dissi-
dents and Communists included. Mandel wasn't afraid of the job, but
he reminded the premier that he was a Jew; his name, like Léon
Blum's, was a red flag: "Wait for things to get worse!" But Mandel
had a place in Reynaud's strategy. He was the man who had sent
traitors before a firing squad.

In this strategy, Reynaud himself would take over as defense and
war minister from the hopelessly well-meaning Edouard Daladier.
There would also be some cosmetic surgery: Marshal Philippe Pétain,
the highest-ranking survivor of the earlier war and now virtually a
monument, would be brought back from his assignment as ambassador to Franco's Spain, to serve as deputy prime minister.

But wasn't Reynaud's choice of a replacement for Gamelin also a
chimney piece? Dominique Leca feared that. For Reynaud had settled
on Maxime Weygand, another survivor. And he was expecting more
from General Weygand than decorative value; he would have to rescue
routed armies, turn defeat into victory. Seemingly no other military
commander had both the qualifications and the prestige that were now
required.

Today Paris policemen began patrolling the streets with rifles—a star-
tling new sight. And, as *Le Matin* would report, a special group of
motorcycle police had been issued machine pistols that could fire
thirty-two bullets in ten seconds, with the order to be on the lookout
for enemy parachutists. Lest citizens get the wrong idea, the prefecture
issued a warning: No one could purchase a firearm without a permit,
and that included hunting and practice weapons.

It was also the day that employees of radio stations, both government and private, were authorized to bear arms.

A. J. Liebling told readers of *The New Yorker* about a young Japanese embassy attaché who said that it was good to be Japanese now,
since no policeman would suspect him of being an enemy para-
trooper.

*　　*　　*

As early as September 1939, the question of evacuating Paris was on the table, the responsibility of a special task force headed by Deputy Prime Minister Camille Chautemps. It was agreed from the outset that there would be no systematic evacuation of civilians, although Parisians who desired to leave would enjoy free movement. Only children, pregnant women, the sick, and the old would receive special assistance.

Now, in the face of the German advance, the Information Ministry issued a warning: The enemy was spreading false reports, not only through regular news channels but via agents provocateurs, to create panic, inciting civilians to flee their homes, even if they lived far from the combat zone. "Their purpose is to congest roads and interfere with Allied troop movements. The result is a slowing down of our columns of soldiers, making it easy for enemy aircraft to attack them and civilians both with bombs and machine guns." One was not to leave home unless ordered to leave. On the other hand, and contrary to rumors, Parisians needed no permission to leave the city, and this despite the decree of May 16 placing the capital in the war zone.

Paul Léautaud's friend Marie Dormoy of the Jacques Doucet Library told him that it was practically certain that the government was deserting Paris, and that wives of cabinet officers had already left. At home at Fontenay-aux-Roses, a stop on the suburban railway line, he reflected:

> When one considers what war has become little by little, with progress, scientific discoveries, inventions, airplanes first of all, etc., it's really a beautiful sight. The battlefield is everywhere. I am here, in this little house, in the middle of a large garden, at a certain distance, all the same, from the true combat zone. A bomb might be dropped at any time to flatten this house, set it afire, annihilate it and everything it contains, including the peaceful, unarmed civilian I am.

Fascist sympathizer Alain Laubreaux was shocked by an advertisement in his morning newspaper:

Mimi Pinson
CHAMPS-ELYSÉES, 79
Dance Hall
Air-raid shelter for 500 persons
Absolute security
Medical service during alerts

"The indecency of this ad!" he told his diary. "For the past week French territory has been overrun, cities bombed, men are fighting furiously, the dead can be numbered in the thousands, and in Paris people dance to the tune of Negro orchestras!" He felt like dashing off with whip in hand to scatter all the loafers and their females dancing "belly to belly." But in that case he'd once again be prosecuted for troubling public order.

Getting ready for his first battle at the command of a tank division, Colonel Charles de Gaulle employed the time at his disposal (while the necessary equipment was being moved forward) to reconnoiter the combat zone, where he acquired a new awareness of the extent of the collapse. He came upon disarmed French soldiers, men who had found themselves in the path of the German advance. The enemy had ordered them to throw away their rifles and to march southward, for the Germans were too busy to take prisoners. "The war begins quite badly," de Gaulle decided. "Thus it has to continue. There is room in the world for that."

He made a promise to himself. "If I live I'll fight, wherever it is necessary, for as long as it is necessary, until the enemy is defeated and the stain on the nation effaced."

And so into battle. On May 17 he ordered an advance with what was available—three battalions of tanks, about a hundred in all, against a considerably larger enemy force. Determination paid off: the French tanks progressed despite enemy artillery and a lack of support from French gunnery, until at last Stuka dive-bombers and truly superior German armor made further progress foolhardy. His armored units did what they were supposed to, momentarily checking the advance of the ubiquitous Panzers. But there could be no decisive victory; one colonel and one division were hardly sufficient for that. De Gaulle was to attack again two days later in an attempt to slow General Guderian's advance, but the Stukas were also back. He pleaded for a chance to engage still more tanks, but it would have taken a second de Gaulle to say yes.

11

SATURDAY, MAY 18

Looking for a story to melt hearts, *Life* correspondent Clare Boothe visited the Gare du Nord, the railroad terminal connecting Paris to the northeast; her ears fairly rang with the names of French cities fallen to the Nazis. "The Germans were hardly seventy miles from Paris," she told herself, before telling her readers. "And fear gripped every heart." At the station's refugee center she watched as an elderly Red Cross volunteer nurse ladled out soup to those arriving from Belgium and northern France with no place to go. "Madame," asked the nurse, "you are an American?" When the journalist admitted to that, the woman went on, "Then you must tell me the truth. . . . Who has betrayed us?" France had sacrificed so much to build the Maginot Line, a line that was to keep the Germans out, but the Germans were coming all the same.

It was the first time Clare Boothe remembered hearing the word *betrayed* in this context. And then she was to hear it often, in cafés, from the lips of concierges. In the minds of ordinary folk, of course, it was the political class that had done the betraying. The reporter saw the expensive luggage piled up in front of the Ritz Hotel, and decided that the wealthy were leaving—the treacherous wealthy.

Compare A. J. Liebling's portrayal of the Belgian refugees now turning up in Paris. "The great, sleek cars of the de-luxe refugees came first," he told *New Yorker* readers. "The bicycle refugees arrived soon after." He didn't like them much better, these "slick-haired, sullen young men" who "shot out of the darkness with terrifying, silent speed." Hotels filled up with large Belgian families, their children taking it as a lark, parents worried about how to earn a living.

Of course there were desperate refugees too, "waxen-faced mothers dragging drowsy babies, and very old couples who remind you of New Englanders—respectable, reserved, and exasperated—lugging cowhide suitcases and parrot cages. . . ."

Clare Boothe found it normal that refugees wearing silver fox coats knew how desperate the situation was. But how extraordinary that the little people knew. Not from the daily press, which "didn't say anything much except that the Germans were about where they had got to yesterday and that France was such a wonderful country, full of wonderful soldiers. . . ." Not even the politicians knew where the front was, not even the High Command. To hear Boothe tell it, "Paris got its information about what France had been doing all day, all night, the way a woman gets hers about what her husband has been up to." That meant that people watched smiles and frowns on the faces of their leaders, listened for inflections in radio speeches; "by a thousand little downward percolating uncensorable gestures and indications, the contagious climate of a mood spread from the top of Paris to the bottom. . . ."

In Berlin, Joseph Goebbels seemed to be all bliss as he confided to his diary: "Panic rises in Paris. They say Gamelin is shaky. Hooray for that. We are kindling the fire."

What Clare Boothe couldn't know was that Parisians were feeding their pessimism not only from their leaders' frowns, but with facts and fiction directed at France by Dr. Goebbels.

It was the day of the cabinet reshuffle. The important thing was to get amiable Edouard Daladier out of the War Ministry. Henceforth, bantam Paul Reynaud was both premier and minister of defense and war; Daladier remained in the cabinet, taking over the Foreign Ministry. Minister of Public Works Monzie was to quip, "Having failed to evacuate Paris on the 16th, Paul Reynaud evacuates his ministers."

Extremist Alain Laubreaux had his own view of the logic of the appointment of Georges Mandel to the Interior Ministry: "For a Jewish war," he told his diary, "they need a Jewish Clemenceau." Mandel would certainly have understood why a Laubreaux would hate him. For his part he felt that the cabinet still contained too many holdovers of the Munich era, appeasers who would become Pétainists. More than once he confided to his assistant Max Brusset his concern about Reynaud, who was too "fragile" for Mandel. (He also worried about Reynaud's relations with the Countess de Portes, who was turning the premier into a young athlete.)

One change in the government everybody understood was the appointment of Philippe Pétain, savior of Verdun. He had been brought out of retirement often enough, most recently as the man most likely to be persona grata to General Franco as France's ambassador to post–Civil War Spain. This morning, in Reynaud's office, he agreed to join the cabinet as deputy prime minister, obviously pleased that France needed him again. But his arrival distressed another military man, Charles de Gaulle, who had served on the marshal's staff between the wars. De Gaulle was sure that Pétain would favor peace with Germany. In the scenario being talked about, Reynaud would turn over the premier's job to a known appeaser of Fascism, Pierre Laval, who would use Pétain to convince the military establishment that France had to bow to German demands.

Pessimism was the order of the day. The Germans had begun to move decisively against key sites in northern France in their relentless drive to the Channel, but they were meeting stiff resistance from better-trained French troops now, and from heavier tanks—the best the French had. But the Germans knew where they were going and had the strength and cohesive leadership to help them get there. In the absence of clear direction or coordinated defense or attack strategy, the French continued to flounder. Paris seemed not to be on the enemy's calendar just then, but who could know that? Senate president Jules Jeanneney's diary reveals his meeting with his counterpart in the Chamber of Deputies, Edouard Herriot, their subject being evacuation from Paris. To go where? The government intended to send everybody to Tours and the surrounding area, on the Loire 140 miles south and west of Paris, but Herriot worried about the vulnerability of that provincial center to air attack. Eventually it too would have to be abandoned. He favored a transfer to the mountains of central France, safer if only because of the greater distance from the capital. Jeanneney pointed out that Tours had been chosen by the general staff after much discussion, and a great deal had already been done to set up temporary offices. All that could not be changed quickly. But he did think that the "governmental core," meaning the President of the Republic, the cabinet, and Herriot and Jeanneney themselves, should be ready for a rapid retreat from Tours to a more remote hideaway.

Stuck with the details, Anatole de Monzie continued to grumble. He was, he told his diary, having increasing difficulty dealing with the impatience of bureaucrats anxious to set themselves up in country castles. He met all such requests with the excuse that he simply didn't have the vehicles. He spent much of his time recuperating motor transport from government agencies that had commandeered it on the day of the Big Scare—and then kept the trucks and buses in their parking lots, just in case. In his own diary Jules Jeanneney recalls that he had asked his staff to pack up essentials on May 16, to comply with government orders. "Since May 16 the two loaded trucks are waiting. For what? For the roads to be congested?"

Events of the day were carefully monitored by the American ambassador. He was advised that afternoon by Alexis Léger, who had not yet vacated his desk at the Foreign Ministry, that Reynaud was drafting a personal appeal to Roosevelt that included a request that the American president ask Congress to declare war on Germany. Bullitt warned that such an appeal would be "far worse" than useless. Roosevelt was doing all he could to help France, but he was also a realist. If he asked Congress to vote, there would be unanimous *opposition* to a declaration of war.

Bullitt spoke frankly, he said, for the United States and the Allies ought to be frank with each other at this grave hour. Should Reynaud ask the United States to declare war, he would only be doing it for the record, to be able to show one day that he had tried, but had been turned down by Roosevelt. That seemed to Bullitt a cheap tactic, and he said as much to Léger. Léger promised to convey the ambassador's feelings, and to block any such appeal from Reynaud. He asked whether Bullitt would be willing to tell Reynaud what he thought that evening. Of course Bullitt would.

When the ambassador and the premier met—at 8:45 P.M., according to Bullitt's record—Reynaud revealed that the Germans were driving toward the Channel coast, intending to cut off one of the best French armies then in Belgium. Eventually the enemy would take all the Channel ports, cutting off France from Britain. Because of German superiority in troop strength and matériel, the enemy would then swing south and eventually overrun Paris. The premier pointed out that if armies had traveled at four miles per hour in the last war, today's armored divisions moved at thirty miles per hour. He concluded dramatically with a prediction that the war could end within sixty days, with total defeat of France and Britain both.

He explained to Bullitt that he had thought of sending Roosevelt a formal message expressing gratitude for all the war matériel France had received. And yet, with the best will in the world, France could not obtain sufficient matériel in this crucial month to match the Germans. But if the French lost the war, Britain would soon be strangled by German submarines based in French ports, by planes from France, the Netherlands, Belgium. Hitler would also set up Nazi regimes in South America. And in the near future the United States would be threatened as France was today. Reynaud was hoping that Roosevelt would make a public declaration to the effect that if France and Britain were defeated, the vital interests of the United States would be threatened. Thus (the president would say) the United States could not permit the defeat of the Allies.

Bullitt resisted, pointing out that in his country only Congress could declare war, and it was not going to do it at the present time. Bullitt knew that Hitler would attack in the Western Hemisphere when he could, but still he believed that American public opinion was unready for war. Americans were aware of their own military weakness, and would not send troops to Europe. Yet, argued the stubborn Frenchman, a statement by Roosevelt would encourage his people and hurt the Germans.

In his subsequent message to Roosevelt, Bullitt admitted that he agreed with the French premier: after defeating the Allies, Adolf

Hitler would indeed turn to South America and "eventually attempt to install a Nazi government in the United States." Despite this, despite Reynaud's plea and his own convictions, the ambassador did not see a statement from Roosevelt along the lines desired by Reynaud. "To have value," he concluded, "such a declaration would have to mean that we would go to war in the near future."

At the end of the day, American and British correspondents turned up at the daily press conference given by Information Ministry official Pierre Comert in a rococo ballroom at the Hotel Continental. Here the press was told officially about the changes in the cabinet. Afterwards a staff officer would remark to A. J. Liebling, "Weygand's ideas are so old-fashioned that they have become modern again."

Liebling worried about Pétain. Would he serve Pierre Laval's schemes as that other old soldier, Hindenburg, had served Hitler's? Still, this correspondent and his colleagues felt more buoyant that evening. They were not expecting victory, but disaster seemed to be moving at a slower tempo.

12

Writing a novel set in these final days, Russian observer Ilya Ehrenburg saw nighttime Paris as a deep forest, now that even the ubiquitous blue lanterns had been extinguished. Pedestrians were being stopped on the street for identity checks. On Rue du Cherche-Midi a lame grocer was arrested because someone claimed to have seen him signaling to enemy aircraft. Parisians swore that there were forty thousand German soldiers walking around the city in disguise.

Ehrenburg described the refugees who then wandered the streets of Paris, so numbed that even the horns of nervous taxi drivers couldn't make them move faster. Exhausted women sat on curbs, as anxious passersby asked where they came from. The war was still far away for ordinary Parisians, and the sight of refugees was the only troubling note.

In Berlin that morning, during Joseph Goebbels's daily meeting with his department chiefs, it was noted with regret that the appointment of Marshal Pétain as deputy premier had had a positive effect on French morale. Countermeasures were called for. Goebbels ordered press and radio to stress that the call to Pétain was only a political maneuver, for a man of eighty-four was in no position to change anything. And they must stress that a Jew had been appointed interior minister to save

Jewish plutocracy by putting down antiwar protests. Both the German press and the underground radio stations were to say (the underground stations were to say it in a tone of indignation) that war criminals like Reynaud were hiding behind the venerable figure of Marshal Pétain.

Goebbels also urged his services to increase their efforts to spread panic. The French-language radio station purporting to be operated by patriotic Frenchmen was to "reveal" a supposed plot against the Chamber of Deputies (an echo of the way the Nazis made use of the Reichstag fire). Reviewing the day's achievements, the propaganda minister noted how the press in London and Paris revealed the "total disarray" in the enemy camp. He was also happy to see that the panicky flight of refugees created traffic jams on highways and even within cities.

It was the day of Winston Churchill's first radio address as prime minister. He had to admit that the enemy had broken through French defenses above the Maginot Line, a breach that the French were trying to stem with the help of the Royal Air Force. If the Allies did what he was confident they would do, "if the French retain the genius for recovery and counter-attack for which they have so long been famous, and if the British army shows the dogged endurance and solid fighting power of which there have been so many examples in the past," he said, the situation could be transformed. But he felt that it would be foolish "to disguise the gravity of the hour." Churchill assured his people that he had the promise of the French, and of France's "indomitable Prime Minister," that "whatever happens they will fight to the end, be it bitter or be it glorious."

When Marshal Pétain walked into Reynaud's office, the indomitable premier alerted the marshal: "I've issued a call to a man you don't like, but this is not the time for personal sympathies or antipathies." The reference was to General Maxime Weygand, and to the lifelong hostility that separated the two veterans, a hostility originating in the rivalry between General Pétain and Weygand's Marshal Foch in the First World War.

Now, after landing in Paris, Weygand took time only to change clothes before showing up in Reynaud's office at the War Ministry on Rue Saint-Dominique. The premier had Pétain with him. The man from Beirut was not told of any change in his responsibilities just then; Reynaud asked him only to talk to Gamelin and Georges, and then to return with his impressions.

Weygand called on General Gamelin at Vincennes. The weary commander-in-chief showed a certain dignity as he told the visitor that after having been defeated, he found it natural that he was being replaced. Weygand replied that all he knew was that Reynaud was unhappy with him. From there Weygand drove up to La Ferté-sous-Jouarre, to find an equally ravaged General Georges, a Georges who confessed that he no longer slept at all. Then the thirty-five-mile drive back to Paris and Rue Saint-Dominique. To Weygand the situation was clear. The initiative belonged to Germany; France no longer controlled its front. Reynaud asked Weygand to replace Gamelin as commander-in-chief, and he accepted the assignment.

Reflecting on these events later, Maurice Gamelin confessed that he hadn't realized, on the morning of May 19, that it was to be the last day of his military career. He had survived difficult moments so many times. And he did not see himself as responsible for what was happening at the front, any more than Pétain could be held responsible for the disastrous Chemin des Dames battle in 1918. He himself thought that the weak link in the French command was at La Ferté-sous-Jouarre, headquarters of General Georges, whose disorderly procedures helped explain that officer's weariness.

For Parisians there had been no change at the top—not yet. It was Sunday, and a different scenario had been written for them. That morning Paul Reynaud, Edouard Daladier, and other members of the government attended a special mass at Notre Dame cathedral. Deputies and senators had also been invited, with the diplomatic corps. They found a sober Notre Dame: its precious sculptured façade had been sandbagged.

A magnificent ceremony, Senator Bardoux called it. The crowd was dense on the vast square outside, dense inside, and it was a devout crowd. Vicar Roger Beaussart wore the bishop's miter and held a staff as he climbed to the pulpit. "What have we come to ask of God?" he intoned. "Victory . . . We ask Him for this because we are fighting a war not for money or worldly power, but to preserve spiritual values without which there is no reason to live." The banner of Joan of Arc, relics of saints, were held high as the procession moved through the nave, then out to the square, a reminder of other processions in times of trouble. Monsignor Beaussart's invocations resounded, echoed by the assembly:

Our Lady of Paris, we have confidence in you;
Saint Michael, protect us in combat!
Saint Louis, protect those who govern us! . . .
Saint Joan of Arc, fight alongside our soldiers and lead us to victory!

William Bullitt stood in the front row. He was one of those observed to be weeping.

But one of the newsmen present, Emile Buré of *L'Ordre,* watching the American ambassador kneel before a statue of Joan of Arc to offer a rose from President Roosevelt, could not resist a profane thought: "It's not prayers we need; it's planes."

Paul Léautaud considered the ceremony "shameful." He told his diary, "Prayer is weakness. . . ." Then he thrashed out the issue over lunch with his loyal friend Marie Dormoy of the Doucet Library. To her argument that prayer was strength, he countered that in the face of danger one doesn't get down on one's knees, one stands to face it. He had no sympathy for the French revolutionaries of 1792, but at a time of crisis they hadn't prayed, they'd raised an army. Better to tell Frenchmen to keep guns at home to defend themselves, and to warn the commander-in-chief, "I give you two days to redress the situation."

But he was not going to forget, all the same, that he was against the Republic. So Léautaud added in his diary destined for eventual publication. Just as "one should send to the firing squad, in case of defeat, all the politicians responsible in one way or another for the defeat."

13

Monday, May 20

Today Paul Léautaud annotated his diary: "This morning's papers put the German armies at the outskirts of Saint-Quentin, tonight's papers in the vicinity of Péronne. They didn't pray hard enough to God yesterday." The critic obviously enjoyed the contemplation of human frailty. A collector of absurdities, he seized upon the editorial that reassured readers with the thought that "the more the Germans advance the more they are in peril, distancing themselves from their bases, while the more we retreat the better we are, approaching our own bases." To that Léautaud added, "Let's retreat all the way to the Pyrenees, then the Germans would be done for."

Correspondent Alexander Werth was nearly as sardonic as Léautaud. He went to the Hotel Continental that day with a story he wished to send to London. A negative reference to Daladier was crossed out by the censor (for after all he remained in the cabinet). While Werth was negotiating with the colonel in charge, new orders were phoned in: nothing could be said about the bombing of Le Havre, nothing on Spain or Italy, or on the probable evacuation of the British colony of Paris.

The reference to Le Havre raised eyebrows. Werth learned that it had been a pretty heavy bombing. At the War Ministry he was told of severe combat "around" Saint-Quentin and Péronne, although the

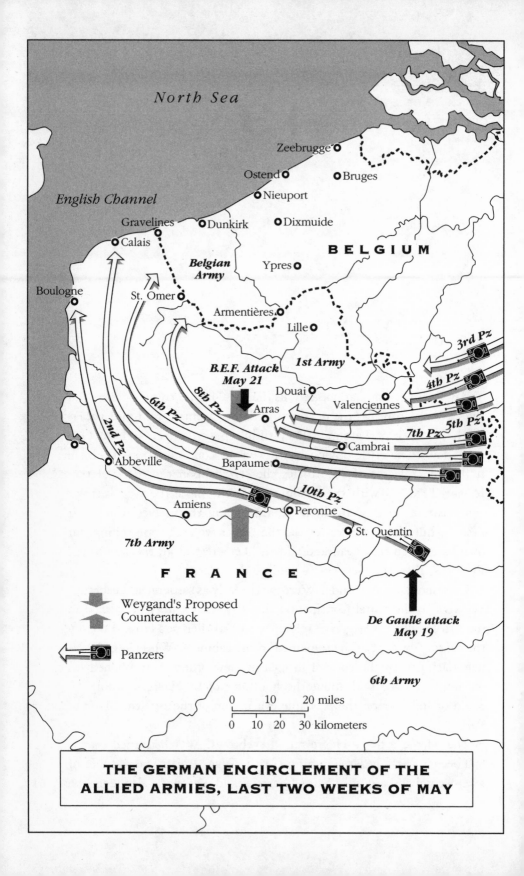

North Sea

English Channel

Zeebrugge
Ostend   Bruges
Nieuport
Gravelines   Dixmuide
Calais   Dunkirk
                    BELGIUM
Boulogne
            Belgian
St. Omer   Army   Ypres

            Armentières
                Lille   1st Army
        B.E.F. Attack
        May 21   3rd Pz
                    Douai   4th Pz
        8th Pz   Arras   Valenciennes
6th Pz   5th Pz
        2nd Pz   7th Pz
                        Cambrai
                Bapaume
        Abbeville
                                10th Pz
        Amiens   Peronne
                            St. Quentin
        7th Army

        F R A N C E

            Weygand's Proposed
            Counterattack   De Gaulle attack
                                    May 19
            Panzers
                                    6th Army

            0   10   20 miles
            0   10   20   30 kilometers

THE GERMAN ENCIRCLEMENT OF THE
ALLIED ARMIES, LAST TWO WEEKS OF MAY

spokesman indicated that enemy progress had been slowed. But Werth was convinced that fighting "around" a place meant that the town in question was already in German hands.

Joseph Goebbels continued to do what he could to prevent the French from feeling overconfident. At that morning's conference with his staff he asked division chiefs to spread the tale that General Gamelin had resigned because he understood how hopeless France's position was, and actually wanted to enter into negotiations with Germany. Another idea: spread the story that the French were handing out counterfeit money to refugees from the war zone. Still another: say that foreign diplomats in Paris had been told to be ready for the evacuation of the government.

In Paris the Communists, forced to lie low by relentless prosecutions, continued to print and distribute illegal tracts as well as the clandestine edition of *L'Humanité.* The May 20 issue made clear that fifth columnists did not have to land with parachutes, for they were already inside the French government. Once again the Communists demanded that France form a "peace government."

Communists aside, Goebbels aside, Premier Reynaud discovered with gratitude that his new appointments had given the French reasons for hope. He turned the pages of the morning papers with the feeling that at last he had done something right. "Pétain," proclaimed the editorial in *Le Figaro,* "is the sublime and victorious resistance at Verdun. Weygand is the soul of Foch."

Rising that morning after a sleepless night, Maurice Gamelin looked around the bare room in which he had lived for eight months: a monk's cell it seemed, in the glorious compound of the Vincennes castle-fort. His orderly packed his bags and at nine he was ready for his successor (Weygand was punctual). "Not a word coming from the heart," Gamelin thought. "Does he have one? Both Joffre and Foch did." This Weygand seemed sure of himself, younger than ever. Gamelin remembered with bitterness that it was he who had appointed Weygand to the Beirut command; did *he* remember that? For his part, Weygand thought he detected relief in Gamelin's attitude— relief to be discharged of all this heavy responsibility.

Gamelin said he would like to write a memorandum on the military situation as he found it that day. Later, much later, when Weygand came upon the report Gamelin had submitted to Reynaud two days before that, with its pessimistic assessment of French chances, he decided that it was just as well he hadn't seen it earlier. The extent of the impending disaster might have discouraged him.

Shortly after noon, William Bullitt turned up at the War Ministry to see Reynaud. Whatever the morning headlines might have done for the premier's morale, he was looking glum again. As Bullitt reported to Roosevelt on returning to the embassy, "The situation is desperate." General Giraud, ostensibly in charge of French defenses in the north, simply had not been heard from. Weygand might well be taking over too late.

To make matters worse, there was a report to the effect that Italy would soon join the war on Germany's side. "My personal opinion," Bullitt told Roosevelt, "is that if Mussolini can be kept from stabbing France in the back, the German drive on Paris will be held." He begged his president to "make a last effort" to keep Mussolini out of the war. "The blow to French morale if he should attack would be terrible."

Mussolini's hesitations had not been feigned. If he had remained out of the war until now, it was because he had not been convinced that Hitler would win, had not believed that Britain could be defeated. But once the risks were reduced, the Duce could swagger. For Italy had to help write history, and never mind that his own generals were telling Mussolini that the state of the country's preparedness was only "forty percent." Fascist Italy had a long list of grievances against the Allies, grievances involving French and British control of the Mediterranean, with Gibraltar on one side, Suez on the other; yet for Mussolini it was "Our Sea." Then there was Africa, with territories once Italian, now French.

It was also true that Italy was not ready, but now Italy would not have to fight to win. Italy's ambassador in Paris, Raffaele Guariglia, was well aware of that. He was busy seeking concessions the French could offer in return for a continuation of Italian neutrality. He thought that the French should prefer peaceful occupation by Italy of some French territory—a part of southeastern France contiguous with the Italian border—to hostile occupation by the Germans. In his scheme, Italy would give up this territory when France made concessions elsewhere. Guariglia tried out the idea on his foreign minister, Count Galeazzo Ciano, Mussolini's son-in-law. Ciano brushed him off.

Ciano didn't even tell him what he was discussing, almost daily, with France's ambassador to Rome, André François-Poncet.

After another trek out to General Georges's headquarters at La Ferté-sous-Jouarre, Maxime Weygand was back at the War Ministry that evening at six. He told a story of errors committed by the French, but felt that something could still be done. The breach could be stemmed at Arras if French, British, and Belgian forces pulled together, and he offered to travel north to meet the commander-in-chief of British forces, General John Standish Gort, King Leopold of Belgium, and of course the French commanders in the sector. Both Reynaud and Pétain thought the journey would be too risky, in view of the speed at which the enemy was advancing. But Weygand insisted, promising to make the round trip in a day.

A secret directive went out that day from the Defense Ministry placing both front and rear echelons on alert concerning enemy paratroopers. Some hit the ground disguised as French officers, carrying all the proper papers, and then proceeded to give orders to French troops in the name of an existing general. German parachutists landed heavily armed. Their mission was to create panic behind the lines by firing at everybody, soldiers and civilians alike. Sometimes they attacked airfields and other vital facilities; at times they were disguised as civilians to mix with the general population, particularly with refugees, to spread panic; this rapidly affected military units as well. They might begin by shouting, "Here come the tanks!" and then start running. Or, disguised as soldiers from neighboring regiments, they joined a column of troops in an attempt to kill officers. They destroyed roads, telegraph and telephone lines. . . .

There were still a lot of imaginary parachutists. In Paris, war correspondent Arved Arenstam found himself in a traffic jam on Place de

l'Alma. The bottleneck was a crowd, visibly agitated, with a report of
the sighting of a German paratrooper racing from ear to ear, shouts of
"Kill him!" But nobody found a parachutist that afternoon. Nobody
could demonstrate that there had been one in downtown Paris.

The war was close, but not that close. The papers that day told
Parisians that ration cards were now available at the city hall. Only
bread tickets would be distributed at first; rationing was expected to
go into effect at the beginning of June. The morning *Le Figaro* offered
kitchen hints, for example how to turn leftovers into stuffed hearts of
artichoke. The papers were full of helpful tips for refugees—offering
shelter, food, even jobs. Youth groups were collecting toys, baby
clothes, chocolate, oranges, to be given away at railway stations.

In her own neighborhood in west Paris, Fernande Alphandery had
watched as Belgians drove into town from their embattled country in
decent motorcars; one needn't worry about them. But now her volunteer Red Cross work took her to the Gare Saint-Lazare to assist the
refugees who really needed assistance. Wearing a prim, official-looking
uniform—which she knew helped to conceal considerable disorgani-
zation in the relief program—Mademoiselle Alphandery took charge
of three Belgian families, first providing food and a place to stay, then
helping them find onward transportation to places south of Paris,
where work might be available.

It occurred to Ambassador Bullitt that the distress of these refugees
might help sway American opinion—both official and public. In a
dispatch to the U.S. Department of State he reported that day:

> Last night by chance I met the wife of the Minister of Blockade,
> Madame Georges Monnet, who had been at Soissons attempting
> to evacuate small children. They were walking on the road to-
> ward Paris since they had no means of transportation and she was
> trying to keep them singing to help their little feet to move. Two
> German aeroplanes came down and machine-gunned them and
> the road was filled with little bodies.
>
> The same story I have from fifty witnesses French and Amer-
> ican.

Indeed. The Red Cross representative in Paris, Wayne Taylor, told Bullitt that German barbarity and French suffering were "ten times more horrible" than even Bullitt was reporting. Taylor estimated that there were at least five million people on the roads, many of whom would die of starvation and illness unless Americans helped—quickly.

It did appear that Parisians had lost their enthusiasm for after-dinner entertainment. At the Casino de Paris, star performer Maurice Chevalier was able to track the advance of the enemy by the diminishing number of spectators in the audience. This evening he and his fellow entertainers played for only a handful of faithful customers scattered here and there in the theater. Many of the performers were missing. The day would soon come when the Casino no longer had a reason to stay open, and so it closed. And Chevalier was off in a little Fiat to join the column of refugees from Belgium and northern France, and increasingly from Paris.

14

TUESDAY, MAY 21

Paul Léautaud had a lady friend who could read English. In that way he learned the details of the rout at Sedan, something the French press could not have given him, and of a whole region "left without defense, without troops, the bridges intact." But his confidante also repeated what she had heard around Paris that morning: Gamelin had been shot. Another woman told him that she had heard the same story. Someone else said that Gamelin shot *himself.*

After lunch, Léautaud's dentist tells him that the Swiss radio has just announced that the town of Laon has fallen. Before the day is over, Léautaud hears more stories, such as that southwest France is overrun with refugees believed to be Germans in disguise. Other Germans are walking around in uniforms of the Polish exile army. A singer tells how he was stopped on the road by a gendarme asking for his identity papers. The singer noticed a general in another automobile and asked the gendarme why he didn't ask to see the officer's papers too, since a general normally didn't drive his own motorcar. The gendarme did go over to ask; the general shot and killed the gendarme. An employee of the Foreign Ministry stumbles upon two suspicious men in a field, questions them, and is shot. True stories? Léautaud wonders. He also hears about workers quitting their jobs or refusing to work on Sundays; he hears too of mutinies in certain regiments. He is convinced that treason lies in wait everywhere.

Goebbels was telling his diary: "All our broadcasts, official and underground, are henceforth involved in a major campaign to stir up panic." He boasted, "I myself write most of the material." There would be a surprise in store for Weygand, added Goebbels: morale was plunging in Paris and London both. It would soon become a kind of "fatalist despair." Meanwhile in Germany everything was rosy. "This people has the absolute conviction of victory."

The theme he gave his so-called Frenchmen-speaking-to-Frenchmen radio stations that day was, "All is lost; we have to end this war." Once again, France's genuine Communists proved that they didn't need a Dr. Goebbels to write their scripts. In Moscow, French Party chief Maurice Thorez drafted a manifesto to spell out his party's opposition to the war. It was for German workers to combat German imperialism, he argued, while the duty of Frenchmen was to denounce those in their own nation who had started the war.

We accuse the French bourgeoisie of having brought on the present war by crushing the German people under the monstrous terms of the Versailles Treaty, an imperialistic punishment for an imperialistic war.

Now that the Communist press was banned, Parisians could not read the Thorez manifesto, and the other papers would not be allowed to print it even had they wished to. The first publicly available periodicals in which it appeared were the Communist Party organs in New York and London, each called *The Daily Worker.*

By agreement the Paris press reduced the number of pages to two on May 21—two sides of a single sheet. This, said an announcement, would economize transport facilities, freeing more vehicles for defense needs.

It happened to be a beautiful day in Paris, as newsman Alexander Werth noted in his diary. Even the morning papers, scanty as they were, were more reassuring than on recent previous days. Werth strolled along the Seine, up and down the old streets of the Left Bank, then ordered excellent duck for lunch, to prepare him for the session of the Senate, where Premier Reynaud was to make an important speech.

"The homeland is in danger," were Reynaud's opening words. He spoke frankly about French mistakes—in thinking that the Meuse River was a barrier to invasion, in failing to blow up the Meuse bridges, for over these bridges passed the *Panzerdivisionen* supported by fighter aircraft, thrown against "sparse divisions badly led and badly trained." It was a stunning indictment of the country's lack of preparation, and Reynaud specifically identified the "Corap army" at the end of his summation.

Hence the appeal to Weygand. "Too late," Alexander Werth heard members of Parliament murmur. Cheers for the Weygand-Pétain combination sounded halfhearted; the gloom persisted. Werth also heard a collective gasp when the premier announced the fall of Arras and Amiens. But Reynaud concluded with an assurance that France and Britain united could not be beaten:

"France cannot die. And if one day I were told that only a miracle could save France, that day I would say: "I believe in the miracle, because I believe in France.' "

Dominique Leca, who had prepared a draft of the speech, winced at that; they were not his lines. The Senate was dominated by lay Republicans who definitely did not believe in miracles. Leca also thought that by admitting faults had been committed, Reynaud opened the door to accusations that France had gone to war unprepared. And in the corridors, deputy Xavier Vallat, who would soon be in charge of the Vichy State's Jewish Affairs Agency, called out to former Popular Front premier Léon Blum: "This is what you got us into!"

For days *The New Yorker*'s A. J. Liebling had been watching the changing expressions on the faces of Parisians. They had become haggard, with cheekbones, noses, and jaws more prominent. He knew that there was sufficient food around, but "people got thin worrying." Yet there seemed to be no immediate danger; Liebling himself only thought of bombs when the news was very bad.

Now however, after hearing Reynaud, Liebling himself was frightened. That evening, in an oppressively hot climate, thunder mixed with antiaircraft shelling. He thought the suburbs were being bombed. Later he was to discover that others had had the same impression.

François Charles-Roux, until then France's ambassador to the Vatican, had been summoned home to replace the hapless Alexis Léger as secretary general of the Foreign Affairs Ministry—the man who kept the diplomatic machine working year-round. A scholar and career diplomat who had passed his sixtieth birthday, Charles-Roux had been his country's ear at the Holy Office since 1932, and in that capacity was qualified to deal with a growing concern of the war cabinet: Italy. Would Mussolini enter the war on Hitler's side? Could he be kept neutral, and at what cost? The first visit of Charles-Roux was to see his predecessor Alexis Léger. The two men agreed that France would soon have a new enemy (Italy) without the hope of getting a new ally for a long time (that would be the United States of America). Charles-Roux went on to the War Ministry, where Reynaud drew him over to a large wall map to brief him on the battle picture—the bottling up of Allied forces in the north, the slim chances of breaking out. "Whatever happens," promised Reynaud, "I shall not surrender."

Those in the know agreed with what Charles-Roux was already thinking, that if France appeared to be losing the war Italy would most certainly attack. But there was another point of view, and it had its champion in the cabinet in the person of the enigmatic Anatole de Monzie. It was a point of view sympathetic to Italy, at least to negotiating with Italy, giving that nation something in exchange for a pledge of neutrality.

Alexander Werth was on the phone at six that afternoon when an air-raid siren sounded; he was cut off. So he left his office to go downstairs to his lodgings in the same hotel, where he started to play the piano. Since he could no longer get a phone connection through to London, he wondered if he should simply stop reporting the war. Other correspondents were using telegrams; he decided to do the same. After the all-clear he went out to the Café de la Paix to discover the sidewalk terrace crowded with pre-dinner drinkers—although the alert had ended only instants earlier.

"My dear darling little wife," Colonel de Gaulle began his letter, following "a long and hard battle which happened to go *very well* for me." He was now in a position to employ tactics he had been advocating, often against the tide, for so long. "My division is taking shape as it fights, and they are giving me the material I need," he told his spouse, Yvonne, "for if the general atmosphere is bad, it is excellent for me."

In fact, de Gaulle's forces could not do much more than the rest of the army was doing—retreat. The best he could do was retreat more slowly, with more dignity, than the others.

15

WEDNESDAY, MAY 22

"The serenity of Paris—with spring more beautiful than ever before—is astonishing," Robert de Saint Jean told his diary.

> Obviously there are Parisians who don't quite understand what is happening, but there are many others who do understand and who nevertheless remain confident in the future of the country, certain that the sun will rise once more tomorrow and that France will also be there.

It was true that one could live almost a normal life in the city during this no-longer-*drôle* war. Certainly a student below military age could, a female student all the more so. In May the university seemed a cocoon; the war was on the outside. For Jeanne Huzard, daughter of a medical doctor, herself a student at the Faculty of Law on Place du Panthéon, the German offensive had come almost as relief—a cloudburst—after months of uncertainty. And then life picked up almost as it had been, with theater, movies, restaurants, even special exhibitions (such as one devoted to Overseas France at the Grand Palais). Classes were at near-normal strength, with students below draft age, professors too old to be called up. Students didn't talk much about the war. Only once was her class interrupted by an air-raid warning, at which time everybody dutifully filed into a cellar. Otherwise, routine. Then came the shock of Reynaud's Senate speech. It was Jeanne Huzard's cold shower.

Simone de Beauvoir was another listener alarmed by what she heard Paul Reynaud confess on the radio. His reference to a miracle signified, to her, that all was lost. Depressed, unable to work coherently, she went to the movies, to the theater, to the opera (for Darius Milhaud's *Médée,* staged by Charles Dullin), for a few hours forgetting the world outside.

A young poet-philosopher, speaking to his own private diary, had detected hope in Premier Reynaud's words. "The violent frankness of the speech," decided Jean Lescure, "carried with it an indirect benefit." He was proud of a people capable of fighting when all seemed lost; it was 1870 all over again, thought Lescure. "But will our leaders know how to use this force, to channel it?"

In his diary Lescure recorded the rumors he was hearing—"rubbish" he called them. Gamelin had at once committed suicide, been killed by a Communist, been shot, been jailed. Lescure's mother-in-law, after hearing what Reynaud had said about the badly led Corap army, added up the rumors to decide that two French divisions had refused to attack the enemy. A somber picture, all in all. Lescure was irritated above all by the habit of looking for someone to blame—most often it was the Popular Front of Léon Blum—for France's present plight.

Stories heard at the Information Ministry, recorded by Robert de Saint Jean, were hardly more reassuring.

The flight of farmers on the highways was provoked by German agents disguised as beggars, blind men, nuns, wounded French soldiers, etc. . . . All this so that the roads become blocked by hordes of civilians, thus rendering them impracticable to French reinforcements.

"The adversary's morale is catastrophic," a jubilant Joseph Goebbels told his notebook. "Our panic plan is now producing quite tangible effects."

The famous playwright Henry Bernstein, walking in the Tuileries garden with Hervé Alphand, a Foreign Ministry officer and future ambassador, ran into a familiar antagonist, the professed Fascist Pierre Drieu La Rochelle. "Cheer up," Bernstein teased him, "the Germans are advancing; you should be pleased." Drieu replied with a couple of punches. The fight didn't go very far; Bernstein was sixty-four and Drieu forty-seven. Indeed, Drieu would become a prominent collaborator with German occupation authorities, while Bernstein was a refugee in the United States.

Walter Kerr had been covering Europe for the *New York Herald Tribune* since the autumn of 1937. He was in Austria the following year to report on Hitler's annexation of that nation, moving on to Czechoslovakia to report the crisis leading to the Munich pact. Already a seasoned war correspondent at twenty-eight, Kerr arrived in France in September 1939, and the phony war there allowed him to travel north to Finland and a truer war. On the day of the German attack on the Low Countries in May 1940 he was home in Syracuse, New York. His editor found him there and asked how quickly he could get to Paris. He traveled the fastest way possible at that time, flying the Pan American Clipper to Lisbon, then overland by train, arriving in Paris on May 22. Like other war correspondents, he first tried to find out where the front was; nobody could tell him. But there was also a war in Paris, with rifle-carrying policemen, plainclothes inspectors stopping people on the street to demand identity papers. He saw bullet holes in the windshields of the automobiles of refugees who had come down from Belgium.

Kerr tried to make sense of the rampant rumors. He was relieved to discover that French food was as good as ever. He only had to remember on which days hard liquor was available.

Vincent Sheean, a senior correspondent Kerr respected, confided to him that France would not last long. Finding that he had said all he had to say about Paris under siege, Sheean himself was packing for London, since the story would henceforth come from Britain.

> I am receiving hundreds of letters daily from French men, women and children, senators, mothers, peasants, imploring me to persuade the Government and the people of the United States to help at this hour not merely with sympathy but with armed force.

Hundreds of letters? Letters from peasants? That ought to be exaggeration, but it is an official telegram signed by Ambassador William C. Bullitt, sent to U.S. Secretary of State Cordell Hull, who, to Bullitt at that hour, must have seemed a stone face unable to be moved. Bullitt's conclusion:

> As the suffering grows, a certain amount of bitterness is inevitable. Up to the present these letters have been couched in terms of gratitude and appeal but there is an undertone. . . . The cry in every letter is for planes.

In a "personal, unofficial, and off the record" message to Franklin Roosevelt, Bullitt had asked whether American reserve pilots could be authorized to fly for France after resigning their commissions, with the understanding that after the war they would be restored to reserve status. Nothing like that was about to be approved by the cautious American government.

Although it wasn't Sunday, a four-day cycle of prayers was initiated at Saint-Etienne-du-Mont, the Late Gothic church behind the Panthéon containing the tomb of Saint Genevieve, who with her prayers turned Attila's Huns from Paris, and became its patron saint. Now Genevieve was needed to protect Paris from another scourge. Monsignor Beaussart, who had led the service at Notre Dame on the previous Sunday, exhorted believers not to judge their leaders, but to give them full confidence.

*   *   *

Sugar was to be rationed. Starting on June 1, it was announced, each citizen would be authorized to purchase 750 grams per month. But bread rationing was postponed. Volunteer reservists were to be organized into territorial guard units, wearing their old army uniforms and helmets. On days when they actually served, they would receive pay appropriate to their grades.

A well-known vaudeville house informed the press:

> Despite present business conditions Mr. Mitty Goldin, director of the A.B.C. Music Hall, considers it a duty, for performers and staff, and mindless of reduced and even negative receipts, to continue performances with the entire cast. Beginning on Friday, at matinees and evening performances, there will be a new comedy show featuring French songs . . . and some of the best stars of the cabarets, the spirit of France and of Paris. . . .

At ten that morning General Weygand had walked into Reynaud's office, to report on his mission to the northern front, a mission not without incident. Not only hadn't the new commander-in-chief slept, he hadn't had time to wash or shave before reporting to the chief of government. "He returns full of spirit," cabinet attaché Maurice Dejean noted. "His entire being gives off energy and decision." The little general told Reynaud something he was surely glad to hear: the situation was certainly serious at the front, but a counteroffensive remained possible, recovery was possible. For this veteran soldier, who would be remembered as the supreme skeptic, had somehow found reasons to hope in the confused battle picture in the north. Despite evidence of inadequate troop strength, lack of coordination between British, Belgian, and French units—and the admission by Weygand's own commanders that their exhausted troops were incapable of mounting a major campaign—the Allies were now expected to attack on two fronts, cutting off the German march to the coast, turning rout into victory. . . . Military historians who reviewed the situation later, knowing at least as much as Weygand knew that day, could only marvel at the veteran soldier's resilience.

At eleven-thirty Reynaud joined Weygand for the ride to Vincennes to meet the British prime minister, who had expressed the wish to see the new generalissimo at his command post. Churchill had brought along Sir John Dill, imperial chief of staff. Weygand had two requests: one to the British for more air support, one to Reynaud for a halt to refugee traffic from the north, for it was clogging essential transportation routes. He recommended that refugees be kept off main roads several hours a day and retained in adjacent fields, and that their ongoing travel be subject to strict rules.

The government was to give Weygand more than he asked for.

MINISTRY OF WAR
ARMY GENERAL STAFF

TELEGRAM
PARIS, 22 MAY 1940

TO THE MILITARY GOVERNOR OF PARIS
FORBID ANY EVACUATION CIVILIAN POPULATION.

CHIEF OF INTERIOR GENERAL STAFF
[GENERAL LOUIS-ANTOINE] COLSON

After a trip to General Georges's headquarters, Weygand was back in Paris before dinner to brief Reynaud again. On a large wall map he deftly pointed out how the battle could be fought and won. The French and British would strike at the Germans from both north and south, piercing the front and thereby releasing Allied forces still penned up in Belgium.

So the day ended in hope.

16

THURSDAY, MAY 23

The heavenly spring that graced the city continued to play counterpoint to ill tidings from the northeast. "Hurray! The bookstalls on the *quai* are open again," Alexander Werth told his diary. "Oh, but why rejoice? For even though Paris looks more normal again, isn't it because the Germans are sticking to their usual one-thing-at-a-time rule? Just now they are clearly concentrating on trapping the Anglo-Franco-Belgian army in Belgium and Flanders." Still it was a delight to stroll along the Paris riverbank. "It's queer to see workmen busy completing the pedestal of one of the statues of the Pont du Louvre. The Fifth Column perhaps want to make Paris look spick-and-span for the Führer, what?"

Newsman Werth entered the Tuileries Park. "How lovely it all looks with the Arc de Triomphe in the distance, and the fountains still playing in the gardens; it is hot in the sun and there is a smell of grass and box hedge." Counterpoint: there were hardly any children around. The fountains played, but children did not. And Werth couldn't help seeing the ubiquitous refugee traffic, cars weighed down with luggage. In one of them he saw a crying woman. He found a group of Belgians in his quayside restaurant. They were reading a Belgian newspaper now published in Paris, and one man appeared to be selling the small truck parked outside. Werth thought he would go down to look at the mob waiting for trains at the Gare d'Austerlitz, gateway to the southwest.

Even the dedicated villain Alain Laubreaux seemed touched by the sun. "Long and lovely days have covered Paris all week," he told his diary. "It's a soft, exquisite spring, a sun that warms without burning, set off by brief storm showers to soften the air, give it a light flavor, as a tender dew in midday." If streets were placid, Laubreaux knew, it was because there were no longer any buses or trucks to trouble the silence. Few soldiers, either. "The girls are pretty. Paris wears the face of peacetime summers."

Then he came upon the policemen with helmets, rifles slung over shoulders. That was war, just as black headlines were war. Still, it was a war competing with eternal Paris. "The sky doesn't care," he concluded. A springtime like this as backdrop to war was a woman forced to accept the attentions of a man she despised.

At fifty-two, Marcel Jouhandeau was the author of a considerable body of admired prose, a leading figure in the literary coterie of the *Nouvelle Revue française,* a magazine, a publishing house, a state of mind. This hardly made him a moral guide. A year earlier he had published a pamphlet called *The Jewish Peril,* actually a collection of his articles beginning with one titled "How I Became an Antisemite." He had told readers that he felt closer to "our former German enemies than to all those Jewish scum considered French." He concluded that "while I have no sympathy for Mr. Hitler, Mr. Blum inspires me with a far deeper aversion."

In his private diary, Jouhandeau revealed a citizen as concerned as any other by the fate of his Paris. He was a privileged observer from his windows on Boulevard de l'Amiral-Bruix facing the Bois de Boulogne park near the Porte Maillot, for it was a boulevard skirting Paris on its western rim, now virtually a highway for troops and refugees moving south. All night, every night, the Jouhandeau house trembled to the movement of trucks and tanks. "Animals sense better than we do any offense to nature," he told his diary. His cat Doudou was paralyzed by fear as the armored vehicles roared past. Human beings, he thought, were better prepared, for they had constructed these machines.

Pierre Drieu La Rochelle was more concerned with his own responses than that of household pets. He had admired the new Europe of the dictators; today that Europe was approaching. Should he stay in France or leave? he wondered. There was a tentative answer in his diary entry of the day.

I am Parisian, I must share the fate of Paris, the fate of the stones of Paris. . . . My only fear is that the Germans will want to apply pressure to me, to use me and thus to humiliate me, but can I be more humiliated than I am already as a Frenchman? And should I not serve as intermediary, and participate in the inevitable transformation of Europe about which I have dreamed so much?

This was in fact the way it would happen. Under German patronage, Drieu La Rochelle would become the lord of literary Paris, as publisher of the collaborationist *Nouvelle Revue française,* managing that monthly magazine as long as he could find credible authors to publish, or readers who would read.

New ways to undermine French morale were put on the table at Dr. Goebbels's daily meeting with his propaganda chiefs. One suggestion was to spread rumors of a cholera epidemic, to make people wary of their drinking water. Housewives would be told to stock up on essential foods.

From the commander-in-chief, Maxime Weygand, to Pierre Héring, military governor of Paris, this Very Secret order:

I am told that solitary soldiers, pretending to be on leave, are moving about in Paris day and night, notably near military barracks.

I request that you take immediate measures to verify the status of these military men. Those who cannot be identified will be locked up; the others will be sent, in groups, to military depots in the Paris region. . . .

At ten that morning, Paul Reynaud called his war cabinet to order, first giving the floor to Armament Minister Raoul Dautry, for the question on the table was how to keep industrial production out of the reach of the enemy. Dautry pointed out that 70 percent of all French arms and aircraft were produced in Paris and its suburbs. Of course there were plans to evacuate these plants to safer regions of southern France, but Dautry stressed the need to avoid spectacular moves that could have adverse effects on Parisian morale. Air Minister André Laurent-Eynac said that he did not plan a systematic evacuation of factories producing aviation equipment, but only gradual deployment. Still, it could not be *too* gradual, with the war going the way it was. All airplane engines were constructed in Paris.

Reynaud broke in. The "psychological situation" was such that the government simply had to keep saying that there would be no evacuations. Let the air minister pursue his deployment, all the while denying that an evacuation was under way. Pétain agreed with Reynaud: There must be no apparent retreat from the capital, otherwise the shock to morale would be considerable. He reminded the cabinet of the situation in April 1918, when there had been similar talk of moving the Citroën and Renault plants. Camille Chautemps, the cabinet officer responsible for evacuation policy, outlined the progress made in planning the transfer of government agencies since the May 16 scare. He worried that certain departures would be contagious, alarming rank-and-file Parisians who had no connection with the government. Civil servants ought not leave Paris before everyone else, for that would give the impression that they were privileged. It was bad enough as it was now, with some government agencies packing and shipping even as the government was issuing statements to the effect that no one was moving.

Better just to encourage parents to send their children, quietly, away from the city.

The premier agreed with his vice-premier. Morale was the priority. There must be a stop to the exodus of the government. Civil servants would stay, war production would stay. And the press would be informed.

Immediately after the meeting, so the diary of his aide-de-camp, Captain Léon Bonhomme, attests, Marshal Pétain ordered him to proceed to Tours to find a suitable castle for the Marshal to reside in when the government moved south. He was back in Paris two days later after having reserved one.

17

FRIDAY, MAY 24

He was in the thick of battle, Charles de Gaulle told his wife in a letter sent off this day—a battle going quite well. "I have the feeling that the surprise has been overcome, and that we are moving toward recovery." Losses were heavy and would continue to be. His own surprise he saved for the end of the letter. "Since yesterday I am a general." Indeed, he had received appointment as brigadier general—acting. Clearly Paul Reynaud was rewarding both the winning doctrine and an officer who was prepared to apply it.

In his diary, Alain Laubreaux mulled over an article in *Paris-Soir* by Eve Curie (whose parents were the discoverers of radium). Laubreaux thinks of her as "Bernstein's bitch," because of her known relationship with the Jewish dramatist. "A new Judith, she calls men to their death for the safeguard of threatened Israel." He was particularly offended by one line in her article: "The sacrifices demanded of us in this grave hour are as nothing and even death seems a recompense." "Vomitory literature," growled Laubreaux.

When one sees in the railway stations, out of danger certainly, but collapsing from exhaustion, weakened by horror and tears, old people, children, girls and women, and when one remembers that the Germans are machine-gunning this weakness and this despair *point blank,* one is so violently revolted that one knows quite well, at that instant, that Germany *cannot* win the war.

It was the kind of positive thinking Parisians needed. They were getting it from columnists such as Germaine Beaumont, who published this in *Le Matin.* Recalling an old Celtic belief, she concluded, "If the men fall, women will take up arms, and if in turn the women fall, the very stones of the road will rise up as in legendary times."

The propaganda specialists assembled around their chief in Berlin had another brainstorm that morning. They would exploit the popular appeal of prophecy. Nostradamus was French, after all, and there was always something to be made of the prophecy in which he mentioned a "Danubian"—Hitler having been born on an affluent of that river— who would fight great battles in the countries of the Francs and the Varangians—those early Scandinavians—to render Germany greater and more powerful than ever.

The notes of Paul Baudouin, Premier Reynaud's deputy who bore the titles of undersecretary of state to the prime minister's office and secretary of the war committee, describe a meeting in Reynaud's office that morning with Weygand and Pétain. Walking in, the generalissimo confided to Baudouin, "The situation is very serious. The British are returning to the channel ports instead of attacking toward the south." He had been told that British forces had abandoned Arras without having been forced to, this despite Weygand's order and the plan agreed to by Churchill forty-eight hours earlier. Weygand was not surprised. Yesterday General Sir William Ironside had been so disagreeable on the phone that Weygand had wished he could slap him. One cannot command an army that is taking its orders from London!

Clearly the British were keeping at least one eye on the coast, on the ports through which escape might be possible if the battle was lost. The Germans were after the same ports to cut off the retreat. Now, at the war meeting, British ambassador Sir Ronald Campbell showed up with a warning from Churchill that the French and British commands were not cooperating as they should be. Charitably, Weygand blamed the French side. General Gaston Billotte, French commander at the northern front, had been killed in a motor accident. His replacement, General Pierre Blanchard, hadn't received confirmation of his new duties in time. Another example of communications failure.

Weygand outlined his battle plan. He began by warning that the forces at his disposal were inadequate, reserves nonexistent. In the absence of British help, a new attack would concentrate on the lower Somme River between Amiens and the Channel, in an attempt to link up with French troops cut off by the German Panzer attack through the Ardennes. If the junction failed he saw no way to avoid the capitulation of Allied troops bottled up in the north. (We now know that Lord Gort had long since decided that there would be no French counterattack. It was time to think of saving what could be saved; the Channel port of Dunkirk was his solution.)

Reynaud asked what would happen if Allied forces in the north were indeed lost. He, Weygand, and Pétain studied various alternative defense positions. So the question of Paris came up again.

The cocky little premier was adamant. The government could leave the capital only at the very last minute, flying if necessary, to avoid the serious consequences of abandoning the city to itself. And where would the government go? The Loire valley, the present choice of the planners, was in truth too close to the front. A harbor, allowing escape or reinforcements by sea, was obviously preferable to a mountain redoubt.

Reynaud made a vow. Even if the northern armies surrendered, even if Italy declared war, he intended to fight until the end. The honor of the army must be saved. He was ready to draft younger men—except that no arms were available for them, or uniforms. The general staff was attempting to reequip the routed Corap army, but didn't even have rifles for it.

From four to seven that afternoon Premier Reynaud, with Marshal Pétain and General Héring, toured the antitank defenses north of Paris, notably at Le Bourget near the airport, in the Ourcq River valley, and at Meaux.

*   *   *

France's predicament led to strange alliances. Ilya Ehrenburg was virtually a historical monument, a longtime Russian émigré, then a Soviet citizen, author, now war correspondent. He was a familiar face in the cafés of the Montparnasse of artists and writers; as a propaganda aide of the Soviet regime he was close to the French Communist Party. As an anti-Fascist (and a Russian Jew) he was on France's side, though a servant of a state now allied with Hitler. Few Russians in Paris were happy with that alliance. The Soviet ambassador had been expelled, but his chargé d'affaires, Nikolai Ivanov, was convinced (or so he told Ehrenburg) that Hitler would attack the Soviet Union. He thought it made sense to be friendly to the Western allies.

On this particular day, Ilya Ehrenburg received a curious telephone call. "Ilya," said Public Works Minister Anatole de Monzie, "it isn't nice to forget old friends. I hear that you are getting ready to return to Russia. How is it that you haven't dropped in to say good-bye?"

Ehrenburg certainly did know Monzie, who had been one of the first prominent French visitors to the Soviet Union, returning to Paris to promote cultural and economic exchanges with the new state. But Ehrenburg also saw Monzie as a somewhat strange individual, at times leftist, at times rightist. He chalked it up to capricious behavior, not Machiavellianism.

So Ehrenburg was off to the Public Works Ministry on Boulevard Saint-Germain. As he recalled the meeting, the pipe-smoking Monzie wasted no time with small talk. "Pétain, Baudouin, and a few others want to surrender," he said. "Reynaud is against that, without mentioning Mandel. We have very few tanks, and above all very few planes. The situation is critical."

Ehrenburg asked him why the government continued to wage war against French Communists, why it angered the working class on which it depended. Monzie admitted that the government had been severe. After some moments he got to the point. "If the Russians sell us airplanes, we can hold on. Do you think that the Soviet Union has something to gain by the destruction of France? Hitler will attack you too."

Ehrenburg walked the short distance from Monzie's office to the Soviet Embassy on Rue de Grenelle to tell chargé Ivanov what the

French were asking for. Ivanov asked him to draft a cable for Moscow.

More is known about these events now, thanks to French Communists whose tongues loosened after the death of Stalin. Monzie had first approached a Frenchman, Charles Hilsum, director of the Soviet Union's Paris-based Banque Commerciale pour l'Europe du Nord; Monzie was friendly with Hilsum's wife, and informal contact was carried on this way. Monzie told Hilsum—perhaps without Reynaud's approval—that France would reestablish diplomatic relations with Moscow in exchange for planes. The banker replied that he had no authority to serve as an intermediary, and it was he who suggested Ehrenburg, a favorite of Stalin who survived when nearly every other Russian Jew who had served Soviet interests abroad was caught up in the purge and executed.

Apparently it was Monzie's idea to send Pierre Cot, air minister in Léon Blum's government, to Moscow to negotiate the deal. Reynaud objected, perhaps fearing what his Parliament would say about employing a Popular Front minister for the job.

Some time before meeting Monzie, Ehrenburg had been picked up by police and taken to the prefecture, locked up with a heterogeneous collection of French Communists and foreign refugees. There an officer responsible for expulsions told him he had three days to leave the country. Ehrenburg began to explain that he had been waiting for an exit visa—but was cut off. The tax authorities were holding up his departure because of funds he had received from Moscow but not declared as income since the money was earmarked for Spanish refugee writers. On another floor of the prefecture he had a chance to explain himself, but this second officer was equally firm. Until the Russian supplied a certificate attesting to payment of tax on the Soviet remittance, and paid a fine, he'd get no exit visa. So he returned to the first officer. After a three-hour wait he had a chance to say that he wasn't allowed to leave. This man didn't care what the other department had told Ehrenburg. He had to leave France *now*.

And despite the war, Sedan, the threat to Paris, Ehrenburg's case wasn't forgotten. He had been summoned to the prefecture again as recently as May 21 and asked why he was still around. There was more shuttling back and forth between offices until air-raid sirens went off and Ehrenburg and other visitors were escorted to shelter. Ehrenburg found himself standing beside the officer who was demanding his expulsion, heard him cursing under his breath. Ehrenburg couldn't decide whether the object of the man's rage was antiaircraft fire, the Germans, or Ehrenburg. This was the context of the summons to the office of the Minister of Public Works on May 24.

Three days after Ehrenburg's request to Moscow for planes, he found himself facing policemen again, this time at his apartment door on Rue de Cotentin. These were no-nonsense inspectors with an arrest warrant; Ehrenburg was sure they had been sent on orders of Minister of State Pétain. The inspectors—one a Russian speaker—did a careful search through his personal papers. Then they led him away, but not before a neighbor had asked whether Ehrenburg was really a spy and a police officer replied, "Germano-Communist plot." One policeman walked behind him with a drawn pistol, warning, "No funny business or I shoot." At the prefecture he was indeed accused of conspiring with other Communists on behalf of the Germans.

The interrogation lasted all day, until the phone rang. An inspector who picked up the receiver all but clicked his heels as he replied, "I hear you, Mr. Minister." Ehrenburg was ushered out politely, allowed to return home. But he demanded a police escort; neighbors saw the conspirator return in style.

It happened that Charles Hilsum, the head of the Paris Soviet bank, lived in the same building. The Hilsums had been coming into the building just as Ehrenburg and his escort left for the prefecture that day. Hilsum immediately phoned Monzie, Monzie called Interior Minister Georges Mandel.

18

SATURDAY, MAY 25

To be a war correspondent in Paris at its loveliest was to be subject to conflicting sensations, contradictory emotions. "Though one of the most decisive battles of history raged to the north," recalled British journalist Geoffrey Cox, "inside the city there was hardly a sign that this was different from any other spring." To attend briefings at the War Ministry on Rue Saint-Dominique, Cox walked across the Tuileries in morning sun, among children playing on the grass. He lunched in the shade at the Racing Club, deep in the Bois de Boulogne park, "while overhead tiny white specks fought for possession of the sky and the radio told of heavy attacks *pour le saillant d'Amiens*." Then he'd walk home again, after a press conference calling up images of blood and bombs, "and the Seine shone like silk beneath the bridges and old men sat and fished from the quays. . . ."

It would have been instructive to read over the shoulder of a Parisian dipping into his daily paper. He might be the kind who turns first to news of the Paris stock exchange. "The week ended with a particularly calm session in an atmosphere not at all pessimistic," reported the business analyst of *Le Figaro*. Indeed, the franc had moved up slightly against the dollar. Another story described the city's official auction house as "this fortress protected against pessimism." A sale of heirlooms, including paintings, brought prices worth quoting.

There was an advertisement for a famous cabaret, Le Boeuf sur le Toit, open each day from 6:00 to 11:00 P.M.—Cocktails, Dinners, Cold Snacks. Thirteen theaters scheduled performances that evening, with *Médée* at the Opéra, *Madame Sans-Gêne* at the Comédie Française, *Carmen* at the Opéra-Comique (all were national theaters). Private theaters still offering entertainment included the Ambassadeurs, Antoine, and Grand Guignol, music halls such as the Pigalle, Alcazar, and Casino de Paris (where Maurice Chevalier's co-star was Josephine Baker). There were still lots of good movies in town, among them *Wuthering Heights* and *Goodbye Mr. Chips,* while *The Hunchback of Notre Dame* and *Ninotchka* ran on and on.

The day ended with a proposal at the highest level of government that France consider a cessation of hostilities.

At seven-thirty that morning General Weygand phoned Paul Baudouin, who of course was watching the war for Paul Reynaud, to report that he felt better about the battlefront. The British and French were working in harmony, and Weygand was able to suspend the order he had given earlier for a retreat to channel ports. Reynaud had just received a telegram from Churchill approving the plan for a joint attack. So far, so good.

But at noon the sky clouded. Bad news from the north coincided with the introduction of a new face into Anglo-French affairs. In a personal letter to the French premier, Winston Churchill explained that since he and Reynaud couldn't see each other every day, he had appointed "an old friend of yours," Major General Sir Edward Spears, to serve as liaison officer on matters concerning the war. Spears had been a liaison officer with French forces in the First World War, spoke French, and thought he understood the French. "You are welcome," Pétain said when he walked in, and Spears took it personally. From that moment on during their first conference Pétain was silent, and even when Churchill's representative turned to address him, the old marshal seemed not to hear. Weygand was cordial, although in the past he and Spears had not been friends. The Englishman found the commander-in-chief wizened—like Reynaud, resembling an Oriental—yet full of energy, showing no signs of the anxiety he must have felt.

Spears began with an attempt to settle one thorny question. Churchill was not holding back on the French, he wanted them to know. If British troops were not in the positions the French expected them to be, the problem was one of coordination. It was possible, after all, that the Allies would not be able to hold out in the north at all. Reynaud had a reply to that: If the northern armies collapsed, it would be extremely difficult for the French in the south to hold the Germans on the long front running from the estuary of the Somme all the way to Switzerland. Even an orderly retreat, from one defensive position to the next, was not conceivable; reinforcements were lacking for that. These gloomy prospects led the French premier to call for a meeting of the War Committee for seven that same evening, allowing a full presentation of the situation by Weygand.

So Weygand was off to La Ferté-sous-Jouarre that afternoon, to consult with General Georges about the kind of defense that might still be possible—defense of the region north of Paris, of Paris itself. The best one could hope for, concluded the commander-in-chief, was to arrest the enemy's progression southward, then to hold a defense line to save both the "heart" of the country and Paris—if only for its arms production.

At three-thirty that afternoon Reynaud called on Jules Jeanneney at the Senate. Again the question was where to go, what to do. Paris was definitely in peril now. Jeanneney said that he didn't want the government to abandon its capital until that became absolutely necessary. And when it was necessary, the retreat had to be orderly, avoiding the spread of panic among civilians. He thought that the best refuge for the government would be Bordeaux, for that southwest gateway to the sea was as far from the Germans as one could get.

Reynaud then told Jeanneney that the enemy, if he overran the Channel coast, might offer peace. Should such an offer be submitted to Parliament? Only, replied Jeanneney, if the cabinet judged the proposal truly worthy of examination. Otherwise there was the risk of going before a Parliament tempted by defeatism. Jeanneney personally hoped that a German offer, if it came, would prove unacceptable, for otherwise it could lead to worse: Prague would almost surely follow Munich (in other words, repeating recent history, after promising nonaggression Hitler would take what he wished to take).

*   *   *

In Madrid the German ambassador read and forwarded to Berlin a report from the Spanish foreign minister of a conversation between Marshal Pétain and the Spanish ambassador in Paris, José Felix Lequerica. When the ambassador had suggested that Pétain embodied the moral authority of France and could find a solution to the military situation, the old man replied that he didn't think the Führer would listen to him.

Generalissimo Franco had wanted the Germans to see this report, should they be at all interested in making contact with Pétain through Lequerica.

At seven, as planned, the War Committee assembled in the premier's office at the War Ministry; it would go on, Paul Baudouin's notes tell us, until ten minutes after nine. Baudouin records the portentous statement of General Weygand, seconded by Pétain, proposing that the British be consulted on whether the war should be continued. In his testimony at Pétain's treason trial in 1945, Weygand would remember that not he but President Albert Lebrun raised the question of separate peace negotiations with the Germans, preferably before rather than after the annihilation of the French army.

The meeting began with a detailed exposition of the situation on the ground, with the attempt of General Pierre Blanchard, the new commander in the north, to regroup French, British, and Belgian units—thirty-eight divisions in all—for a counterattack, and then the effort of French troops above Paris to hold a line literally running across France. That line must not be ruptured, Weygand affirmed; the troops must fight until "exhaustion" to save the country's honor. Reynaud agreed with that. "This being said, it isn't certain that our adversary would grant us an immediate armistice, and isn't it indispensable to avoid the capture of the government if the enemy enters Paris?"

The fall of Paris was now on the table. The discussion turned to alternative capitals—Tours again, Bordeaux again. Baudouin's minutes of the meeting, found in National Archives records sealed up for years and not tampered with, show that President Lebrun had indeed asked how France would go about dissolving its commitment to Britain. Before accepting a separate peace, Reynaud affirmed, France would have to consult its ally. Why not right now? Weygand wanted to know. So Reynaud revealed that Churchill promised to continue the war alone while waiting for the intervention of the United States. The premier had asked William Bullitt how France could best formulate its plea for American aid; his reply was yet to come. In closing, Weygand stressed that the French army had to be preserved, for it was the only force that could maintain order among Frenchmen.

France's ambassador to Rome, André François-Poncet, drafted a secret telegram to Paris that evening. A good source reported that during his March meeting with Hitler at the Brenner Pass, Mussolini had agreed to declare war on France. In the first stage of hostilities, Italy would try to seize Corsica, Tunisia, Malta, and Egypt. The Allies could still dissuade Mussolini if they paid the price, a price sufficiently high to permit the Duce to justify staying out of the war to his own public opinion, and to be able to tell Hitler that the benefits to Italy from abstention ruled out war. Ambassador François-Poncet felt that the outcome of the battle of Flanders would weigh heavily on the decision of the Italian dictator, because he would either join the war to take advantage of France's weakness, or would hesitate if it appeared that the war would drag on.

Foreign Minister Edouard Daladier sent his own telegram that night—to the French embassy in Washington. He asked French ambassador René Doynel de Saint-Quentin to coordinate an approach to President Roosevelt with Britain's ambassador, Lord Lothian. They were to ask Roosevelt if he could find out from Mussolini what precisely he hoped to obtain in the Mediterranean, "guaranteeing to Italy the satisfaction of its legitimate aspirations in that sea."

19

SUNDAY, MAY 26

War correspondent Quentin Reynolds was getting his information from Colonel Horace Fuller, the American military attaché, "the only man in Paris," thought Reynolds, "who knew what was coming." And Fuller was apparently telling people to get out of the city while they could. He didn't think the French army would "bother" to defend the city.

Young Maurice Kahane, something of an iconoclast, seemed to relish the disarray of fellow Frenchmen. Seeing Paris policemen with their helmets and old carbines, as they waited for infiltrated parachutists, he reflected, "The combat will be unequal!" He was clearly delighted by the spectacle of city garbage trucks equipped with heavy machine guns, manned by overage troops. "Who had that idea? Perhaps Reynaud himself, he's a smart one!" The Germans were approaching Paris, and inside Paris helmeted house porters waited for them with brooms. "We'll overcome! As at Verdun." The humor of a man who was to thrive in German-occupied Paris (using his mother's name, Girodias), and with impunity.

The morning's *Le Figaro* made a contribution to its readers' peace of mind:

FOR NATIONAL SECURITY
Arrests of undesirable individuals
Inspection of refugees
Punishment of lapses

A reporter had gone in search of news of the "fifth column" and landed at the Interior Ministry, "where night and day Mr. Mandel gives the example of the vigilant effort that he preaches to his staff." *Le Figaro* was able to report that the police were carrying out regular roundups, arrests, and house searches, at a rate and rapidity rarely achieved. A new technique, said the reporter, was to stage surprise raids on cafés, restaurants, and other gathering places, to verify the identities of everyone caught in the net.

The Interior Ministry was aware of public suspicion of refugees as possible spies and saboteurs. This fear, the reporter was able to say, was exaggerated. Just to screen the refugees was an enormous task, but now they were being directed to regions of the country whose authorities would have more time to look for enemy agents among the innocent. A separate news report revealed that since Georges Mandel's appointment as Minister of Interior a week earlier, more than two thousand hotels and cafés had been inspected, more than 62,000 persons interrogated. As a result of questioning, some 500 persons had been arrested; of that number, 334 were foreign suspects, and no time was lost in dispatching them to concentration camps.

A more ominous note was the warning from the office of Premier Reynaud published in the middle of the front page:

In order to create disorder behind the lines and even at the front, the Germans are spreading—by tract or telephone—orders or instructions signed with the name of a French authority or even with the name of the prime minister, minister of national defense and war.

So the premier's office wished to remind Parisians that no government orders were ever issued in the form of tracts, and that no one should obey an order given by phone.

Such warnings could only heighten anxiety. An editorialist in the same *Le Figaro* pleaded for indulgence for innocent people, French or foreign, who needed or simply desired to leave Paris. He cited the example of a woman of foreign (but friendly) nationality who required police permission to travel, but found a mob ahead of her at the local police station, a mob of native French people who knew that soon they too would need exit permits to leave. The editorialist was aware of the frightful exodus from the north, resulting in traffic bottlenecks prejudicial to the military. "But Paris, which is calm, whose calm derives from its courage and also from a situation which gives no grounds for alarm, Paris should not be committed to regulations allowing no flexibility."

This Sunday would see another appeal to the city's patron saint, she who had saved the city at least once before. Starting on Wednesday the faithful had been called to prayer at the monumental tomb of Saint Genevieve inside the church of Saint-Etienne-du-Mont. Today, for the first time in many years, the saint's relics were removed from the sanctuary to comfort believers, as in times past when the reliquary had been carried through the streets of Paris to ward off disaster.

Long before the announced hour a crowd estimated in the tens of thousands filled the square before the church, spilling over to the Place du Panthéon and adjacent streets; more worshipers, and the curious, leaned from windows and balconies. The scene had a touch of the medieval as Monsignor Beaussart once again led the chant:

> *Our Lady of Paris, Our Lady of France, pray for France!*
> *Saint Genevieve, pray for France!*
> *Saint Louis, courageous in combat, help our military chiefs!*

When the monstrance was held high over the church steps to trace the sign of the cross, worshipers fell to their knees—where there was room to kneel. And then, after seeing the reliquary safely into the church again, Parisians broke into a *Marseillaise*.

But at least one observer, Quai d'Orsay diplomat Jean Chauvel, was not quite convinced by the demonstration. He was reminded of how, as a high school student, he had lit a candle before taking final exams.

He suspected that the government was behind this sudden burst of religious fervor, or else how explain the presence of Léon Blum, representing the government, at the ceremony at the Sacré Coeur basilica? Now, at Saint-Etienne-du-Mont, he discovered "a neighborhood crowd of spinsters and housemaids." Only two hundred yards away on Rue Soufflot the outdoor cafés were jammed, with women in summer dresses, men in shirtsleeves and hats tipped back, seated before mugs of beer. . . .

Or, as Senator Jacques Bardoux saw it: "The spectacle of the relics of Saint Genevieve promenaded on the Place du Panthéon before a silent, stunned crowd which had lost its voice and couldn't even sing the *Marseillaise* correctly, running through prayers as if by rote, is not exactly comforting." The shadow of another defeat, 1870, was spreading over the land. . . .

"I should like to give you my most private opinion on the present military situation for your most private ear," William Bullitt began his secret cable that noontime, marking it Personal and Secret for the President Only, to keep it from prying eyes in the State and War departments.

> I believe that the British, Belgian and French armies in Flanders will be obliged to surrender within two or three days and that there is no hope that they may be able to cut through to join the main body of the French Army.
>
> Within five or six days the German mechanized divisions will have mopped up the remains of these allied armies and have been reformed for the march on Paris. The Germans meanwhile are concentrating huge masses of infantry just to the north and south of Laon. When the German mechanized divisions are ready to advance, they will sweep easily to the Seine at Havre and Rouen. If the French should send the full reinforcements they have to meet this threat of envelopment of Paris from the northwest the striking force now being concentrated in the Laon area will break through on the direct road to Paris by Soissons, Compiègne, Senlis, Chantilly and Meaux.
>
> It appears, therefore, that Paris will be in danger of occupation

in about ten days and, however bravely the French army may fight, it is difficult to imagine circumstances which will enable Paris to be defended successfully. I regret deeply to feel obliged to express such an opinion but I think you ought to know just how serious the situation is.

It had become painful to be an American in Paris, so correspondent Clare Boothe decided. As an awareness of the peril grew among Parisians, there were increasing and anxious questions about how America was going to help. Would the United States send warplanes? Boothe had to confess that she was not sure the planes even existed. So her French friends begged her, "Go home now, and tell everybody, anybody, that we've got to have them! In God's name, can democracies never learn?" Indeed, Boothe would have to go home to tell America what France needed, since censorship prevented cables or broadcasts that spelled out the urgency of the need.

While Americans were being asked to help, the British were being criticized. Clare Boothe observed a rise of anti-British feeling among Parisians, who blamed the ally for the defeat on the battlefield. Boothe herself admired the French for their courage, for the way they helped refugees, cared for the wounded, or simply stood up under stress.

Her own countrymen were now scarcer in Paris. The toughest of correspondents, those who had already seen war in Madrid, Warsaw, Prague, Helsinki, and Oslo, were still around—mainly in bars, exchanging gossip. One night, when the German advance seemed to have opened the road to Paris, much of the surviving foreign press corps gathered at the Hotel Ritz—in the "brightly lit, pretty little blue and white salon" which was part of her suite. One veteran newsman, H. R. Knickerbocker, spoke in anger about America's neutrality. "Is it important for America to keep Hitler out of Paris?" he asked, obviously believing that it was. "Why don't people in America please stop being 'sorry for refugees' and 'ninety-eight per cent sympathetic to the Allies,' and answer that question God-damn quick?"

Boothe asked him, "You think it is our war?"

"Hell, yes," he replied. But when she advised, "Write them that," he replied with violence, "That's not what my editors want, it's not what my readers want. They want 'local color' from Paris! They want to read how all the taxicabs have been requisitioned to send troops to the front . . . how people are examined by armed police in the cafés to find fifth-columnists. How crowded but calm the subway shelters are in an air raid. How the grass in the gardens of the Tuileries hasn't been cut this spring. . . ."

Premier Reynaud flew to London that morning. He was ushered into Churchill's office for a private meeting, after which the two heads of government were joined by other officials. The talk was of Italy, of how to prevent Mussolini from joining the war. Since the chief grievance of the Italians was British sea power in the Mediterranean, Reynaud wondered whether it would be possible to promise Mussolini a share of control of the sea, should he keep out of the war. Reynaud reminded Churchill how dangerous it would be for Britain if France, faced with the combined strength of Germany and Italy, lost the war. The two leaders discussed a formal appeal to the Italian dictator by Roosevelt. In it the American president would ask Mussolini to spell out his demands. The Allies knew that Italy was concerned about the Mediterranean, and they were prepared for a settlement that would take effect at the end of the war.

Roosevelt went along with that. In a cable from Washington the American ambassador in Rome, Wendell Phillips, was instructed to "communicate immediately and orally" a message from Roosevelt to Mussolini expressing America's concern about the extension of the war to the Mediterranean. "If you are willing to inform me of the specific desires of Italy in this regard in order to insure the satisfaction of Italy's legitimate aspirations in that area," said Roosevelt in a clumsy burst of diplomacy, "I will communicate them to the Governments of Great Britain and of France." He did not convey the Allies' offer of a settlement, but made his approach in the form of a U.S.-Italian dialogue. The president preferred it that way.

It was time for Major General Spears to take a sounding of his old friend the marshal. He paid a Sunday call on Pétain at his office in a smallish pavilion on the Boulevard des Invalides, an office that seemed to the Englishman unreal in its pastoral calm. Pétain reminded Spears of the time in the First World War when Pétain commanded an army corps on the front east of Paris. The same site was back in the war communiqués, added Pétain with a bitter smile. While he did not intend to interfere with General Weygand's conduct of the war, Pétain himself felt that the situation was hopeless. There was no reaction in Pétain's face as he said this, observed Spears; it was as if a man happened to observe unfortunate events in a distant branch of his family. Was it a sign of age?

Churchill's emissary returned to Pétain's office that afternoon, this time to accompany a British liaison officer bringing news of the front. Spears found Pétain alert this time, and more than alert. At one point the old marshal asked whether General Gort could take command of Allied forces in the north, which Spears decided was an idea that had come to him on the spur of the moment, and was not an insidious attempt to pin the blame for eventual defeat on the British.

Then, as Spears was getting ready to take leave, his host called him over to a window recess for a private word. Did the Englishman know that Weygand feared a revolutionary uprising in Paris? Spears replied that this seemed to him a matter of politics rather than a military question. He himself did not think any such danger existed; he had spoken with Interior Minister Mandel, who after all was the person directly responsible for such questions, and Mandel hadn't appeared worried. As far as Spears was concerned, Weygand had enough to do as it was, getting the army to obey him, and could well leave civil affairs to others.

Louis Rollin, who had replaced Mandel as minister of colonies, drove out to Weygand's headquarters at Vincennes. The general quoted Roman history to him. When the barbarians invaded ancient Rome, the Senate had continued to deliberate. When a Gaul pulled a senator's beard and was rebuffed with a stick, the entire Roman Senate was massacred. But the behavior of the Romans was courageous all the same. Weygand added, "You know, I didn't sleep all last night. I did a lot of thinking. There are no two ways about it, the government must remain in Paris to be taken prisoner."

That came as a shock to the minister. So struck was he that he stopped off at the Elysée palace to tell President Lebrun what he had just heard. "He's just crazy," Lebrun declared.

On hearing what Weygand had told Rollin, Paul Reynaud pointed out that not all of the ancient Roman senators had stayed in the city waiting for the enemy, but only the old men incapable of bearing arms.

For A. J. Liebling of *The New Yorker,* each week of crisis contained within it "an Indian summer of optimism." Over lunch he exchanged expressions of relief with French friends that the Germans hadn't gotten as far as Paris after all. The only question seemed to be where General Weygand was going to counterattack. They talked, and Liebling stayed on for tea, then for supper, until time for the final radio news at eleven-thirty. Earlier bulletins that day had been inconsequential, but this time the speaker's voice was ominous, and Liebling and his hosts were upset before he had said anything significant. Finally it came out: "Whatever the result of the battle in Flanders, the high command has made provisions that the enemy will not profit strategically by its result." What did that mean? That the Allies would retreat across the Channel? "Now they are coming to Paris," said Liebling's hostess, sobbing. "Now they are coming to Paris."

It was the middle of the night in France when President Roosevelt delivered his Sunday radio talk—on Sabbath evening, as he called it. He told the American people of the plight of European civilians under the Nazi onslaught. Many Americans closed their eyes to these events, some in good faith, for they believed that "what was taking place in Europe was none of our business." Whatever the reason for shutting out the problem in the past, Roosevelt warned, there was a rude awakening now. For America was no longer "remote and isolated," no longer "secure against the dangers from which no other land is free." Today the United States had to be prepared for the worst, and the president was asking Congress to vote the largest military budget ever proposed in peacetime. "In this era of swift, mechanized warfare," he explained, "we all have to remember that what is modern today and up-to-date, what is efficient and practical, becomes obsolete and outworn tomorrow." In the United States the manufacture of war matériel was the job not of government but of private industry; now the government would help industry develop this production. "We defend and we build a way of life, not for America alone, but for all mankind," concluded Roosevelt. "Ours is a high duty, a noble task."

20

MONDAY, MAY 27

General Weygand sat down with the military governor of Paris to make sure that he was covered closer to home. It was not only a matter of protecting Paris from the Germans; for the politically conservative Weygand, maintaining order *inside* Paris was a priority. Today the two generals discussed possible scenarios.

At the moment, the enemy was still at a safe distance from the capital, and indeed a French army stood in its way. But a surprise attack by tanks, a parachute drop, even a move by the "fifth column" already inside Paris, was always possible. Then, should the French be forced to retreat to positions immediately to the north of the capital, defense of the city would become the concern of the armies in the field. At the moment Paris was protected by a defense line that ran from Vernon on the Seine to the lower Oise River, the lower Ourcq, then to the Marne as far as Château-Thierry; along this line concrete defense positions protected all access roads. Now Weygand and Héring worked out an extension of the line, west from Vernon to Pacy-sur-Eure and the Eure valley, east from Château-Thierry to Montmirail and Esternay. The line existed. What lacked was a credible defense force; the best men were farther north at the front.

It happened that Interior Minister Georges Mandel shared Weygand's fear of civil disturbances, and it was his job to put them down. Today he was to dispatch a liaison officer to Vincennes with a request for three infantry regiments equipped to deal with "trouble" in the vicinity of Paris. He met a sympathetic ear in Weygand—but where would the soldiers come from? Finally Vincennes was able to detach two battalions of Senegalese colonial troops, a small cavalry group, a few tanks, several platoons of gendarmes, plus one thousand *gardes républicaines*. Weygand took the opportunity to ask the government to release the *gardes* who were "abusively employed" as orderlies in government buildings. Which is to say that he was scraping the bottom of the barrel.

Today it may seem odd that France's highest authorities, military and civil, were so concerned in the middle of the Battle of France about keeping order in Paris—which is to say keeping Parisians in order. The political establishment clearly saw the people of Paris, with its working-class majority, as a danger requiring the allocation of precious manpower. At lunch, William Bullitt had a confidential talk with his friend Edouard Daladier, with whom he shared these fears. They also shared the conviction that Paris didn't have much more than a week to live. Now Daladier said something more. Should the French government evacuate Paris, the Germans would not enter the city immediately. Instead they would stand by as the Communists took over, to "burn, pillage and murder everyone decent who might remain in the city" (Bullitt's words, repeating Daladier's words). The foreign minister saw a solution: the French government should remain in Paris even if it meant capture.

Daladier also told this ambassador ready to listen that while the Germans would not pillage the American Embassy or kill Americans remaining inside, Goebbels would arrange to have Communists do the job before the Germans marched in. "This may be possible," Bullitt reported to Roosevelt that evening, "but I have no intention of leaving Paris and neither have the other members of the staff. Such happenings would be unpleasant, but brief, and no one here would have any great objection to anything except being treated like Schuschnigg and fed atropine and bromides in order to disintegrate. In such a case anyone would count on you for immediate action."

After saying these things, Bullitt offered his opinion that he really didn't think the Germans would do anything of the kind.

He and Daladier talked about something else at their lunch, for the Frenchman went back to his office to draft a secret telegram to France's ambassador in Rome describing the message Roosevelt had sent to Mussolini. There had been another warning from Ambassador François-Poncet to the effect that Italy's attack on France was imminent, and the only hope of heading it off would be a concrete offer of concessions. Conferring with Reynaud and with François Charles-Roux of the Quai d'Orsay, Daladier concluded that Roosevelt's message contained just such an offer.

So the disappointment was general when news came in that when U.S. ambassador Phillips had tried to deliver Roosevelt's message he wasn't even allowed to see Mussolini. He got second best, the dictator's son-in-law and foreign minister, Galeazzo Ciano. And Count Ciano was ready with the Duce's negative response. His position, explained the count, was that Italy didn't only want to obtain its legitimate aspirations, but that Mussolini was determined to honor his commitment to Germany.

Phillips asked Ciano whether he fully understood the significance of the communication from President Roosevelt. Yes he did, but nothing would change matters. Ciano couldn't say precisely when Italy would enter the war; it might be in a few days or a few weeks, but it would happen "soon."

Before the day was over, Reynaud's cabinet came up with a true concession to Mussolini: an offer of French African territories, such as the Somali coast, the railway line between Djibouti and Addis Ababa, revisions of the frontier between Tunisia and Libya to the latter's advantage. At the Quai d'Orsay, Charles-Roux, when he had a draft of the message in hand, saw it as an impulsive act, owing to the consternation that another piece of news (from Belgium) had created. At three in the morning he woke the foreign minister to say just that. Daladier told him not to do anything until morning. By then cooler heads had prevailed. And the British were to warn that no concession to Mussolini would satisfy him; it would only convince him that the French were on the ropes. So no offer went to Rome at all.

*   *   *

The shock had come in the late afternoon. At six-thirty General Weygand rang the War Ministry to say that he was on his way over to talk to Reynaud. "It's grave," was all he would say. The grave news was the capitulation of the Belgian army. Reynaud summoned his cabinet for a meeting at eleven that evening. It opened in an atmosphere of crisis, with expressions of anger directed at King Leopold, for he had asked for help and French troops had been sent to help. If the French hadn't gone to Belgium even earlier, when there was still hope of success, thought Charles-Roux, it was because of Leopold's neutrality, his repudiation of existing alliances with Britain and France.

There was some anxiety in the cabinet that ordinary French men and women would blame the hundreds of thousands of Belgian refugees on French soil for their sovereign's betrayal. The morale of the French army was satisfactory; the problem was the morale of French civilians. They were already saying, "We've been betrayed." If Belgian refugees (the able-bodied men among them) weren't put in uniform and sent to the front, French public opinion would "explode."

21

TUESDAY, MAY 28

Belgian journalists who had taken refuge in France found the right word for the King of the Belgians: Leopold was the traitor king. His father Albert I, a stalwart ally of France in the earlier war, had been the warrior king. For now everybody knew that Leopold had surrendered his armies in mid-battle, without advance warning to his allies. *Le Matin* published the assurance by Premier Reynaud that the Belgian cabinet had resolved to carry on the fight; a new army would be formed of Belgians on French soil.

In Paris, depressed, weeping members of the Belgian exile community flocked to the equestrian statue of Leopold's father on Cours-la-Reine off Place de la Concorde, to lay black-ribboned wreaths: one of the saddest ceremonies he had ever witnessed, thought American correspondent Walter Kerr.

Reynaud caught Parisians at breakfast with his radio speech. "I must inform the French people of a grave event," he began. "France can no longer count on the cooperation of the Belgian army." Leopold's surrender had been an act unprecedented in history.

Hearing this, a Belgian refugee sat down on the nearest curb to weep. It was seeing him, as much as the incessant flow of motorcars topped with mattresses, that brought the war home to one Parisian, Annette Sireix. Now it was everybody's war.

Another witness, newswoman Clare Boothe, discovered a less sympathetic reaction. "Enraged Parisians began to throw Belgian refugees out of their houses, and to burn their poor carts in the streets, and heckle and buffet them in the stations and on the highroads. . . ." "We always knew he was pro-German!" so Parisians said of King Leopold. (A. J. Liebling heard that. And another comment: "All the refugees probably are spies.")

At Joseph Goebbels's morning conference a new leitmotif was offered to the men responsible for disseminating propaganda in the direction of France. "Let's end it!" Clandestine broadcasts to France were to suggest that the French could have an honorable peace now if they really desired it.

Things *had* changed. "We don't look at things in the same way anymore," the writer Léon-Paul Fargue suggested to readers of *Le Figaro*. Up to a week ago Paris had been calm. Now it "had been shaken up suddenly, like a sleeping person awakened with a start from a tranquilizing dream." Parisians had been "philosophical" about it all, stoical, even dilettantish. Now a cold wind had swept all that away.

"The tendency of the market was dull yesterday," the same paper's stock exchange report announced. "Yet government bonds . . . held up well, and for other French commercial paper the variations were generally not considerable. Even coal mines had not depreciated noticeably." (The northeast coal mines were now in enemy hands or under direct threat.)

The New Yorker's Liebling took a stroll around elegant Place Vendôme. There the luxury shops reassured him, reminding him of prewar normality, of prewar tourists. He saw a collection of summer neckties at Charvet. The salesman there looked sad enough as it was, so Liebling decided not to bring up the subject of the war—but the vendor did. "We are an indolent people, Monsieur," he said pleasantly. "We need occurrences like this to wake us up."

At eleven that morning Paul Reynaud asked William Bullitt to call on him at Rue Saint-Dominique. He needed the ambassador's opinion on an appeal to be made to Roosevelt jointly by King George VI of the United Kingdom and President Lebrun of France. Reynaud had already scribbled an opening line: "The armies fighting to preserve the liberties of the world have been stabbed in the back." The reference was to Belgium's surrender. Reynaud drew his visitor over to a wall map to point out positions that had been held by the Belgians, extending from the Channel coast down to the French frontier. As soon as the Belgians ceased to defend the line, a German armored division slid through, cutting off the entire British army, and France's best soldiers in the bargain. They'd fight to the last cartridge, he assured Bullitt, but now could do nothing more than die well.

And when these trapped soldiers were wiped out, Reynaud went on, the Panzers would descend on Paris, probably via Laon—the direct route from southern Belgium, without bothering to take Rouen or Le Havre first. The French would fight to the bitter end, but the end would come quickly. Hence Reynaud's appeal to Roosevelt. It was clear to the Frenchman that after defeating France and Britain, Hitler would strike at the United States.

After hearing him out, Bullitt acknowledged that the British sovereign and the French president had the right to address Roosevelt directly. Still, he thought it would be wise for the Allies to consult first with Britain's ambassador to the United States, Lord Lothian (Philip Henry Kerr), before deciding "just what should be said and what should not be said." Of course, Reynaud knew that even if the United States declared war on Germany tomorrow, it could not fly an army to France in planes that didn't exist. But there *was* an American fleet. He implored Bullitt to ask Roosevelt to order the Atlantic fleet into the Mediterranean. That might at least prevent "another stab in the back" from Mussolini.

Cabling Roosevelt an account of his meeting with the French premier, Bullitt added his own plea for an American presence in the Mediterranean:

I believe as strongly as I have ever believed anything that you will be unable to protect the United States from German attack unless you have the cooperation of the French and British fleets. I believe that one of the surest ways to obtain such cooperation would be by sending our Atlantic fleet to the Mediterranean.

"Solemnly and urgently" he begged for a cruiser to be sent to Bordeaux, carrying submachine guns and ammunition for the French, taking away French and British gold reserves for safekeeping (there were 550 and 100 tons of it, respectively, waiting to be saved).

In separate meetings with Bullitt, Reynaud and Mandel explained that the required small arms—between five thousand and ten thousand .45-caliber Thompson submachine guns—a 1928 model, as it happened—were to be employed to protect Paris, not from Germans but from French Communists. Both the premier and his minister of the interior expected "a Communist uprising and butcheries in the city of Paris and other industrial centers as the German army draws near." And the Paris police possessed only antiquated single-shot rifles. Bullitt himself felt that their appraisal of the situation was accurate, the need for the small arms justified. He hoped that the arms would be put aboard an American cruiser the very next day—arms to be borrowed from U.S. Navy stocks if necessary.

"Incidentally," the American ambassador told his president, "we have exactly two revolvers in this entire Mission [the U.S. Embassy] with only 40 bullets, and I should like a few for ourselves. . . ." Submachine guns were what he meant. When the American vessels were finally ready, they sailed not to Bordeaux but to Casablanca, where they found the gold reserves. The submachine guns never got into the hands of Paris policemen.

Once again Charles de Gaulle was in the vanguard, once again not to win a battle but to prevent it from being badly lost. At Abbeville, just below the Channel coast, the Germans had breached the Somme River line to threaten the integrity of Allied armies in the north. De Gaulle's modest mission was to wipe out that dangerous pocket. He had 140 tanks to do it with, backed by six battalions of infantry and supporting artillery. The attack was sprung as soon as the division was in position—which happened to be no earlier than five that afternoon. Losses were heavy, but before dark the enemy had been routed. De Gaulle followed up with a predawn offensive, when German aircraft could not be brought into play. His men attacked again and again, approaching Abbeville without attaining the city. The intrepid officer could nevertheless see his final combat as a victory.

The point now was to save what could be saved from the disaster in the north. It was no longer a matter of re-forming a battered front for a counterattack, but simply of holding the line to allow as many Allied soldiers as possible to reach the Channel port of Dunkirk. In the French view, British and French soldiers alike would be evacuated by sea from Dunkirk for immediate transportation to points west and south, where they would disembark on French soil to rejoin the war.

But it soon looked as if the British were sailing away with their soldiers to defend their own soil, as if they had written off French chances. The dramatic evacuation of Dunkirk under enemy fire was pursued over the following week, and in the end it would be seen as a victory, just as holding on at Verdun had been a victory in an earlier war. In a historic operation by boats large and small, some 330,000 soldiers (less their heavy equipment) would be picked off the French coast to sail to the English side of the Channel; some 130,000 French troops were among them. They lost not only their armor and their big guns but some of their best fighting men, those who defended the bridgehead until the end.

22

WEDNESDAY, MAY 29

Perhaps he was only telling the Duce what he wished to hear, but a report now sent to Rome by Italy's ambassador to France, Raffaele Guariglia, merits reading as an example of what was passing through Fascist minds:

> While the [French] government, press and parliament seek to blame the wise Belgian king for events which are solely the responsibility of the politico-military deficiencies of France . . . public discontent is growing—if below the surface. It still can't express itself and even less can it produce immediate and signif- icant practical consequences, but it has led the government to reinforce precautionary measures, and to seek to accredit the illusion of a possible defense on the Somme and Aisne. Perhaps only when the illusions fall away and Paris also falls will French- men comprehend the guilt of those who pushed them into a situation without an exit, and then a serious reaction could occur.

Guariglia reported rumors, contradictory rumors, including the likelihood of a Pétain-led cabinet prepared to accept peace with Ger- many.

Concerning Italy, some believe that a French retreat after the fall of Paris along the Loire and Rhone river valleys will not so much open the possibility—but will impose the necessity of Italian occupation of France's frontier districts before the Germans reach them. . . . This Italian occupation could take place, according to this hypothesis, even without a formal declaration of war by Italy against France, but for us in any case it would constitute a decisive asset to have in hand when the time comes for a general peace settlement.

Almost at the same moment the papal secretary of state, Luigi Cardinal Maglione, was contemplating Paris and the war from quite another point of view. He called in the Italian ambassador to the Holy Office, Count Bernardo Attolico. Would the count kindly ask the Italian government to request of Germany that it not bomb Paris, that it consider Paris an open city? And not to bomb the horde of refugees who will certainly try to flee Paris before the Germans march in? Count Attolico promised to try (and we know from the diplomatic archives that he did try).

This same day Benito Mussolini issued an order to his armed forces: They had one more week to prepare. From June 5 onward, he explained, he could declare war at any moment.

All the chips seemed to be on the table as the month of May drew to a close. General Weygand was now ready to say as much. First he sat down with Marshal Pétain to be sure that the two generals had no significant difference of opinion on the issue. Then (on the afternoon of May 28) he drafted his memorandum. Next morning at nine he showed up at Reynaud's office to read the memorandum aloud to the premier, beginning with a reminder of what was now at stake. France was about to commit to battle all of its remaining forces, divisions that had survived setbacks in the north and along the Meuse. Orders were being given to hold firm—to take no step backward. But this also meant being ready for a later and still graver decision.

For it was possible, Weygand pursued, that despite heroic efforts on the French side, the Germans would make their breakthrough. Then, thanks to planes and Panzers, the enemy would quickly attain "the vital centers of the country," Paris included, with its density of armament factories. In such a case France would no longer be in a position to continue to assure "a coordinated defense of its territory." In the First World War it was always possible to stem a breach, since neither side then possessed a coordinated tank-and-plane capability. Today, even if France had the proper equipment, the enemy would not give it time to teach troops how to use it.

They'd of course try to hold the line, and this despite the defection of Belgium. But even to do this they would need British troops, tanks, planes. Hence the brutal conclusion:

> It's also important that the British know that the time may come when France would find itself, despite its best efforts, in the impossibility of continuing a militarily credible fight to protect its soil.
>
> This moment would be preceded by the definitive breach of positions on which French forces had received orders to fight without thought of retreat.

In retrospect, so Weygand would say, he was glad that he had written this memorandum. For it served to explain, before the final battle, the reasons for France's defeat.

Ambassador Bullitt lunched with Chamber of Deputies president Edouard Herriot at the home of a mutual friend. Bullitt told the table guests that only days before, King Leopold had asked the United States to place his children under American protection, and Roosevelt had agreed to bring them to Washington and to treat them like his own family. Opinion was becoming firmer in the United States (so Herriot remembered hearing the ambassador say). The United States was sending everything it had to Europe, leaving it with no more than 150 pursuit planes and 150 bombers; more planes were being turned out as quickly as possible.

In Reynaud's office that day there was talk of a final appeal to

Roosevelt, a personal phone call from Reynaud that might bring airplanes, together with American pilots to fly them.

The morning's issue of *Le Matin* carried a notice directed to American residents of France from Ambassador Bullitt. All those desiring to return to the United States could sail on the SS *Washington,* which could take up to 1,500 passengers in Bordeaux on June 4.

If one was not at the front and not in government, it was still possible at the end of May to fail to relate to even the most brutal headlines. Thus writer and journalist Emmanuel Berl, despite his influential friends, shared the collective apathy. He knew in his heart that the Germans would win, and yet he had not even thought to send his English mother-in-law back across the Channel. From his country house north of Paris, Berl could watch the flow of Belgian refugees and, increasingly, French refugees from the embattled northeast; this spectacular movement of populations took on for him the terrifying aspect of a geological cataclysm.

It was also true that everyone around Berl expected a miracle, a repeat of the victory on the Marne in World War I, which of course had not been so much a victory as a holding action.

Berl was a French Jew. Uncanny examples of what can only be described as euphoria came from Jews, who for the seven years of Hitler's reign had been choice targets of the Nazis across the border. Even Jewish refugees from Germany and Eastern Europe seemed afflicted by what today must be seen as irrational behavior. If asked, they would say, "But it can't happen in France." Annette Sireix, then twenty-seven and employed as bookkeeper-typist, stayed in Paris with her two brothers until the Germans were within artillery range; and even when they left the city with friends, their Polish-born parents stayed on. Lacking the provincial ties so many Parisians enjoyed, where would a Jewish family go? Statistics suggest that proportionately fewer Jews than non-Jews joined the exodus from Paris, and this was even truer among recent émigrés—the most vulnerable.

One could still leave Paris as easily as if going off on holiday; an identity card or other proof of nationality was the only document required. It was even possible to travel in style, if not in one's private automobile, then in first- or second-class sleeping car compartments, although these never left Paris empty. It was easier to find a seat in a third-class carriage, for the less affluent were not the travelers.

The writer Julian Green told the story of actor and dramatist Sacha Guitry, known for his egocentric worldview, arriving at the Gare d'Orsay to find himself at the rear of a pushing and shoving crowd. "Aren't you all ashamed of yourselves!" he cried. In his commanding tone he had soon restored order. And then the extravagant showman moved with his baggage to the front of the line. "What about you?" came the complaint from the crowd. "It's different for me," Guitry replied. "*I'm* afraid."

Reporting for *Life,* Clare Boothe covered the other side of the story at the train stations—the refugees from the north. "They came off the trains with their bewildered faces, white faces, bloody faces, faces beaten out of human shape by the Niagaras of human tears that had flowed down them." Exaggerated? These were people who had lost homes, and a country, often a loved one fallen in battle. At the very least they were separated from family members and friends and saw no end to their misery. "With bicycles and bundles and battered suitcases, holding twisted bird-cages, babies, and dogs in stiff arms, or holding one another up, they came and came and came. . . . The great stations echoed with the saga of their suffering and numbed your brain and sometimes almost your heart."

Parisians did help. The Nord and Est stations were staffed with volunteers, Boy Scouts, Red Cross nurses, even "rich American expatriates," observed Clare Boothe, surprised to learn that there were so many good hearts in this group. The Americans asked for lists of needed supplies and then bought them with their own money. Ambulances often bore the names of American donors. Only there were not enough scouts or nurses or rich Americans, not enough medicine or milk or beds or ambulances. Told by a fellow reporter that there weren't enough shelters in all France for these refugees, let alone sufficient food, Boothe countered, "The American Red Cross will send them money." "They need material, not money," came the reply. "How can we send that? In our ships? You know the neutrality law."

"A way will be found," Boothe insisted. "Yes," replied her colleague, "but not in time." She had not thought of that before. Help would not reach France in time.

A different kind of support was coming from the American Hospital of Paris, an institution founded before the First World War to serve Americans residing or traveling in Europe. Although still a comparatively small facility at the outbreak of war in August 1914, the American Hospital had treated wounded French and British soldiers, and then of course American soldiers when the United States joined the battle in 1917. History was to repeat itself in 1939 when the American Hospital of Paris and its seaside clinic at Etretat on the Channel coast were transformed into war service hospitals for French soldiers—with some beds reserved for American civilians all the same.

After the German attack on May 10, a base hospital was opened in Angoulême, some three hundred miles southwest of Paris, in a school building. By early June, doctors, nurses, and equipment had been dispatched to the base in American Hospital ambulances, and soon the staff was receiving wounded directly from the battlefields. The main Paris hospital was still open, its ambulances performing feats that would earn a citation, rushing through the night without headlights to carry French wounded away from the advancing enemy.

One could help without being an institution. Indeed, Hélène Azenor was the least institutional Parisian one might encounter, even in the heart of French Bohemia, between-the-wars Montparnasse. She lived in her painter's studio on Rue Campagne-Première, which seemed terribly far from the war. Yet the street was only steps away from that major north-south artery, Boulevard Saint-Michel, and cut into another urban highway, Boulevard Raspail. So she became an involuntary witness to the refugee flow, watching with fascination the vehicles buried under furniture and mattresses, bicycles and birdcages; inside, there were always one or two passengers too many. The column of fugitives grew denser each day; soon the traffic through Paris was bumper-to-bumper. Most impressive were the horse-drawn wagons, each with a household of belongings, accompanied by women, children, and the elderly. Younger men walked alongside the horses; dogs were tied to wagons and helped to drag them along, or so it seemed.

The war had also come to the painters' studios. Windows had to be painted blue; for artists with skylight windows this represented a considerable surface, and when Hélène Azenor, with her concierge's help, got her windows painted, her studio became sinister. She wondered if the time had come for her to join the exodus. One day she actually walked alongside the procession, making her way south to the Porte d'Orléans among the autos and wagons and bikes, now finding many refugees without any wheeled transportation at all—walking, sometimes pushing wheelbarrows, or baby carriages occupied not by babies but by personal belongings. One had to push one's way along, or yield to stronger pushers (the motorized and horse-drawn vehicles). All this in extreme disorder, with the biggest bottlenecks she had ever seen, the highest noise level, what with the shouting, crying children and neighing horses, and of course the inevitable automobile horns. She got back to her studio as fast as she could, bucking the crowd. She now knew that she would never leave Paris. Friends asked her to, promising to make room for her in one or another motorcar. "We'll camp out," they said. "Come along; the Germans are going to commit horrors as they did in 1914." She didn't believe it, partly because she didn't believe the Germans would ever reach Paris.

Now she had fewer neighbors with which to share that conviction. Her street, and her beloved artists' compound at number 9, were emptying. On the corner of Boulevard Raspail a large empty building had been turned into a refugee shelter, and it did not take much curiosity to discover that these unfortunate people were in total disarray. With the help of her concierge, Azenor determined to make as many of them as possible comfortable. For there were dozens of empty studios in her building, their occupants having left keys with the concierge as they departed for the exodus. Of course she gave priority to women with infants, the old, and the helpless. Neighborhood shopkeepers donated milk and bread. For those sufficiently fit to be able to survive the bedless shelter on Boulevard Raspail, Hélène Azenor and her concierge offered blankets, and food when they could.

All this while the world was changing, for the day came when even the district administrative center was deserted, the local police station and hospital seemed emptied of personnel. The Montparnasse painter was more alone than ever, alone with a concierge in a compound containing more than one hundred flats and studios. The concierge had sworn to high heaven that she would never leave. And then she did leave, a day before the Germans marched in.

Julius P. Winter was manager of the Paris office of Western Electric, an American company specializing in sound equipment for movie theaters, and recording equipment for making films. He had some one hundred employees, he the only American among them. Winter's association with Paris began in 1918, when he arrived as an American soldier. Billeted just behind Quai de la Rapée near the Bastille, he was soon going out with a French girl who lived across the yard. When they married he moved in with her family. He was still living there in 1940 (and fifty years after that he was *still* living there).

When war broke out in 1939, Western Electric stayed open, although chiefly for maintenance work. Even that ended with the May 10 offensive. By now the Winters had two grown children, a son over twenty-one, a daughter of fourteen. They were all very French while he, citizen of a neutral nation, felt that he had nothing to fear. There was no reason to flee.

Julius Winter lived a French life; he knew no other American not on official business who stayed in Paris. Later he would feel that staying had been an error, for to avoid compulsory labor in Germany his son went into hiding and died of malnutrition. When the Germans approached Paris, Winter drove to Bordeaux to place company funds in a safe deposit box there. His driver refused to take him back to Paris with the Germans so close, so Winter found a braver man to fight the tide of refugee traffic. In Paris he was able to get a certificate from the American Embassy to hang on his front door, attesting that the apartment and its belongings were American. Of course the day would come when such a sign was a handicap, and another day when just being an American in Paris was dangerous, but French friends helped Julius Winter live through them.

Then there was the Rogivue family, old Burgundians with Swiss relations. The war caught the children—girls of sixteen and twenty, a boy of eleven—on a visit to Switzerland, but in May not even Switzerland was a guaranteed sanctuary, and the youngsters returned to Paris. Their father, Henri, was a public works engineer who had been supervising the construction of a landing strip near Evreux. There he had been able to observe the exodus up close, and that strengthened his resolve not to flee. He acquired a revolver, all the same, to defend his family.

Sixteen-year-old Michèle remembered the day her father gathered the family together in their living room. Of course Paris was emptying, of course the Germans would soon enter the city. Nobody knew what they'd do, said Henri Rogivue, but did it make sense to take chances on the highways? Roads were being bombed; besides, they had no place to go in France. Everyone voted to stay. "On one condition," Michèle's father said. "That we stick together."

The day came when they were virtually alone on their shuttered street, Rue Albert-Samain near the Porte de Champerret, they and their concierge. To enter the building they used a signal, so no intruder would pass.

No one did a head count of departures from Paris during the Battle of France, but the statistics that happen to be available make it possible to arrive at a convincing estimate. The last official census was carried out in 1936. But in May 1940, when one had to sign up for ration cards, most honest people did, which certainly meant most people. At the beginning of the German occupation an informal head count was undertaken by civil defense block wardens, and then a more thorough tally was carried out by the police in German Paris during the night of June 26 to 27, brought up to date for rationing purposes in July. A city hall officer, Eugène Depigny, later compared the results.

CENSUS	PARIS	SUBURBS	TOTAL
1936	2,830,000	2,130,000	4,960,000
End of May			
1940	1,860,000	1,640,000	3,500,000
June 16–20	807,000	737,000	1,544,000
June 26–27	983,718	753,396	1,737,114
July 7	1,051,506	887,326	1,938,832
July 14	1,101,030	967,433	2,068,463

The city neighborhoods that lost the most population were the more affluent, such as the seventh *arrondissement* (district, or ward), which saw 87 percent of its inhabitants disappear, and the sixteenth (but also the thirteenth and fifteenth, although higher percentages of the population of these districts were working class and white-collar). The neighborhoods that lost least population were the lower-income nineteenth *arrondissement* (54 percent), the first, second, third, and fourth districts (of shops and small businesses). Departures averaged 130,000 a day, and perhaps were as high as 300,000 a day on June 11, 12, and 13.

The desolation did seem more total in the upper-class sections of the city. "For the honor of the French bourgeoisie went away—disappeared—in the ugly panic organized by its leaders." This from a disgruntled war correspondent, Jacques-Henri Léfebvre, ruminating over the collapse in German-occupied Paris.

The Spanish Republican émigré Wilebaldo Solano, in forced residence in Chartres, watched the exodus from Paris along the much-traveled route to the safer southwest. One refugee stopped long enough to explain it to him: "Paris is moving out."

23

THURSDAY, MAY 30

At that time Memorial Day was celebrated in the United States on May 30 of each year. Originally conceived as a commemoration of the Civil War dead, it had since become the occasion for honoring the fallen of all American wars. This year Premier Paul Reynaud made a point of being in the front line of the commemoration, and his appearance that morning alongside Ambassador William C. Bullitt as the American lay a floral wreath at the tomb of France's Unknown Soldier was a front-page event for Parisians.

It was a very American day for Reynaud, who spent part of his afternoon discussing the pros and cons of a telephone appeal to Roosevelt. Would it be wise to bother the American president again? Could it do any good? Was Roosevelt in a position to offer help? Did the United States possess the matériel France needed, and could it arrive in time?

In earlier years Americans in Paris who belonged to the American Legion would travel to the battlefields of the First World War to place wreaths at the graves of comrades killed in the fierce trench warfare of 1917 and 1918. But of course there could be no such travel this year. Instead, at the American Episcopalian Cathedral on Avenue George V, the Legion erected a row of marble crosses, each symbolizing one of the military cemeteries, each decorated with a floral wreath from American organizations and institutions based in Paris. The presence at the ceremony of Military Governor Héring, Minister Louis Marin representing the government, and the prefect of the Seine district, Achille Villey, was remarked. A sign of the times: The account of the commemoration in *Le Figaro* bore evidence of censorship. Ten lines had been excised, apparently from the speech of Ambassador Bullitt.

What he felt that day we know. To Roosevelt, in a Personal and Confidential dispatch, he sent his gloomiest assessment of the war to date. "This may be the last letter that I shall have a chance to send you before communications are cut," he began dramatically.

The morale both of the French Army and the civilian population is a vast credit to the human race; but there are four German soldiers to every one French, and there is no longer either a British or Belgian army, and supplies of material are already running low.

When the Germans strike on the Somme and Aisne, therefore, in spite of all the courage and character that will go into stopping them, the Germans may reach Paris very soon.

Again Bullitt indulged his particular preoccupation. "Everyone," he said, including both "hardboiled" Interior Minister Mandel and "softboiled" Radical Socialist Edouard Herriot, was sure that as soon as the French government withdrew from Paris, "the Communists of the industrial suburbs will seize the city, and will be permitted to murder, loot and burn for several days before the Germans come in." The ambassador did not think he would have much influence either with the Communists or the Nazis, but he would do his best to save as many lives as possible, and to "keep the flag flying." He expected that the German occupation would be "stern, cruel, but orderly"; he would be prevented from making his own contacts, and would probably have to work through the counselor of embassy, Robert Murphy. In that case, thought Bullitt, he himself might be more useful in Washington, handling French affairs from there.

No American Ambassador in Paris has ever run away from anything, and that I think is the best tradition that we have in the

American diplomatic service. But if the calm of death descends on Paris, I should like to be in very active life trying to prepare the USA for Hitler's attack on the Americas which I consider absolutely certain.

Rambunctious Bill Bullitt ended this communication to the President of the United States by saying: "In case I should get blown up before I see you again, I want you to know that it has been marvelous to work for you and that I thank you from the bottom of my heart for your friendship."

Shortly after noon in Washington (by then the day was coming to a close in Paris) Roosevelt held a press conference, accompanied by his civilian and military advisers. The meeting was, as tradition then demanded, off the record, although White House correspondents could sum up the proceedings. This procedure allowed the president to speak his mind. "Now just one word—my Lord, I seem to have talked an awfully long time—one word about the present situation," said Roosevelt at one point (and today we can read the transcripts of the conference). He confided to reporters that because German personnel and matériel were superior, Hitler and his ally Mussolini could well win the war against France and Britain. "It would hurt their morale terribly if we mention it out loud, but it looks very serious."

And if the Nazis won, Roosevelt went on, they would set up their own trade zone, including friendly South American nations such as Argentina, and in that way dominate the world.

On the other hand, a victor of that kind may think at the beginning that he is not going to conquer the whole world but, when the time comes and he has conquered Europe and Africa and got Asia all settled up with Japan and has some kind of a practical agreement with Russia, it may be human nature for victors of that kind to say, "I have taken two-thirds of the world and I am all armed and ready to go, why shouldn't I go the whole hog and control, in a military way, the last third of the world, the Americas?"

He drew the lesson: "So there is the situation, and that is what we have got to prepare for."

The State Department appeared more positive than either Bullitt or Roosevelt that day. A message sent out from Washington, signed by Secretary Cordell Hull, informed the American ambassador that a way had been found to transfer munitions from the War and Navy departments to the British and French, making use of private manufacturers as intermediaries. The equipment would include five hundred of the 75-millimeter guns the French so badly needed.

Precisely at the moment that message was being cabled to Paris in code (ten o'clock that night), Bullitt was writing to Hull, and to Roosevelt, with a less gloomy view of affairs than he had sent that morning. The British and French were displaying heroism at Dunkirk, where they were evacuating the trapped northern armies under fire. They had better pilots and, when numbers were equal, were showing superiority in the air. The Germans didn't dare face them in combat. "This war is not lost," concluded the volatile diplomat, "and every plane that can be sent today will be worth a hundred next year."

Italian ambassador Raffaele Guariglia began to hear reports that morning concerning a final French effort to keep Italy out of the war. Cabinet minister Jean Ybarnégaray, one of the right-wing additions to the Reynaud government, called at the gracious town house on Rue de Varenne that served as the Italian Embassy; his intention was to make the Italian ambassador listen to reason, but Guariglia found his bombast slightly ridiculous. Anatole de Monzie, reputedly Italy's best friend in the government, phoned to suggest that Guariglia keep himself free that evening. And then at 8:00 P.M. Foreign Minister Daladier was on the line: Could Guariglia come over to the Foreign Ministry? He could, at once.

Daladier had the Italian envoy read the message the French wished to transmit to Rome. Guariglia read it, and slipped it into his pocket, saying he would pass it on. But Daladier wanted more than that, he wanted the Italian to comment on the note then and there, confidentially. So Guariglia told the minister that he thought the note was fine in principle, but not a serious basis for negotiation.

Back at his embassy, Guariglia took another call from Monzie. "Daladier tells me that our note didn't satisfy you," said Monzie, who proceeded to explain the French position in detail. Guariglia stopped him short, saying that it would make more sense for them to meet. He walked the few steps separating Rue de Varenne from the Public Works Ministry on Boulevard Saint-Germain. While he sat with Monzie, the Frenchman phoned Daladier and tried to persuade him to let Guariglia tell Rome that in addition to France's formal note, a more concrete negotiation would take place on a strictly verbal basis. But Daladier couldn't accept that. Guariglia sat through the telephone dialogue, which lasted over half an hour. When it was over, Monzie raised his eyes to the ceiling, his way of commenting on Daladier's failure of will. It was understood that Guariglia shared Monzie's point of view.

Still, before another twenty-four hours had gone by, Daladier would phone the Italian ambassador again, and this time tell him he could inform Rome that he had learned from French sources (but please not to mention Daladier) that the French were ready with concrete proposals.

Mussolini received the message, gave it a glance, and asked his secretary to file it, just as Guariglia's own dispatches arguing the good faith of the French had been filed away.

From his exile in France, Count Carlo Sforza, who had been Italy's foreign minister in pre-Fascist days, drafted a prescient appeal to King Vittorio Emanuele. Conceding that France was losing the war because of its own ineptitude, he warned that Britain would never surrender, and that the United States would eventually enter the war. Was it being said that the United States was divided, antimilitarist? "Don't believe, sire, these fables. . . . America will astonish the world with a military and economic development before which everything will bend." If the King endorsed Mussolini's plan to declare war, it would end with "the most devastating ruin for Italy."

Vittorio Emanuele approved the declaration of war. Indeed, when informed that it would be announced on June 11 (Mussolini's original date), he was delighted, because that was his saint's day, and his serial number in the army had been 1111.

That day the military authority responsible for the defense of Paris drew up an inventory of barriers blocking access to roads leading into the city from the north, each such barrier composed of concrete blocks with emplacements for heavy artillery or machine guns. The barriers allowed passage of traffic until the time came to shut and defend them. They were located at strategic intersections—on Route Nationale 1 at Saint-Denis, for example, as well as at bridges spanning the Seine. There were fifty-three of them in all, running along a line defined by the towns of Cormeilles, Argenteuil, Saint-Denis, Noisy-le-Sec, Neuilly-sur-Marne, and Joinville.

Soon army engineers discovered that the wooden railway ties employed to close the passages could be destroyed by tank fire, so measures to hide them were called for. The ties could be concealed, for example, behind trucks parked across the openings in the concrete blocks.

24

Friday, May 31

Unpredictable Bill Bullitt. His reports to Washington oscillated between the darkest pessimism and ingenuous hope. Now, on the morning of the last day of May, surely after an invigorating walk to the American Embassy from his official residence on Place d'Iéna, he had to express the poetry of springtime Paris in his secret telegram to the U.S. Department of State:

> The calm of the people of Paris, who realize fully that they may be killed within a few days, is as extraordinary as it is noble. I think the President and the Postmaster General will be especially interested to know that the outdoor stamp market in the Champs-Elysées is still functioning calmly. Children are still riding the same eight old donkeys in the Champs-Elysées and others sit daily in the sunshine watching the Punch and Judy show.

He concluded: "The French at this moment do honor to the human race."

And as if that were not enough, he drafted another cable, this one "Strictly Confidential for the President and the Secretary [of State]," reporting "the magnificent resistance of the French and British armies at Dunkirk," which he considered "of a quality that astounded even the leading members of the French Government." Allied air power provided sufficient protection, while the Germans (according to the French) had lost their three thousand best pilots. German infantry was attacking "in the most crude mass manner"; French 75s were inflicting tremendous casualties.

Parisians could read just about the same thing in their newspapers that morning. The official communiqué indicated that Allied forces were pursuing "with vigor, in the middle of incessant combat, and in good order, the execution of movements decided by the high command." It just didn't indicate the direction in which Allied troops were moving. A British communiqué was somewhat clearer:

> As a result of augmented German pressure on their northern and southern flanks, British and French troops operating in the north had been obliged to withdraw toward the coast in the midst of heavy fighting.

Clare Boothe had been looking for a way to return to New York for some time. The fast way was the Pan American Clipper flight from Lisbon, but obtaining Spanish and Portuguese transit visas was not an easy process. Ambassador Bullitt wished her to go to Bordeaux to wait for the SS *Washington,* which was making a special voyage to evacuate American nationals, but she feared that she might still be waiting for the ship in Bordeaux when the Germans showed up. She decided to fly to London, which itself involved considerable red tape, and spent the day waiting at Le Bourget airport for a flight. There she met a French diplomat returning to his job at his country's embassy in London. "Something good must come out of all this," he told her. "This is a world revolution, and when we peoples of the democracies see what we have lost in money and life and human dignity by not sticking together, we will start our own counter-revolution to unite the world. . . ." He concluded, "There are no desperate situations, there are only desperate men."

Boothe's last cable from Paris appeared soon after that in New York's *Life* magazine. She was writing it, she said, on an unusually calm day, although no Parisian was really happy, for everyone wondered how it happened that they had not been hit by enemy aircraft. "Everybody in Paris and London knows that if they haven't been badly bombed it's not because Hitler admires the contents of the Louvre or has a sentimental attachment for 10 Downing Street, anyway not since Chamberlain left." This is why there was no dancing in the streets.

While the British were picking men off the beach at Dunkirk, General Weygand was visiting the Quai d'Orsay to pick the brain of diplomat François Charles-Roux on Italian intentions. In fact both men expected Italy to enter the war, and soon. "We'll resist," the general assured the diplomat, "but I am still obliged to remove men from the Alpine army to the northern front." Charles-Roux, with understandable curiosity, asked what were the real hopes for France in the north. The general-in-chief explained that he had been obliged to shorten the front in order to be able to protect it with the fifty divisions remaining. This meant holding the line on the Somme River. "Stopping the Germans there is not impossible, but I can't guarantee that it can be done."

This same morning Charles-Roux was summoned to the Rue Saint-Dominique to talk to Paul Reynaud. Pétain and Weygand were there, Admiral François Darlan too, and soon Foreign Minister Daladier joined them. Once more a message to Mussolini was on the table. In it France would promise a postwar settlement of Italy's complaints about the way the Allies controlled the Mediterranean sea. It was agreed to coordinate the note with the British before sending it.

Walking out with Marshal Pétain, Charles-Roux took advantage of the opportunity for another expert sounding on the war. It all depended on the Somme line, Pétain told him—and already there were small breaches in it. "The objectives of the Germans are the lower Seine and the Marne, so as to enclose Paris in the two jaws of a pincers."

The message to Italy was ready at last, modified by London, and handed to Ambassador Guariglia for transmission to Rome. The text was also cabled to the French ambassador there. In Paris, Anatole de Monzie put in his own phone call to the press attaché of the Italian

Embassy. "They gave in!" he cried triumphantly. "They" were his own cabinet colleagues. Monzie ought to have guessed that the French were tapping the phones at the Italian Embassy.

Daladier told his friend William Bullitt why he approved the French offer to discuss Italy's grievances. For either Mussolini would make such outrageous claims that the whole of the French empire would be swept by a wave of patriotism, or Mussolini would refuse to reply, in which case the French would realize that their government had done everything possible to head off Italy's intervention. In its final form the French note expressed astonishment that Italy could consider making war on France, for hadn't the Duce always said that Italy would serve only its own interests? The French felt no incompatibility with Italy because of the difference in regimes. More, the French were prepared to discuss Italy's desiderata for the Mediterranean basin. "It is still time to avoid the worst between us," concluded the French message. "Our gesture should not be seen as a sign of weakness. . . . It is only meant to show that we have tried everything that could bring together and safeguard the interests of both of our nations."

Once again Ambassador François-Poncet made his way to the Italian Foreign Ministry to explain the French position. Ciano told him to expect no reply from the Duce. Italy was determined to declare war on France; he just would not say when.

Ciano snapped to the British ambassador, "Even if France offered us Nice, Corsica, and Tunisia, we'd declare war."

When he heard the Italian reply—or rather the refusal to reply to the French message—Ambassador Bullitt asked Secretary Hull, "Is it possible for the President now to speak the truth in public about Mussolini?"

Adolf Hitler also had something to say to Mussolini. On Thursday the Duce had asked the Führer when he thought Italy should enter the war. He was considering June 5, but was prepared to postpone a declaration of war to suit Hitler's planning. The Italian people, added Mussolini, were eager to join the Germans in the fight against their common enemy.

In reply, the Reichsführer began by summing up the military situation. The war against the British and French armies in the north would end that day, May 31, the next day, or the day after that at the latest, virtually wiping out the Allied armies. The Germans had captured an enormous number of enemy soldiers, an enormous quantity of equipment. Just to move all of the prisoners had required five German infantry divisions. The Duce could be sure that as soon as German forces could be reorganized, the attack would resume.

Hitler felt that there might be some advantages in a postponement of Italy's declaration, at least for three days. German aviation had located new French airfields, and was about to destroy them. Should Italy declare war now or France feel threatened, the French might move their planes, and thus render a German attack on them fruitless. Hitler hoped to finish off the whole French air force in a week's time.

For this reason, said Hitler, he hoped that Mussolini would wait until the end of the following week, say until the sixth or eighth of June. The seventh would also be possible but that was a Friday, a day not considered by Germans an auspicious time to begin something.

One wonders how much Hitler really wanted Mussolini in the war. Hitler's offensive in the north had been ordered for May 10, a Friday. German troops moved into Paris on June 14, a Friday.

Paul Reynaud waited two days before replying to General Weygand's warning that France might have to lay down its arms. Reynaud wrote it now. He would tell the British ambassador this very day what Weygand had said about the decisive battle on the Somme. But even if the French could no longer defend all of their national territory, he added, he hoped that remaining forces could withdraw to a more defensible region, a redoubt including a military harbor. His recommendation was the Brittany peninsula.

Weygand dismissed Reynaud's scheme as unrealistic, militarily impossible, requiring men and equipment—such as antitank and antiaircraft weaponry—that didn't exist. As it was, there wasn't enough matériel to defend the front.

It would be easy to explain things to the British. Churchill showed up for a meeting of the Supreme War Council, composed of the two chiefs of government and their military advisers. The British prime minister was accompanied by Clement Attlee, leader of the opposition Labour

Party and a member of the war cabinet, the same Attlee who would unseat Churchill after the war. Then William Bullitt walked in for an appointment with Reynaud, to find him still conferring with his British visitors. Churchill wished a word with Bullitt, so the ambassador was ushered into the conference room. "The news is encouraging," Bullitt informed Roosevelt in a rush telegram two hours later. "As a result of the superb courage of the troops in the Dunkirk area it has been possible to save already 150,000 British troops and 15,000 French troops. The French with their customary spirit are holding the lines to enable the British to leave first."

Churchill asked Bullitt to transmit a message to Roosevelt. "Now that it was almost certain that unless you could frighten Mussolini, Italy would declare war on France," Bullitt explained to his president, "the need for destroyers for France was enormous and vital."

Earlier that day Bullitt had asked Roosevelt if he could turn over twenty-four old destroyers to the French, and that as soon as possible. When he suggested that America move the Atlantic fleet into the Mediterranean to intimidate Mussolini, Roosevelt had to tell him that there was no Atlantic fleet to speak of. Bullitt worried that the United States would seek a modus operandi with Italy. "To believe that the Government of the United States will be able ever to cooperate with Mussolini is as dangerous to the future of America as would have been the belief that our Government could cooperate with Al Capone."

Now, after sitting in on the Allied Supreme War Council, Bullitt assured Roosevelt: "Everyone present at the meeting was full of fight and determination. I shall say no more about it, but merely repeat that this war is not (repeat not) lost."

Such optimism continued to flare at dinner that night in the British Embassy. Reynaud was there, with Georges Mandel and other cabinet members. Afterwards Churchill paced the room with Armament Minister Raoul Dautry, who would remember the prime minister's words: "We shall fight in the hills, we shall fight in the fields. We'll burn the Black Forest with our incendiary bombs, we'll destroy the Rhine bridges with our floating mines. . . ." Dautry noticed that as a precaution all the furniture and rugs had been removed from the embassy's main drawing room.

25

SATURDAY, JUNE 1

By now lucid Frenchmen could see the handwriting on the wall. Not all Frenchmen, however. Roger Peyrefitte, then a young officer in the diplomatic service, satirized the moment in a postwar novel, staying as close to the truth as he could to portray one of his superiors in the Information Ministry, the eternal optimist. Air-raid alerts appeared to please this man, for they led him to reflect on how much Britain's air force was helping France. Peyrefitte's chief had been comforted by the ceremony at Notre Dame: faith would save Latin and Christian civilization. The somewhat ridiculous official seemed to believe his own ministry's propaganda; he believed for example that the French army was using specially designed blankets to throw over enemy tanks in order to hinder their movements, and pouring carob tree oil on roadways to clog tank treads. Paris need not fear attack by enemy parachutists, explained this optimist, since the police were now equipped with rifles, while garden benches and garbage trucks were lined up on public squares at night. He also knew that the military governor had ordered regular inspection of the sewer system to catch fifth columnists.

Then there were the congenital pessimists. Everybody saw the venerable Marshal Pétain as one of them. He was aware of France's inferiority in men, matériel, and air power, so he confided to François

Charles-Roux at the Foreign Ministry. Pétain's response to the crisis seemed to be limited to getting rid of old political nemeses, Daladier among them. Speaking that day to Reynaud's aide, Paul Baudouin, another old soldier, Maxime Weygand, made it clear that he did not think of himself as an ally of Pétain; he, Weygand, was a loner.

Circumstances would soon draw them closer together.

Perhaps it was to place himself under the spell of a more positive thinker that General Weygand called in Charles de Gaulle just then. The junior general had recently been given a chance to apply his theories in battle, and he had indeed demonstrated that there was a way to hold and even to push back the enemy, using the same kind of armored force the Germans had so successfully employed against the French. De Gaulle was also to see his patron, Paul Reynaud, on this trip; had de Gaulle requested the appointment, or had Reynaud summoned him? What we know is that on Friday night de Gaulle told his aide-de-camp, Captain Paul Nérot: "Tomorrow morning at five we're off to Paris!"

The drive down from the front took a good part of the morning. As they entered the capital, de Gaulle ordered his driver to stop on Avenue de La Motte-Picquet for a rapid visit to Petitdemange, then one of the city's best military tailors; he went upstairs a colonel and came down a general, with a spanking new tunic, the two stars of a brigadier, a fancy kepi with oak-leaf brocade. Nérot guessed that the new general had ordered the outfit in advance. He told de Gaulle: "I'm going to enter the history books as the first person to see you as a general." Risking his luck, he added, "And if I now go upstairs I could come down a major."

"It isn't that you don't deserve the promotion," de Gaulle replied sternly. "But this is hardly the moment."

They drove to the War Ministry on Rue Saint-Dominique, where de Gaulle was to meet Reynaud. "Wait for me; I'll need an hour." With de Gaulle's permission, Nérot employed the hour to speed out to Versailles to let his family know that he was alive. On his return to the ministry, de Gaulle still hadn't come out of his meeting. When he did he was more generous with information. Reynaud, he said, had offered him a choice: he could take command of all French tank divisions, or join the cabinet as undersecretary of war. Nérot remembered that de Gaulle preferred the government post. And while historians dispute the date that Reynaud invited de Gaulle into the cabinet, it happens that de Gaulle read and approved Nérot's memoir of the episode.

"Mr. Minister," declared Captain Nérot with mock solemnity, "I congratulate you."

It was now that they drove out to meet Weygand. This time General de Gaulle invited his aide-de-camp to join him for the talk. Thus he stood by as the diminutive General Weygand took the giant Charles de Gaulle by the shoulders to embrace him, this despite the coolness each man was known to feel for the other. "De Gaulle," said the generalissimo, "you have saved our honor." He asked what de Gaulle thought should be done with the twelve hundred recent-model tanks still available on the French side. The younger general was ready with a battlefield strategy: the tanks should be divided into two groups, one placed to the north of Paris, the other to the east, below Reims. Each group would have its own motorized infantry, its own artillery. Both groups would be prepared, when the German armored divisions slowed their advance, to strike at their flanks.

The lucid Maxime Weygand told de Gaulle: "I shall be attacked on June 6 along the Somme and Aisne rivers. I'll have twice as many German divisions on my back as we dispose of. This will tell you that our prospects are dim." But if things didn't move too quickly, if he could get back the French troops evacuated at Dunkirk, if he had sufficient weapons to give them, if a reequipped British army also returned to the battlefield, and if the Royal Air Force committed itself in France, "in that case we have a chance." Otherwise . . .

De Gaulle sympathized with this old soldier who'd been given a job he couldn't fulfill, for by the time he took over effective command on May 20 it was already too late. Weygand wasn't prepared for modern tank warfare, and he was too old to learn.

To follow up his meeting with Reynaud, de Gaulle put some of his general philosophy on paper for the premier's further consideration. Pleading for the combined tank and air offensive that might still save France, he concluded, "Above all, we must flush away notions of the defensive. . . . We must have a strong will and impose it on the enemy. It isn't too late. But it will be too late tomorrow." For at this moment the enemy—motorized ground troops and aviation both—appeared to be exhausted.

De Gaulle was staying on in Paris. He told Captain Nérot to return to the division, and gave him messages for his staff. When they separated, it was for the duration. Nérot didn't follow his chief to London, but commanded a resistance movement in German-occupied northeastern France.

That day General Héring, as military governor, signed an order calling for a new defense line around the city. Its principal component would be felled trees whose tangled branches faced the enemy: abatis, in military idiom. The tree-cutting would be carried out in the forests lining the left banks of the Seine and Oise rivers; priority would be given to placing obstacles on main roads. To cut down the trees, soldiers stationed in the immediate vicinity were to be utilized along with civilian workers, and professional loggers when available.

In Rome, Foreign Minister Ciano sent for American Ambassador Wendell Phillips to give him Mussolini's verbal response to President Roosevelt's message. Italy had already decided to enter the war, declared a defiant Mussolini. He did not agree that the United States had interests in the Mediterranean, any more than Italy had, say, in the Caribbean sea. If the United States increased its aid to the Allies when Italy attacked France, that, added the Duce, was America's problem. It did indicate that the United States had chosen the Allies; for his part, Mussolini intended to respect his own commitment to Germany.

The Italian dictator made it clear that he did not wish to feel further "pressure" from the United States. Ciano warned Phillips that such pressure could only stiffen his attitude. Mussolini knew how Roosevelt felt; Ciano thought that Roosevelt also knew how Mussolini felt.

26

SUNDAY, JUNE 2

It was an exquisite Sunday, almost a peacetime Sunday. "A brilliant summer's day that momentarily chases away the war-clouds," an English expatriate, Peter Fontaine, described it for his diary. He sat with his friend the count at the Rond-Point des Champs-Elysées, just outside the Jockey Club, protected from the sun by leafy trees. Then he and the count strolled up the Avenue des Champs-Elysées, passing sidewalk cafés crowded with Parisians "sipping and gossiping." There was a jarring note at Place de l'Etoile: an antiaircraft gun perched atop the Arch of Triumph, while François Rude's famous statue of *La Marseillaise* was buried beneath sandbags. These sights, and the men in uniform who were part of the Sunday crowd, were the only reminders of war on that delightful day.

Indeed. This month of June 1940 was to be the eighth hottest June since 1874, and the sixth driest. There was to be more sun, 288 hours of it, than in any other recorded month of June except in 1887 and 1893; weather bureau records don't lie. "Never had the city been more beautiful or calmer," diplomat Jean Chauvel exclaimed, before returning to practical matters. "The weather was constantly fine in these days when we should have liked torrents of rain to sink the German tanks into the mud."

Such gorgeous weather seemed to mock the misery of many souls under the Paris sun that day, as Chauvel observed on leaving his Sunday tour of duty at the Foreign Ministry. Crossing the Seine on the way home via Cours-la-Reine and the Champs-Elysées, he passed the legendary Ice Palace skating rink, now a shelter for Belgian refugees. Here were people without personal belongings, without homes or a country. "Some were seated on benches along the avenue, extenuated, in soiled clothing, slumped over, with empty eyes. Before them, under the trees, passed the prosperous Sunday crowd, the vain gentleman, madam showing off her unnecessary fox furs, bored child. Between these human wrecks and the strollers there were no exchanges, no contacts."

Parisians were still spending Sundays in the country, still finding reasonably convenient and even comfortable ways to get there. But there was also an impressive gathering up in Montmartre, for the third successive day of prayers for France's salvation. Parisians crowded into the Sacré Coeur basilica, spilling over to the monumental stairway, the terrace dominating the skyline of Paris. Inside the church Emmanuel Cardinal Suhard, who only that week assumed his charge as archbishop, chanted high mass, then told the faithful that their prayers were as vital as armament for French victory. The cardinal led a procession down the steps, and from the high-perched terrace blessed all of Paris.

Reading their Sunday papers, Parisians learned what it meant to live in a combat zone. Henceforth they would not be able to make a telephone call from any public place—and that included post offices as well as cafés. Power for the phone lines had been cut. One could still call from home, but only within the Paris region. Beyond that, authorization was necessary.

One could still listen to the radio, of course. Thanks to the Germans, there was more choice than before. One of the German pirate stations, called Reveil de la France and ostensibly operated by patriotic Frenchmen, broadcast an unambiguous message:

A great defeat has just been inflicted on the Allied armies, and in this battle France lost thousands of lives, young hopes of the nation. This government, whose incompetence has become dramatic, is hiding the sad truth from the country.

It offered its own hate list:

We accuse the Daladiers, the Reynauds, and all the scum of the political snakedom, for they are responsible for the misfortune which has struck us.

A new strategy was discussed at Propaganda Minister Goebbels's daily meeting with his aides (Sunday was no holiday at the Propaganda Ministry). The subject on the table was the German-operated Radio Humanité, which pretended to be the voice of France's underground Communists. Until now Goebbels's Communist station had actually been run by former French Communists on the German payroll. But Goebbels found these men too intellectual, unable to speak to workers in their own language. So he called on one of Germany's most famous ex-Communists, Ernst Torgler, the Communist member of the German parliament accused in 1933 of attempting to burn down the Reichstag building; he was now a Nazi asset. With him on the staff, Radio Humanité would be a more efficient weapon of the class struggle.

Perhaps the most singular outing that Sunday was the convoy of limousines transporting Premier Reynaud, General Weygand, Marshal Pétain, and their staffs on a tour of the front, which by now did not require a very long drive; any Frenchman with an automobile could have gone that far for Sunday lunch in peacetime. It was still a very calm front, for the Germans were making no attempt to gain ground before the French capital; all energy was being applied to the battle around Dunkirk now. The main stop for the excursionists was Pierrefonds, a village at the eastern edge of the Compiègne forest, a little over fifty miles northeast of Paris. Known to tourists for its restored medieval fortress castle, Pierrefonds now served as field headquarters for General Aubert Frère, who commanded that exposed sector. From there the party drove on to Compiègne, where the commander of the divisions holding that sector seemed to lack confidence. "How do you expect to defend villages built with mud walls against tanks when we don't even have the materials to build solid barricades?" Reynaud and Armament Minister Raoul Dautry promised to dispatch what was needed. The very next day Dautry ordered up a trainload of quarry stone. But the problem of finding laborers to do the heavy work remained. In fact it was easier to recruit the muscle than to feed and to shelter it.

Read today, the secret Defense Ministry directive signed that day by General Louis-Antoine Colson underlines the atmosphere of the hour. Military personnel were ordered to make use of every weapon at their disposal against enemy aircraft. They were to be prepared to shoot from a ditch or a truck, or while on a rest stop along the road; the point was to react quickly. "Indeed," explained General Colson, "the rifle is a dangerous arm for low-flying aircraft." But this required that as many men as possible shoot their rifles at the attacking planes at the same time, to create a cone of fire.

That evening the weary marshal had an English visitor. Edward Spears thought that he knew his Frenchman. Today he found Pétain not only tired from the day's outing but cross; decidedly the marshal hadn't appreciated what he found at Compiègne. Pétain spoke badly of Weygand—out of resentment? He would not have set up the defense of Paris the way the commander-in-chief had. But Pétain also warned that if the British did not increase their support, they would be giving Weygand an excuse for possible failure. The British, in other words, were setting themselves up as scapegoats. Pétain added that Weygand wasn't wrong to complain about the way Britain was holding back on the French. Churchill had not engaged his forces totally in this battle.

Churchill's emissary pointed out that His Majesty's Government was reluctant to commit more resources without knowing what was really happening; it did not like to make promises that could not be kept. "Our difficulties in the north are largely due to faulty French Command," he said. "We all know that now, but I have heard nothing but praise of the French commanders from General Weygand."

As Spears remembered it, his own anger built up until he burst out with: "No doubt the French are fighting bravely, but if I hear any more of Weygand's sneers about our people, I shall tell him what I think of him to his face and then return to England. . . . This attack on the Prime Minister, the best friend the French ever had, is really too much."

That night London phoned Spears to inform him that a telegram had been sent by Weygand to the French military attaché in London requesting that he insist that the French rear guard at Dunkirk not be sacrificed—that it be evacuated along with the British.

Before the day was over, Benito Mussolini had dictated and signed a message for Adolf Hitler. Italy would join the war on the tenth of June.

A. J. Liebling, who had spent a truly peacetime Sunday on a country estate near Melun, thirty miles south of Paris, heard something ominous on the train that took him back to the city that evening. A group of women in his compartment were talking about leaflets dropped from German planes, which warned that Paris was to be bombed the next day. The word "bombing" of course evoked the worst memories of the war so far—the destructive German air raids on Warsaw and then on Rotterdam.

There were no taxis in sight when Liebling arrived at the Paris terminal, drivers finding it too dangerous to move around in the blacked-out city. It took him nearly an hour to get back to his hotel on Square Louvois.

27

Monday, June 3

Did the French have the right to complain that the British were abandoning them to their fate on the beach at Dunkirk? Winston Churchill dictated a message to Paul Reynaud as the evacuation drew to an end this morning. More boats were sailing over to pick up French soldiers caught in the pocket, he promised. But he asked that the operation proceed with speed. Last night British vessels had landed and had waited in vain, taking heavy damage, running the risk of capture.

Churchill's message was passed on to Admiral Maurice Le Luc, Admiral Darlan's chief of staff. He snapped, "One can't at the same time make war and sail away."

In the end, all the surrounded troops got out of the trap. Not a single soldier remained at Dunkirk to fall into German hands.

A curious message moved through the coded channels of German diplomatic communications that day. The German Embassy in Madrid sent Berlin a telegram based on information received from "Wilhelm," which was the code name for the Spanish foreign minister, Colonel Juan Beigbeder Atienza. Beigbeder was passing on a report from the Spanish ambassador in Paris, José Felix Lequerica, after he had had "another long conversation" with Pétain. According to Lequerica,

Pétain felt that a coup d'état would be necessary for him to take power. But the President of the Republic, in France, was only a creature of the political parties, and Pétain could not expect him simply to hand over his office. "They must therefore wait." Pétain believed that France's military situation was approaching the desperate. He showed the Spanish ambassador, on a map, the front running from the Somme River to the Maginot Line along which he thought French resistance would be possible. It was as if Pétain were at that instant in direct contact with the enemy; "Wilhelm" made sure that he was.

Charles de Gaulle was also dreaming. He drafted a message to Paul Reynaud; later he could not remember whether he had actually delivered it. "We are on the edge of the abyss and you carry France on your back," he opened his heart to his patron. The enemy was winning, explained de Gaulle, because they were applying de Gaulle's methods while the French were not. Reynaud was in charge, but "you are abandoning us to men of another time. I don't ignore their past glory and merits," he went on, alluding to Pétain and Weygand without bothering to mention their names. "But I tell you that these men of another time—if we let them—will lose this new war."

If these reflections did reach Reynaud, they could only confirm what the embattled premier already thought. A British visitor who called on him at his private quarters opposite the Chamber of Deputies (a smallish bachelor flat up a narrow flight of stairs, which the premier clearly preferred to his official residence) found Reynaud pale, "his face puffy with fatigue. . . ." He "radiated a quiet defiance" all the same. The premier's éminence grise, Countess Hélène de Portes, was alongside him, and that—for the British visitor, and for so many other spectators of his private life—was the problem. She was "expensively dressed, with an unusually athletic build for a Parisienne and with dark hair brushed into curls, giving an impression of tousled, restless energy." For unsympathetic observers she represented both Reynaud's and France's dark side, "a sort of Lady Macbeth in reverse, constantly urging surrender. . . ." De Gaulle on one side (the good angel), and then all those old men, and this athletic woman, on the other.

*　　*　　*

It seemed time to accept the consequences of Paris's inclusion in the war zone. So General Weygand informed General Héring that should the French armies in the north retreat toward the city's perimeter, the defense forces under Héring's command would be integrated into the battle. Of course Héring had been preparing to defend the capital for long months, and was now as ready as he could be. He believed that the city could be held with the three divisions at his disposal, considering that he had a solid first line of defense in the concrete antitank pits and, closer in, a second line protecting all the approaches to the city. Between the two he had established a staggered line of resistance points at strategic road crossings. On this day he was able to report that the Labor Ministry was giving him ten thousand workers to cut down trees to be used as barriers, and for other defense construction.

He also planned to destroy the Seine River bridges, should the enemy come that close. This was a more controversial operation, as the engineering corps didn't fail to warn him. For one thing, in the absence of preliminary mining, a powerful explosive would be necessary for each bridge, and this would damage nearby buildings and kill civilians. For another, hasty destruction of structures such as the new Saint-Cloud bridge, the Pont de Neuilly, the viaduct of Auteuil, the new Pont des Saints-Pères, would create considerable technical problems: the debris from the damaged bridges could be used by the enemy to cross the river anyway, and it would block navigation on the Seine, should the French resume the offensive.

To assist General Héring in his rapidly expanding role, Weygand recruited Lieutenant-General Henri Fernand Dentz, then serving on the Alsatian front. The fifty-eight-year-old officer had been first of his class at the Saint Cyr military academy, one of the youngest at the War College, before distinguishing himself in World War I. Pending a more specific assignment, he was to be General Héring's deputy.

In an ironic comment on the all-but-peacetime Sunday Parisians had just enjoyed, a French-language speaker on the German radio told listeners, "You were right to take advantage of your last Sunday."

It was nearly half past one that afternoon before the German bombers attained the region of Paris, more than two hundred of them, assigned to specific targets such as the Renault and Citroën factories now entirely devoted to war production. The plants were inside the city or on its rim. More than one thousand bombs were dropped during an attack lasting nearly an hour, striking objectives—or missing them—in the fifteenth and sixteenth *arrondissements* (in the west and southwest sections of Paris), in suburban Billancourt, and in Maisons-Lafitte. Visibility was poor as the planes reached the outlying suburbs, and because they flew at high altitudes they were not spotted until the first bombs began to fall.

Explanations, excuses, would come later. The first thing was to see what damage had been done. Armament Minister Raoul Dautry reached the Citroën compound on Quai de Javel within thirty minutes of the attack, bringing with him virtually the entire war cabinet. They had been meeting at the Quai d'Orsay for the regular daily conference. Pétain was in uniform, for he and Dautry were to have visited tank production lines that afternoon. Instead they were inspecting a partly demolished factory, still smoking from fires extinguished only moments earlier. By the time they arrived the dead and wounded had been evacuated, and workers were returning to their jobs in buildings that hadn't been hit. Destruction at Citroën was heaviest on an assembly line producing shells for the 75-millimeter cannon, and Dautry made sure that everything possible was being done to get the line moving again.

The center of the city hadn't been touched, not even the operational center—the ministries. Except for one, the Air Ministry, not in the center at all but on the city's southern edge at Boulevard Victor. Ambassador William Bullitt happened to be visiting the building, attending a lunch in honor of an American delegation that had come to town to discuss aid for the French aviation industry. The ministry dining and reception rooms were located on the top floor, and Bullitt and the other guests were sipping sherry before lunch when the sirens sounded. Unable to believe that Paris itself was the target, the American party moved out to the balcony to watch the action.

A first bomb struck a field just one hundred yards away from the Air Ministry building. A second bomb dropped through the roof of the reception room Bullitt and the other guests had just abandoned (but this bomb didn't explode). Bombs continued to fall over the ministry as the lunchers made a hasty descent to the basement shelter, and shattered glass and plaster threw up a cloud. When they finally climbed out of the cellar an hour later, the Americans and their host, Air Minister André Laurent-Eynac, discovered that two official automobiles in the courtyard had been demolished, but not Bullitt's. "I am entirely uninjured," he assured Washington moments after his return to the American Embassy, "and lost only my hat and gloves, which are sitting at this moment close to the unexploded bomb."

The near miss was worth a headline:

A BOMB

FALLS AT FEET

OF MR. BULLITT

WITHOUT EXPLODING

It was "providence," the press quoted the ambassador, and the papers made much of his telephone call to Roosevelt, of the president's emotion, the anger and relief of the American people. Privately, to his diary, correspondent Alexander Werth growled: "Well, they shouldn't have built the damned place of glass."

Not everyone managed to be that close to the action. But the alert, the drone of enemy aircraft, even the distant thunder created a community of witnesses at the four corners of the city. It was the first event everyone remembered later. André Maurois, who resided in one of the city's better neighborhoods, lived over a garden facing the Bois de Boulogne park. So the famous author and his family were front-row spectators that afternoon. "Look, a swarm of bees!" one of his children cried out, for that's what he made of the massive formation of enemy warplanes against a brilliant sun. Maurois and his wife guessed that the Germans were only trying to frighten Parisians (nobody in the family heard the exploding bombs). Later, when they got the news, they toured the bomb craters, the damaged and destroyed buildings, the still-smoking factories.

When *Manchester Guardian* reporter Alexander Werth finally realized what had taken place, he jumped into a taxi to reach the scene, getting stuck in a traffic jam on Pont Mirabeau, for all Paris was trying to get to the site. A crowd gathered to watch firemen put out a fire. "The pigs, we'll get back at them!" an old woman shouted, shaking her fists. Werth noted that an apartment house off the Avenue de Versailles had been badly damaged, all windows shattered. The street was littered with glass. He saw bits of brown paper in the debris, and realized these were the paper strips used to protect windows against blasts; obviously they didn't help much when the bombs were close. In front of the Café Mirabeau—whose windows were also shattered—workers were filling up a crater dug out by a bomb.

He went on to Rue Poussin. "A large house bombed to hell," he observed, "the front of its three top stories gone; the whole thing like a badly cut piece of cheddar." There was a mountain of rubble in front of the building. Werth also noticed bedcovers protruding through ceilings, pictures hanging without their supporting walls. It reminded him of Madrid under siege not so long before. "Bomb craters marked the elegant Boulevard Suchet, where the Duke and Duchess of Windsor had had a house," correspondent Geoffrey Cox remembered, "and maids in uniform and footmen in livery came out from expensive flats to empty dustpans of broken glass and china into the gutter."

Fernande Alphandery was working in Neuilly when the attack came. As the business manager of a pharmaceutical firm, she had been confronted with the hasty departure of its British owner, and the need to help sixty employees divide up the assets the man had left behind for them. Her maid phoned from home with the news that a bomb had fallen next to the corner bakery, but hadn't exploded. There was a crater in the middle of the street. Later, neighboring apartment buildings were evacuated as police began to disarm the bomb. Fernande Alphandery's house was just across the Seine from the Citroën plant, and no tall building obstructed the view of the column of smoke she perceived as she returned to her flat.

She was in a war zone, but she also realized that it was only bad luck. For she could easily see the limits of the German attack, and already realized that ninety-nine Parisians out of a hundred couldn't even guess that bombs had been dropped on the city at lunchtime that day. To engrave the scene in her memory, she decided to make a tour of the neighborhood. On Rue de Ranelagh she came upon the old Lycée Molière. "High school ravaged, rooms blown out, collapsed stairways, gaping crater," she noted in her diary. Although the school year was not quite over, the building had obviously been empty at the moment of attack.

One of the German targets, intentional or otherwise, was the Saint-Denis Hospital. There the chief military surgeon, Professor Louis Digonnet, had just concluded an operation with the assistance of Dr. Pierre Daunois. They had washed and were on their way to the officers' mess when the sirens sounded. With no proper shelter anywhere in sight, the two military doctors leaped into a trench dug near the guard post at the hospital entrance. Captain Digonnet was just offering Daunois a cigarette when two shells went off, one near the gate, which killed a nurse who was coming in to take up her tour of duty. The other bomb fell outside the operating room that the two medical officers had left a few minutes earlier, and destroyed it. As for Daunois, he got the blast right in his face, and nearly swallowed his cigarette.

General Spears remembered that day. He was to lunch with a Polish count, a longtime friend of British Intelligence, high above the Champs-Elysées. The guests were leaning over superb dishes when the sky began to rumble. While the other guests rose from the table, the count and Sir Edward finished their desserts before moving to the balcony, each with a glass of remarkable cognac in hand. Spears saw no bombs, but flames rose from the Quai de Javel, a column of smoke pierced the sky. There was no sign of panic in the streets below. He remembered the First World War in Paris; then the bombs had come closer one day at lunch.

Later a senior British air officer who had been at the Villacoublay military airport at noon told Spears that French air defense had been virtually nonexistent. Spears informed London that the apathy of the French air force was troubling.

A man at street level could confirm that there was no panic that day, certainly not in the center of the city. Young professor Henri Quéffelec was lunching alone at the Méditerranée restaurant on Place de l'Odéon when the sirens went off. No one moved from his table or was asked to. Paul Léautaud heard both sirens and antiaircraft batteries, and took shelter in a doorway of the Passage Dauphine near the Seine. A well-dressed man soon joined him; the man didn't wish to descend into a cellar any more than Léautaud did. He turned out to be an American, resident in France. When Léautaud complained about the war, the American countered, "What have you and the British been doing since September? Nothing. Just speeches. You should have destroyed Berlin on the first day."

They heard an explosion; the American identified it as a bomb. An hour passed; Léautaud found himself falling asleep standing up. Finally he decided to go to his office. "With all these things happening . . . my cat Poupou sick, the war and everything I'm obliged to listen to on the subject," he complained to his diary, "I have so little time to think about my literature and about the fact that I am a French writer now publishing the diary of my literary life in a literary magazine." Later, when a former companion now safe in Brittany wrote to say that she was worried about Léautaud, he reflected, "I believe that things are more frightening seen from a distance, reading about them in the press. When one is there, on the scene, one just waits for them to be done."

Pietro Nenni, the exiled Italian Socialist leader who had fought in the Spanish Civil War, looked at the German attack bombers through field glasses, although he was too far from the targets to realize how serious the air raid had been. The realization came to him only that evening with the radio news. The figures—the release of one thousand bombs—impressed people more than the actual event had, he told his diary. It left everyone feeling that he had escaped mortal danger. The effect was to speed up the exodus. There was no panic, but roads leading south, away from the German threat, were now filling up with Parisians who joined the columns of refugees from farther north.

Another émigré, anti-Stalinist revolutionary Victor Serge, stood with his companion at a balcony as the antiaircraft batteries puffed away at the German invaders. "At the thought that innocent blood is being shed at this very instant on our side," he thought, "one is seized by a feeling of such disgust that one can think of nothing else." He was relieved, later, to discover that Parisians hadn't lost their morale.

Thanks to the sun, the city had even retained its "holiday mood."

Yet it was certain that the exodus was going to accelerate now. The official French communiqué on the June 3 bombing reported 200 civilian victims, 45 dead. But Parisians could piece together evidence bringing them nearer to the truth, the truth being that there had been 906 victims, 254 of whom had died, 20 of them children. That would lead parents to think hard. The state was taking charge of the evacuation of school-age children; schools would close shortly. Newspapers made the point that the claim that the Germans had struck only military objectives contradicted the evidence: schools and hospitals were hit. Most victims were not in Paris proper, but in the north and northwest suburbs. The official German communiqué spoke of airfields in the Paris region, airplane factories. The Germans claimed to have destroyed 104 French planes in combat, and three hundred to four hundred more on the ground. They lost only nine of their own.

Editor Pierre Lazareff, whose job was to understand the man on the street, was convinced that far from creating panic, the German air raid had solidified morale. Marxist sociologist Georges Friedmann, then attached to a military hospital outside the city, came in on a visit and reported the same to his diary: "Paris doesn't seem demoralized, on the contrary, it is roused, disgusted, revolted (depending on one's disposition). . . . The destructions have stimulated morale."

At five that afternoon, William Bullitt cabled the president of the United States to report that the air minister had told him that the French government believed that the air raid "marks the beginning of a systematic attempt to destroy Paris and that we shall have further raids tonight." A prediction—two predictions—that would prove wrong.

Bullitt also told Washington that the extreme accuracy of the bombing, notably in the pinpoint attack on the Air Ministry, seemed to indicate that the enemy had obtained "in one way or another" the secret bomb sight developed for the U.S. Air Force.

Paul Reynaud's cabinet aide Dominique Leca remembered that the premier regretted the language of the High Command communiqué released at six that day, for it stated that the Germans had concentrated on military targets. This seemed to turn the adversary into decent warriors who avoided civilian casualties. (In truth, the High Command communiqué had clearly indicated that the Germans had attacked "Paris and the population of Paris." It was rather the premier's communiqué which commented that the German raid was "probably directed at military objectives.")

And when the cocky premier was ready to inform his British partner of the day's events, his message to Churchill, which has remained secret until now, was worded: "Paris, the Paris region and its industrial facilities have just been bombed by 300 German airplanes. A similar treatment of the Berlin region would be 'greatly appreciated.' " (Reynaud put the final two words in the language of his correspondent.)

We can also now discover that French military authorities knew in advance that the Germans were going to bomb Paris. Their source was the enemy's own directives, intercepted by French military intelligence thanks to their ability to outfox the most secret of coding machines, Enigma. On May 27, French intelligence deciphered a German air force dispatch concerning a massive air raid code-named Paula. In the following days there were more references to Paula; by May 30 it became clear that Paula was Paris. A French intelligence officer personally warned air force General Joseph Vuillemin on June 1 of the coming raid, specifying the time and place of assembly of the German air fleet. The answer came that all fighter planes were committed to the front.

It could have been worse; today it is not clear why it was not. Joseph Goebbels himself, in his diary, was mostly concerned by the thought of Allied reprisal raids against Germany. "From the propaganda point of view," he told himself, "we don't intend to do anything regarding this first attack. We shall see what the enemy does. . . ." And they would wait for a second German attack before attempting to create panic among Parisians.

Cleaning up after the raid took time. German bombs had even interrupted the superbly efficient Paris Métro, with damage to a subway tunnel between the Chardon-Lagache and Mirabeau stations. But, as

Raoul Dautry was proud to report, nearby Citroën was back in production twenty-four hours after the attack.

The report on the raid in next morning's *Le Figaro* contained two blocks of white space, indicating that military censors were not letting everything pass. The business column let it be known that the Paris stock exchange session had been "noticeably shortened" by the German incursion. "The market was dull and few stocks proved the exception to the rule." Gold mines were one of the exceptions; they did do well on June 3.

The same newspaper offered some lessons drawn from the experience. The courage of Parisians had been admirable, an editor declared. Yet they were often too ready to take chances. Too many people peered out of windows, too many people—those who should have served as examples of discipline—stood at their balconies. There were too many people in the streets, too many who thought taking shelter meant ducking into a doorway. Wise Parisians, explained *Le Figaro,* got off the streets, closed shutters, sat in their cellars. Moreover, after the raid was over, many Parisians rushed to the scene of the bombing, getting in the way of police and firemen. Not all bombs go off right away; one should not crowd around if one is not sure that the explosion had occurred.

The paper repeated the warning soon after that: "Close shutters and open windows. Close gas and electric meters. Carry a gas mask and identity papers. At night wear a coat, carry a blanket." There was a lot more. One was not to light a flashlight on a stairway going down to a cellar. If surprised on the street, one should assume a prone position, even in the gutter. Inside a shelter: "Don't move around, don't speak unnecessarily, don't smoke, don't bring pets into the shelter."

One of those who was observing a stepped-up exodus of Parisians was Ilya Ehrenburg, who was still not being allowed to go home to Moscow. The day came when he and his wife were all alone in their apartment house on Rue de Cotentin. In Moscow the story was spreading that he refused to return. He couldn't correct that, because communications with the Soviet capital had long since been interrupted.

"Long files of cars with mattresses on the roof stretched as far as the Portes d'Italie and d'Orléans," observed the Russian. "Everybody said that the Germans were approaching." Later on, scholars would ask themselves what had precipitated the flight of Parisians. There had been no order, no decree. And if at first departures appeared to be compensated for by the arrival of family members and friends from exposed regions of northeast France, streets were patently emptier after June 3. Even residents of the suburbs immediately outside the city's northern gates began to migrate to the center. Paris was the hub. "The movement grows from hour to hour," observed city official Eugène Depigny. "The crowd becomes agitated, with a kind of morbid anguish, irrationality, panic; a psychosis of flight is developing." This precise man noted all the types of vehicles being used by fleeing Parisians: automobiles, trucks of all kinds, horse carriages, carts, taxis, delivery vehicles, pushcarts, drays, coffee vendors' carts, hay wagons.

All the while, the exodus from the north, into and through the city, went on. Sylvia Beach, the American bookseller whose Shakespeare & Company had succored a "lost generation" of Americans and Britishers, was keeping her bookshop open on Rue de l'Odéon, minutes away from the Boulevard Saint-Michel, that much-traveled road of refugees on their way south. Through tears, Miss Beach and her bookseller companion Adrienne Monnier watched the grim procession, moved especially by the spectacle of cattle-drawn carts piled with household effects, with children and the old and the sick, with pregnant women and women with infants, chickens in their coops, cats and dogs. At times farmers stopped at the Luxembourg gardens to let their cows graze.

Marcel Duhamel, then a young movie actor, joined friends who were driving to safer climes in southern France. He discovered that everybody who left Paris chose the main highway, Route Nationale 6, either because they were sheep or scared out of their minds.

Raymond Martin was an engineer employed in a research division of French Railways when at the beginning of June he was reassigned to the regional command post for southwest France based at the Gare d'Austerlitz, alongside the Seine in eastern Paris; it was the terminal for Tours, Limoges, Bordeaux, Toulouse, Montluçon, Béziers, in a region far from Germany and far from Italy. France's railroad system was divided into five regions, which since 1938 had been combined into a single government corporation. In Paris, each region was managed from one of the city's main stations. Raymond Martin's new job was to head up one of two task forces operating at the regional command post at the Gare d'Austerlitz to deal with the extraordinary movement of Parisians out of their city.

The point was to keep the trains rolling, rolling as they had never rolled before; each of the task forces had a twelve-hour duty day for that. As soon as a train reached a provincial destination with its wagons packed with fugitives, it would unload and return to the Gare d'Austerlitz; timetables were thrown out. Martin and his inspectors had a constant reminder of the challenge in the queue of would-be passengers, four or five abreast, extending from the waiting room all the way out to the Boulevard de l'Hôpital.

He shared a camp bed and a sink with the other team chief. The staffs could go home, but the two chiefs were obliged to remain in the station night and day, so that in an emergency one could relieve or assist the other. And there *were* emergencies. They could get lunch at an employee restaurant staffed by nuns from a nearby convent (which gave the place a name, Vatican Palace). For dinner they found a local bistro, but that became harder as the days went by. In the final hours of the exodus, Martin had to walk all the way to Rue Mouffetard to find a place to eat.

What the emergency teams discovered, on the day they received their mission, was that neither the government nor the railroad was working with an evacuation plan, certainly not for the civilian population, for this would have implied that a military defeat was possible. Martin received new directives as the need arose, say to prepare a train for the transfer of a particular government department, so many railway cars for personnel, so many for equipment and files. To keep ordinary passenger traffic separate from government transport, freight stations were generally used for the latter.

Before long the men at Austerlitz realized that each government department was making its own plans, not necessarily coordinated with the others. So the command post in turn drew up its own schedules for evacuations to key centers such as Tours (or beyond Tours to Bordeaux and La Rochelle), Limoges (with Toulouse and Perigueux), Bourges, and the Massif Central mountain range. From main stations along each line they obtained indications of the capacity of each town to handle more evacuees.

Certainly no one tried to keep Parisians in Paris. Even when it became evident that the city would not be defended and thus would not be the scene of violent combat, the legion of candidates for departure did not let up. Toward the end the task force began to reduce the distance each train traveled from Paris, so that it could make a round trip faster and get more people out of the capital, even if fewer passengers would be able to travel as far as they hoped to. This did not seem to bother most passengers, for they didn't know where they wished to go, only that they wished to get out of Paris.

Raymond Martin and his men lived like monks. Paris became the view from his office window over the station platforms.

Clearly the educational system had its own agenda; this may have contributed to public peace. High school teacher Simone de Beauvoir, for example, wanted very much to leave Paris for the south, to be close to her companion, Jean-Paul Sartre, when his military unit was ordered to retreat. But she was a teacher first of all. After the June 3 air raid her closest friends left town, but she had to stay at least another whole week, for on June 10 she was supposed to supervise baccalaureat examinations—the apotheosis of a public-school career. Sitting at the Café du Dôme on Boulevard de Montparnasse, she pondered these things. The Germans would come and she'd be trapped. Yet morally she was obliged to stay.

On June 3, hours before the appearance of German bombers over Paris skies, the Sorbonne opened its doors for an exceptional examination for young men scheduled to be called up for military duty. There were some 250 candidates for the *licence* (the bachelor's degree), and 35 for a higher degree in classic studies (French, Greek, Latin). These were written tests; orals were scheduled for the following Friday and Saturday.

"An epidemic of spy-mania has broken out," announced Peter Fontaine in his diary entry for the day. "Policemen are stopping people in the streets to ask for their papers." Belgian-Russian-international revolutionary Victor Serge attributed the severity to tough Interior Minister Mandel; Serge called it "the purge of Paris." He described a veritable roundup, with helmeted gendarmes bearing carbines surrounding student cafés on Boulevard Saint-Michel; foreigners without proper papers were herded into trucks. Many happened to be anti-Nazi refugees, noted Serge, "for of course the other foreigners have the proper documents." He feared that there would be new prisons for anti-Fascists, prisons in a French Republic that had been their last hope on the European continent, but that was now "losing its head in its death throes."

Arthur Koestler was one of the victims. He seemed to have every possible fault. He was an Eastern European, a Jew, a former Communist propagandist. At the beginning of the war he was arrested and interned. Released in January 1940, he was obliged to report regularly to the French police. He spent his time writing *Darkness at Noon,* which would be one of the most effective anti-Stalinist books ever published. Now, as the Germans approached Paris he was arrested again, although he managed to bluff his way out of the internment camp. He hid in the Paris flat of Sylvia Beach's friend Adrienne Monnier, moved on to the local PEN chapter before making his escape south. This time he joined the Foreign Legion, and that gave him a ticket to North Africa and freedom.

Later that day, newsman Alexander Werth dropped in at the swell Hotel Meurice on Rue de Rivoli, where a reception was under way for Alfred Duff Cooper, Churchill's minister of information. Werth broached the matter of the fifth column: Was there anything like that in Britain? Duff Cooper replied that England also had its Nazis, but he felt that British morale was healthier than what he was seeing in Paris.

28

TUESDAY, JUNE 4

At an off-the-record press conference President Roosevelt was asked by a White House correspondent whether he had a comment to make on the bombing of Paris.

Shaking his head "no," the president nevertheless said, "Except that I am very glad the Lord has his arms around Bill Bullitt."

Paris had changed in one way: it was quieter. "One moves about only on foot," observed the young publisher Maurice Kahane, "and everyone sticks to his neighborhood." It was a Venice on dry land, a Venice without noisy motorboats. From his skylight window under a roof he could see the empty streets, with only an occasional housewife braving the silence, shopping basket in hand. Now one could hear the "silence"—and the birds thriving on pure air.

Born of a British father, Kahane noticed something else. English had become a foreign language, an unknown tongue, in the cafés where it was lingua franca only a short month before.

Calm even at the stock exchange. The day following the air raid was as normal as one could hope for. As the financial editor of *Le Matin* told it, the session of the Paris Bourse was hardly reportable, for it took place under "absolutely banal conditions." Even stocks likely to be affected by a Mediterranean war hadn't been affected. Some did well.

This newspaper carried the usual advertising, even if the language in some of the ads seemed to have particular relevance. THE OPTIMIST DRINKS CINZANO, read one such. In smaller print readers were assured that the wines utilized to make this aperitif came exclusively from the French empire.

YOU ARE BITTER, DEFEATED, read another advertisement. YOU SEE EVERYTHING IN BLACK! The remedy was Carter's Little Liver Pills. A third ad offered diet pills; apparently a woman could still be overweight in June.

Correspondent Alexander Werth kept himself busy following up the previous day's raid. At the regular War Ministry press conference, reporters heard the official version of events but also exchanged unofficial gossip. The foreign press was clearly impressed with German air power, the speed of the attack. The official spokesman confirmed earlier reports that the enemy had aimed "chiefly" at military objectives in and near Paris, although at the height they flew they could not help damaging nonmilitary targets as well. The casualty figures were now 254 dead, 195 of them civilians; 652 injured, 545 of them civilians. A fortnight earlier, German bases had been 250 miles away from the city. Now they were mighty close, "no farther away from Paris than Calais is from London," thought Londoner Werth. He also decided that the way the attackers had protected their bombers with a fighter escort should be a lesson for the British.

Joseph Goebbels was ready with his own evaluation of the June 3 raid. He was pleased to note that Paris recognized that the Germans had struck only at military targets. But the British had reacted differently, he discovered. They spoke of barbaric methods and called for reprisals (because, chuckled Goebbels, London was less accessible to German bombers).

In America [he told his diary], some indignant reactions of course, but fewer than I expected. In this war everything is the opposite of what one expected. Ambassador Bullitt, who was nearly touched, is acting the hero, and Duff Cooper, who was having breakfast, says on the radio that he had to wait a long time to be served. They are all crazy as loons.

Parisians were drawing their own conclusions. "Next time I'll go down to the cellar," was the headline over one press story; the speaker was a woman who hadn't been quick enough, and so suffered injuries. Paris began to review civil defense procedures. Thus one civil defense unit, responsible for the neighborhood embracing the Invalides military complex, had sent inspectors up to an eleventh-floor roof to look at the city the way hostile aircraft might see it. The inspectors discovered that lights were burning all over the Hôtel des Invalides headquarters. Alerted, Military Governor Héring warned that offenders would be found and punished.

The use of Métro stations as shelters was reviewed. As early as December 1939 a confidential study had determined that two stations right in the center of town, Place Saint-Michel and Ile de la Cité, would actually be dangerous in the event of air attack; steps had been taken to make sure these subway entrances were closed quickly after an alert. A month later a number of other stations were added to the list. As late as June 2, inspection of five stations showed that only one had sufficient personnel to deal with large numbers of persons seeking shelter; this was Porte de Vanves, with a capacity of 3,500. But the station beneath the Gare d'Austerlitz, which, when suburban trains arrived with full loads, might have to provide shelter for as many as ten thousand commuters, lacked a first-aid station, and could muster only ten policemen and five soldiers to maintain order.

"We lead a rather anxious and active life here," Philippe Pétain wrote to his wife (then still at the Madrid embassy). In Paris he was staying with friends, living the life of a bachelor, taking meals at a modest neighborhood restaurant—"but prices have doubled," he reported.

He spent no lunch money on June 4, for he was the guest of the American ambassador at the official residence on Place d'Iéna. They took their coffee in the garden. Suddenly Pétain asked Bullitt whether the French government had ever told Roosevelt how bad the situation really was. Bullitt replied that he thought Reynaud and Daladier always spoke frankly.

Still, the marshal wanted Roosevelt to know what he was thinking. The Germans not only outnumbered the French in manpower three to one, but aviation was going to decide the outcome, and France was hopelessly outnumbered in the air. The Germans were about to attack on the Somme River and close to Laon and Reims, but the French had nothing to oppose them save their courage. Roosevelt should be told, said the marshal, that he expected the Germans to cross the Somme and the lower Seine River and envelop Paris. To add a complication, Italy was about to enter the war, and France simply had no planes to defend itself against Italian raids. Italy could easily take the French Alps. Worse yet, the British were holding back on France, insisting on embarking their troops first at Dunkirk, and now that they had few soldiers on French soil, they were not flying as many planes as they had been.

Reporting this to Roosevelt, Bullitt summed up Pétain's attitude toward the British:

Under the circumstances he was obliged to feel that the British intended to permit the French to fight without help until the last available drop of French blood should have been shed and that then with quantities of troops on British soil and plenty of planes and a dominant fleet the British after a very brief resistance or even without resistance would make a peace of compromise with Hitler, which might even involve a British Government under a British Fascist leader.

Clearly no love was lost between Pétain and the allies across the Channel. The marshal made it clear that he was going to repeat these thoughts to the War Council the next day. Unless the British sent aircraft and adequate troop reinforcements, Pétain warned, the French themselves would come to terms with Germany, whatever happened to Britain. Bullitt told Roosevelt, "He added that it was not fair for any French government to permit the British to behave in a totally callous and selfish manner while demanding the sacrifice of every able-bodied Frenchman."

In London, Winston Churchill stood before Parliament to report on the evacuation of Dunkirk. A victory of sorts, although he was the first to say, "Wars are not won by evacuation." He mentioned the possibility of an invasion of the British isles; they would be ready. "We shall go on to the end," he declaimed,

> we shall fight in France, we shall fight on the seas and oceans, we shall fight with growing confidence and growing strength in the air, we shall defend our Island, whatever the cost may be, we shall fight on the beaches, we shall fight on the landing grounds, we shall fight in the fields and in the streets, we shall fight in the hills; we shall never surrender.

Even if the enemy got the best of them. He promised:

> Then our Empire beyond the seas, armed and guarded by the British Fleet, would carry on the struggle, until, in God's good time, the New World, with all its power and might, steps forth to the rescue and the liberation of the old.

That Englishman in Paris, Peter Fontaine, who was seeing the last of the city, could actually feel French resentment at the way French soldiers were left waiting on the beach as British troops were embarked at Dunkirk. "I have been noticing gradual rifts in the Entente," he noted in his diary. "Little pin-pricks at first." People were comparing the wages paid to French soldiers to the amount Tommies received.

Alexander Werth heard it from his hotelkeeper, who was otherwise a cheery soul. The woman felt that the British were running out on France. "Having lost the Channel ports, they aren't quite so interested in France any longer, she says. There's some truth in it; and the French people feel it instinctively—even without the insinuations of *Paris-Soir.*"

29

WEDNESDAY, JUNE 5

At sunrise the decisive phase of the battle for Paris and the French heartland got under way. Following several aborted counterattacks by the combined French and British forces, the last a desperate thrust against a German bridgehead at Abbeville, it was the turn of the Germans now. They threw six armored divisions against Somme River defenses at Amiens and Péronne, in an advance that was to take the first wave of attackers as far as the valley of the Oise River and the lower Seine, launching pads for the drive on Paris.

General Weygand phoned the bad news to Reynaud at 7:00 A.M., then drew up an order of the day that concealed his pessimism:

The battle of France has begun.

The order is to defend our positions without thought of retreat.

Officers, noncommissioned officers, soldiers of the French army, let the thought of our wounded homeland inspire you with the unshakable resolution to stand your ground. . . .

After receiving a briefing, Weygand did what one had to do to communicate with the field: he went out to the field, in this case to

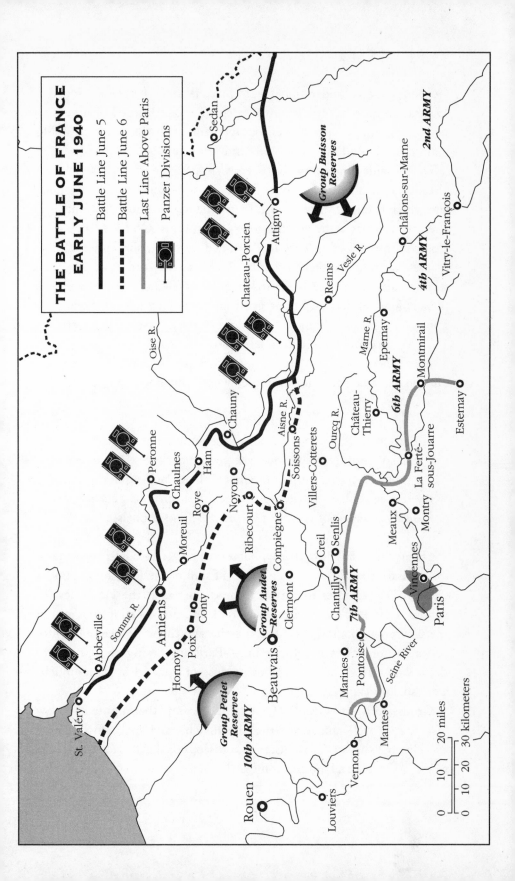

THE BATTLE OF FRANCE
EARLY JUNE 1940

Battle Line June 5
Battle Line June 6
Last Line Above Paris
Panzer Divisions

Sedan

Group Buisson
Reserves

2nd ARMY

Châlons-sur-Marne

4th ARMY

Vitry-le-François

Attigny

Vesle R.

Chateau-Porcien

Reims

Oise R.

Marne R.

Epernay

Montmirail

6th ARMY

Chauny

Aisne R.

Ourcq R.

Château-Thierry

La Ferté-sous-Jouarre

Esternay

Peronne

Ham

Soissons

Villers-Cotterets

Chaulnes

Noyon

Roye

Ribecourt

Compiègne

Creil

Senlis

Meaux

Montry

Moreuil

Clermont

Chantilly

7th ARMY

Vincennes

Amiens

Conty

Beauvais

Marines

Pontoise

Paris

Hornoy

Poix

Group Audet
Reserves

Seine River

Group Petiet
Reserves

10th ARMY

Mantes

Abbeville

Somme R.

St. Valéry

Vernon

Rouen

Louviers

0   10   20 miles

0   10   20   30 kilometers

General Georges's operational headquarters at La Ferté-sous-Jouarre. Well aware of what the troops needed, Weygand urged Georges "to neglect nothing, appeals, encouragement, rewards," which could maintain "resolution, emulation, and tenacity."

On one side, an enemy that seemed impossible to stop, which had already vanquished and all but obliterated some forty Allied divisions, and which had now turned south to get the rest. Behind the front line, a reserve German army waiting to exploit success. On the French side, a hastily improvised defense line manned by weak, shaken units. The marvel was that the French fought as well as they did now. The men seemed less unsettled by Blitzkrieg tactics—the Panzers and the planes; foot soldiers and their good artillery—the famous French 75 guns—made each kilometer expensive for the best of the Germans along the Somme between Amiens and Péronne.

Everywhere, one could encounter justifications for one's worst fears. On the walls of Paris, for example, where this poster appeared:

The Military Governor
of Paris appeals to the vigilance of the population to notify without delay military authorities, the gendarmerie, and the police of the presence of parachutists or enemy planes landing in the countryside, as well as of the appearance of suspicious persons near military installations, factories, bridges, and tunnels.

"Everything smells of defeat," observed an active officer called back from Alsace that day to become chief of staff of the Paris region under General Dentz. After reporting to headquarters at the Hôtel des Invalides, Colonel Georges Groussard took the afternoon off for a tour of the downtown boulevards. Of course he saw the unbroken column of private automobiles heading south—Parisians fleeing the city. And those who stayed, out of duty or because of fear of losing too much, wore solemn expressions.

Groussard was received by General Dentz only that night. He knew his superior well, and was struck by his changed appearance; Dentz was clearly exhausted, exhausted and discouraged. "I'm expecting the worst," the general officer confessed. Dentz made it clear that his assignment was to maintain order inside the city, yet Groussard was alarmed by the absurdity of the organization of the Paris region. In peacetime the military government was largely a symbolic institution, but with the war it had assumed tangible duties. As commandant of the Region of Paris, Dentz would in fact share responsibility for the city with the military governor, and yet be his subordinate. Groussard also saw the defense plan for the capital as "a masterpiece of illogic." The outer position was the responsibility of a general who reported to the Region, that is, to General Dentz. But the inner position was subordinate to the military governor, who didn't even have a staff of his own.

As he went through the files, Groussard was to discover another reason for alarm. Fortifications that should have been built long before, during the respite offered by the phony war, were only now being put up. And of course it was too late. They had sufficient labor, but workers couldn't be moved to the defense lines fast enough, nor could they be fed there, and there was a dearth of supervisors. This army of unemployable laborers only served to complicate the job of the real army.

The press that day prepared Parisians for the evening's entertainment. The Opéra, for instance, was doing *Thaïs*, the Massenet work based on Anatole France's story of an Egyptian courtesan become devout. The Comédie Française happened to be resting that day, but promised *Le Cid* for June 6; its sister theater across the Seine scheduled *Andromaque* and *Le Médecin malgré lui*. Two private theaters were open, the George VI and L'Oeuvre, with the cabarets Le Boeuf sur le Toit and Ciro's. At the movies one could see Leslie Howard in *Pygmalion*, Greta Garbo in *Ninotchka*. In fact Parisian screens still offered thirteen films with their original English soundtracks, among them *Wuthering Heights* and *The Hunchback of Notre Dame*. (*Goodbye Mr. Chips* was playing in a French version.)

PRECIOUS STONES
AND JEWELRY
WILL STAY IN FRANCE

The above headline in *Le Matin* seemed to announce good news. In fact it was a warning. A new decree banned the removal from French territory of gold, platinum, silver, gilded silver, and finished jewelry.

After leaving General Georges and stopping off at headquarters for late news, General Weygand ordered his driver to take him to the Rue Saint-Dominique for the daily meeting presided over by Premier Reynaud, doubling as war minister. The general-in-chief told the group that in his opinion the Germans were seeking to draw France's remaining reserves to the Oise valley, and then to launch attacks simultaneously in the lower Somme toward Le Havre and Rouen, and in the region of Rethel, directed to the Marne. He would not be surprised if the enemy avoided a frontal attack on Paris and bypassed it to the east and west, moving toward an assembly point at Orléans, over sixty miles south of the capital.

Reynaud warned that they had better plan for the worst case: the government would certainly have to evacuate Paris so as not to fall into German hands. Where to go? Not, warned Weygand, to a last stand in Brittany, for that made no military sense. If the worst did come, Weygand declared solemnly, if the battle was lost and the Germans moved to overrun most of the nation's soil, true courage would lie in negotiating an armistice. Pétain agreed with that.

But Reynaud did not. He was certain that the Germans would not offer France an acceptable peace. The French army would have to fight as long as it possibly could, and then the government would continue the war from bases outside France. He revealed to Weygand his plan for a new cabinet. It was time for a government of public safety. He had wanted to remove Daladier, to replace him as foreign minister with Pétain, but Pétain hadn't accepted. Weygand told Reynaud that Pétain was right to refuse, for the army would not understand why their marshal was removing himself from the war.

Reynaud was soon face to face with the British ambassador, Ronald Hugh Campbell. He told the visitor that when Pétain had learned that the British would not send a substantial number of aircraft, he had commented, "Well, there is nothing left but to make peace. If you do not want to do it, you can hand over [the government] to me." Reynaud refused that, so Campbell reported to Churchill.

* * *

Ministers got their official telegrams at dinner: there was to be a meeting of the full cabinet at 11:15 P.M.; no reason was given. The encounter between Daladier and Reynaud prior to the meeting was predictably painful. The old Radical Socialist asked only that he be allowed to depart with honor. It was enough for him, Daladier told the assembled ministers, that he enjoyed the esteem of his children. Reynaud praised his patriotism, his four years as war minister before his move to the Quai d'Orsay.

And as if the dramatic cabinet confrontation hadn't been enough to fill the evening, Reynaud now braced himself for a momentous telephone call. Bill Bullitt was there to assist him. So was Eve Curie, a frequent visitor to the United States. Making a call to Washington, even when one was a premier calling a president, was still a technical feat, subject to frustrating delays. Reynaud was hoping to speak to Roosevelt "man to man," and when at last they were connected he promised that France would fight to the last soldier. Not only France's destiny but freedom and democracy the world over were at stake in this battle. He ended by asking for aircraft and destroyers. Roosevelt said he would get guns and ammunition.

"Reynaud was enormously pleased by his conversation with you on the telephone this evening," Bullitt cabled Roosevelt (at midnight, on his return to the embassy). The fighting was going well, as Reynaud had assured Roosevelt that it was, and this despite German superiority in equipment, especially in aircraft. Reynaud had let Bullitt know that he had sent "the stiffest note that he could compose" to Churchill to protest the removal of British aviation from French skies. The premier described this act as "utterly shocking," and said that Churchill's excuse was that British planes had to be based in Britain, for it would be imprudent to make use of French airfields now. Since RAF planes could not be effective in the present stage of the fighting if they didn't fly from French fields, they could not be used at all.

If Churchill continued to hold back his air force, warned Reynaud, the reaction on his part would be fierce. Britain could not withdraw planes any more than King Leopold could, with honor, withdraw Belgian soldiers. And should Italy enter the war, Bullitt explained to Roosevelt, the French need for aviation would be desperate.

Personally, I feel that the question of sending the British pursuit planes to participate in the present battle is the touchstone with regard to future British policy. If the British continue to refuse to send their planes I believe it indicates that they have decided not to give any further serious support to France in her terrible struggle against Germany (and potentially, Italy), but to give just enough to keep France fighting to the bitter end.

That, concluded Bullitt—shooting from the hip—suggested that Britain intended, either before the Germans attacked England or shortly thereafter, to install a Fascist government "and accept vassalage to Hitler."

30

THURSDAY, JUNE 6

NOTICE
to the people of Paris

The Ministry of National Defense and War advises:

"Several measures concerning traffic in Paris and other sites
were taken this morning. These measures should not alarm
inhabitants of the city.

"It is normal that precautions be taken against the possibility of landings of parachutists and enemy transport planes.

"It would be an error to attribute another meaning to these
measures."

A notice, thought correspondent Walter Kerr, worded to reassure
Parisians. But it was having the opposite effect. He walked past steel
girders that had been placed across the Avenue des Champs-Elysées
and other streets, evidently to prevent the landing of troop-carrying
aircraft. Kerr decided that the government, which knew what was
going on, was more frightened than the people, who did not.

So the city was beginning to resemble the war zone it was. Robert
de Saint Jean, who that day joined the staff of the new information
minister, Jean Prouvost, with responsibility for foreign affairs, spotted

the rows of steel girders on the vast plateau of the Place de la Concorde as he walked to his office in the requisitioned Hotel Continental on Rue de Rivoli. Saint Jean also took note of the dense auto traffic, each of the passing vehicles bearing a charge of valises, crates, even furniture.

The all-too-visible defense measures, noted Peter Fontaine, were combined with a new round of arrests of Communists. "So much the better," a French count of his acquaintance commented. "Our danger is as much from within as from without. The Stalin-Hitler pact has unsettled the populace. If they ever get the upper hand, there'll be rivers of blood flowing in the Paris streets."

Fontaine himself felt that much of the unhappiness of workers came from the order to remain where they were, while more fortunate owners of private means of transportation were strapping bedding on car roofs and leaving town.

A headline in *Le Temps* that afternoon: CRACKDOWN ON SUBVERSIVE ACTIVITIES. It introduced a report that 101 Communist activists had been taken to internment centers since Georges Mandel joined the Interior Ministry.

Reveil de la France, the German radio station pretending to be French, broadcast from Brussels:

> Long live the national revolution! Frenchmen, at the dramatic moment when Hitler's hordes prepare to march on Paris, at the moment when all the warmongers, the Daladiers, the Reynauds, all the incompetents, have pushed France over the cliff, we appeal to all to join us in creating a national revolution.

This signified eliminating Reynaud, Mandel, and "all this Jewish underworld which has invaded France and sucks its blood." The Boches (the German broadcast actually used this term) were winning the war.

> Frenchmen, to compensate for the faults of our government, to block all attempts to continue to spill blood, rise up against this war caused by the Jews, led by the Jews.

*   *   *

Scholar Jérôme Carcopino, an authority on ancient Rome, was in his third year as director of the French School in Rome. It was time to wind up the operations of this prestigious institution. The problem was to obtain Italian exit visas for the French personnel; that took some time.

But Carcopino was home in Paris on June 6, and surprised, for the capital seemed as far as ever from the battlefield. Visiting his friend François Charles-Roux at the Foreign Ministry, Carcopino discovered immediate confirmation of his feeling that Paris was living in a cocoon, for Charles-Roux spoke with admiration of General Weygand and his determination. Did he still think that France had a chance?

Life did seem to be going on as usual—school life, for example. Only the youngest children were being provided for. After the bombing of Paris, during which several schools were hit and some children killed, the government decided at last to shut down primary schools in Paris and the suburbs—effective at the end of the day on June 8. Examinations for high school diplomas for vocational students were scheduled for the eighth and ninth. School administrators were free to advance the dates of examinations whenever local conditions seemed to warrant. Moreover, a student qualified to take an examination could take it wherever he or she happened to be.

City buses began to evacuate children on June 6. When they could do so, parents took responsibility for their own. The tempo of the exodus accelerated.

When he woke that day, General Weygand was informed that French defenses were holding. All he could do now was to perfect the defense plan and encourage the defenders. At 8:00 A.M. he was ready to accompany General Georges to his field headquarters; at 10:30 A.M. he was back in Paris for the morning war conference.

Whatever he had been told, French positions were not holding. A member of the headquarters staff later complained that Weygand's generals simply didn't commit all the forces at their disposal to the front lines. And the men who were ordered to hold their ground knew quite well that retreat was in the cards.

Churchill's liaison, General Spears, walked into the War Ministry conference with a reply from London to the French plea for additional support. Troops were promised, but Churchill had to say frankly that the evacuation at Dunkirk made it necessary to call a temporary halt to air operations for the next four or five days. At best, two fighter squadrons—say twenty-four planes—could be flown over. "There should be no limit to human effort when it's a matter of not dying," replied Reynaud with drama. "And that is the issue, since the decisive battle has been under way since yesterday."

Weygand asked Spears to tell the British prime minister that if he could see the condition of French troops now being sent into battle he would not hesitate to throw in his fighter squadrons, no matter how unready they were. After the Englishman's departure, Weygand briefed Reynaud on the military situation. It was generally satisfactory, said he, although once again the British were disappointing them. At the extreme left of the line, along the Channel, the single British division engaged in battle had moved back. Was that on orders from London? It did seem so. Again the question was raised about what to do if the lines on the Somme and Aisne rivers failed to hold. Could the war continue, the general in chief wished to know, if the Paris region was captured, and 70 percent of the nation's war production with it? Reynaud replied that arms would come from the United Kingdom and the United States, but for that to happen they would have to resist somewhere in France. Weygand could not agree with that; no French redoubt would be credible. "Then if a peace agreement respecting French honor and vital interests is refused us," the pugnacious premier told him, "we'll carry on the war in North Africa." Weygand didn't like that idea either. Pétain supported Weygand. If the present battle were lost, he said, there would be nothing left to do but to negotiate with the enemy—if they obtained suitable terms.

Ambassador Bullitt and his British counterpart, Sir Ronald Campbell, lunched together. Campbell confided that if Churchill was not sending his country's remaining pursuit planes to France, it was because at the present rate of destruction none would be left after a fortnight of battle. Based on what Weygand was saying, there was no hope of preventing the Germans from occupying Paris and destroying the French army; therefore Britain simply had to hold on to its air force. Bullitt warned Campbell that the French would consider this a betrayal. And that could lead to an early peace with Germany, and French hostility toward Britain. Campbell was aware of that danger. As a matter of fact, Churchill was prepared to go further than any of his advisers in supporting the French, but the planes simply were not there, and in any case the Germans couldn't be stopped.

The hopelessly Francophile Bullitt couldn't agree. The French *could* stop the Germans. But if the British didn't help them and the Germans weren't stopped, then Britain too would be lost.

After lunch, just to be sure, Bullitt called on Reynaud. Was it true, as Sir Ronald had said, that Weygand was pessimistic about the outcome of the present battle? That, Reynaud declared, was a lie. The French were holding magnificently; the only breach in the line had come about because of Britain's sole division committed to the battle. Reynaud said that he was shocked that the British refused to send over their pursuit planes.

Reynaud's deputy, Colonel Paul de Villelume, made a suggestion to his premier, and it was not the first time he had brought up the question. This was the time, he said, for the evacuation of the top echelon of officials of government departments, and to be ready for a general retreat of the whole cabinet from Paris. Villelume reminded Reynaud that in Poland and Norway the Germans had done everything they could to try to capture the governments.

Reynaud was adamant. The cabinet would not leave Paris. But he authorized Villelume to negotiate a transfer of the premier's office and the Defense Ministry to the Palais de Chaillot, a safer place to be in the event of further air raids. Air raids indeed! muttered the frustrated officer.

Reynaud spoke to France by radio at 7:45 that evening. He conceded that his previous two speeches had conveyed bad news, the capture of Amiens on May 21, the treason of the Belgian king on May 28. Today there were reasons for hope. First, the northern armies had not been annihilated as the Germans threatened, but had been evacuated at Dunkirk, showing what mastery of the sea signified. Second, the morale of Parisians had not been affected by the June 3 bomb attack. Because the bombing had not been precise, women and children and the old had been victims. But Parisians had carried on. "We now know what a massive raid signifies: for the soul of Paris, it is nothing." Nor had the attack gone unavenged, for Britain had since bombed factories in the Ruhr, Frankfurt, Düsseldorf, Cologne, Essen. "The same thing will happen every time a French city is attacked in the future."

And now, the Battle of France. "The entire world is following the vicissitudes of this battle with bated breath, for the combats of June 1940 will decide its fate, as Hitler put it, perhaps for hundreds of years."

For the next five years, as a starter.

If Reynaud was not a pessimist, William Bullitt could hardly be one. In a new message to Roosevelt he expressed his pleasure that the president approved the speech Bullitt was to deliver in the little village of Domrémy-la-Pucelle, where Joan of Arc had been born. "I shall make it Sunday, the Lord willing, and it will help." Quite certainly the ambassador believed that. "The French troops have held again magnificently today," he told Roosevelt, virtually repeating the language of the official communiqués. "Everyone is full of fighting spirit and hope."

Still, Bullitt thought it wise to brief the president on a delicate matter. Perhaps Washington was not aware of it, but all of thinking Paris was. "While the French soldiers and civilians are displaying a courage and character beyond praise," he began, "strange things are going on at the top. Paul Reynaud, who has great personal qualities, is completely dominated by his mistress, the Comtesse de Portes, who has the virtue of being sincerely fond of him."

Then, in this undiplomatic diplomatic telegram, suitably coded and marked Personal and Confidential, Bullitt spelled out the problem. The changes in the French cabinet had been dictated by Hélène de Portes. She hated Daladier, and so he had been removed; she liked Paul Baudouin, and he had been upgraded. "The people of France, who are fighting with an absolute selflessness," wrote the ardent ambassador, "deserve better at this moment than to be ruled by a Prime Minister's mistress—not even a King's! In the end she will be shot. Meanwhile, she will rule the roost."

There was more. When Reynaud had put in the telephone call to Roosevelt, revealed Bullitt, he had forbade his mistress to enter the room, but she had walked in anyway, and had refused to leave. Bullitt advised Roosevelt not to talk to Reynaud by phone anymore, "since the lady in question will repeat [the phone conversations] all over town in exaggerated form."

He concluded:

I trust that this sort of gossip will not seem to you unworthy of the tragic days through which we are passing. I thought that you would like to know that there is still some continuity in French life, and that the mistress of the ruler again directs the State as she has since time immemorial.

We had another air raid at five o'clock this morning, and I was delighted to find that I could sleep peaceably in my sumptuous wine cellar.

Good luck and love to you all.

Perhaps Bullitt was seeing too much of his friend Daladier; perhaps he was only nursing a private grudge. There is the story that when Bullitt wished to deliver an oral message to Reynaud—that Roosevelt would give him one hundred planes if France sent an aircraft carrier to pick them up—Bullitt put through a phone call to the premier, but the countess got on the line to say that he was ill. When Bullitt showed up at Reynaud's flat all the same, she insisted on being present during the talk, and even argued against sending a French vessel; it was all Reynaud could do to overrule her. The planes remained at Martinique during the war (revealed in his memoirs by François Charles-Roux).

Was she really that bad? Later Reynaud's daughter Evelyne, seeking to protect her father's reputation, painted a contradictory picture of a Countess de Portes who was certainly neutralist, and certainly bossy, but who was totally without influence on Reynaud's decisions.

31

On the following day, Bill Bullitt had more to say about Premier
Reynaud and his obtrusive lady friend. Bullitt explained that he was
still thinking about his eventual return to the United States, leaving
the embassy to Anthony Drexel Biddle, Jr.

"Tony is just as eager to get to work in Paris as I am to get to work
in the United States," Bullitt cabled his president in another Personal
and Confidential message, "and I can promise you with my customary
modesty that from my experience here, I now know more about how
to get ready for war than anyone except yourself."

The ambassador assured Roosevelt that Biddle, until now ambassador to Poland, and like himself a member of high society back home,
would be as sociable as he had been. "In fact, the Comtesse de Portes
already has had her eye on him and has done everything possible to
introduce him and Margaret [Biddle] into the select circle which
gathers nightly in her apartment." He added to that, "Seriously, the
job to be done here now consists in part in flattering the King's
mistress."

But Madame de Portes was not the only personality whose action at
center stage all but obscured the war. Paul Baudouin records the
appearance of Marshal Pétain in his office that morning. Pétain had

come early for the daily conference at the War Ministry so as to be able
to unburden himself of his feelings concerning Charles de Gaulle. He
begged Baudouin to insist to Reynaud that the new undersecretary for
defense and war not be admitted to the war conference. Pétain, as by
now everybody in the government knew, still had it in for de Gaulle
because of an old quarrel. When de Gaulle was attached to Pétain's
staff, he had written a book about the army that the marshal was to
publish under his own name. But when Pétain did nothing with the
manuscript, de Gaulle took it back to publish it as his own. "He's
vain," Pétain told Baudouin, "ungrateful and bitter."

Later that day, when Reynaud chewed over the plan for a last-ditch
defense in Brittany, de Gaulle supported the scheme, for it would
facilitate contacts with both Britain and the United States. Colonel de
Villelume opposed the plan and said so to Reynaud but not to de
Gaulle, because he refused to talk to de Gaulle.

The war conference began at ten-thirty that morning, without de
Gaulle, but with a Weygand clearly pleased at the way the battle was
going. French troops were performing well, and only the weak British
element on the left end of the line merited criticism. Its General
Fortune (Major General V. M. Fortune, commander of the 51st High-
land Division) should be called General Misfortune, quipped Weygand. The British were asking to be replaced at the front by
reinforcements, as if reinforcements existed!

Reynaud's aide, Dominique Leca, thought that he had uncovered a
secret concerning the clique (Weygand and Pétain were part of it)
lobbying for an armistice. They were the same people who wished to
keep the government in Paris. This was only the first step; later the
same men insisted on remaining in Bordeaux rather than transferring
the government to North Africa to pursue the war from there. To stay
in Paris, later to stay in France, meant to wait to be captured.

The day ended in disaster. Weygand's staff phoned to report a "technical" problem at the front. Two German armored divisions had broken through to attain Forges-les-Eaux, opening the Seine valley, the
road to Rouen.

Baudouin reached Reynaud at home. "Is it possible that our hope is collapsing like this?" Reynaud moaned. Everyone could relate to Forges-les-Eaux, a charming little spa surrounded by forest some seventy miles due north of Paris; everybody drove through the town on the way to favorite beaches. Its fall would have more than military significance.

Each afternoon American and British correspondents filed into a briefing room at the War Ministry so that a colonel speaking English could give them a report on the military situation.

When the officer mentioned Forges-les-Eaux, it became apparent to Walter Kerr than none of the Americans knew where it was. And when asked, the colonel couldn't find it on the map.

That day Lieutenant Georges Friedmann, the sociologist attached to a military hospital outside the city, drove into town on an errand. His diary recorded what he saw.

Love and death float over this crowd at once Parisian and insouciant, over these women in summery dresses, over these bodies deprived of their lovers and over us who observe them. . . .

32

SATURDAY, JUNE 8

The news came with the morning communiqué, heard by everybody with a radio, and those without one would read about it that afternoon in *Le Temps* or *Paris-Soir*, or next morning in *Le Matin*.

MASSIVE PUSH OF THE ENEMY
BETWEEN AUMALE AND THE AISNE
An enemy tank group
attacks Forges-les-Eaux
The Roughest
Days
Of the War

Two hours from Paris in the family motorcar . . . Suddenly the reason for all the commotion on the outer boulevards of Paris became apparent. An English resident of the city thought he could hear the battlefield cannon (what he apparently heard was the firing of antiaircraft batteries directed at enemy aircraft overflying the Paris region).

"Night of anguish," noted Marcel Jouhandeau in his diary. "Uninterrupted parade of trucks under our windows." For of course the residential boulevard in front of his house on the Bois de Boulogne was now a north-south highway. When he opened the shutters that morning, Jouhandeau saw a truck parked across the roadway to bar the route to the enemy. When his wife showed herself at the window, a sentinel stationed before this pathetic barricade shouted up, "Oh, madame, please excuse us for the noise. . . . We're your protectors."

That evening the reclusive couple ventured out to accompany a neighbor to the Gare d'Austerlitz. "The train she's taking, in which rich and poor pile in willy-nilly, has no announced destination," he reported to his diary. Upstairs in the station's command post, Raymond Martin and his task force had felt the new tension, had seen the crowd swell, after the scare word "Forges-les-Eaux" began to spread that morning.

"Paris begins to resemble a city under siege," noted the pamphleteer Alfred Fabre-Luce. "The cannon fire is almost continual." Restaurants were emptying fast. The Ritz with its last guests seemed like a resort hotel on closing day. Fabre-Luce went to one of the few surviving theaters, the Oeuvre, where a comedy played to a dozen spectators out for a good time. The title of the play translated as *No Friends, No Problems.* Fabre-Luce overheard a wag call it "No Audience, No Critics." During the performance he was reminded of a low mass served by a distracted priest. The handful of spectators weren't watching the scheduled performance, he thought, but the tragedy of the war.

Because contradictory reports were circulating, the daily press was asked to inform readers that the only evacuation being encouraged by the government concerned children under fourteen years of age and pregnant women. Free transportation was available in these cases, and it covered the travel of a mother or guardian accompanying a child under fourteen, as well as children between fourteen and eighteen traveling with brothers or sisters under fourteen.

At 11:15 that morning a radio announcer read out a warning: The Germans were using their captured Brussels radio transmitter to broadcast French-language programs pretending to be anti-Nazi. But beneath that disguise the Germans were spreading false news and subversive comments. The French had their own news station, the announcer reminded listeners.

The press carried confirmation of the presence of the enemy within the gates. TEN YEARS IN PRISON FOR SPREADING FALSE REPORTS, one story was headlined. (The defendant had told stories likely to affect the morale of Parisians.) Another defendant was sentenced to two years for propagating Communist ideology, a third got eighteen months for anti-French remarks. THE APPEAL OF DEATH SENTENCES BY FOUR SPIES IS REJECTED, read another headline. (Two of the accused had German-sounding names.) THE GERMAN SPY FRITZ ERLER HAS BEEN SHOT. (His accomplice, a Swiss woman journalist, was pardoned.)

There was an appeal to veterans to volunteer as national guards "to deal with an enemy lacking scruples." In the suburbs some members of civil defense teams had abandoned their posts (presumably to join the exodus). The prefect warned that they faced sanctions.

Newsman Alexander Werth, after taking his afternoon tea near the Opéra ("There are still plenty of cakes; but very few customers") told his diary:

I hear there is terrific dissatisfaction among the Paris working class. They have been given the strictest orders to stay where they are; if they leave Paris they'll be treated as deserters. Naturally, they don't like to see the other people buzz off like this.

Polish-born Perla Epstein was twenty-nine years old. Her husband, Joseph, also born in Poland, was then at the front. He was urging his wife to leave Paris, saying, "You don't know the Germans." *He* knew them: he had fought in Spain in 1936 as a volunteer in the International Brigade helping the republican government resist Franco; wounded, he was evacuated to France, then returned to Spain to fight again. At the outbreak of war he had tried to enlist in the French army, but as a foreigner he could only join the Foreign Legion—which he did. Now he was at the front, but he knew that civilians in Paris were also in danger, and that as a Jewish émigré, Perla Epstein was in more danger than most other civilians.

Joseph himself didn't seem to mind dangerous situations. After capture by the Germans he would escape to Switzerland, arm himself with French identity papers, and return to Paris to carry out sabotage against German occupation authorities, taking charge of operations in the militant Communist resistance movement called Francs-Tireurs et Partisans. When the Gestapo finally found him, they tortured and killed him.

Because no Communist paper was being published in wartime Paris, Perla tuned in to Moscow radio, although it told her more about Soviet harvests than about her day-to-day concerns. She certainly did not believe official French propaganda, which assured her that France would win because it was the stronger side.

She was the manager of a pharmacy on Rue Cambronne. The Corsican owner had long since withdrawn to his island. Perla got along well with the employees, even though she was a foreigner; they were all under the knife together. Yet she could still laugh, and occasionally even go to the movies or to see a play when the theater was still functioning.

After Dunkirk she saw things differently, and then came the bombing of Paris on June 3. But even after that she lived as she had. The grocer and the dairy, fruit and vegetable, and butcher shops remained open and hospitable. Of course there was some hoarding of sugar, sardines, and other staples. Having no memory of an earlier war and no children to feed, Perla Epstein saw no need to stock up.

Eventually, because shopkeepers were also tempted by flight, flight made easy for them because each possessed some kind of motor transportation, finding food became a challenge in these last days of free Paris. Even pharmaceutical supplies were running short—but so were customers for them. Nearby shops closed, one after the other, and most businesses on this traditional market street were boarded up by the time she closed the pharmacy—handing the key to the concierge. She made the decision to close when the neighborhood doctor drove away.

She was not to return to the pharmacy in German Paris, wary of Nazi and Vichy state restrictions on Jews. As a matter of fact, she never did register as a Jew at the local police station, as one was supposed to. Her husband had warned her about that too.

At the morning war conference, General Weygand explained what had happened at Forges-les-Eaux. The Germans had broken through with two armored divisions, followed immediately by infantrymen riding in troop carriers, soldiers who protected the flanks of the tank thrust and thus thwarted French attempts to cut off the Germans from behind. Weygand had been at headquarters of the defending army when German planes attacked in support of the ground offensive. "The power of German aviation is terrifying," he told Reynaud and Pétain. All communications had been cut; the French could neither receive messages nor transmit orders.

Now they would have to rebuild their defenses farther to the south, along the Seine, all the while harassing the enemy. Reynaud drafted a new message to Churchill that described the new defensive position around Paris, and again begged for planes.

Colonel de Villelume, who remembered urging his premier to employ "a tone of considerable brutality," since milder notes had fallen on deaf ears, kept a copy:

> Rouen and Le Havre are under direct threat and with them the food supply of Paris and of half the army. I appreciate your efforts, but the situation calls for even greater ones, requiring also that the pursuit squadrons be based in France so that they can be utilized with maximum efficacy. . . . My duty is to request that you commit all your forces to the battle just as we are doing. In friendship.

And in Reynaud's archives a copy of Churchill's response can be read:

> We are giving you all the support we can in this great battle short of ruining the capability of this country to continue the war. We have had very heavy and disproportionate losses in the air today, but we shall continue tomorrow.

Meanwhile, Weygand was preparing the transfer of the high command to more secure quarters south of Paris, on the Loire. He would try to stop the Germans along the Seine River, even if he was forced to rely on exhausted troops. The Germans were not exhausted, and they had reserves.

The question remained: Should the government leave Paris? Armament Minister Raoul Dautry said a loud no to that. Paris was France's factory, Paris had both the plants and the skilled workers required to produce arms, and there was no way to move men and equipment to safer territory. He asked that the government announce it would stay in the capital and that factories would continue to function in the region.

As Dominique Leca saw it, the government was preparing to withdraw from Paris, but without saying so, even to itself. In no case would anyone try to evacuate the population of the city; that was simply not realistic. Nor would the city be defended (another thing not said aloud).

Léon Blum remembered that Saturday. As soon as his friends heard of the latest German breakthrough they began to besiege him with phone calls. They told him, erroneously, that the enemy had reached Magny, Pontoise, Senlis. They told him, erroneously, that the government would abandon Paris that very night. Blum was not naïve about the military situation; he knew that Le Havre and Rouen were in danger, even that Paris was vulnerable. But he took the government seriously when it said that Paris would be defended. So how could it be evacuating government departments?

To answer that one, Blum went to the source—and some of his political allies were inside the cabinet, for the patriot Reynaud had made it a point to bring representatives of all democratic parties into his war cabinet, and that of course included Socialists. What he learned was that ministers were staying on in Paris while arranging for the departure of their staffs. Each department was assigned to a particular estate in the Loire valley pleasure castle country centered on Tours. But Blum also recalled that Reynaud had once told him that Tours would hardly be far enough if the Germans approached Paris, and that it would make sense to increase the distance between the enemy and the government. Vichy, for example, would be a safer choice. Later that day Blum talked with Police Prefect Roger Langeron, who shared his concern at the lack of a serious plan for the defense of Paris—since, after all, the government did say it would defend Paris.

Visiting General Weygand with his new information minister, Jean Prouvost, Robert de Saint Jean was struck by the relaxed behavior of the generalissimo, and by the monastic calm of his surroundings. His was the office of a modest civil servant, its cement floor covered with a straw mat. No telephone broke the silence; officers moved about as if they were in a peacetime army.

Weygand's placidity was reassuring, but what he told Prouvost was not. Paris would soon have to be evacuated, and Weygand thought it was reckless of the government not to be preparing for the move.

Getting ready for a journey to London as Reynaud's emissary, General de Gaulle also called on Weygand that day, finding the older man "calm and master of himself." But the visitor quickly realized that Weygand expected to lose the war, that he was ready to talk peace with the Germans. When de Gaulle suggested that the French continue the war elsewhere—in the French colonies—Weygand snapped at him, "That's childish! As for the rest of the world, when I've lost this battle, England won't wait a week before negotiating with the Reich." De Gaulle also remembered hearing Weygand say, "Ah, if I could only be sure that the Germans would leave me sufficient forces to maintain order. . . ."

The cabinet was convened for five that afternoon. Now at last Reynaud spelled out how the government would deal with a German drive against Paris. While it was the duty of the cabinet to remain in the capital even under bombardment, the government could by no means allow itself to be captured. Thus plans were ready to send the President of the Republic and his cabinet ministers to Tours. Reynaud would stay in Paris with the ministers of interior, air, and navy, for as long as the situation allowed.

Information leaked quickly. That night at nine-thirty the Italian ambassador sent off a coded message to Count Ciano. Reynaud's aide, Baudouin, had confided to him "with some bitterness" that France was now fighting alone, that there was only one British division in France. Despite this the French would pursue the war until only a single battalion, a single cannon remained. It was not stubbornness but a matter of honor.

Ambassador Guariglia also told Rome that up to that moment no decision had been taken on the evacuation of the government, or on the defense of Paris.

At ten, so the writer Fernand Gregh remembered, a friend attached to a cabinet ministry phoned him and his wife at home.

"My friends, if you don't wish to see the Germans in Paris, it's time to go."

"We'll leave tomorrow."

"Better leave now."

The sixty-seven-year-old writer set his wife to packing their bags. At midnight another well-placed friend phoned, confirming the advice. At 2:00 A.M. the Greghs, their baggage, two servants, and their Maltese spaniel drove off in the old family Ford.

That evening Simone de Beauvoir attended the Opéra with her friend Bianca to see *Ariane et Barbe-Bleue,* an early-twentieth-century work by Paul Dukas and Maurice Maeterlinck, in which the heroine, Ariane, marries Bluebeard to deliver his five previous wives from captivity, although they do not seem to care either way. Hardly inspiring, but Beauvoir saw it as a final patriotic demonstration of defiance. The weather was stormy and the two women were on edge. Bianca was striking, thought Simone, in her flaming red dress on the grand staircase of the theater. On the way back to the Left Bank, on foot, they talked of the coming defeat. Bianca said that one could always kill oneself. Simone replied that generally one did not.

That night Ambassador Bullitt scrawled another rush message for coding and cabling, marking it Personal and Secret for the President.

Will you please have put on the next Clipper twelve Thompson submachine guns with ammunition, addressed to me for the use of this Embassy. I am fully prepared to pay for them myself.

There is every reason to expect that if the French Government should be forced to leave Paris, its place would be taken by a communist mob.

How deal with an ambassador so undiplomatic? How contradict him, when he was on the scene? How deny his request, when he not only wrote it out, but then telephoned it to the president of the United States?

Secretary of State Cordell Hull replied, in a Strictly Confidential for the Ambassador. Instructions had been given to the commanding officer of an American warship moored in Lisbon to make available "the material you require." Bullitt was invited to send a trustworthy representative to Lisbon to pick up the guns, which would be labeled as official supplies for the embassy. "Every precaution should be taken to avoid publicity," advised Hull.

33

SUNDAY, JUNE 9

William Christian Bullitt left Paris early that morning for the long drive to the tiny village of Domrémy-la-Pucelle, Domrémy the Maiden, the birthplace of Joan of Arc in the Vosges hills of eastern France, a site virtually under the eyes of the invader now. The occasion was a ceremony in a village church that Joan herself might have known, for she was baptized at its fountain. After a mass served by Monsignor Roger Beaussart, who had made the trip from Paris with the ambassador, Bullitt offered a statue of Joan to France, and to God, explaining that it was the work of Maxime Real del Sarte, who had become something of a specialist in likenesses of Joan, and that it had been acquired thanks to donations from American Catholics and Protestants both. "Americans know on which side are wrong, cruelty and bestiality," he declared. "From one end of this earth to the other, every civilized man is praying, after his fashion, for the victory of France."

Bullitt followed up with an invocation:

"Saint Joan, France remains worthy of you!

"Worthy are its soldiers, who do not yield before fire, nor even before treason!

"Worthy are the pilots who rise in the sky as you rose to the ramparts of Orléans. . . ."

Then, in the name of the American president, he placed a rose at the feet of the saint.

Next day Domrémy was in German hands.

It was a truly splendid June Sunday in Paris. "Fine, cloudless," noted the weather bureau (but, in order not to make it easier for the enemy, did not publish the information). "The sky was bright," recalled an observer; "most Parisians were convinced that the Germans would never reach Paris, because a peace agreement would be signed before that happened." The battle seemed farther away, incursions of enemy aircraft rarer. Sidewalk cafés on the Champs-Elysées and other favorite promenades were crowded, even if uniforms were much in evidence. Was it possible, wondered André Maurois, that the Germans were only half an hour away by car?

He happened to be having lunch in the garden court of the Ritz Hotel, on Place Vendôme; every table was occupied. The only sign that something was amiss appeared on Place de la Concorde, where trucks were lined up in front of the naval ministry. When Maurois ran into the editor of one of the Paris dailies, he asked whether the presence of the trucks signified evacuation. The journalist told him that the government was still divided on the subject. Then Maurois went to the movies, where he found the theater nearly full. Newsreels showed both the battle of Narvik in Norway and the bombing of Paris. Thought the writer: Last week's tragedy has already become spectacle.

Perhaps it depended on one's neighborhood. In the less affluent quarters of the Left Bank a brooding Ilya Ehrenburg also walked that Sunday. He was more likely to come upon closed restaurants and cafés, signs announcing that they'd stay closed "until further notice." He caught a bit of Parisian monologue: "We bought a car, but we can't get gas. If only we could find a horse somewhere. . . ."

Drawing a lesson for this too-peaceful Sunday, the daily *Petit Journal* was to tell its readers:

Yesterday resembled all fine-weather Sundays. The air was mild. The sky was pure. The sun was bright and pretty.

Yet this was nevertheless a wartime Paris. At nightfall trucks and buses were lined up to form barricades, guard posts were manned, ramparts of bags of earth went up. . . .

Italian exile Pietro Nenni had lived through other crises, other wars. Now, after Madrid, he looked on as another capital was threatened by the forces of darkness. "One always expects a miracle," he told his diary. He confessed to feeling relieved when friends assured him that Weygand knew how to deal with Germans, but of course he was skeptical. He observed signs of defeat in the breakdown of food distribution, the presence of retreating troops at the very gates of the city, not to speak of the saturated roads leading south. He also noted that soldiers who had lost contact with their units were mixing with the civilian fugitives. The stragglers claimed to have lost their arms, and said that at the front they no longer saw a French plane or a French tank, that their officers had abandoned them. The word *treason* was pronounced.

Writing to a friend, that other exile Victor Serge confessed to finding a resemblance between the deserted city and what he remembered of Saint Petersburg under siege in 1919. But while the people of Saint Petersburg had been "fiercely linked one to another and to grand principles, here the people hold to nothing, dwell in an absence of faith. . . ." It was an "every man for himself" that spelled disaster.

A friend of Jean Cocteau stood in attendance during the elaborate preparations for the departure of the extravagant artist-poet for safer climes. It seemed that Cocteau had forgotten to stock up on containers for his opium, and without opium he knew he couldn't survive. So he would stay. "The Germans will shoot me," he said, "for they detest poets."

So his complaisant friend trekked through the abandoned city looking for jars to hold Jean Cocteau's opium. Shop after shop where such things might have been purchased were closed, but he found one in the end. The jars were wrapped and brought back to the artist's rooms facing the Palais Royal gardens. The friend found Cocteau "prostrated," but he shook himself awake, hastened his preparations, and was off.

* * *

Paul Léautaud was even fussier. Although his best friend, Marie Dormoy, was packing to follow her library to a safe haven in the south, he refused to join her. How could he, with his cats, his precious possessions, his job at *Mercure de France*?

Ever precise, Simone de Beauvoir records her movements on this Sunday: the morning devoted to reading, then to music (she listened for free at a record store opposite the Luxembourg Garden). She saw a double feature at a local cinema. Then to the Café Mahieu on Boulevard Saint-Michel, a favorite of the intellectual left since Lenin, to write a letter to her man at the front.

She could hear antiaircraft fire. Looking up, she saw puffs of white smoke. The café terrace rapidly lost its Sunday crowd. She felt the enemy advance as "a personal threat," for she would be cut off from Sartre.

She returned to the record store for more music, then to her hotel to find a note from a friend who was waiting for her at the Café de Flore on Boulevard Saint-Germain, waiting with important news. There were no taxis; she took the Métro. Her friend explained that a well-placed officer had informed her father that a retreat was planned for the following day. School examinations were canceled, teachers were free to leave. So the Germans would be in Paris in a matter of days, thought Beauvoir. And they'd take the Maginot Line from the rear, meaning that Sartre would be a prisoner, would be treated badly, and she'd get no news of him. For the first time in her life, she remembered, she had a nervous fit. It was the worst moment of the whole war for her. She was ready to leave Paris.

A glance at the morning paper for that day reveals that Simone de Beauvoir saw her double feature at the Ursulines, a cinema dear to students. It was one of fourteen theaters still advertising English-language films that day. Thirteen others showed French films or foreign films in French versions.

The theater was almost all official now, the Opéra with *The Magic Flute,* the Opéra-Comique with *Carmen* at two, *Mignon* at seven. The Comédie Française was doing *L'Avare* and *On ne saurait penser à tout* at two, the Odéon *Le Cid* and *Les précieuses ridicules* at two-thirty, *L'Ami Fritz* (a sentimental sketch about Alsace) at seven-thirty.

Indeed, that morning *Le Matin* was sufficiently intrepid to publish the program of the national theaters for the rest of the week: Beethoven's *Fidelio* at the Opéra, scheduled for the following Saturday, June 15; Massenet's *Werther* for Sunday, June 16, at the Opéra-Comique. The Comédie Française would do *Polyeucte,* the Odéon *Le Cid* again, and *Tartuffe.* Actually, on June 9, after the newspapers had gone to press, the subsidized theaters received their marching orders. Sunday, June 9, was to be their last day.

In Roger Peyrefitte's novel *La Fin des ambassades* the nonchalant young diplomat who is Peyrefitte himself goes to the Comédie Française that afternoon. "He had been warned that this would be the final performance: this comedy playing to a sparsely filled auditorium took on a tragic aspect." The Marivaux playlet that followed Molière, and whose title translates as "One Can't Think of Everything," had never seemed less appropriate—or more ironic.

"The curtain falls slowly, heavily, like a solemn farewell," remembered an observer—not Roger Peyrefitte, but an officer of the troupe who stood watching in the wings. Everybody was affected; the public filed out of the theater in silence. Outside, small clusters of Parisians were scrutinizing the sky. Some were convinced that they could see German parachutists.

CHILDREN
MUST
LEAVE PARIS
With Schools Now Closed
This Departure Cannot
Be Delayed

The above reminder appeared in the morning newspaper *Le Jour,* as if Parisians with little ones still needed the prodding.

The schools of Paris closed their doors yesterday. In the morning the lower classes passed elementary school examinations, a month ahead of the habitual date. It is estimated that there are still some 200,000 children in the city.

With the school year closed, nothing should keep these children in a place where they are unnecessarily at risk.

For a woman who had just lived through a war, close enough to hear the exploding shells, the Battle of France as experienced from Paris held no fears. Marguerite Orlianges, born in Paris of parents from the mountains of central France, had been raised in politics, with her father a Socialist activist. She met her husband-to-be when she was eighteen; he happened to be Spanish, and when insurrection flared in his country in July 1936, he, as a reserve officer, returned to Spain to join not the rebel army under Francisco Franco, but the besieged government. Marguerite followed him to Madrid, and when Franco took the capital she was repatriated to France, pregnant with Jean Monino's child.

When the baby was born, in December 1939, she lived not far from Paris at Melun with her mother, commuting to a job at the City Hall. In May 1940 her mother took the infant south to the region of Nevers, and soon after that Marguerite moved in with friends on Place Saint-Michel. That of course turned out to be an extraordinary observation platform for the war as a civilian could know it, now that it had become the main road from northern to southern France. Otherwise, for a woman who had been taught to use a rifle to defend Madrid street by street, this was not much of a war.

She and her friends, committed anti-Fascists, lived these days of June in individual cocoons. They practiced a form of self-censorship; one didn't talk war. The silence in her case was agonizing, for she had no idea what had happened to her husband after his capture by Italian troops assisting Franco.

Marguerite Monino didn't believe a word of the reassuring French war communiqués, or the speeches, knowing that the Germans were now too close not to enter Paris.

And the day came when she was told about a city bus taking children south of the Loire. There was room for her and her sister; now she would be able to see her own child. They got out of Paris all right, but by the time the bus reached the Loire valley, they were caught in crossfire. Then the French army stopped all civilian vehicles to make room on the roads for the retreat of troops. Abandoning the bus convoy, she and her sister managed to cross the bridge over the Loire at Gien on foot. She remembered stepping over the bodies of French African soldiers.

The bad news Maxime Weygand woke to that morning had been anticipated. The Germans were fanning out to the east, extending the front to a length of more than 250 miles, with enemy thrusts toward the Seine to the west, the Champagne region to the east. The only thing he could hope was that his line would hold fast. There were reports of valiant behavior on the part of the 14th French Infantry, led by one of France's best young generals, Jean de Lattre de Tassigny, as Weygand wrote out the day's watchword:

> The order remains for each soldier to fight without thought of retreat, facing forward, there where the commanding officer placed him.

Then the dramatic appeal:

> Officers, noncommissioned officers, and soldiers, the safety of the nation demands of you not only your courage but all the persistence, all the initiative, all the fighting spirit of which I know you are capable.
> The enemy has suffered heavy losses. He will soon reach the limits of his effort.
> We have reached the final quarter hour. Hold fast.

Henceforth the so-called Army of Paris, composed of troops formerly commanded by the military government of the capital, assumed responsibility for the central segment of the front from Vernon on the Seine to Boran on the Oise. After a visit to field headquarters, the commander-in-chief drove back to Rue Saint-Dominique to report to Paul Reynaud his conviction that the French army had reached the limit of its possibilities, fighting under air attack by day, marching at night. He painted a picture of exhausted officers "advancing as if in a trance, sometimes incapable of hearing an order, only having the strength to advance and to accompany the advance of their men who were thrown, literally, to the other side of the barbed wire of the new position to defend, who fell asleep on the battlefield, and had to be awakened to get them to begin shooting."

Weygand felt, or so he would say after it was over, that Reynaud wasn't listening to him.

Of course, Reynaud marched to a different drummer.

Pietro Nenni worried about Weygand's declaration that France had reached its final quarter hour. It was more likely to inspire fear than courage.

The Region of Paris circulated a plan for the destruction of all gasoline depots in Paris and its suburbs, a destruction that—when ordered by the army—would be accomplished by the simple expedient of setting fire to the contents of the tanks.

A report in *Le Matin* told how Italian cities were preparing for night-time blackouts. Museums were closed. In Milan, underground shelters were ready for air raids.

Only in Paris did the noise of war in Italy seem remote, and one had to be privy to state secrets to know about the feverish diplomatic activity, the speculation on when and how (not whether) Fascist Italy would enter the war. As early as May 26 the Italian ambassador in France, Raffaele Guariglia, had opened negotiations with the French Foreign Ministry for the repatriation of the Italian diplomatic community. One possibility was a simple exchange, one Italian authorized to leave France for each Frenchman released from Italy. Or would it be all Frenchmen for all Italians? For there were not only embassy personnel to consider, but teachers, as well as employees of tourist offices, chambers of commerce, and shipping companies. There happened to be more Italians in France than Frenchmen in Italy.

At ten-thirty that morning, during the day's war conference, Marshal Pétain read out a memorandum in which he explained why he thought the nation's leaders should not abandon Paris at the very moment that everyone's chief concern should be to conserve the moral and intellectual heritage of the nation. The old soldier expressed his anxiety about

the difficult position in which the army found itself, its lack of mo-
bility. It was handicapped by the proximity of the fighting to Paris,
deprived of the reserves still holed up along the now useless Maginot
Line. He hoped the government would consult with Weygand on
what to do when Paris was captured—an event he considered inevitable.

Pétain knew what he would do. He would ask for an armistice.

Reynaud replied that one could not expect the Germans to offer
honorable terms. Hitler wished to annihilate France, period. And it
would be wrong to break with France's allies. Pétain had his answer to
that: French interests came first; Britain was responsible for France's
present circumstances.

It was now that Weygand arrived with his bad news. He read out
his order of the day with the clinching "final quarter hour," and
showed the group the draft of a memorandum not quite in final form
in which he pointed out that the French were now making a last stand,
fighting the last possible defensive battle; if it failed, the French
armies would inevitably be broken up. But couldn't some of the
surviving divisions be transferred to Brittany? a discouraged Reynaud
asked. For there they could meet up with British reinforcements sent
from across the Channel. Weygand replied that the survivors of the
present battle would be in no condition to march to Brittany.

Reynaud suggested replacing old General Héring as military governor, but Weygand thought it was the wrong time to do that, just
when the battle was to begin on positions he had prepared. And
Héring now had a capable deputy in Dentz. The discussion turned to
details concerning the defense of Paris. Still, Reynaud wanted to
know, shouldn't President Lebrun and government departments not
involved in the war be evacuated to the Loire valley now? Weygand
thought that this was a good idea. Armament Minister Dautry asked
about men of military age—about 100,000 of them—who were on
special assignment to work in factories in and around Paris. Those
under the age of thirty could now be sent to safety. Agreed. Dautry
praised the morale of workers and factory managers. The plants were
humming; no one spoke of fleeing.

* * *

The law required that the presidents of both houses of Parliament be consulted on any transfer of authority outside the capital. So Reynaud dispatched the necessary letter to the presidents of the chambers.

I have the honor of informing you that the commander in chief advises that in view of the military situation he deems it prudent to call for the evacuation of Paris by the authorities.

When Paul Baudouin walked into Reynaud's office at six that evening, he learned that the situation in the field had again worsened, and that the advance forces of the enemy were now as close as l'Isle-Adam, less than twenty-five miles north of Paris. The evacuation would have to proceed at a faster rate. Baudouin phoned the Quai d'Orsay, which had begun to send personnel away earlier that day, to prepare now for total evacuation. Then he went to pack his own bags.

At six, Georges Mandel had phoned Senate president Jules Jeanneney. The Germans were approaching Pontoise, less than twenty miles away, if they were not already inside that town. The cabinet session that was to have been held the next day to make a final decision on the departure of the government was moved up to this very evening at nine.

The ministers listened to Weygand's advice, and Pétain's failure to advise. President Lebrun remembered rousing a tired old man. "Don't you wish to give your opinion, Marshal?" "I have nothing to say." Pétain had been brought into the government to give it strength, Lebrun mused, but he was pulling in another direction.

Over the objections of some ministers, the cabinet at last agreed to leave the capital, ministers and their staffs and other governmental agencies to take up assigned quarters in castles and villas along the Loire. A departure without a fight, thought Dominique Leca. Which meant that Paris was an open city. But still no one was ready to say that it was.

Raoul Dautry was thinking that just two days ago he had promised that the government would stay in the capital, and that factories would continue to operate in Paris and vicinity. Now he'd have to call the same factories to order them to evacuate, with as much of the manpower, tools, raw materials, and finished goods as they could carry.

At ten-thirty that night, alone in the Senate, President Jeanneney—having heard from no one—phoned his counterpart Edouard Herriot, who was as ignorant as he concerning what the cabinet had decided. So they called the Elysée, to learn that the cabinet session had ended some time earlier, and that President Lebrun was driving off early the next morning for Tours. Jeanneney arranged for his own departure just before sunrise.

On leaving the cabinet meeting, Reynaud was informed that the situation on the ground had not changed. This meant that no further decision need be made concerning his own departure until the next morning.

Bullitt was waiting for him. Reynaud explained that he would remain in Paris until the last possible moment, together with his ministers of the navy, air, and armament. He hoped Bullitt would tell Roosevelt that the point was not to prepare to surrender, but to make it possible to fight until the bitter end. Reynaud knew that he and the remaining ministers would soon have to leave Paris all the same; he hoped Bullitt would join them. Here he added remarks flattering to the American ambassador, so flattering that the ambassador decided not to put them into his cabled report of the conversation.

Bullitt told Reynaud that no American ambassador in history had abandoned Paris. Nor would he, as long as he thought that he could be of use to the city. Reynaud worried that without Bullitt he would no longer have a way to communicate with Roosevelt. So Bullitt told him, in strict confidence, that should the American ambassador be cut off from Reynaud because of the capture of Paris, Ambassador Anthony Drexel Biddle, who was going to Tours with the government, would act as Bullitt's deputy.

The two men discussed the latest reports from the front. Reynaud revealed that despite eleven telegrams and seven phone calls he had not been able to persuade Churchill to commit more than a fourth of available British fighter planes to the battle. He hoped that Roosevelt, through the British ambassador in Washington, could express his surprise that the British had not offered more planes when all the blood flowing to protect civilization was French. Reynaud wished to phone Roosevelt once more before leaving Paris, to assure him that the French would fight to the end. Reporting this to Roosevelt, Bullitt commented, "Whether or not you accept such a call is entirely up to you."

Charles de Gaulle had spent the day in London, talking to Churchill. It was their first meeting; was it love at first sight? In any case, de Gaulle saw at once that this man was a fighter, and he told Churchill that the French cabinet was determined to pursue the war even if it had to move to the French colonies to do it. The Englishman was not totally convinced. Nor did he believe that France could save its home territory, which is why he could not risk a significant number of aircraft in this lost battle.

One story illustrating the cabinet's disarray was too good to remain secret; it was told often and not always the same way. Jean Prouvost, the newspaper and magazine publisher, was not very comfortable in his temporary job as information minister, working from the least governmental of governmental offices, the internationally famous Hotel Continental, overlooking the Tuileries gardens. As his editor-in-chief, Pierre Lazareff, told the story, Prouvost was talking to a group of American correspondents that afternoon, reassuringly. "Whatever happens, the government will not leave Paris," he promised them. "Stay with us. If you have something to ask of me, come in to see me—tomorrow, the day after tomorrow, whenever you like—you'll always find me." At that point the Associated Press correspondent John Lloyd, who was president of the Anglo-American Press Association, invited the minister to be guest of honor at the association's lunch the following Wednesday. Prouvost promised to be there.

Minutes later the phone rang on Prouvost's desk. He was advised that the government would leave Paris that night. Editor Lazareff walked in just then, to find his boss looking distressed. "They've made me put my foot in my mouth," the publisher explained. "They've made me say that we're staying when we knew that we were leaving. . . . We're not leaving, we're fleeing!"

A British witness adds some spice to the incident. As Prouvost was assuring a group of British reporters that there was no question of the government leaving Paris, two burly porters entered the room to pick up a filing cabinet and carry it out. "What are you about?" the minister asked them. One of the porters explained, "We're leaving for Tours. We have orders."

Information Ministry staffer Maurice Martin du Gard, journalist and critic, had gone to work as usual that wartime Sunday, walking across a hushed Place de la Concorde, stopping to watch as Parisians entered the square from the Champs-Elysées just to stare at the trucks lined up alongside the naval ministry (trucks, he guessed, overflowing with naval secrets). On the corner of Rue Saint-Florentin he passed the shuttered Hôtel Talleyrand, town house of Baron Edouard de Roth-schild; there a policeman with a carbine on his back waited for his parachutist. . . .

Newsman Alexander Werth, writing up his diary notes, found he had little to say about that day. At a morning news briefing an officer had mumbled something about this being a crucial day, and Werth could hear gunfire distinctly now. He put final touches on the day's story and cabled it:

PARIS IN ITS ANGUISH CALM AND BEAUTIFUL THESE DAYS STOP DURING DAY NUMEROUS LUGGAGE LADEN CARS SEEN LEAVING TOWN WITH PASSENGERS HAVING TEARS IN EYES STOP. . . . GOVERNMENTS DECISION CASE PARIS IMMEDIATELY THREATENED BEING AWAITED STOP BUT TIS TOO EARLY DWELL ON THE DARKER POSSIBILITIES OF COMING WEEK

When the spokesman was asked at the press briefing at the Quai d'Orsay whether the government had decided to leave Paris, he replied, "I don't know anything about that." But everybody else knew. Werth was invited to see Information Minister Prouvost together with other British correspondents that afternoon, but saw no point in going.

The first minister to leave Paris was Philippe Pétain, who drove out of the city shortly before midnight, escorted by two motorcycle police guards. His aide-de-camp noted that traffic was heavy near Fontaine-bleau, but that was because of Parisians returning from Sunday outings. (Not a joke: Captain Léon Bonhomme recorded the observation in his diary that very night.) The marshal and his party were to proceed to Briare, headquarters of the transferred high command. But no accommodations were available there, and Pétain spent the rest of the night in the bed of a railway inspector at the Gien station.

Pétain was not running a ministry; his was a relatively easy move. As seen by Colonel Georges Groussard from the office of the military governor, the cabinet's sudden decision to evacuate had been ill-advised and even dangerous. At once every surviving means of transportation disappeared, with no concern for military requirements. In the previous war the taxis of Paris had been requisitioned, but that had been to move soldiers *toward* the front. To make things worse, ordinary Parisians who realized what the government was up to began to utilize whatever transport *they* could muster up to join the exodus.

From the point of view of the Region of Paris, responsible for the defense of the capital, available vehicles were to be used above all to rush supplies to troops assigned to the protection of the city, and then to provide for the civilian population. Only after that could they be used to evacuate government files and equipment. Despite these logical priorities there was constant pressure on the military from government departments; everybody seemed to have the right to requisition transport. The result was chaos. Soon there would not be a single vehicle available to carry munitions to fighting units, no way to bring food to the towns and villages surrounding Paris, or even to move wounded soldiers. New war matériel would be abandoned because there were no trucks to take it away.

Had there been a plan, the government could have staged its departure in an orderly manner. The abrupt flight, decided Colonel Groussard, was nothing less than catastrophic for the people of Paris, left without directives or even advice. Now there could be genuine panic.

Groussard witnessed an example of inadequate planning at the Air Ministry, whose personnel had been moved out earlier in the month by rail and truck. But the bureaucrats had forgotten the files, and by the time they remembered, it was too late; the Germans got them. The same neglect concerned young men of draft age assigned to vital war industries. They received a succession of orders and counter-orders;

some were sent out of Paris without instructions, on foot, while others were left to their own devices in their factories, without orders to destroy machinery that could be of use to the enemy.

A nightmare. The worst of nightmares, thought Groussard, when one's whole career was spent preparing for a war that seemed increasingly inevitable, to find that one's best efforts, and the best efforts of so many others, served no purpose. Some were to speak of treason in remembering these hours. It had not been treason, but simply incompetence.

Night and day Groussard's office was plagued with phone calls and unannounced visits from people whose superiors had gone off without leaving instructions. His invariable reply was, "Stay at your post and do your job." Few obeyed, and how blame them, with the example of their chiefs?

When Jean Chauvel arrived at the Foreign Ministry that morning, his superior informed him that they were all leaving Paris that afternoon at five. After clearing out his office he found that he still had time on his hands. So he took a walk along the Seine, past bookstalls still open on Quai Malaquais. He bought a book on Vermeer, sat at a café opposite the Louvre. On return to the Quai d'Orsay he met the colleague who was to drive with him and his wife out of the city. When they went to pick up Madame Chauvel at their apartment on Rue Mignard, he took a last look around. At that instant they still believed that Paris was to be fought for, and therefore that they would never see this building and these possessions intact again.

Taking leave, they walked by neighbors and concierges, who in turn observed the departure of the diplomats "with a bit of surprise, a bit of mistrust. They felt abandoned. And we also felt this abandonment—a painful feeling."

Jérôme Carcopino, who since his return from Rome had spent his time looking up old friends, and finding them hopeful on the whole, got a shock that day. A couple he knew was to drive him to the country so that he could visit his mother. When he reached their apartment on Rue Bonaparte at nine that Sunday, the concierge told him that his friends had left at dawn, with large packages, for a castle on the Loire.

His friend was inspector general of historical monuments; Carcopino guessed that he had been entrusted with an urgent mission having to do with the removal of precious works of art.

Léon Blum, at sixty-eight elder statesman of the Popular Front, conscience of the Socialist Party, was still in Paris as the city emptied. A man of many talents, a journalist and literary critic before conversion to Socialism, prime minister of the first Popular Front government in 1936, Blum played no active part in the war or for that matter in politics now; no one would have expected that of the frail, cautious intellectual—least of all the pugnacious Paul Reynaud. During the day, friends in the cabinet had gotten in touch with him, one after the other. He was advised to pack; his political associates did not wish to leave Paris without him. Were they now leaving? "No, not yet, the decision hasn't been taken, but it can be from one minute to the next." "Then I'll wait," he said. "Perhaps we'll have another May 16th" (the day of the Big Scare). He was advised, in any case, to keep car and driver ready, with a full tank of gas. And Paris? "Our departure won't change anything; Paris will be defended to the end." Members of the cabinet still believed that.

People were calling Blum for advice: Should they leave? He felt that anyone asking such a question already had an answer, and merely wanted approval of the answer.

At about seven, Blum paid a call on a friend whose husband was in the Council of State, the supreme administrative court. From her he learned that the members of the council were leaving for Angers the next morning. He was still at his friend's house when Georges Monnet, minister of agriculture in Blum's 1936 cabinet and now minister of the blockade, found him by telephone. "Leave," pleaded Monnet, "leave right away; you can't stay in Paris." Blum protested, "But nothing has been decided; the cabinet is meeting tonight." "Quite true," replied Monnet, "but the matter has already been settled; leave, I beg of you. As the hours go by, the roads are getting more clogged. We in the government will get through easily, but you had better go now." The friends he was visiting put in their own plea for the exodus of this man who, as a prominent Socialist and a Jew, represented anti-Fascism in his country. He was sure to be a victim both of the

Nazi invaders and of their French sympathizers when the enemy took the city.

When Blum returned home he discovered that his housemaids, after getting an earful from Minister Monnet, had packed his bags and summoned his driver; the car was waiting outside the door. Friends had dropped in; he sat talking to them, surrounded by familiar possessions in this still tranquil house. If he left, when would he come back? "That is true," a friend responded, "but you can't fall into German hands, you don't have the right to do that." At eleven, Georges Monnet was on the line again. "The cabinet meeting is over. We leave for Tours at this instant, except for Paul Reynaud and Mandel. My car is outside. But we can't and we won't go while you stay in Paris." And Reynaud agreed with Monnet. Monnet's wife took the phone, sobbing, to wrest a promise from Blum. He saluted his friends and got into the waiting automobile. The surprise was an empty road. The only delays were at police checkpoints.

President Lebrun couldn't sleep that night. At dawn he was ready for the drive to the castle of Cangé, near Tours; he remembered thinking how lovely it would be to live there in other circumstances. Driving out of Paris, he was in effect transferring French sovereignty from its age-old capital. And no Frenchman, no Parisian not privy to state secrets, knew it.

Everybody turned up in Tours, or in one or another of the nearby villages and towns. There seemed to be a palace or a cottage suited for each rank and dignity. Thus Chamber of Deputies president Edouard Herriot, who had finally gotten away at 4:00 A.M., arrived at the charming wine village of Vouvray at eight, and was soon settled into the fifteenth-century castle of Moncontour.

Of course the American ambassador would receive early word of the departure of the diplomatic corps. Henri Hoppenot had telephoned from the Quai to tell him that the Foreign Ministry was sending letters to all embassies advising them of the imminent departure of the government. When Bullitt informed the State Department of this new development, in a rush telegram at 7:00 P.M., it was his understanding that the Germans were now only twenty-five miles from the city.

Roosevelt read the telegram at four in the afternoon on June 9, Washington time. A reply was drafted in his name, perhaps by the secretary of state. Since all or most foreign diplomats assigned to Paris would follow the government to Tours, Roosevelt was to say, he had decided that Bullitt should also leave Paris—contrary to the earlier understanding. For one thing, the Germans would probably not cooperate with the American ambassador in making things easier for Parisians who stayed behind. Most important, Bullitt needed to be in direct touch with the French government "in the event of certain contingencies arising" (without doubt, surrender was the contingency referred to).

Roosevelt may or may not have drafted the message, but in the end he disapproved it. It was not sent, nor read by Bullitt.

That morning the steamship *Washington* left its moorings at Bordeaux, en route to the United States. Some fifteen hundred Americans were on board, temporary or permanent residents of France. Bullitt and the State Department had seen to it that U.S. citizens received priority in booking passage.

Peter Fontaine found only "bustle and confusion" at the British Embassy that day, as offices were emptied and trucks waited outside on Rue du Faubourg Saint-Honoré to be loaded with filing cases. At times the sound of gunfire was quite audible at this sanctuary in the very center of the city. "An uncanny feeling of impending disaster grips us all," the Englishman told his diary. "Yet Paris is still supposedly in a state of defence. Are we about to witness her death-throes, or is there still hope?"

Writing for the Italian daily *Il Giornale d'Italia,* correspondent Sergio Bernacconi watched the city closely that day and on the following days, although because of what was about to transpire between his country and France, his report was not sent out right away. He remembered June 9 as the last day that French troops could sustain a true defensive line; immediately thereafter would come rout, disorderly and desperate. Some soldiers had thrown down their arms to make their way back to their home towns and villages. Others sought to find their retreating leaders, leaders a thousand times guilty of France's defeat. The Fascist reporter named Léon Blum first of all, then Daladier, Chautemps, Herriot, Reynaud, Mandel, men who he said had exploited and destroyed their country. None of them had appreciated the merits of Fascism, added Bernacconi, or realized that it was to seal the fate of democracy.

So, on that last Sunday of democratic Paris, the Italian journalist watched endless columns of vehicles proceeding south, west, and southwest. Along the Champs-Elysées, under a tepid sun, old people and women strolled wearily; at outdoor cafés British officers and airmen drank whiskey in the company of unserious women. At one point a long column of Paris city buses repainted in camouflage colors drove by with soldiers on the way to the front. The Sunday crowd looked on with a certain indifference (said Bernacconi); there were few gestures of farewell to the passing soldiers from the Champs-Elysées crowd, no banners, no songs. And the Englishmen at their tables did not seem to notice this final act of the tragedy. For these soldiers were to die because the British wished it, and continued to wish it.

At sunset Bernacconi heard cannon fire, distant but insistent. At ten that night German aircraft overflew the city, and for the last time French antiaircraft guns fired away furiously. It was their swan song, for next day these guns too would abandon Paris, to protect the government in its new quarters.

There was an equally voluble German witness to this day. Wilhelm Ritter von Schramm was an aide-de-camp on the staff of General Georg von Küchler, commanding the 18th Army approaching Paris from the north. That day its field headquarters was at Clermont, in the Oise district some forty miles north of the capital, at the edge of the forests of the Ile de France.

Seen from von Küchler's headquarters, the war was all but over. The French troops they now encountered were virtually harmless; at the first sight of the invaders, to hear von Schramm tell it, they would salute and ask to be taken prisoner. It was definitely not the First World War all over again; this time the miracle was German. (Perhaps von Schramm was scribbling his observations from the Clermont villa occupied in the earlier war by General John J. Pershing, commander of American forces; in this villa he had received Clemenceau, Foch, and Pétain to plan American participation in the final and victorious offensive.)

That morning, von Schramm noted, the Germans had captured a French colonel who declared defiantly that the Germans would never take Paris, even if they succeeded in occupying all the rest of France. Paris would be defended to the last Frenchman. Toward evening the captured colonel's vow seemed to receive confirmation, for radio intercepts indicated that the French were regrouping for heavy resistance. From the terrace of their temporary headquarters the division's general staff could observe an uninterrupted series of flashes from enemy artillery positions. The French were dug in, with concrete pillboxes and trenches, barricades reinforced by barbed wire. Then there was the Oise River, a formidable barrier at that point, with the swampy bottom of the Nonette River still farther south. From now on it would not be child's play; the French were not yielding, and the German advance seemed to have been checked.

Perusing military documents on the French side, one learns that the swampy Nonette was not a natural barrier, but a long-planned tactic of the army responsible for the defense of Paris. The first stage of flooding of the Nonette basin had been ordered as early as May 17, the second on June 1, followed by a third and total flooding, supervised by army engineers, forty-eight hours later.

Certainly French lines seemed credible at that moment, with (in addition to what Wilhelm von Schramm observed) concrete shelters for big guns, antitank pits spread over miles of terrain, special antitank obstacles ready to be drawn over roadways. For on June 9, and despite what some people thought they had heard, nothing had been decided, nothing had been said officially, about abandoning Paris, declaring it an open city. If French lines held, Paris might just be saved.

Before going to bed, Maxime Weygand drafted another memorandum for the government. He would sign it or not sign it depending on what he learned about the front lines the following morning. In his draft he reminded the cabinet that the decisive battle had begun on June 5, and the French were fighting it heroically; the enemy suffered heavy losses. But there simply weren't enough French soldiers to make it possible to relieve front-line fighters with reserves; fatigue would take its toll. On the morning of the sixth day of battle—that would be Monday, June 10—he had to accept the truth that enemy attacks were driving the French back, lengthening the offensive line eastward, and the Germans could still call on fresh troops. At one place German armor had forced a wedge, threatening the lower Seine. The French were still holding along the river, holding north of Paris, holding on the Marne River too—this forming a last line permitting resistance.

Weygand went on to recall his earlier memorandum, dated May 29, in which he had warned that the time could come when the French would no longer be able to stand fast. That time would come when the Germans broke through lines along which the French had been ordered to fight without retreat. It could happen "from one moment to the next." The enemy could now attain the Paris region by crossing the lower Seine, or break through in Champagne with tanks, or pierce French lines running from the Seine to the Marne.

If such an eventuality occurred, our armies would continue to combat up to the moment of exhaustion of their strength and their means. But their dissolution would only be a matter of time.

34

MONDAY, JUNE 10

Parisians who hadn't heard it on the radio could now read the commander-in-chief's stirring order of the day in their morning newspapers. "We have reached the final quarter hour" all but leapt from the front pages. In these meager dailies, single sheets printed front and back, only essentials now had their place. News of the war was printed side by side with calls for participation in the war. Thus readers this morning found an appeal by the Ministry of Veterans' Affairs for volunteers from the ranks of World War I soldiers, either to join a territorial guard or to fill various vacant posts at their local prefectures. Workers temporarily unemployed who were willing to participate in activities connected with the defense of the Paris region were asked to make themselves known.

There was also a warning: with the exception of certain aircraft plants being transferred to safer ground, no defense factory was to evacuate without written orders. The Public Works Ministry issued a request for the reduction of electricity consumption, whether for business or home use.

It was the stock market's final day. The Bourse was to close down at 1:15 P.M.; brokers would be advised when the exchange was ready to reopen. And this last day of trading under the Third Republic was a calm one. What little action there was indicated a certain stability, as in shares of the Bank of France and the Compagnie de Suez. Electricity, coal, rubber, gold mines showed "resistance," in the sober language of Le Temps, the preferred newspaper of business interests. Today's reader comparing quotations of June 7, the Friday before the weekend, with those of Monday, June 10, may be surprised to find that some stocks rose in value.

The press reported further trials of French Communists, thirty-three of whom were going before the Paris Military Tribunal that day, including the chief editor of L'Humanité, Robert Blache. He was one of eleven persons indicted for treason, risking a death penalty for the distribution of forbidden tracts and pamphlets urging workers in defense plants to carry out systematic sabotage. The twenty-two other defendants were being tried under the September 1939 ban on the Communist Party, for they had continued to spread Party propaganda in defiance of the law.

Four defendants convicted of treason and espionage, including a former aviator and a German national, lost their appeals and were to be executed. A man convicted of spreading false reports harmful to civilian morale received a ten-year prison term. Another accused of disseminating Communist propaganda got a two-year sentence, a third eighteen months for defeatist remarks.

In these days when paid advertising was reduced to a few column inches at the bottom of the second (and last) page, Le Figaro carried an ad for Creed, a men's tailor on Rue Royale:

OFFICERS
In three days your uniform fitted by the
most famous tailor in Paris. . . .
Special prices for military personnel.

Three days was indeed all the time they had.

Latvian correspondent Arved Arenstam was warned by an Englishwoman who had reason to know that he ought to leave Paris at once. (She knew, for example, that the government had already gone.) Arenstam's cook told him of the atmosphere of panic at her morning market, and of rising prices. His English friend insisted that he accompany her to Bordeaux that very day, but he had to be at the Information Ministry at three for the daily press conference.

But of course there was no conference. He became one more witness to the disarray, the empty offices and scattered papers, and to the expressions on the faces of foreign correspondents who had been left high and dry. Some of them, advocates of France's cause, felt that they had been abandoned to German reprisals.

Arenstam found it hard to get home, in the absence of taxis and buses. When at last he did, he learned that his English friend had booked sleepers that night for Bordeaux, leaving from the Gare d'Austerlitz.

The train leaves in four hours' time [he told his diary]. About 20,000 people are massed in front of the station, most of them seated on their belongings. It is impossible to move, and the heat is unbearable. In its present state of nervous tension the crowd has lost all its charm, and has none of the friendly gaiety that usually characterizes the French en masse. . . .

The human body can evidently stand much more than one suspects in normal times. I have now been standing wedged in this seething mass for over three hours. . . . A woman standing near us has fainted. Two *agents* force their way through, and carry her off over the heads of the crowd. Children are crying all round, and the many babies in arms look like being crushed to death. The Police Officer in charge of the entrance gates orders all babies to be handed over to the Police within. This human baggage is gradually passed over the heads of the crowd by outstretched arms, and the babies are assembled on a table within the Station gates, until their mothers can get through to collect them. . . .

All this while loudspeakers attempt to reassure the mob: everybody will leave, there will be more trains. . . .

A. J. Liebling actually found a taxi, or rather his hotel porter found one after a two-hour hunt, so that Liebling could get to the Spanish consulate to apply for a transit visa, to get through that country into Portugal and home. From there he went to the police prefecture for a

French exit visa. There a clerk told him to leave his passport and return for it in four days. "By that time, Madame," said Liebling, "the Germans may be here and the Prefecture may not exist." He did not leave his passport with her.

At the bar of the Hotel Crillon, a Canadian general told Liebling, "The French still have a fine chance. I am leaving for Tours as soon as I finish this sandwich." The *New Yorker* reporter went from there to the Continental, where he ran into a reporter leaving the hotel. "If you're going up to the ministry, don't bother," the man told him. "The government left Paris this morning." His colleague told him more: "You remember when John Lloyd stopped Prouvost last night and invited him to the Wednesday luncheon? Well, Prouvost was in a hurry because he was leaving for Tours in a few minutes." Liebling replied that maybe they had better go too. They did.

"The government leaves Paris in a hurry without saying where it is going or why," mused the *Herald Tribune*'s Walter Kerr. So the inevitable happens—Parisians also rush away. "Where is the enemy?" wondered Kerr. "Is anyone fighting back? No one seems to know or care." He could not help noticing posters for two American movies on the Champs-Elysées. One was *Going Places,* the other *You Can't Take It With You.*

Kerr was not going places. The policy was that the head of each news bureau was to follow the government to Tours; Kerr happened to be a number two.

It was a day Simone de Beauvoir had to memorialize. She rose at seven, managed to flag down a taxi to take her to the Camille Sée high school in the southwestern part of the city. There she found a handful of students who had turned up to see whether the final exams would be held after all. Of course they would not be. Professor Beauvoir was handed an evacuation order: her high school was transferred to Nantes in southern Brittany. Back in her Latin Quarter she ran into students of a neighborhood school who seemed unable to repress their joy, for today had become an unexpected holiday, "this examination day without examinations." Young people who thought they were to confront the most rugged trial of their school career suddenly found themselves free, albeit in a dying city. Outdoor cafés were virtually deserted now;

the action on Boulevard Saint-Michel was the parade of fleeing Parisians. At a favorite bistro the owner confided that he was leaving that very evening. So were the lavatory attendant at the Café Mahieu, the grocer on Rue Claude-Bernard. The quarter would soon be deserted.

Simone de Beauvoir was to leave with a friend. They waited at the Café Mahieu for the car that was to pick them up, wondering if it were already too late. She found this "interminable farewell" to Paris unbearable. The parade of fleeing motorists continued before their eyes, with horse-drawn wagons too, and bicycles. The weather was hot and damp, both women had slept badly. She remarked that a man was carefully cleaning the street lamps on the opposite sidewalk—"His gestures created a future in which it was impossible to believe." Finally their driver arrived and they piled into the car, not before hearing a last street rumor: "The Russians and British have just landed at Hamburg." The man spreading the story was a soldier from the nearby Val de Grâce military hospital; it made them feel that all was not lost as they maneuvered their way out of Paris via the Porte d'Orléans.

André Maurois was an author of considerable repute, one of the pillars of Paris society; he happened to be a French Jew. Three well-placed friends phoned him early that morning to advise that the government was leaving the city. It was recommended that Maurois's wife leave at once, while Maurois himself would be sent on a mission to London.

His wife suggested that they take a last look at their beloved city. They were out of doors at eight that morning. As they walked, past the gilded dome of the Invalides, along the Seine to the Louvre and Notre Dame, they realized that other Parisians were also taking a last look at their city. Certainly there were tears, but no despairing words were pronounced. Both husband and wife were certain that a civilization which had produced so much beauty could not die.

Home again, they wondered what they could take away with them, not more than would fill up an automobile. That afternoon, when Maurois left for the airport, the city appeared deserted. But the roads leading out of the city were not.

Fernande Alphandery, the woman who lived close to the bombs that fell over Paris just a week ago, no longer had a job to go to; no one was manufacturing pharmaceutical products now, and even the Red Cross group in which she was helping refugees had disbanded. So she decided to leave, since everybody else was leaving, aware (so she told her diary) that it would be the final chapter of a life. But not before recording her feeling of "deep disgust," of "total helplessness."

She had seen so many refugees and their distress; now everyone was a refugee. When your government has left Paris, how can you stay, especially if you have a way to leave? As one of the privileged, with a car of her own, she invited friends to join her—a woman teacher, a German Jewish journalist and his wife. She herself wasn't leaving because of her religion; indeed, she had the feeling that a higher percentage of Jews than non-Jews were staying on in Paris simply because, as recent arrivals, they didn't have family or friends in the provinces. These refugees had been running a long time, and now wished to stay put and to hold on to what they had.

She herself was back home in Paris in October.

The Gurewiczes stayed. Mirra Gurewicz was eighteen and a student at the La Fontaine high school at the Porte de Saint-Cloud at the city's western edge; she lived nearby with her Russian-born parents. She herself had been born in Warsaw in 1922. In Paris they found a congenial environment of Russian Jews and German Jewish refugees. Among themselves the Gurewiczs spoke German—until September 1939, that is. After that it was not good to be taken for a German.

When Parisians were issued gas masks, the family didn't get any—for they weren't French.

Mirra was in her final month of her final high school year when the German offensive began in May. Soon she was part of a volunteer student group that assisted refugees at the Gare du Nord, pouring coffee, getting them the practical information they needed, taking care of old people and parents with children. Once she joined her class in an invasion of a boy's high school, helping move out desks so that classrooms could be used as a refugee shelter.

Rumors about final exams were contradictory: they would or would not take place. In the end they were postponed. Mirra didn't complain. She enjoyed the excitement of those days. When a child was taken down to a shelter and missed the flashes and the blasting in the sky during an air raid, he or she felt deprived of a bit of fun. Even the bombing on June 3, which came so close to their house, failed to disturb Mirra.

But the day came when the war ceased to be fun. Too many shutters were shut, too many buildings in the neighborhood stood empty. In their own eight-story house, with its four stairways and sixty-four apartments, only a handful of tenants remained. It wasn't that people feared what the Germans might do to them as Jews; the worry had been that Paris might become a battlefield. When truly close friends got ready to leave, Mirra and her mother began packing their own suitcases, but her father said he was not going anywhere. "Here I know what's in store for us," he explained. "But we don't know what it will be like somewhere else." So mother and daughter stayed with father.

Denise Khaitman was a teenager, living in a largely Jewish neighborhood near City Hall with a father born in Russia and a mother born in Lithuania. Her parents owned and operated two shoe stores, and at the time of the German attack, young Denise was in charge of one of them. What happened in the north, even when news arrived of the German approach to Paris, didn't seem to concern daily life—nor did it seem to perturb their neighbors. No one believed that the Germans would actually enter the city; those who left were people who happened to have somewhere to go.

The Germans were within a couple of days of Paris—at the rate they were advancing—when at last Denise's father prepared the old family Citroën for their departure. There would be Denise's parents, her grandmother, her sister and aunt and uncle and cousin, a friend with two young boys; there were thirteen in all in the automobile. They drove for forty-eight hours straight, at times paying for the water they used (an experience that runs like a thread through the souvenirs of so many refugees), until at last they reached a hilltop in the Corrèze mountains, where they could sleep in somebody's barn.

Friends followed them in a truck filled with shoes from the two Khaitman stores. So they would leave their barn each Saturday morning at four to go to an open market at Bort-les-Orgues, riding in a horse-drawn cart packed with shoes. Before summer was over, Denise returned to Paris; her parents joined her a month after that. It didn't occur to them that Jews might not be welcome. Later they found out. During the occupation Denise joined an underground movement that provided false papers and hiding places to Jews and others on the Nazi blacklist.

If you were an ordinary citizen going about your business, why not continue? That was the attitude of Marguerite Bouchardeau, then thirty-three. In peacetime the Bouchardeaus lived on Rue d'Arsenal, running a small workshop that made lampshades to order. Now, with husband Jacques in the army, Marguerite carried on the business alone. And business was lively, for companies were ordering dark blue lampshades for office use during blackouts (the color was called "civil defense blue").

Indeed, there was so much for Marguerite Bouchardeau to do that she slept on a camp bed in the workshop, her only child having been sent to stay with her parents in a village just south of Paris. In peacetime Jacques made his deliveries with a Peugeot sedan, after removing the rear seats. But his wife never got a driver's permit and couldn't make use of the car (though he had taught her how to drive). So she delivered her lampshades by subway, even though some of them were a yard or more in diameter. She just had to get a driver's permit! When she made an appointment for an examination she was given the date of June 10. Then when she showed up for the test there wasn't an examiner in sight; official Paris was no more.

So she continued to carry her outsized packages down the Métro steps, and used the same subway to call on customers to collect bills. Only now she was coming up against a lot of locked doors. It was time for Marguerite to think of leaving. She shut down the workshop, drove off in the Peugeot, and never mind that she was driving without a permit; she picked up her child and her parents on the way, to proceed to what seemed a safer place, Saumur on the Loire. Following the armistice, driving the family back to their village below Paris, she worried that she might be stopped and asked to produce a driver's permit. The Germans did stop them, but her father's World War I veteran's card got them through.

*   *   *

Then there was the woman with one hundred children—orphans in a girls' school. It was the responsibility of teacher Anne Jacques to move them out of Paris and to safety. She approached the Gare d'Austerlitz with a fast-beating heart this morning, to find that she was not alone. The line was so long she estimated it would take her two hours just to reach the ticket window. Finally she was able to get directions to the office of a stationmaster; the man inside seemed overwhelmed by the immensity of the challenge. "I have a hundred children to evacuate," she began. "I need a whole railway car." "No," he replied. "There are some sick children, some handicapped. . . ." "It's not possible." "I have no one to help me." "We can't reserve trains anymore." He returned the list she had given him. Suddenly her hand trembled so violently the paper rattled. "You'll get the last available train," the stationmaster said at last. After a silence he added, "You have a terrible responsibility." She replied, "So do you." He took the hand that had trembled and shook it.

Then Mademoiselle Jacques had to get through to the ticket clerk. It took only an hour to reach the window, but there she was asked for the dates of birth of each of her wards. She tried to write, leaning first on a trunk, then on a bench, but the crowd was too dense around her. She left the station and crossed the avenue to a café, ordered a drink she couldn't touch, and began writing names, inventing dates of birth. A man seated nearby saw what she was doing and helped; he dictated notional dates, she handed him the drink she had ordered. Then she had to return to her suburb to pick up the children and accompany them to the Gare d'Austerlitz in two rented buses. Traffic was dense; the final half-mile took an hour, and only two hours remained before the departure of the train. With the help of a policeman and a station employee the buses were directed to the adjacent freight station. Inside, the children and their teacher drank water from a barrel, all using the same glass every departing Parisian used that day.

Their train was already on the platform, so Mademoiselle Jacques rounded up her group and the two nuns who were to accompany the children. But their wagon was already occupied; would-be passengers had simply broken the seals and rushed to fill all the seats. The stationmaster had to be called to get them out again. Anne Jacques saw her children off, then found it nearly as difficult to get out of the station as to enter it, for candidates for departure were leaning against the iron gates. The stationmaster suggested she try to leave through the subway, but that too had become a refuge. When she did at last attain the Boulevard de l'Hôpital she walked home in a summery night that seemed disconnected from the pandemonium she had left behind her.

Young Information Ministry officer Roger Peyrefitte had been invited to lunch by the ex-king of Albania, whom he had met on a previous embassy posting; the improbable venue of this improbable lunch invitation was fashionable Chez Maxim's. Nothing seemed to have changed there, thought Peyrefitte as he approached the famous restaurant, although he quickly discovered that he was wrong. The elegant automobiles outside the door were filled with valises; obviously they belonged to Parisians who were treating themselves to a final splendid meal before joining the exodus. The doorman was at his regular spot, greeting arriving clients with the usual "Good appetite!" And Peyrefitte had to admit that the food smelled good. Soon his royal host had ordered a savory lunch for his party. Peyrefitte, not privy to his own country's secrets, had to learn from the Albanians at his table that the diplomatic corps was being asked to join the French president in Tours; a nearby villa had been set aside for the Albanian legation.

But while most of the diners at Chez Maxim's that day seemed in a hurry, King Zog and his guests were not. Peyrefitte himself didn't know what to advise. King Zog wasn't going to leave Paris at all.

Peyrefitte walked back to the Hotel Continental to confront a strange silence: empty corridors, doors wide open. Was it the effect of a mysterious spell that had been cast over the place? (So wondered the hero of the novel Peyrefitte wrote about the experience.) An air alert? His superior brought him back to earth. "Go pack your bags," he said. "The last special train for government agencies leaves the Gare d'Austerlitz for Tours at six."

When he rose at daybreak, dapper Maxime Weygand found a visitor at the door, his chief of staff, back from a mission to the lower Seine valley. The news was good and bad. No, the Germans hadn't crossed the river. But soon they would; French defenses would not resist. So Weygand picked up the memorandum he had drafted for Reynaud, signed and dated it; he would hand it to the premier at the morning conference. He found Charles de Gaulle there, attending the war meeting for the first time (Pétain was now somewhere along the Loire).

Reynaud was in a fighting mood. He would carry on the war. If they couldn't hold the Germans before Paris, couldn't prevent them from invading the French heartland, he still intended to concentrate remnants of the army in Brittany, which would allow continued contact with Britain—and they would again try to bring the United States into the war. Weygand had yielded to Reynaud's stubborn dream—in that he had been thinking about Brittany. But to close off the Breton peninsula meant to defend a line 120 miles long from Channel coast to Atlantic Ocean, and they no longer had the means to hold such a line. When they were ready, the Germans would puncture it in a day.

Paul Baudouin, Reynaud's deputy whose responsibilities included the cabinet's war committee, grumbled under his breath about his cumbersome rival, Charles de Gaulle. He was sure that de Gaulle was the one encouraging Reynaud in his Breton "fantasy." Meanwhile de Gaulle was reporting to the committee on his mission to London of the previous day: Churchill could not deprive the British of its air force, but would do what he could; that is, he'd sent eight squadrons— nearly one hundred planes. They would cross the Channel every day for missions in France, to return to British bases at night. Churchill no longer saw hope for the Battle of France. Reynaud put in that British respect for French military skill had been lost when the Germans crossed the Meuse.

Before handing his note to Reynaud, General Weygand briefed the meeting on the military situation. France had now reached the limit of its resistance; in some cases soldiers had simply stopped fighting. He blamed fatigue, after eight days of battle without respite. German air superiority had taken its toll, telephone lines had been cut between Paris and Evreux and Caen, cities which were actually on the French side of the Seine. Even the retreat of French troops was blocked as bridges were destroyed behind the lines. The British defenders of Rouen had given up; the Germans were pushing toward Reims. . . . The general-in-chief added that he wasn't surprised at what was happening. The enemy had entered the battle with eighty divisions in reserve, while the total strength of the French was only sixty-five divisions. "It should be said," Baudouin heard him say, "that the sense of discipline and devotion lacked in many cases. We're paying for 20 years of lies and demagogy."

After reading Weygand's memorandum Reynaud remarked that it lacked a positive side. Baudouin pointed out that if Pétain were present he would have insisted that they now talk to the British, and then to the Germans, about a possible armistice. "The situation is worsening from day to day." "If the situation is worsening," countered de Gaulle—visibly irritated by Weygand's paper—"it's because we let it get worse." "What do you suggest?" Weygand asked. According to Baudouin, de Gaulle replied that it was not his job to suggest anything.

De Gaulle's recollection of that instant is spicier. He remembers snapping at the general-in-chief, "The government has no suggestions to make, only orders to give. I expect it to give those orders."

Reynaud asked Weygand when he thought the Germans would enter Paris. "If the Germans knew just how weak we are, in twenty-four hours," he replied. "But it could take a little longer, and it is probable that the Germans won't attack Paris frontally. They'll begin by surrounding the city."

Even the plucky Reynaud was discouraged now. Before the morning was over he gave instructions for everyone to be ready to pull out at a moment's notice. Suddenly William Bullitt was beside him. He made it clear that he was going to stay; he'd share the fate of ordinary Parisians. Dramatically he added, "An American ambassador can be more useful dead than alive."

Now Reynaud asked his embarrassing question: Could he talk to Roosevelt by telephone? It was not possible that day, the ambassador replied, for the American president was on his way to make a speech in Charlottesville, Virginia. Then could Reynaud give Bullitt a personal message for Roosevelt? Reynaud wrote it out, with Bullitt looking over his shoulder.

Mr. President: I wish first to express to you my gratitude for the generous aid that you have decided to give us in aviation and armament.

For six days and six nights our divisions have been fighting without one hour of rest against an army which has a crushing superiority in numbers and material. Today the enemy is almost at the gates of Paris.

We shall fight in front of Paris, we shall fight behind Paris; we shall close ourselves in one of our provinces to fight and if we should be driven out of it we shall establish ourselves in North Africa to continue the fight and if necessary in our American possessions.

"You know who dictated that," Bullitt added slyly, in relaying the message to Roosevelt (the handwritten original that Bullitt had asked Reynaud to sign for him). "Please keep this for me," Bullitt asked Roosevelt, "or for yourself if I don't turn up." Quai d'Orsay archives reveal that a first draft of Reynaud's letter had been written by Americanophile Eve Curie with Roland de Margerie, Reynaud's liaison with the Foreign Ministry.

Reynaud concluded with a request for even greater assistance from the United States. Roosevelt responded by releasing Reynaud's stirring appeal to the press.

Events accelerated. At noon, French ambassador to Rome André François-Poncet telephoned to report that he had been asked by Count Ciano to come to the Italian Foreign Ministry at four-thirty, most certainly to be told that Italy was declaring war on France. Reynaud turned to Bullitt: "What really distinguished, noble and admirable persons the Italians are to stab us in the back at this moment." The expression would soon be flashed around the world. Reynaud asked his secretary to arrange for him to address the nation by radio that night. To Bullitt the premier confessed that everyone was trying to get him to leave Paris now. He intended to stay until the last possible moment, but didn't himself know when that moment might come.

By now the Germans were crossing the Seine in two places, and were also taking Fère-en-Tardenois, sixty-five miles east of the capital.

* * *

Back at the embassy Bullitt had a caller, Armament Minister Raoul Dautry. The minister had already sent his staff to Mont-Doré, and had met for the last time with factory owners and managers who would try to continue tank production in the provinces. Now he felt that he had a final duty to carry out. He knew that Bullitt had done all he could to help, knew that he couldn't supply more machine guns and rifles because America didn't have them. He also knew that Bullitt was trying to obtain 75-millimeter cannon that the U.S. War Department would sell as "scrap metal."

For his part, said Dautry, he wished to show gratitude. So he was handing over, then and there, secret plans for France's best tank, the B. I *bis,* as well as for France's best antitank weapon, the 47. "When you enter the war on our side, as you will certainly do," explained the armament minister, "these weapons will be useful to you." Visibly moved, Bullitt embraced the Frenchman. It was only after leaving the American Embassy that the minister would call on Reynaud at Rue Saint-Dominique to tell him what he had just done. Reynaud, who was busy ripping up papers, warmly approved Dautry's gesture.

Bullitt appointed a team to follow the French government wherever it went. It was headed by Ambassador Anthony Drexel Biddle, Jr., assisted by a senior diplomat, H. Freeman Matthews. Robert Murphy would stay with him in Paris, along with several diplomatic aides and the military and naval attachés.

The ambassador would be criticized for what he was doing, even by some Frenchmen. "To let Paul Reynaud leave without accompanying him signified, on the part of the United States representative, the opposite of an encouraging gesture," Reynaud's Dominique Leca would say later. Secretary of State Cordell Hull, to whom Bullitt was ostensibly reporting, in retrospect blamed Bullitt for not following the French. Had he gone with the cabinet he might have kept France in the war, with its fleet operating from North Africa. Robert Murphy, who stayed, thought that Bullitt deserved at least some of the credit for saving Paris from destruction.

At 4:55 Ambassador François-Poncet telephoned again from Rome. War was indeed what Count Ciano had wanted to tell him about. Italy was declaring war both on France and the United Kingdom, effective at midnight. Reynaud gave orders that the air force and navy be alerted. Everyone tuned in to hear Mussolini's bellicose speech.

He began calmly enough. Italy's conscience was tranquil, insisted the Duce. The world was his witness that his country had done everything humanly possible to avoid war. But now Italy was prepared to confront the risks and sacrifices of war for the supreme purposes that History had assigned to the nation.

Not very far from where the Reynaud group sat listening to the radio, in front of the Italian Embassy in its historic town house on Rue de Varenne, angry Parisians began to assemble. Reynaud's deputy, Maurice Dejean, scrutinizing the faces in the crowd, thought he read scorn rather than hatred. He also remembered what France and Britain had agreed to do the day Italy declared war: to launch an attack by British bombers based in southeastern France, and French and British warships, against Italy's industrial north. But Air Force general Joseph Vuillemin vetoed the plan, fearing reprisal raids. For the moment only the bombing of Genoa was authorized.

Sergio Bernacconi, the Italian Fascist newsman, had that morning been at the Information Ministry, which is where a foreign journalist was supposed to get his news. He noted—and he could not have been surprised—that it was all but empty now. Through half-open doors he saw deserted desks, scattered papers. Nobody bothered to find out who he was. Phones rang, and no one was there to pick them up.

He did find a young censorship officer, even a telephone operator, and he was able to put a call through to Rome. Then a call came in for the censorship officer, after which, with a resigned expression, he informed Bernacconi that the government was leaving Paris, and the telephone was being cut off. The Italian asked if he could phone Rome with *that* information. "Impossible," snapped the officer. Then, after a pause, he said more softly, "There is no hurry to send out that kind of news. At least let the few Frenchmen in the world who still believe in France have another hour of hope and tranquillity." A few minutes after that the Continental offices were closed down, forever.

Bernacconi observed Paris as Paris listened to Mussolini on the radio, speaking from his balcony on Piazza Venezia to his armed forces and his Black Shirts. The hour of destiny had arrived, the Duce was saying. This was a just war against plutocratic democracies and Western reactionaries who stood in the way of Italy's prosperity. In the opinion of Bernacconi, of course, Mussolini's words were a fair sentence. He noted that Frenchmen hearing the speech did not react, did not threaten or insult Italy. They listened with bowed heads, blaming only themselves. Italians in Paris didn't conceal their enthusiasm, but listened to the Duce with tears of joy and pride. Leading personalities of the Italian colony directed their steps to their embassy for an impromptu celebration. Earlier, when Italian ambassador Guariglia called at the French Foreign Ministry with a copy of Italy's war declaration, he had found no one to talk to. He had gone on to the Brazilian Embassy, which had agreed to protect Italians and their interests in the absence of diplomatic relations. Then it was time to return to his embassy for what he called, in his report to Ciano, "the historical words of the Duce."

As soon as Mussolini finished speaking, Guariglia heard cries coming from the street. He rushed to a window to see that French police had surrounded his embassy and were preventing anyone from entering. The "Jew Mandel," as Sergio Bernacconi called him, informed Guariglia that as the only representative of the French government remaining in Paris, he was placing the Italian ambassador and his staff under arrest. An embassy secretary was threatened by a police officer with a revolver. Henceforth the embassy on Rue de Varenne was a prison.

Russian gadfly Ilya Ehrenburg had a privileged observation post, the Soviet embassy on Rue de Grenelle, quite close to the Italian Embassy. Walking in the garden of his embassy he could hear happy shouts and singing coming from inside the Italian compound. He could even identify the song, the Fascist hymn *Giovinezza*.

At seven o'clock Maurice Dejean informed Premier Reynaud that the Germans were inside Dreux, with motorized units on their way to Houdan—this was thirty miles southwest of Paris. The capital was now virtually surrounded on three sides, and the departure of Reynaud and his men could not be put off much longer.

But Reynaud was not an easy man to budge. People—reasonable

people—had been trying for the past forty-eight hours to persuade him to leave the city. He would go, he promised, but only so as to be able to continue to run the war from headquarters, which had been transferred from Vincennes to Briare along the Loire, some twelve miles upriver from Gien. People around him on Rue Saint-Dominique were packing, burning papers, making sure that nothing of value to the enemy remained in desks and safes.

Outside on Boulevard Saint-Germain, Maurice Dejean had the feeling that Paris was in mourning. The sky had taken on a yellowish hue, veiling the sun. Everything, including people's faces, had become unreal. Dejean didn't know why.

He paid a final visit to the Foreign Ministry. This building, which had linked France to the rest of the world, offered "a spectacle of desolation," he noted. In the garden, roses had somehow survived the burning of secret documents on the lawn. Someone was picking the flowers; the Germans wouldn't get them.

Reynaud's radio address, preceded by the opening notes of *La Marseillaise,* was somber. "We are in the sixth day of the greatest battle of history," he began. He still saw hope everywhere: "The ground gained by the enemy is strewn with destroyed tanks and downed airplanes."

> The trials which await us are heavy. We are ready for them. Our heads do not bow.
>
> It is at this precise moment, while France, wounded but valiant and standing, struggles against German conquest, and fights for the independence of all peoples as for itself, that Mussolini chooses to declare war. How judge this act? France has nothing to say. The watching world will judge.

France had met rougher challenges in the course of history. "It is then that it always astonished the world. France cannot die."

The French were not overreacting, reflected Italian exile Pietro Nenni. A few Italian shops and restaurants were early and easy targets for anger, and so there were damaged fixtures and merchandise. As for the city's Italian colony, it was divided.

*   *   *

The French radio called for the immediate departure from Paris of all males aged eighteen to fifty. Workers from eighteen to forty-five were to leave even if they had to use their feet to get away.

A singular convoy left Paris for Vincennes, turning south, that day. It included a city bus, a truck, a dozen automobiles carrying files and equipment. Their cargo included the Second World War's biggest secret of all, accompanied by the spymasters in charge of the operation. Had their convoy been intercepted then or later, had their cargo been compromised at any time during the German occupation of France, the war would not have been as surely won by the Anglo-Americans and their allies. French intelligence officers were transporting expertly crafted replicas of the German Enigma encoding machine. The operation, which allowed the deciphering of German High Command and air force messages, was to be baptized Ultra. In their island fortress the British also possessed the Enigma machine and techniques allowing them to read its codes. But its use by the British, then and later, required that the Germans remain unaware that Enigma messages could be read. Capture of the French intelligence staff, with its materials and documents, would have put an end to the British operation as well.

The story of Ultra began nearly two decades earlier, closer to the First World War than to the Second, when a German working in his country's code department offered his services to French intelligence, for money. Hans Thilo Schmidt, then thirty-three years old, was given the operational name H.E., or Asche. He happened to have a brother who was to rise in the military to become one of Hitler's elite Panzer generals, and a vital source of intelligence thanks to indiscretions to his spy brother. In the view of the French, H.E. was the most important spy of World War II (more important even than Richard Sorge in Tokyo, for Sorge was gleaning scraps of the big picture for his Soviet spymasters from far-off Japan, while H.E. was in Berlin, with access through his brother, at least once, to Hitler himself). H.E.'s chief contribution to Allied victory was the help he provided to cryptanalysts cracking Enigma—early documents describing the workings

.of the machine, later information on periodic changes in the keying of the encoding device.

But before that happened, a second operation was necessary, this a Polish initiative. Poland had been preparing for the next war ever since the last one; by deduction the country's military codebreakers guessed that the Germans were using a coding machine, which turned out to be a modified version of a device available on the market to transmit business secrets. Wizards in Polish intelligence succeeded in reconstituting the German military adaptation of Enigma, and by the time Hitler came to power in 1933 they were cracking the codes of their future enemy—thanks to help from the French and their agent H.E. (The French offered H.E.'s booty to the British too, but at the time the British merely riffled through the papers and filed them away; Britain was not yet ready for the part it would play as the second war's supreme codebreaker.)

By 1939, when war seemed inevitable, the industrious Polish team possessed seventeen Enigma machines of their own making. In July of that year, when Hitler's attack on Poland was only weeks away, the Poles invited French and British code experts to Warsaw, and there unveiled the reconstructed machines. They gave two of the machines to Captain Gustave Bertrand, the French officer who had been handling H.E. from the beginning; Bertrand kept one of them for French intelligence and personally carried the second one to Colonel Stewart Menzies, then deputy chief of M.I. 6, the British intelligence office. When the Nazis did at last invade Poland in September, the Poles destroyed the remaining Enigmas to protect their secret. However, leading members of the Warsaw codebreaking group managed to escape with two replicas of the machine. Thanks to Captain Bertrand, they were put to work alongside their French colleagues.

This was the situation on the eve of the German offensive of May 1940. By then the French, as well as the British at their secret decoding facility at Bletchley Park, between Oxford and Cambridge, were decoding German messages, although on May 2 the latest round of German modifications of encoding procedures temporarily rendered the codes unbreakable. The silence persisted through the first dozen days of the Blitzkrieg, until Bletchley Park managed to break the code again on May 22. Knowing where the Germans were and what they were about to do could have made a difference, had not the French command structure been disorganized, dispersed, demoralized.

The French ran the Enigma operation not from military intelligence headquarters at 2 *bis* Avenue de Tourville in the Invalides quarter, but from a country manor, the castle of Vignolles, a turn-of-the-century rococo house in a large park of its own, some thirty miles southeast of the city. The staff numbered seventy, including fifteen Polish crypt-analysts and seven Spanish Republican refugees, plus a British liaison officer. Bertrand managed to enroll his Spanish contingent in the Foreign Legion, while the Polish exile army in France took the Polish team under its wing, thereby assuring that there were no civilians at Vignolles. Thanks to Enigma, France was able to keep up with changes in the German order of battle, precious information for an army able to make use of it. No army in history ever had better intelligence—so Bertrand was to recall later, with bitterness.

Packing up at the Vignolles command post began early in June. Bertrand couldn't find anyone to initiate an order to evacuate, so he drafted it himself, and was told to take it up with General Weygand. When he arrived at Weygand's office he was told by one of the general's aides, "The general has decided to die on the spot rather than retreat; do the same." Bertrand knew that he couldn't do anything of the sort to his men, to his Poles and Spaniards and British liaison, nor to his secret. So he made his way to the army car park at Vincennes and sat at the wheel of a brand-new city bus. His driver at the same moment was making off with a new five-ton truck loaded with jerry cans of gas. They drove the two hijacked vehicles to Vignolles and began loading. With the new bus and truck they formed a convoy of a dozen vehicles, and that day, June 10, got as far as La Ferté-Saint-Aubin in the Loiret. They quickly set up their equipment and were soon intercepting and decoding German secrets again, through June 14, the day Paris fell. On the following day they resumed their journey southward, to reach Agen on June 19. They installed a new command post in the Grand Séminaire de Bon-Encontre.

Bertrand sent the British officer back to London from a military airport near Bordeaux, got the Polish and Spanish teams evacuated to Algiers. In Bordeaux, when the French cabinet set up a temporary capital there, French intelligence officer Major Henri Navarre ran into the French secret agent who had originally recruited H.E.; the agent was an extroverted, extravagant personality whom Navarre knew would be better under wraps; he begged the man to leave France at once (in addition to everything else, he was of German origin). The agent—known as Rex—ignored the recommendation, and turned up at Agen. After the armistice Rex was ordered to lose himself on the French Riviera.

With a collaborationist government in Vichy and the consolidation of German hegemony over France, it was going to be an extraordinary feat to keep the Enigma codebreaking operation safe. Remarkably enough, the work was pursued throughout the years of German occupation, not only in the seclusion of Britain's Bletchley Park but in occupied France. No German, no collaborationist Frenchman, ever got a hint of it. By October 1940 the Bertrand group had moved into the castle of Fouzes near Uzès, an estate purchased with false papers, and big enough to house a major codebreaking operation. There were thirty-two persons in the castle—seven Spaniards and fifteen Poles, seven French auxiliary personnel, Bertrand and his wife and his chief deputy—supplied with food thanks to a recruit in the local town hall (whose Vichy-appointed mayor remained ignorant of the operation). Although Weygand, defense minister in Pétain's first Vichy cabinet, had approved clandestine operations of French intelligence, neither he nor any other Vichy official was briefed specifically on the Enigma decoding. Only three army officers knew what Bertrand was doing: the chief of military intelligence (which had been allowed by the Germans to continue to exist), the chief of a so-called antisubversives office supposedly working for Pétainism but actually a cover for anti-German intelligence, and his deputy.

All the while, Captain Bertrand's command post at Uzès read German secrets and transmitted intelligence to London, while his Polish team kept its own London-based exile government informed; some information (with no indication of its origin) went to the French army in Vichy. Even when the Poles were arrested during an attempt to leave France through the Pyrenees, they were not questioned by the Gestapo about Enigma. And when the extravagant agent known as Rex was at last picked up by the Germans, and after long interrogation revealed the activities of super-agent H.E., he did not give away the Enigma operation. H.E. was arrested, and died in captivity; his brother, General Schmidt, was disgraced. The Germans obviously could not believe that their codes were readable, and a lack of coordination between the Gestapo and German military intelligence did the rest.

When counterespionage officer Paul Paillole was in Britain during preparations for the Normandy landings of June 6, 1944, he was confronted with none other than Stewart Menzies, by then head of M.I. 6. Britain's intelligence chief told Paillole that the Allies were engaged in extensive operations to fool the Germans about the actual landing site, so that they would be required to spread defense forces all along the coast from Belgium to the tip of Brittany. Thanks to Ultra, the Allies could find out if they were indeed fooling the Germans. But if the Germans *knew* that their codes could be read, they would be the ones doing the fooling, at the cost of countless lives, the failure of Operation Overlord. Paillole did what he could to reassure the Allies. And so their best secret weapon, Ultra, after surviving the fall of Paris and the occupation of France, remained inviolate.

With the government out of Paris, it was time for the press to move. The city's dailies had been preparing their evacuation at least as thoroughly as the government had. Advance teams had been sent to south and central France to look for towns with printing plants and enough hotel rooms to take care of editors and printing personnel. Some dailies ceased publication in Paris on June 10, others the next day. A few simply shut down, including the Socialist organ *Le Populaire*.

Even Jean Prouvost, the information minister who seemed so firmly committed to Paris, was one of the early planners. He had sent staff members of his daily *Paris-Soir* out of Paris weeks earlier—on the tenth of May, in fact—to look for a suitable refuge. The best choice seemed to be Clermont-Ferrand, where Pierre Laval was offering hospitality at his own newspaper plant. Later *Paris-Soir* moved on to the more cosmopolitan city of Lyon.

In the final days in Paris, when most of the eight hundred employees were safely away, *Paris-Soir* editor-in-chief Pierre Lazareff worked with a skeleton staff and a handful of street vendors. Remaining editors took their meals in Lazareff's apartment in the Palais Royal. Cars and drivers were never far away. The last issue of the paper appeared at two on the afternoon of June 10, dated ahead as usual (to June 11). Outside the building on Rue de Louvre, Parisians stood waiting for copies. At three an officer of the military government drove up to urge the remaining staff to leave Paris. One of the editors who drove off that day was young, still unknown author Albert Camus, with the manuscript of the novel that was to make his reputation, *The Stranger,* in the trunk of the car.

The last issue of *Paris-Soir* carried the headline

Our Troops Resist
With Ardor and Heroism
WITH INCREASING VIOLENCE
The battle continues from
the sea to the Argonne

As always, the second and last page contained information on entertainment available to Parisians that week. There would be *Médée* at the Opéra on Wednesday, June 12, *La Bohème* at the Opéra-Comique, *Le Misanthrope* at the Odéon on Thursday. The Théâtre de l'Oeuvre was still open, as were a theater called Humour and a music hall called Eve. Twenty-one cinema theaters listed English-language films, thirty-three showed French ones.

Employees of *Paris-Soir* often spoke of the elevator operator as an odd fellow. After the arrival of the Germans he showed up in the uniform of a German officer, and became the publisher of the Paris edition.

"A great exodus from Paris started this morning," Englishman Peter Fontaine began his diary entry—as if the exodus were only beginning that day. But he also called it a stampede. He watched as cars and taxis piled high with baggage and mattresses came "tearing along" the streets of Paris. Shops and restaurants closed, and so did banks.

It reached the point, observer Pierre Audiat discovered, that those who were remaining in Paris of their own volition seemed suspect to those who were leaving. Could they belong to the fifth column? Audiat watched the evening strollers, seated on benches or at outdoor cafés, as the exodus continued, looking at the flight of fellow Parisians "with feelings in which pity had less and less of a place." One convoy of twenty-five buses with curtained windows was the object of particular curiosity; policemen stood on the rear platforms. These, Audiat knew, were inmates of the Santé prison.

"Oh, this parade of vagabonds and martyrs all night long!" exclaimed Marcel Jouhandeau; the reference was to French soldiers retreating along the avenue beneath his windows. Some of the soldiers seemed ashamed of the way they looked now; the most exhausted simply sat down on the sidewalk, resting their heads between their knees.

But the Jouhandeaus stayed. It was because of his wife Elise's stubbornness, her husband concluded; it was her proprietor's instinct, her desire to sit in and hold on to her house. She was the only one Jouhandeau knew who refused to leave, although he couldn't imagine how they would continue to live, with the school at which he taught shut down, his publisher gone. "It seems that everyone is going off on a long journey and we are alone, in the middle of an ocean of abandoned homes." It could indeed seem that way in Jouhandeau's affluent neighborhood.

Night had fallen on Paris by the time Franklin Delano Roosevelt appeared before the graduating class at the University of Virginia in Charlottesville to talk about the state of the world. Of course his speech had been written earlier, but now Roosevelt saw the opportunity to react to Mussolini's entry into the war. He wrote his comments into the speech, but Undersecretary of State Sumner Welles, finding the president's language undiplomatic, struck them out; Roosevelt put them back in.

On this tenth day of June 1940, the hand that held the dagger has struck it into the back of its neighbor.

On this tenth day of June 1940, in this University founded by [Thomas Jefferson,] the first great American teacher of democracy, we send forth our prayers and our hopes to those beyond the seas who are maintaining with magnificent valor their battle for freedom.

Before dinner, Police Prefect Roger Langeron called on Georges Mandel at the Interior Ministry on Place Beauvau. "I'll have completed the job of getting my cabinet colleagues out of town this evening," Mandel told him. "Then I'm leaving." They were alone in the minister's office, an office Langeron had been visiting, he reflected, over a period of thirty years, the last seven as head of the police. Mandel was one of his oldest friends, for they had been together as young men in Clemenceau's cabinet. Now the minister told the policeman, "With the prefect of the Seine district you will represent the government and France in dealing with the invaders. I need say no more. I know you well enough to be sure that you will handle the job well." Langeron replied that the assignment would be possible, if not exactly easy, only if Mandel remained in the cabinet. Mandel assured him that he would.

Langeron had found Paris calm that day. Apprehensive, but calm; no incident troubled public order. The only police problem concerned the columns of refugees from rural France crossing the city. At City Hall, Langeron had consulted with Seine Prefect Achille Villey to find that administrative structures were intact, food supplies adequate. From there he visited headquarters of the Garde Républicaine and the mobile gendarmes, to tell their commanders that their men now formed part of the army of Paris, and were to stay in Paris. The morale of these officers, of the Paris police as a whole, was all one could ask for.

All that afternoon Mandel had been talking to Paul Reynaud by phone. He needed two hours' notice to clear the roads for the premier's trip south to the Loire; precautions were to be taken so that the chief of government did not fall into the hands of enemy paratroopers. De Gaulle joined Reynaud's aides in an effort to persuade Reynaud to set a time for his departure. Reynaud promised to be ready at ten that evening, following his radio reply to Mussolini's declaration of war.

For de Gaulle, June 10 was "a day of agony." He had hoped that Paris would be defended, that a determined military governor would be put in charge of operations. He took a dim view of Ambassador Bullitt, who offered not encouragement but a farewell; de Gaulle was one of those who felt that Bullitt's decision to stay was wrong, for it let the French think that the United States didn't think much of the country's chances.

It was ten-thirty by the time Reynaud and de Gaulle were ready to climb into the limousine that had been waiting and waiting for them. A dozen automobiles formed the convoy, escorted front and rear by motorcycle troopers. They had soon caught up with the southbound traffic. "This immense river of men and machines flows slowly . . . in almost total darkness," remembered Reynaud aide Maurice Dejean. "The slightest sign of headlights brings loud and indignant protests from these people who in their exodus have already been bombed or machine-gunned by enemy planes." The official party got only as far as Orléans that night. Reynaud was put up at the prefecture, sleeping in the prefect's bed.

The question for actors and actresses at the Comédie Française was, should they be considered employees of a state institution subject to evacuation, or civilians expected to stay home? After the final matinee of *L'Avare* on Sunday, director Jacques Copeau told the cast they should plan to leave. They were to keep in touch with a field office in Toulouse, in the event the troupe was to be assembled again. Their costumes were also supposed to go to Toulouse, but with the exodus clogging all roads, that would turn out to be unfeasible. The administrator of the theater, playwright Edouard Bourdet, was driven to Bordeaux, and Jacques Copeau also got away. The theater's account books and treasury reached Bordeaux in the automobile of heiress Mrs. Frank Jay Gould, protected by her American passport.

On June 10, when the financial director of the Comédie showed up at the theater, he was surrounded by members of the stage crew, wardrobe assistants and the like. He explained that the government was closing the theater, but failed to be specific about what its employees should do. Finally the chief of the stagehands asked permission to drive one of the theater's tractors with the trailer used to move scenery. He would drive as many people as he could as far as Etampes, thirty miles southwest, where they could still find trains to take them farther southward. The financial director reminded the volunteer that when *he* had suggested using the tractor to evacuate costumes, the man had said the machine wouldn't survive a fifteen-mile drive. But the chief of the stagehands said he would try.

There were eighty candidates for departure. Since only half that number could fit in the trailer, it was decided to make two trips. But the tractor never got back to Paris; on the return from Etampes a German machine gun opened up on it. Two hitchhikers the driver had picked up were killed immediately; the driver suffered a broken shoulder. The German who had fired on him apologized; when he saw the tractor with the canvas-covered trailer, he had assumed it contained military equipment.

A group of Parisian legislators, all of whom happened to be in a right-wing minority, decided it was their duty to stay behind. Most were also members of the City Council. Calling on Georges Mandel that afternoon, the group won from him the assurance that the government was not ordering legislators to leave, only "urging" them to do so. The senior of these seven stubborn men was Jean Chiappe, himself a former prefect of police; Paul Reynaud sent him a note to approve the group's decision. Soon the members of the group—by then reduced to four—had set up camp beds in City Hall.

Whatever had been said (or thought) until now, it became more obvious with every passing hour that Paris was not going to be defended. But no one bothered to say as much to the people whose responsibility it would be to fight for the capital. It was almost as an afterthought that the supreme commander, General Maxime Weygand, informed Premier Reynaud that the capital was an open city de facto, or, as he put it in his memoirs, "that Paris was an open city in the sense that the capital had no defense of its own, but that it was protected at a distance of some 20 miles, by an advance security zone. . . ."

But the term *protected* did not in fact appear in Weygand's letter to Reynaud of this day, which concluded, "In order to preserve the quality of Paris as an open city my intention is to avoid any defense position encircling the city on the line of the ancient fortifications."

This seemed an incomplete declaration of the city's status, and how would the enemy know? How would friends know? For until then neither Reynaud nor Weygand had informed Paris's official defenders, Generals Héring and Dentz, that they were not expected to fight for Paris, first in the northern outskirts, then at its gates, then street by street. Reynaud did pass Weygand's letter on to the two prefects, and they showed it to the president of the City Council. It may have been an oversight, on a day of confusion, that the military commanders were kept in doubt. It would have been Weygand's job, not Reynaud's, to tell the generals; on the other hand, the decision to declare Paris an open city ought to have been Reynaud's.

35

TUESDAY, JUNE 11

Darkness in midday, strange smoke clouds veiling the sun, the atmosphere charged with soot: images that recur in the memories of those who stayed to witness the last days of free Paris. The curious warping of normal June weather, day turned into night, heightened the perception of doom, the anguish; for those whose minds turned to philosophy, it was a fitting symbol of the fading away of the world's most glorious city, its surrender to the world's most wicked empire. It "announced, without question, some Apocalypse," in the expression of museum curator Yvon Bizardel.

At first nobody knew why it came. Even when daily papers were still being printed, they weren't publishing weather reports that might serve the enemy. *Paris-Soir* had already shut down when editor Pierre Lazareff looked out his window to discover that the sun hadn't risen. "Low in the sky, a thick layer of black cloud hung over the tragic city, as far as one could perceive what had been the sky. And this added to our anguish." Readers phoned the newspaper to report their observations, offering contradictory explanations for the soot-filled sky. Some said that the gas depots just north of the city had been set afire; others thought it was the reservoirs of cooking gas, hit by shells at Saint-Cloud to the west. Lazareff himself believed that the Germans had laid down smoke screens to cover their offensive. A few callers believed that the French had set off the smoke screens themselves, to hide their retreat.

Lazareff was impressed by the woman caller who, "in a voice from the tomb," insisted that it was the beginning of the end of the world and that God, to indicate his displeasure with the folly of man, had banished natural light.

English expatriate Peter Fontaine experienced it as a "peculiar black fog." Peculiar indeed, for it began to come down as speckled rain. Hélène Azenor, the Montparnasse painter, found that her light beige trench coat was "riddled with tiny black points." Literary scholar Henri Quéffelec discovered a "black sun." Emmanuel d'Astier found this new sun "almost supportable to the eyes, as if seen through smoked glasses."

More prosaically, a functionary at City Hall analyzed the phenomenon as "impalpable molecules of soft coal which settle everywhere and blacken everything; hands and face are impregnated with it, walls and furniture stained."

Young Odette Daviet obeyed civil defense instructions to leave windows open (so that they didn't shatter in the vicinity of exploding shells). So she woke that morning covered with soot. American newsman Quentin Reynolds called it a smoky fog "so thick you could reach out and grab a piece of it in your hand." He too believed it was "a man-made fog, a smoke screen thrown over Paris to hide the railroad stations from the bombers."

Observant Florence Gilliam, longtime American resident in Paris, had first spotted the phenomenon the previous evening at about seven; it was then a pall of smoke. Next morning she and friends woke "coughing with the black soot they had inhaled all night, to find the high brilliance of the sun reduced to a sulphurous glow, like the ominous light before a hurricane."

Even a military man could be fooled. "It was an emission of artificial fog of the kind the Navy uses," Major Georges Benoit-Guyod noted in his diary. "My orderly, a former sailor, gave me this explanation and it was subsequently confirmed. The fog was made by us, not the enemy." He was to revise that judgment. "It seems that yesterday's cloud came from Rouen, where enormous quantities of fuel have been set afire." Police Prefect Roger Langeron hadn't been given any better information. After speculating on the possibilities, he told his diary that he was informed that the cause was German bombing of gasoline reserves.

If Parisians couldn't read about their fog, Americans could. In New York the *Herald Tribune* was able to publish a very precise account by Paris correspondent Walter Kerr. "At 9 a.m., from the Rond-Point on the Champs Elysées, it was so smoky that you could not see the obelisk on the Place de la Concorde or the Arc de Triomphe at the Place de l'Etoile," he reported. "The smoke began to pass away about eleven o'clock, and before noon it had been cleared away by a fairly strong wind, and the sun shone. It was hot the rest of the day."

"I see that in blowing my nose I come away with a tinted handkerchief." That from airman Pierre Mendès France, who knew the detail was important. (But he too thought that the Germans were using smoke screens to facilitate their crossing of the Seine.) When Interior Minister Mandel arrived in Tours, he and his party were "black as coalmen," so one of his secretaries remembered.

In his report to the *New York Herald Tribune*, Walter Kerr described the smoke cloud as observed by everyone. In his personal notes he remembered waking with the taste or "feeling" of the black dust. Later he would watch the unbroken file of refugees crossing Place de la Concorde, fascinated by this parade of old-fashioned farm wagons, each drawn by three horses in single file. As cars broke down they were abandoned right there, on the broad boulevards; their owners simply pursued their journey on foot. Kerr saw two women driving a donkey cart, another woman with four dogs on a leash and a suitcase in each hand, other men and women with pushcarts. He wondered where they were going. To Bordeaux, perhaps. But could you walk four dogs or shove a pushcart to Bordeaux?

Men and women in the subway on the edge of tears: the vision that appeared to writer Victor Serge that morning. He heard what they were murmuring: "Those rats!" For the newspapers proclaimed Italy's entry into the war—the dagger in the back. "One morning paper expresses everybody's thought," noted Pierre Mendès France, "in condemning 'those who stole clothing from the wounded.' "

* * *

Despite all, there were people who came back to Paris that day. One was Léon Blum, who at the urging of well-wishers had left town on Sunday. This party leader often criticized for a weak response to Fascist aggression, notably in Spain, in the name of the pacifism then dear to French Socialists, was now a fighter. He was disappointed that the Reynaud cabinet hadn't seized the initiative by declaring war on Italy first, instead of waiting for Mussolini to choose his day. France could have attacked across the Alps and won decisively.

But he'd had what he called an "irresistible desire" to return to Paris. A political friend had told him that the ministers of war—that was Reynaud himself—and of the navy and air had postponed their departures. He had felt ill at ease as an escapee, and now wished to become involved. His friend Marx Dormoy, who had been interior minister in Blum's cabinet in 1938, decided to return to Paris with him. They drove the 180 miles from their relatively safe haven in Montluçon in south central France. As they crossed the Loire River at Sully, engineer troops were mining the bridge, and there were soldiers everywhere, roadblocks, a barricade in the Fontainebleau forest. They took a detour to Paris via Melun, and Blum's knowledge of terrain he had walked and biked through helped them now. Still, the last miles, bucking the exodus of civilians, were rugged. They entered Paris from the east to find empty streets, shuttered shops, and shut windows. The chief activity seemed to be the loading of automobiles and motorcycles and motorbikes in front of apartment houses.

Blum and Dormoy called on a friend on Rue de Varenne. Here they remarked that no one was loading up a car, but this was because residents had long since abandoned the neighborhood. A few policemen stood guard at the Italian Embassy. Blum made use of his friend's telephone: no reply at the premier's office, at the War and Interior ministries, or at Reynaud's flat. Finally Marx Dormoy was able to reach Police Prefect Roger Langeron, and learned from him that Paris was now in the care of Langeron himself, Seine Prefect Achille Villey, and the military governor. Langeron, who was touched by this call from men he respected, invited them to lunch at a restaurant near the Madeleine church, Lucas-Carton (then one of Paris's best, with three stars in the Michelin guide). On the way, Blum and Dormoy discovered astounding scenes of desolation. Blum was reminded of Strasbourg, which had been officially evacuated, and where the commanding general had taken him on a tour of the empty city. Paris, after all, had not asked civilians to leave.

They drove up to a shuttered Lucas-Carton, the owner standing outside in the uniform of an officer. "Can't you give us something to eat?" "Impossible—all my people have gone." They were directed to nearby Rue Boissy d'Anglas, where a bistro favored by theater people was still serving (even if Michelin gave it only one star). At that point Prefect Langeron showed up. Over lunch—meatless, to respect the Tuesday rule—the politicians questioned the policeman, "as if we had left Paris long weeks ago," remembered Blum. With the government gone, Langeron found it difficult to keep up with the military situation.

But he did believe that Paris was to be defended; the official position on that hadn't changed. And still it was as if the official position had not been intended to be taken seriously, for where was the defense? Blum wondered whether the government had dropped the idea of military protection in order to preserve this beautiful city.

Langeron urged Blum to explain the dilemma to the government—if there was still time. Meanwhile he suggested that they call on General Héring at the Invalides. "Think of yourself," Langeron begged Blum. "Protect yourself. Consider yourself in danger. It's your duty to the country." His warning was actually directed to both men. Blum survived the occupation; Marx Dormoy would be killed a year later by French Fascists he had brought to justice before the war.

On their way to the Invalides, Blum and Dormoy stopped at the American Embassy. Bullitt received them at once. Blum had felt close to the American ambassador from the day Bullitt arrived in Paris. The diplomat told his visitors that he expected the Germans in Paris any day now, any hour. So what would he do? "What a question! I'm staying. As you can see, the house is full of Americans I have to help get out of France, with visas, cars, gasoline. I'll do what I can for everybody, but for my part I'm staying." He admitted that he had minced no words in telling President Roosevelt of his decision. "If you cable me to leave, I shall disobey you," he said he had told his president, who had replied, "All right, Bill." The State Department was asking him to leave; he refused. And he was sure that Roosevelt was still thinking, "All right, Bill." He'd stay as long as he was needed. "There are things I can prevent with my presence, and if I can't prevent them, I must at least bear witness to them."

They embraced, Blum and Bullitt, as if they might never meet again.

The Invalides, at least, was alive. Blum found General Héring "as calm and serious as ever, with his face of a professor with spectacles." The officer explained that he was leaving Paris to take command of the army defending the city in the northwest, an army now under attack on the Seine near Vernon, on the Oise at Persan. The ranks were thinning out, the men sleeping on their feet.

Although Blum now saw the question as academic, he asked all the same about the defense of Paris. Nothing, officially, had changed, said Héring; there had been no order to evacuate or even to prepare for the departure of the military garrison. Communication with headquarters on the Loire was difficult and rare. Héring had tried to reach Weygand by phone and had barely been able to hear his voice.

Blum couldn't help saying that Paris could and should be defended, as it had been in 1914. The troops now in the north could take up positions in and around the city; this would represent the pivot of French defenses. He felt that Héring agreed with him.

Dormoy took temporary leave of Blum to drive to the Belleville blue-collar neighborhood to pick up the mother of one of his staff at the Montluçon town hall (Dormoy was mayor). He returned to tell Blum that he had discovered a quarter as lively as it had ever been. Parisians living on small budgets hadn't gone away.

There were other round trips that day. Actor Jean-Louis Barrault, attached to a camouflage unit as befitted his stage experience, took advantage of a mission to Paris to call at his home, hiding under the canvas top of a military truck. His unit was to begin its retreat anyway, so he didn't see himself as a deserter. The truck drove him through the mysterious black smoke, which now covered the road as a fog. They reached Paris at seven in the morning. There he discovered that actress Madeleine Renaud, whom he was to marry—the wedding had actually been set for Friday, June 14—had already joined the exodus, on orders of the Comédie Française. He wandered through the apartment, trying to decide what he would take with him, finally settling on a notebook with a flower from their garden slipped between the pages. The truck returned to pick him up; when it stopped again he peered out to find himself at the gate of Père Lachaise cemetery, where his mother had been buried the previous year. The driver gave him time to place the flower he had plucked on his mother's grave.

Jacques Cléret de Langavent, junior officer in a battalion of tanks—in fact part of Colonel de Gaulle's Fourth Armored Division—was at once courageous and devil-may-care, as befitted the scion of the upper class. On a reconnaissance patrol he found himself face to face with five German motorcycle troopers; he immediately shot down three of them and took two survivors prisoner. But his unit was in full retreat; Cléret's commander told him there wasn't much they could do with prisoners except to take them along.

The itinerary of their retreat took them into Paris. What to do with two enemy soldiers? Cléret took them home—to the home of an aunt, as it happened, where he knew he'd get food and a bed. His prisoners dined at the table with him, and they too slept over. Next day the insouciant officer pursued his journey southward, turning the Germans over to a military police officer at Chambord.

When he met another soldier from his division, Henry Lemarié, Cléret's tunic still showed bloodstains from the skirmish with the motorcyclists north of Paris.

From the sixth of June the Saint-Denis Hospital in Paris's working-class northern suburb was part of the war zone. This meant a new assignment for Dr. Pierre Daunois: henceforth he was to receive and examine wounded soldiers before sending them on to the appropriate military hospital for treatment. Even if the team at Saint-Denis had wanted to, they couldn't do more, for the two doctors—Daunois and his captain, Louis Digonnet—had a single assistant, a civilian nurse who administered anesthetics. Since there was no relief crew, they were on call round the clock, gulping down meals, dozing when someone from the medical ward could relieve them.

They followed developments at the front through their patients. On June 7 a charming English girl drove up in her ambulance with eight

Senegalese soldiers wounded during a skirmish at Grandvilliers, twenty-five miles south of Amiens, meaning that the front had been breached. Then the wounded began arriving in greater numbers, sometimes by ambulance, more often in trucks or requisitioned private motorcars. Most of the soldiers had been hit by aircraft guns, or antipersonnel bombs dropped from Stuka dive-bombers.

On June 10, a day marked by soot-colored sky, Daunois's wife, a nurse at the Beaujon-Clichy Hospital, turned up with a colleague. The two women were leaving for the Corrèze mountains despite Daunois's plea that his wife didn't have the right to abandon her job in the emergency ward. Paris was now prey to the panic that had stripped northern France of its civilians. Then, on the eleventh, the Digonnet unit received a group of soldiers wounded by warplanes on the road near Pont-Sainte-Maxence. They had been crammed into a truck normally used for hauling sand.

There were fourteen soldiers in all. After a rapid examination, Daunois determined that five were seriously injured, beyond the capabilities of Saint-Denis. He had them sent on to the Foch Hospital, aware that it was a race against time. The nine others could be saved if operated on at once, with immediate blood transfusions; if they were sent away, at least half would die. Daunois found Captain Digonnet and told him the story. The officer reminded him that their orders were that they must not perform surgery, but to do the dispatching to hospitals that could. But when he saw Daunois's reaction to that, he added that to operate on nine seriously wounded men filled with shrapnel demanding detailed X-ray examination would require ten to twelve hours of continuous work. "Yes, Captain, but if we don't operate on at least the worst cases they'll die." "Then get them in here, call the staff together, and we'll operate."

They began that afternoon at four, continuing into the night, completing the job at six the following morning, working with aides who had long since finished their tours of duty. There wasn't sufficient blood for transfusions, so members of the operating unit volunteered theirs, while staying on the job. A nurse gave a total of 800 grams while continuing to work. Daunois expected her to faint and asked one of the male nurses to keep an eye on her, with a chair ready to slip beneath her should she weaken. They managed to operate on eight soldiers, saving all of them. The ninth was still on a stretcher in the corridor when Digonnet collapsed. Daunois explained the situation to the wounded soldier, who replied, "I'll wait; you've already done so much." Daunois himself stretched out on a cot, too tired to remove his surgical smock spattered with blood or even, he realized, his nasal mask. At 9:00 A.M. he was shaken and told that a general officer of the medical corps had arrived for an inspection. Unshaved, in his bloody smock, Daunois was obviously a disturbing sight; the senior officer asked to see the captain. Both Digonnet and Daunois received a scolding for operating without orders. "What will you do with your patients when the Boches arrive—tomorrow, perhaps?"

The captain replied sharply that he did not expect the Germans to cut everybody's throat. He and his assistant had acted according to their consciences, and that was as good as the rules. He turned to his assistant to say, "Daunois, you will continue the visit with the general; I am very tired and I am going to rest, because we have more hard work to do."

The general was speechless. When Digonnet walked out of the room he told Daunois, "Your captain has a truly bad character." So Daunois told him the whole story—about how long they had been standing at the operating table, about Digonnet fainting. He added, "My captain is not an ordinary captain." Indeed, he was a full professor at the Faculty of Medicine, his father-in-law was a director of the Pasteur Institute, *and* he was a friend of the head of the army medical corps. At the end of his tour of inspection the general asked Daunois, "Will you ask Professor Digonnet to come to see me before I leave?" It was to apologize, and to agree that they had been right to proceed as they had. So the two doctors went in to operate on the remaining stretcher case, and on three additional wounded soldiers who had arrived that morning.

Bill Bullitt had a brainstorm. At ten that morning he was drafting another Personal and Secret cable to his president.

> In order to receive messages from the United States after occupation of Paris and possible destruction of our official radio receiving set at the Chancery, it is suggested that commercial radio

stations broadcasting shortwave programs to Europe broadcast
such messages at the end of their normal broadcasts. To let us
understand that the message is designated for us, have the announcer broadcast: The following is from Pearl Smith to her
mother, father, etc. The employment of any girl's name will
signify that the message is intended for Paris and of course the
same message should be broadcast several times at different hours
to ensure reception on our ordinary radio sets.

There is evidence that the American government took him seriously; the State Department, so a note in the National Archives tells
us, contacted the Federal Communications Commission, which in
turn passed the word on to private radio stations. The system was
never used.

At noon the American ambassador had a still more solemn announcement for Washington.

I have talked with the Provisional Governor of Paris, who is the
single governmental official remaining, and it may be that at a
given moment I, as the only representative of the Diplomatic
Corps remaining in Paris, will be obliged in the interest of public
safety to take control of the City pending arrival of the German
Army. . . .

I shall, of course, refrain from any proposals to do this unless
it should prove to be absolutely necessary in the interests of
saving human lives. Incidentally, Reynaud and Mandel just before their departure requested me to do this, if necessary.

An American taking control of Paris . . . In this penultimate hour
the flamboyant ambassador was at his best. He told his listeners, an
official Washington straining to hear anything one could say about
Paris:

The Germans are now approaching my house at Chantilly and in
my garden is the last line for the defense of Paris. In this city
today . . . there are sights that tear the heart. . . . I cannot

exaggerate what it has meant to those who stay behind to know that I am here.

The defense line running through his garden was the little river called the Nonette.

Bullitt had some things to ask for, such as aid for French and Belgian refugees. Roosevelt was to have requested funds from Congress, but then postponed his appeal because the American Red Cross was asking for voluntary donations. But Bullitt knew that the Red Cross ship hadn't even left the United States. (On June 7 *Le Figaro* reported that the first Red Cross ship carrying food, medicine, and clothing for refugees, the *McKeesport,* would sail only the following week for Bordeaux. At that point seven million dollars had been raised in a campaign that set as its goal twenty million.) "There are now six million persons in southwestern France who will die unless American aid for them is organized immediately with the utmost efficiency," cabled Bullitt. He considered the negligence of the American Red Cross "criminal," its officers incompetent. He wished to see the task wrested from that organization, to be given to the best available admiral. At least two ships a week must dock at Bordeaux. "You cannot tolerate today the incompetence of any individual or organization which is preventing supplies from reaching dying French men, women and children." If that was not the way to talk to a president, it ought to rouse the attention of his subordinates.

Bullitt didn't impress Jean Chiappe and other members of the Paris City Council who called at the embassy that day. As diehard rightists they tended not to like what the Third Republic was up to, and had resolved—a hard core of them—to stay on with the people of Paris. As deputy and councilman Noël Pinelli remembered the meeting with Bullitt: "This man whom we knew had done all he could to push France into the war received us almost in good humor." Bullitt told them that the fighting had reached the estate he rented near Chantilly, and he found that funny (or so Pinelli understood). The ambassador led the delegation on a tour of portraits of his predecessors as ambassador, repeating that none had ever abandoned the capital. He too would stay.

* * *

Prefect Langeron remembered something else about that day. He had been warned that his predecessor Jean Chiappe, whose reputation had been made for all time when he leaned toward the extreme right during the antiparliamentary riots of February 1934, expected that the German occupation forces would appoint him governor of Paris. Langeron had little sympathy for Chiappe, whose son-in-law's neo-Fascist weekly *Gringoire* attacked him regularly, but he refused to believe that Chiappe intended to become "master of Paris" with German backing. So Langeron got him on the telephone, and assured him that they were in this together. Chiappe took that well. Later in the year the Vichy regime appointed him High Commissioner to Syria; on his flight to Beirut an RAF fighter shot his plane down.

"The capital has retained an appearance of serenity," journalist Jacques-Henri Lefebvre observed. "It's only in the railroad stations that you find disorder and panic." A writer in *Le Temps,* now published in Angers on the Loire, described a Paris "emptied of all those not responsible for its preservation and defense." In some ways the city had been purified; bawdy night life, for instance, had disappeared. Parisians refrained from their reputed mocking humor.

> There are no longer any foreigners. Those who came to town for high and joyous living have stayed home. Those who came to Paris for work and learning have left the Latin Quarter. Those who came for business and fashion, what would they do here now? . . . We are alone with ourselves. . . .

One stranger was still around: correspondent Sergio Bernacconi of the Fascist daily *Giornale d'Italia*; he describes that day darkened by smoke (he thought that fleeing French soldiers had set fire to oil reservoirs). As the day went on, the sound of shellfire became more intense—the enemy approaching. French fighter planes could no longer be seen, reported Bernacconi, and for three days running there had been no air-raid sirens. The city was now considered lost; no one bothered about it anymore. Tumultuous, clamorous Paris no longer existed, and the silence was the most impressive, the saddest thing.

Was this enemy softening? Not really, for Bernacconi goes on to describe the martyrdom of Italian residents of Paris and its region, who had been herded into the Buffalo Stadium (where German refugees had been taken the previous month). The head of the Italian Catholic Mission had turned up at the arena demanding to be interned; his place, he said, was with the prisoners. Few women had been arrested, noted Bernacconi; most of those inside the stadium were there because they hadn't wanted to be separated from their husbands. Their tears, said the correspondent, were testimonials to the health, solidarity, and morality of "our race."

Inside the Italian Embassy on Rue de Varenne, the situation hadn't improved. The second-in-command of the Brazilian Embassy had managed to talk his way inside, to find 120 Italians virtually interned— the embassy staff and guests. The Brazilians carried in some food (and, a grateful Italian ambassador reported later, refused payment). The problem for Italian ambassador Raffaele Guariglia was that he no longer had a Quai d'Orsay to complain to. He had to persuade hostile police to help him locate relatives of embassy employees and escort them to the Rue de Varenne. Thus he brought in ten Italian nuns from Vitry-sur-Seine, ten more from Noisy-le-Grand, others from Saint Vincent de Paul hospital in Paris. Room was found for all the sisters on the embassy grounds. Guariglia hoped to keep everybody there until the Germans arrived, for that seemed less perilous than evacuating personnel and families on a train vulnerable to attack. But the French police wanted the Italians out immediately.

After receiving orders to report for duty at the Bordeaux air base, Pierre Mendès France took a moment to reflect—as he packed—on the "moral divorce" between those who were leaving Paris, or trying to, and those staying on. "These last already feel alone. With the public authorities, the government, the press, the capital gives the impression of being abandoned."

For someone like Mendès France, born and raised in Paris, leave-taking was bitter. As he looked around his apartment he wondered who the strangers were who would profane these rooms and their familiar objects. Wondered also when he would see them again. What I am seeing now, he thought, I'll never see again. A loved one found after several years of separation is no longer the same.

*   *   *

Peripatetic Peggy Guggenheim later confessed that she had not done much to be proud of during these weeks. She had a new man friend, a married man she just calls Bill. She sat in cafés drinking champagne with him, doing nothing to alleviate the misery of the refugees she could see all around them.

She did have one of the great collections of contemporary art, and hoped she could hide it in one of the caches to which the Louvre was evacuating its collections. But curators of the museum said her art was too modern—not worth saving. The paintings not worth saving included a Kandinsky, several Klees and Picabias, one each by Gris, Léger, Marcoussis, Mondrian. There were Surrealist works by Miró, Ernst, Chirico, Tanguy, Dalí, Magritte, and Brauner. Among her sculptures were works of Brancusi, Lipchitz, Giacometti, Moore, Arp. In the end her friend Maria Jolas, who had rented a castle at Saint Gérand le Puy near Vichy (where she watched over fugitive James Joyce and his family), agreed to store the Guggenheim treasures in her barn. The Germans never bothered to look inside. Then Miss Guggenheim herself, with maid and Persian cats, drove off in her Talbot in the direction of Megève. By the time they reached Fontainebleau they were barely averaging a mile or two an hour.

Victor Serge, who until that moment had thought he could hang on in Paris, making enough money to survive by writing for the left-wing press, realized that there was no longer a reason to wait. Paris had become a vast departure lounge. The writer in him couldn't fail to record his last images of Paris—the bluish smoke, of course, deserted shops, "people on doorsteps listening to the distant sigh of cannon." Down below in the subway he detected "animal anguish." Métro trains were delayed; he, his companion Laurette, son Vlady, and a Spanish comrade decided to walk. "An atmosphere of mutiny around the Gare de Lyon, for there are no more trains, they say, in any case no more room in the station. . . ."

While wondering how they would ever get out of town, Serge and his party suddenly found themselves before the open door of a taxi. Laurette had been waving and waving for one on the deserted boulevard, and then this one-eyed driver stopped for them. It turned out that he had slept all day and didn't know what was happening; he was just coming out for his night on the job. First Serge asked him to drive to a station—but there were only the crowds, no trains. Then, for a fee, the driver agreed to take them all the way to Fontainebleau. That got them on the right road. After that it was hitchhiking, camping along the way, telling each other that they were living "an end of the world combined with an involuntary vacation."

From the diary of Englishman-in-Paris Peter Fontaine:

> Troops come drifting into the capital, stragglers without rifles, ragged and dispirited—many of them wounded. A defeated rabble! Some are drunk and babble wild, incoherent tales of the rout. There are shouts of "Down with war," etc.
>
> At the offices of the Southern Railway near the Madeleine a small knot of stranded Britishers—men and women, on the verge of panic—are besieging a lonely official who is engaged in locking up the premises.
>
> "No trains at all—we can make no arrangements or reservations—the authorities have left us high and dry—go and see for yourselves at the stations," he keeps reiterating to their clamorous questioning.
>
> "Caught like rats in a trap," says one of them.

One foreign institution occupied a singular place in Paris, indisputably American, rigorously nonofficial. At the American Church in Paris, a Protestant institution, pastor Clayton E. Williams spent a good deal of his time in early June ferrying Americans who considered themselves vulnerable out of Paris. In his absence he was replaced by Edmund Pendleton, who had been the church's organist and music director since 1934, and who was to stay on as director of this institution during the early months of German occupation, leaving Paris only when the United States entered the war. Now the church was a shelter, for its own personnel first of all. Kazar Nergararian, a Frenchman of Armenian origin, had been its custodian for a decade. When he learned on June 11 that the village outside Paris to the north in which he resided was to be evacuated by the army, he appealed to

Edmund Pendleton for help and got it—not without some hesitation, he later recalled. Next day, while Nergararian was on duty at the American Church, his family and neighbors received orders to leave their homes within two hours; they simply closed the doors and began walking toward the city. Nergararian took his family into the church house, where they took over classrooms, sleeping on chairs or on the floor, with use of a kitchen. Pendleton moved up to the pastor's large apartment, which had space for a British woman who had been a member of the choir, and her mother and her sister. The three women kept the pastor's quarters in running order. Pendleton spent the final hours before the arrival of the Germans going through papers, destroying everything that might be seen as anti-German.

Paul Léautaud's village, although not north of Paris, was emptying all the same. "If this continues," he told his diary, "there won't be many more people in my street." First the neighbor to his left had gone, then the neighbor to his right, she with her "three abominable screaming brats." Also the tax collector, and a couple employed in a defense factory—obliged to follow their plant south. Everyone left one or more cats and a dog, asking Léautaud to make sure they were fed.

The gardener of two wealthy women living close to Léautaud's house had gone off that morning on foot, with wife and child, pushing their belongings in a wheelbarrow, not knowing where they would wind up. His employers asked Léautaud to take their dog; he refused.

He rode the suburban Métro line into Paris that morning to walk about as usual. On Boulevard Saint-Michel, at his subway station, there was a steady stream of vehicles of all kinds, automobiles piled high with baggage, trucks, bicycles, pushcarts with dog attached, farm wagons, one of them with half a dozen cows tied to it. Later, on Boulevard Saint-Germain, Léautaud saw a man on a bicycle, his belongings secure behind the saddle. In front, sitting on a blanket before the handlebar, a small dog was perched; he seemed happy. Léautaud couldn't help calling out a compliment to the man, a simple worker, for taking his pet away with him.

When he spotted milk trucks bearing the names of villages in the Eure district northwest of Paris he thought, The encircling of Paris has begun. In the Métro he found evacuees from Pontoise who were crossing Paris to find a train at Massy-Palaiseau that would take them southward. Where would they all find a place to stay? he wondered.

He would stay. He had always known he would, he was surer now than ever. He didn't want to give up his pets. He didn't know where he'd go. He had a bad character; he couldn't live just anywhere, with just anybody. He wanted to be sure his house wasn't looted. It was not a matter of bravery; rather was it a mix of sangfroid, reason, indolence, and a don't-give-a-damn attitude. He took precautions, stocking up on tobacco as he had already done on coffee.

"It is forbidden to weaken," so Marcel Jouhandeau resolved. "Faced with the migration of a whole people marching under our windows, we are holding each other tightly. . . ."

> Suddenly a wagon stops and the whole procession is blocked: a woman stands in the middle of valises and a moving farmyard. She shouts that she has lost her little Louise, and everybody in her group turns back toward Neuilly, calling Louise as horses whinny and horns are tooted; stray farm dogs throw themselves at the gates of houses along the street as they let off a death howl.

Ilya Ehrenburg now spent much of his time in the relative security of the Soviet Embassy on Rue de Grenelle. He heard the rumor that the USSR had declared war on Germany, and that was greeted with obvious enthusiasm by workers outside.

Sometimes he left the embassy to watch the exodus; it could be observed at his favorite cafés in Montparnasse. "Opposite the Rotonde café stands the statue of Balzac by Rodin," he remembered. "A mad Balzac seems to want to step off his pedestal. . . . Suddenly it seemed to me that Balzac was also leaving, with everybody else."

On his own Rue de Cotentin the corner grocer abandoned his store without even closing the door. Bananas, canned goods were strewn about. This wasn't departure, thought Ehrenburg, but running away. The radio was broadcasting contradictory messages and appeals, he noted. Some called for an orderly evacuation of Paris, others recommended staying home and remaining calm.

*   *   *

It depended on which radio program one tuned in. At his morning meeting with his propaganda aides in Berlin, Joseph Goebbels ordered the underground stations broadcasting in French "to spread panic by every means."

A Parisian landmark, the *Herald Tribune* was then the French edition of the famous New York newspaper of that name. It had its own publisher in Laurence Hills, a patriarchal figure who made his own rules. He didn't want to shut down, for example, when all the other Paris dailies were closing and moving. To the consternation of his assistant, he planned to produce the paper even when the Germans occupied the city. That would certainly mean a loss of independence, and might even compromise the survival of the Paris edition when the Germans were driven out.

So from New York the paper's owner and publisher Ogden Reid settled the matter in a peremptory cable to Hills on June 7:

DO NOT BELIEVE HUNS WILL REACH PARIS THIS CENTURY BUT IF THEY
SHOULD YOU AND MRS. HILLS SHOULD BE ELSEWHERE. WE WILL NOT
PRINT PROPAGANDA AND UNDER INVASION COULD NOT PRINT
NEWSPAPER.

This was the signal for remaining staff to leave. Yet when the French government ordered the press to suspend operations, Ambassador Bullitt won special permission for the *Herald Tribune* to continue—for at least one more day. The final issue, put together on June 11 for printing in the early hours of June 12, was a single sheet, and only the top side contained news. There was one signed story, by Walter Kerr—who in fact was reporting for the New York edition—on the exodus. Kerr observed, on one of his last visits to the Paris edition, that the military censors were still at their desks ready to censor— probably because no one had remembered to tell them to move out along with everybody else.

Since the regular delivery service no longer had any trucks, the paper was not distributed to regular outlets. It was time for the last holdouts to pick up and go. Some, along with correspondents of American newspapers and magazines, had taken advantage of the sailing of the SS *Washington* from Bordeaux. Among those who had stayed were the correspondents of the Associated Press, the United Press, and the *Chicago Tribune,* plus Walter Kerr, the Paris *Herald Tribune's* stubborn Laurence Hills, and a sports columnist of the same paper known as Sparrow Robertson.

Seen from the German side, the Battle of France hardly concerned Paris alone. The front was broad enough to encompass the French capital, but also to circumvent it, as the Germans advanced to the east and west of the city. Again it was the Panzers that proved Germany's best weapon. French defenses were most efficient in populated areas; the Germans had their way on open ground. Battle records, division logs, show that German forces continued to meet heavy opposition on June 9 and 10. Then, on the night of the tenth, the Germans reached the Aisne River, and after their crossing the French side could no longer offer credible resistance. By the morning of June 11 the Germans had also crossed the Seine at Elbeuf, Les Andelys, and Louviers. To the east they had taken Reims. There was nothing for the French to do now but to retreat in orderly fashion, protecting as much of the heartland as possible.

For the French could no longer put a first-class army into the field between the enemy and Paris. The so-called Army of Paris consisted of the 84th North African Corps, a group certainly in fighting form, but hardly prepared for the Blitzkrieg. They were now reinforced by a reorganized Tenth Corps of Moroccans and Senegalese. Another group, the 25th, assigned to hold the Oise River line, consisted of men salvaged from the decimated Tenth Corps, and another North African division mixing Frenchmen, Algerians, Senegalese. They all fought well, but with no hope of winning. Meanwhile German propaganda would glory in this evidence that France was defended by inferior races.

When General Weygand reached Briare at dawn on June 11, he found the staff at the new headquarters working under less than ideal conditions. (He lived and worked at the castle of Muguet, some miles out of town.) Weygand was soon hearing enough about the military situation above Paris to convince him that he had been right to withdraw from the capital. The Germans advanced steadily, unspectacu-

larly but steadily, north of the city, east and west of the city, with no
chance that the French could stop them. Rather than wait for rout,
Weygand chose orderly retreat, giving him a hope of saving the army
for the defense of what he called "the heart of the country," which no
longer included the country's capital city.

By now France's governing bodies were spread out along the Loire
valley over a wide area. The distance from Georges Mandel's Interior
Ministry in Tours to Briare headquarters was 115 miles along the best
local roads. Paul Reynaud was settled into a museum piece of a castle,
the medieval-style Chissay, east of Tours. Arriving at Langeais, a
small, attractive castle town with abundant castle lodgings and castle
offices for the Foreign Ministry, Reynaud's deputy, Paul Baudouin,
spent the morning learning how to communicate with the rest of the
government. Thus Foreign Ministry offices were installed in the nearby
Châtagneraie castle, which had only one telephone line (connected to
the Langeais post office). To contact other components of government
one was better off visiting them in person, fighting traffic all the way.
One of Baudouin's first visitors was Sir Ronald Campbell, the British
ambassador, in search of the latest news. Baudouin had none to give;
Campbell proved to have more, thanks to a field radiotelegraph unit
set up in his nearby castle embassy; he was in direct touch with
London.

Churchill found his way to the French, all the same, his plane
making a wide detour around German-held territory, protected by a
dozen Hurricane fighters. Before taking off he cabled Roosevelt:

> Everything must be done to keep France in the fight and to
> prevent any idea of the fall of Paris should it occur becoming the
> occasion for any kind of parley. The hope with which you inspire
> them may give them the strength to persevere. They should
> continue to defend every yard of their soil. . . .

On the flight over France, General Spears observed a frowning
Churchill, ruminating on the imminent tragedy, and then, at the
deserted Briare airstrip, brightening as he was greeted by the French
as if he were absolutely delighted to be at that particular place at that
particular time. The prime minister discovered that the castle in which

the heads of the French and British governments were to spend a momentous evening possessed a single telephone—in the lavatory. "It was kept very busy," he remembered, "with long delays and endless shouted repetitions."

He made it clear at the outset that whatever happened, Britain would continue the war. He even hoped that the Germans would attack Britain to give France some respite. And then he asked the French, point-blank, to defend Paris. Should the Germans then try to take the city, they would have to fight house to house, thereby pinning down considerable forces. He reminded his hosts of Clemenceau's vow: "I shall fight before Paris, in Paris, and behind Paris." That did not go down very well with his French listeners now.

In turn, Generals Weygand and Georges described the dimensions of the disaster. After praising the heroic French effort, Churchill wondered if the line could be held a while longer so that Britain could put its own troops back in the field. He remembered the dramatic turnaround in the First World War. Weygand agreed with the British position. But they only had hours, not days, and in the present war the French had no defense against the enemy's combined air and tank offensive. It was when he opened the door to a possible armistice that Reynaud jumped on him. That was a political decision, not within the competence of the military. Churchill wondered whether they could pursue the war with guerrilla tactics, at least in those parts of France where such a thing was feasible. Pétain replied that this would lead to the destruction of the country.

Just before noon an emissary of General Héring, General Emile Barazer de Lannurien, had turned up at Weygand's headquarters in Briare to try to find out precisely what was expected of the Paris command. Was Héring supposed to move out at the head of an army, or sit still in the Invalides? Weygand told Lannurien that Héring commanded the Army of Paris and would "follow its fate," whatever that meant. The general-in-chief was giving Héring's previous responsibility as military governor to General Dentz, so it was Dentz who would remain in the Invalides, even if the Germans entered the city.

But would Paris be defended? For this was the question Héring wanted answered, this was why Lannurien had traveled all the way down from Paris. Now, for the first time telling Paris what Paris was to do, Weygand said he intended to declare the capital an open city. This meant that the approaches to the city would not be defended, that nothing inside the city was to be destroyed, that retreating French troops could not march through Paris, but would have to find their way around it.

To Weygand's thinking, Paris would have had military significance as a bridgehead, had the French been able to hold along the Seine downstream from the city, and on the Marne. But once the Germans had shown that they could penetrate French defenses, and when it became clear that Weygand couldn't marshal sufficient troops to throw them back, Paris could not and should not be held. Should not, because of what that would cost in lives and national treasures. There had been combats at the gates of Paris in 1814, and the city had been besieged in 1870, with minor damage. Modern warfare would inflict enormous destruction.

The dialogue between Weygand and Lannurien continued as they strolled in the castle garden. Elsewhere in the same garden, Paul Reynaud and Philippe Pétain were also pacing the ground as they waited for the arrival of Winston Churchill. Weygand brought Lannurien over to Reynaud and told him and Pétain what he had just decided to do about Paris. Neither Reynaud nor Pétain reacted; they simply yielded to what had become obvious.

So General Lannurien made his way back to Paris, arriving at Invalides headquarters at ten-thirty that evening. He brought no written instructions, but could give Héring an oral report of what he had elicited from Weygand. It was, of course, Héring's first official notification of the status of Paris as an open city, as well as his first indication that Dentz was taking over as military governor. Later Héring would say that he spent that night asking himself whether to obey; the idea of running out on Paris was too much for him. But at one that morning a report came in that the Germans had reached Evreux, behind his left flank. That was the signal for him to move; he could not let the bulk of remaining French forces be enveloped because of a breach in his front.

*   *   *

In Washington a president who was having second thoughts about his ambassador's decision to stay in Paris drafted a message to William C. Bullitt. He strongly recommended that the ambassador follow the other ambassadors to France's temporary capital, but he did grant his friend the final decision, "and assume you will make your decision in the best interests of the United States and of humanity." But Roosevelt couldn't see Bullitt acting in the place of the French as governor or guardian of their capital city. "No authority can be given to you to act as a representative of the French government or local government but, again, being on the spot, you will, as a red-blooded American, do what you can to save human life."

36

New Yorkers woke to the headline:

GERMANS AT THE MARNE, PARIS BARRICADED;
BRITISH RAID LIBYA, ITALIANS BOMB MALTA:
U.S. CLOSES MEDITERRANEAN TO OUR SHIPS

Parisians woke to almost no headlines at all. Of the score of Paris dailies, only the one-page *Herald Tribune* could be found at a few major boulevards near the Place de l'Opéra. It was dated "2 A.M. EDITION," fifty-third year of publication, number 19,244. Number 19,245 would appear on December 22, 1944, four months after the liberation of Paris. A headline crossed the front page:

ITALIAN BOMBERS TAKE WAR TO ASIA, AFRICA;
GREAT BATTLE FOR PARIS AT CRUCIAL STAGE

There was also a ray of hope:

ROOSEVELT PLEDGES
ALLIES UTMOST AID

Walter Kerr told Parisians what they could see for themselves, that their city was virtually deserted. (He had actually written his story for American readers.) "Fouquet's went out of business yesterday afternoon. Hotels are closing fast, the Plaza Athénée today and the Crillon tonight or tomorrow." He mentioned the American flags at the windows of American citizens (but also over the Belgian Embassy, now under American protection). Men were still digging air-raid shelters near the Grand Palais exhibition hall.

Overleaf there were only a few small advertisements, one for Tiffany, the jewelers on Rue de la Paix, another for the National City Bank of New York on the Champs-Elysées (calling attention to its safe deposit boxes); the Rue de Rivoli bookstore W. H. Smith and Sons advertised its tearoom. There was a listing of forthcoming sailings of Italian steamships.

By afternoon, as a lifebuoy thrown to drowning men, vendors were offering a newspaper in French. It was the product of volunteer crews of three daily newspapers that normally competed, *Le Journal, Le Matin, Le Petit Journal*; they called it *Edition Parisienne de Guerre*. Readers starved for print found the usual single sheet printed on both sides. Alongside the date, June 12, there was a "Number 1," as if there might be a number two tomorrow.

HOLD   ALL

ON   THE SAME

readers were exhorted from the top of the front page. The main story told of violent attack, valiant counterattack; there was a hopeful headline:

American Opinion

Evolves Rapidly

In Favor of the Allies

Thanks to the departure of the army, *Edition Parisienne de Guerre* was unique in another way: it was published without censorship. One of the things the editors could now talk about was the weather, usually

a taboo subject in wartime. So there was news of yesterday's "apoca-
lyptical sky"—the smoke fog hiding the sun. Parisians wondered, said
the editors, whether the cause was a smoke screen, or a fog caused by
the constant flow of automobiles through and out of Paris (clearly this
writer had no answer to the riddle). The paper also passed on advice
from the military government: young men not yet of draft age but over
seventeen should evacuate the Paris region. And all men who had been
exempted from military service because of war work were to leave
Paris, unless they served in the police, the subway system, or the gas,
electricity, waste disposal, or water services. The prefecture of police
had issued a requisition order to all bakers, pharmacists, food stores.
Vendors in any of these categories who ceased activity were subject to
prosecution.

Overleaf, a brief item reported that a man riding the subway dressed
as a monk had been heard to say that Russia had declared war on
Germany, which (he added) proved that Maurice Thorez and André
Marty—two Communist leaders then fugitives in Moscow—had been
quite busy. The same rumor, said the newspaper report, had been
heard on another subway line. The writer said that the false report had
first been broadcast on the German-controlled Brussels radio.

Advertising in *Edition Parisienne de Guerre* seemed left over from
prewar times: a lotion to prevent gray hair, a kennel selling both
watchdogs and household pets, a potion against rheumatism.

In Berlin, Propaganda Minister Goebbels had important things to say
to specialists who were broadcasting to the French. They were to
criticize those who sought to fortify Paris and thereby resist the German takeover of the city; they were to call for peace demonstrations to
"avoid the worst."

Goebbels asked his military liaison to find out from Hitler's High
Command whether the German attack forces preferred that Paris civilians evacuate the capital or remain in place; future broadcasts would
be planned to conform to the desire of the military. This, said Goebbels, was the moment for all-out effort. It would be the crowning of
the work of many months if they succeeded in "unleashing revolution
in Paris."

*　　*　　*

Stay-behind correspondent Walter Kerr, who was paid to know what was going on, realized that he no longer did. He did not know, for example, where the front was. Still didn't know if Paris was to be defended by the armies that presumably were now falling back under the German assault. In a cityscape of straggling soldiers, refugees in a still unbroken column crossing from north to south, Kerr decided to call on the American ambassador. Bullitt was too busy with a continuous stream of visibly anxious visitors, so Kerr went to see Colonel Horace Fuller, the military attaché. "I think I've got it figured out," said the officer (who on earlier visits had appeared less certain). He rose from his chair and walked over to a wall map. "I've been wondering where the French armor is—why it hasn't counterattacked. But I now think it's concentrating over here," he explained, pointing to an area about a hundred miles southeast of Paris. "I expect it to hit the German flank any time now, perhaps today or tomorrow."

So there was hope. Comforted, Kerr went over to the Invalides to find that General Héring and members of his staff had left. Was it for the north, repeating the move of Gallieni in 1914? No one seemed to know. Or to the south? Several noncommissioned officers shrugged their shoulders, and then nodded—affirmatively.

Pietro Nenni visited the headquarters of the exiled Italian Socialist Party at 103 Rue du Faubourg Saint-Denis. There he was informed by fellow Socialists of the French police roundup of Italian nationals. One of the group had been slapped by an angry Frenchman, but that was an isolated incident. Italians were being asked to declare their loyalty to France, which Nenni felt was a generous way for the French to treat his countrymen. They were not being required to join the army.

But it was time for him to leave all the same, to join his family at Alençon. The French government had made it relatively easy for this eminent opposition figure to escape the Nazi invaders; he was booked on an evening train for Tours. By then a light rain was falling. He drove through an empty city, even up in working-class Belleville, but the impression of abandonment grew as he passed Place de la République, continuing west along the boulevards to Place de l'Opéra. There he found the usual traffic policeman, whose white stick was guiding not fancy motorcars but "a picturesque chariot drawn by oxen." And then the expected mob scene at the Gare d'Austerlitz, with shouting, swearing candidates for departure, wailing children, grumbling older people. His train got under way four hours after the announced departure time, with long and exhausting stops, incessant complaints, always the crying children. Nenni was shocked by the reactions of fellow passengers. Workers spoke of revolution, but it sounded to Nenni like a form of complaining.

Seen from City Hall by financial director Eugène Depigny, June 12 was the last day of massive exodus, the day when even small shopkeepers got into their pickup trucks to drive off. Everything one heard confirmed the impression that Paris would be a battlefield, the city to be defended street by street. Everyone knew that men were out in the suburbs digging trenches. That was evidence enough, evidence that was nevertheless creating doubts, worry, simple fear—because one could see how inadequate the preparations were after all.

No one anywhere near Paris was producing food now, no food was coming into the city, stocks were diminishing, distribution systems had all but shut down. There would be no more fresh milk, for example, no more meat. The small farms surrounding the suburbs had been abandoned; lettuce and peas stayed in the ground. That morning at the eastern and western gates of the city, flower vendors were selling small carrots from the suburban farm patches; lines formed until supplies ran out. That evening Eugène Depigny's favorite bistro could offer only an onion broth and noodles. An hour later the owner of the establishment was driving out of town with the neighborhood fruit and vegetable dealer—who had been the last surviving shopkeeper in the neighborhood. Concerning the city as a whole, the military supply service had been evacuated, leaving behind only a couple of days of foodstuffs, which, thanks to the city's reduced population, could be stretched out to six or eight days. The prefectoral decrees requisitioning food stores covered shops in which condensed milk, flour, and fresh and refrigerated meat could still be obtained. The two prefects added a personal touch to the official language of the requisition:

> We remind you that every shopkeeper, like all citizens, should remain at his job, today more than ever. Economic activities

continue normally. . . . The authorities will provide the necessary protection to all those who do their duty.

Surprisingly—it was a surprise for the police prefect, who watched them daily—food prices remained stable. Few sought a quick, illicit, unpatriotic profit. Miraculously, too, there was no health crisis, no epidemic. First-aid stations staffed by civil defense authorities, as well as the police prefecture, kept close watch. Stocks of pharmaceutical products were requisitioned, guaranteeing that there would be no interruptions in delivery during the exodus. Because of the decline in population within the city, there was actually less serious disease being reported than in normal times.

The police continued to watch the city's prostitutes, sufficiently so that there was no discernible increase in venereal disease. Abandoned dogs were picked up as insurance against an outbreak of rabies.

The desertion of Paris by the well-to-do, while less fortunate citizens remained to face the Germans, was to provide ready-made propaganda to the enemies of Republican France. Less than a month after the Germans marched in, a pro-German Paris weekly, *La Gerbe,* published what it said was the letter of a twenty-five-year-old Parisian describing these days:

> I grabbed my bike to take a little ride. I covered all of the 8th and
> 16th *arrondissements* of the city, the center, the 9th and 10th and
> a bit of suburb. This is how it was: In wealthy neighborhoods,
> nothing, not a soul, all the windows shut tight, especially in the
> 16th. Lots of people in lower-class neighborhoods. It was the
> people of Paris who stayed. . . . Those who have a wallet instead
> of a heart and who tremble for their lousy golden complexions
> were gone. We don't want to see them come back. Working
> people who don't let themselves be influenced by propaganda
> remained faithful to their duties as Parisians. . . .

Police statistics, which show that only 983,718 people remained in Paris on June 26 of a prewar population of 2,829,746, are eloquent. Only 24.9 percent of the population of the upper-class sixteenth *ar-*

rondissement remained. The fourth *arrondissement,* with its rundown streets and lower-income population (including much of the city's Jewish population), retained 45.9 percent of its peacetime population.

Odette Daviet was fifteen in June. She had received her elementary school diploma that spring and would have continued school if the arrival of the Germans hadn't put an end to that dream. She lived with her parents on Rue Charlot (another less-privileged neighborhood, only a couple of streets from the fourth *arrondissement*). Her father refused to believe that his family was in danger; not even a fifteen-year-old female. He said, "You mustn't listen to what people say." They were a close family; they'd stay together. They didn't own a radio, got their news from the street, also from newsreels at the movies—which means they received an optimistic interpretation of events, and accepted it. Communiqués always said that the French were withdrawing to prepared positions.

As early as the Munich crisis in the fall of 1938, the Daviets were stocking up on sugar and cooking oil (they simply didn't have the cash to hoard other things). They saw themselves as lucky—not to be bombed. (On June 3 they weren't even aware that an air raid was going on.) Those who were leaving Paris, they believed, were those who happened to have ties to the provinces. Odette Daviet and her family were 100 percent Parisian without relatives anywhere else, so where could they have gone? Papa was called up in 1939; already forty-five, he was assigned to guard duty at the Gare de Lyon, but had already been released before the German offensive began in May 1940.

The Daviets were not Jewish, but many Jews lived in their neighborhood. Those who could leave had already gone. But even some of the Daviets' Jewish friends refused to believe that the Germans could capture Paris, or, if they did, that they would bother Jews or anyone else. Some Jews who left Paris soon returned—under the German occupation. There had been an Italian family in their building; it disappeared when Italy declared war.

Marcel Jouhandeau, one of the survivors in the affluent sixteenth *arrondissement,* walked to the post office on Rue Saint-Ferdinand to mail a package. Just as he arrived—a little before noon—the iron shutter was being rolled down. Postal employees were embracing, sobbing as they embraced. It was not "just" panic flight, Jouhandeau told his diary, for even those who had been most determined to stay were now on their way out. On broad Avenue Malakoff only one shop remained open—apart from the faithful pharmacy.

On a corner of the nearby Avenue de la Grande-Armée, Jouhandeau watched as a woman waved to a passing soldier on a bicycle. At once the man jumped off the bike and began shouting that she had given a Fascist salute. Jouhandeau intervened to prevent a veritable lynching.

Paul Léautaud was in Paris that morning to observe the flow of refugees along Boulevard Saint-Michel; he continued to be attentive to those with household pets. He spoke to a farm couple, husband and wife each leading a horse cart, with a cow attached to one of them. Where were the dogs? They were in another cart, the farmer assured him; they'd catch up with it at the Porte d'Orléans. Léautaud hadn't asked about cats; everyone left those "poor creatures" behind.

The city and its immediate surroundings seemed protected by a cocoon, one that the enemy made no effort to penetrate. Rather than pushing due south to the capital, the Germans continued to gain territory east and west of Paris. To the east, Guderian's armored columns had broken through in Champagne, reaching the gates of an important junction town, Montmirail. To the west the Germans crossed the Seine at Vernon, threatening Evreux.

This, decided General Weygand, was the signal for the retreat he had spelled out in his directive of June 11. He now told General Georges to execute the order. The Germans didn't know, of course, precisely what Weygand was planning. On this twelfth day of June it still looked from their side as if Paris would be defended. German divisions positioned to move against Paris from the north continued to meet artillery fire. When they advanced they encountered concrete pillbox defenses, trenches, barriers of felled trees reinforced with barbed wire.

Soldier Wilhelm von Schramm, his army's bard, was present at General von Küchler's headquarters when a noncommissioned officer in charge of the radio burst in. He had just picked up a broadcast on the official Paris radio that suggested, without saying so outright, that Paris was an open city. Yet reports from the front continued to indicate resistance; German units crossing the Nonette and Oise rivers were meeting enemy fire. That afternoon von Schramm saw some of the action for himself. The bridge at Creil was under French fire. Then another bridge at Pont Sainte-Maxence was attacked by low-flying French planes. None of this suggested abandonment.

On the Loire that morning, Churchill and his party had a final meeting with the French over breakfast. Returning to the matter that troubled him, Churchill asked why Paris and its suburbs couldn't be used as an obstacle to cut enemy lines in two, slowing the German advance as in 1914, or in the way Madrid served Spanish Republicans in the recent Civil War. And would not that allow time for a French-British counteroffensive on the Seine west of Paris? Couldn't the French hold out at least until the United States entered the war?

For his part, General Weygand saw no objection to planning for a counteroffensive. He simply didn't see where the troops would come from. Reynaud again pleaded for more British air support, and Churchill promised to submit the request to his War Cabinet as soon as he returned to London. But he did think that it would be a fatal error to deprive Britain of its vital defense force. Reynaud put in helpfully that the real problem was the need to manufacture more warplanes, and here the United States with its vast industrial potential was their only hope. Churchill promised to make that point to Roosevelt.

And indeed Churchill took up the French request with his War Cabinet that very afternoon. He was not optimistic about French chances, although he thought that if the front collapsed, Reynaud might turn to Charles de Gaulle for leadership. (Clearly Churchill had been impressed by that junior general.)

And he sent the promised message to Roosevelt, urging the American president to help Reynaud's resolve to fight on. "If there is anything you can say publicly or privately to the French, now is the time."

At lunch, Reynaud recalled later, Weygand blurted out, "The country will not pardon you if, to remain faithful to England, you turn down a chance at peace." Pétain agreed.

In Paris that morning General Henri Dentz was mulling over the dilemma in which he had been placed. He had been brought back from a command on the eastern front to assist General Héring in the defense of Paris, had then been appointed to replace Héring as military governor—at the very instant Paris was declared an open city. He had become its chief only to surrender Paris. Since Héring's emissary to Weygand, General de Lannurien, was returning to Briare that morning for further instructions, Dentz wrote out an appeal to the commander-in-chief, asking him to appreciate the lamentable situation in which he had been placed. He wished that Weygand would reconsider the decision; at the very least he desired written confirmation of his status.

When he read that letter, Weygand decided to reply by telephone all the same. "My decision is final: you must stay in Paris." Later Weygand would say that he had handpicked Dentz for the job precisely because of his authority, his spirit of sacrifice, his sangfroid.

Weygand's instructions as to the status of Paris, telephoned at fifteen minutes after noon on June 12 and recorded by Héring, were as follows:

1. Paris is declared an open city.
2. There will be no defense on the outskirts, or on the city's rim, or inside the city.
3. There will be no destruction of bridges and no defense preparations within the city.
4. In the event of retreat, fighting troops must not cross the city.

The general-in-chief was not, at least not now, calling for immediate withdrawal of French forces holding the line north, northeast, and northwest of the city. But he did ask Héring, if his army failed to hold along the Nonette River, to withdraw to the capital's "safety" position, which, at Aulnay-sous-Bois, for example, was a scant nine miles from the Gare du Nord inside the city. And then—for of course there would be a "then"—the French were to retire to a line extending from the Rambouillet forest to Juvisy-sur-Orge; both of these positions were *below* Paris.

"To defend Paris would have given the city up to fire and destruction without the slightest utility," Dentz would confide to his own notebook. "As to having the people of Paris take up arms—and what arms?—to resist tank divisions which had just chopped up French armies—such talk would only have led to a massacre."

The decision had been Weygand's, and he stuck to it, later justified it. Thanks to Paris's status as open city, it would be the only great European capital to conserve its beauty intact.

General Héring was now to join his active command. But he knew what that meant. Weygand had employed a euphemism in speaking to Dentz on the telephone: "The commander of the Army of Paris follows the movements of the army group." Movements now meant nothing more or less than retreat. At six that evening Héring bid farewell to Dentz at the Invalides, turning the city over to him. He understood what was going on in the mind of his successor, but Dentz uttered no protest; he was, decided Héring, a good soldier. At the end of the war, when Dentz went on trial for treason, accused of aiding the Germans fighting the Free French and the British in Syria, Héring testified on his behalf. Dentz received a death sentence that Charles de Gaulle commuted to life; Dentz died not long after that in a prison hospital.

Prefect Langeron drafted a message to be plastered on the walls of the city.

TO THE
PEOPLE OF
PARIS

In the grave circumstances now being experienced by Paris, the Prefecture of Police continues its mission.

It must preserve security and order in the capital.

We shall carry out this duty until the end.

Parisians, I count on you, as always, to facilitate my task.

Count on me.

Once more I assure you of my deep affection and total commitment.

Roger LANGERON
Prefect of Police

Paris, 12 June 1940

At the Invalides the military governor's deputy, Colonel Groussard, had identified a source of trouble: French deserters fleeing from northern battlefields, but also workers who had been recruited for the defenses hastily being erected north of the city. He had arranged to have this unwanted population shunted off to camps in the suburbs of Colombes, Maisons-Lafitte, and Massy-Palaiseau. Within three days the camps were saturated, and there were no officers available to lead the soldiers back to the front, no arms to give them, no trains to move them south. But it was vital for order and tranquillity that the "horde" now gathering above Paris not enter the city. If it did, from the point of view of the military government, one could fear the worst. Colonel Groussard ordered that fugitives be channeled not through but around Paris.

The forces of law and order could hardly be content with their mission. Ferdinand Dupuy, chief clerk of the police station on Place Saint-Sulpice responsible for the sixth *arrondissement,* knew that city patrolmen had expected to be evacuated from Paris along with other official corps. Individual policemen had actually packed suitcases to be ready at a moment's notice. But now, on June 12, they had this circular signed by Prefect Langeron:

> My dear friends,
>
> In the grave circumstances now being experienced by Paris, we have received the order to pursue our mission.
>
> We must preserve security and order in the capital.
>
> We shall carry out this duty until the end.
>
> Once again, dear friends, the people of Paris counts on you.
>
> Once again your Prefect assures you of his confidence and deep affection.

Despite the warm tone of the message—and Ferdinand Dupuy could not remember any other quite like it—its meaning came as a shock. The government was asking some fifteen to twenty thousand men, most of them armed or able to bear arms, to place themselves under the thumb of the Germans. Some policemen grumbled that they'd leave all the same, if only to join the army. Some did leave, despite the best efforts of the district commissioners.

Langeron was well aware of what was going on in the minds of his men; he understood the pressures being brought to bear by families, friends, neighbors. He called a meeting that very night of as many men of all ranks as could fit into the main auditorium of the prefecture. About a thousand officers showed up, a capacity crowd. Langeron explained the position of the government. He too hated the idea of sitting to wait for the enemy's arrival, but the police had a duty to protect Parisians, even to protect them from themselves—which meant to prevent them from causing incidents that would bring German reprisals, and to watch for looting. Langeron would facilitate the departure of certain family members, young girls for example, and mothers of young children, as well as men from Alsace-Lorraine, and all officers who had handled espionage cases. (Many of these men were to refuse to leave all the same.) But everyone else had to stay and serve.

The men seemed to understand. The meeting ended with cries of "Long live France!"

Roosevelt's directive to Bullitt, sent from Washington the previous evening (when it was already close to sunrise in Paris), was decoded and read by the ambassador at breakfast. He penned the most eloquent reply he could under the circumstances.

He began by reminding the president of an evening they had spent together at the White House over two years earlier, during which Bullitt had said that he was sure there would be a war and that the Germans would threaten Paris, the State Department would want Bullitt to leave, and Bullitt would not leave. He had then said to Roosevelt that he hoped he would not be given such an order, for he would have to disobey it. Roosevelt had promised, during that evening discussion, that Bullitt would not get any such order. "As I said to you when you telephoned me the night of Sunday the ninth, my deepest personal reason for staying," pursued Bullitt, "is that whatever I have as character, good or bad, is based on the fact that since the age of four I have never run away from anything." He added, "If I should leave Paris now I would be no longer myself."

And if this sounded too much like forging national policy out of capriciousness, Bullitt set the record straight:

> I am certain it is my duty to stay here.
>
> This Embassy is the only official organization still functioning in the City of Paris except the Headquarters of the military forces Governor and the Prefecture of Police.
>
> Thousands of people of all nationalities, French, Canadian, English, Belgian, Rumanian and even Italian are turning to us in despair for advice and comfort. The fact that I am here is a strong element in preventing a fatal panic.

He might soon be of even greater use, he added, for General Héring was to withdraw with his army, leaving General Dentz in charge.

> Owing to danger of fire and mobs, they have decided to leave the policemen and the firemen of the city at their posts until the Germans shall have occupied the city fully. They have stated to me that at a given moment—not far off—they will ask me in writing, as representative of the diplomatic corps in Paris, to act as guardian of the civil authority of this community during the transition from French Government to German military occupation, and to treat [sic] the General commanding the German forces for the orderly occupation of the city.

Bullitt even thought of broadcasting a message announcing that at a specific time an American Embassy automobile would drive slowly along the road to Chantilly. In it would be the American military and naval attachés, prepared to discuss the orderly transition to German rule. Bullitt believed such a procedure would save thousands of lives; he hoped the president would not object.

He used every argument, every entreaty, his imagination could command. "The French are still holding the line of the Nonette in my garden at Chantilly but the Germans have crossed the little river near Senlis and the position is difficult," he reported to Roosevelt. "The French all along the line are fighting with the same incredible courage in the face of four times their numbers."

He was sure that Tony Biddle could handle contacts with the French government at Tours.

> I have said nothing in this cable about the tradition that the American Ambassador does not leave Paris. Remember Gouverneur Morris and his wooden leg in the Terror, Washburne in the Commune, Herrick. It will mean something always to the French and the [United States] Foreign Service to remember that we do not leave though others do.
>
> J'y suis. J'y reste.
>
> Love to you all.

Late in the afternoon the ambassador called on Prefect Langeron to confirm his intentions. "We are bound by friendship," Langeron told his diary. "Cordial, courageous, intelligent, he is a man with his heart in the right place. We work together warmly."

Apart from the help Ambassador Bullitt and his staff could offer, there could be little protection now for British subjects, for if the United States was a neutral nation, Britain certainly was not. Englishman Peter Fontaine was to spend the day in an attempt "to beg, borrow, or steal a car and petrol," as he told his diary. He was not going to succeed. He walked over to the British Embassy, where he saw files stacked outside the office of the military attaché. The porter told him that the remaining staff expected to retreat well beyond the French government's temporary quarters at Tours.

Out on the street Fontaine watched as military trucks picked up men not quite of military age—to get them out of the city.

Bertha Pons was a British subject who hoped to stay, for she had a reason: her husband was a French soldier at the front. But the day came when even she knew that it was time to go. When she called at the British Embassy that morning, she found no one who could help her. She was told to go around the corner to the American Embassy, which was taking on the task of putting British civilians on a train for Saint-Malo on Brittany's northern coast, from which harbor they could sail across the Channel. But a train for Saint-Malo had been strafed by enemy planes, so no more trains would be dispatched in that direction. Next day on the way to the American Embassy she saw posters proclaiming Paris an open city. Finding no other way out, she and her mother-in-law packed bread and sardines and rode off on bicycles, until the traffic bottleneck forced them to walk.

Florence Gilliam was one of the Americans who stayed, after watching so many of her countrymen leave. Addresses were exchanged, last wills and testaments verified. She wondered about all those Americans who, like herself, preferred to remain in their beloved Paris. For some it was a kind of duty; they had enjoyed peace and pleasure in France, and could not desert in time of danger. "But for most of them it was the sort of feeling that had kept some of the French from joining the exodus," she decided, "the thing that keeps people living on the slopes of a volcano, because it is their volcano."

Yet there were good reasons for leaving, even if one was a Swiss journalist unlikely to suffer under the Germans. Edmond Dubois later realized that he had left "because Paris had suddenly changed: One can't imagine how the street sweeper and the woman selling newspapers can stabilize confidence in a street. The day when the sweeper doesn't show up, the newsstand remains closed, the street becomes tense. . . ." Late that day, Dubois came upon a herd of cows roaming freely on Place de l'Alma in the heart of an elegant neighborhood (the cows happened to come from the nearby Ferme d'Auteuil). The animals were hungry, and their mooing raised sad echoes on the deserted streets. The rare passerby hardly bothered to look. It was probably this vision, he thought later, that persuaded him to go.

If we believe Sergio Bernacconi, writing for *Giornale d'Italia*, his countrymen rounded up at the Buffalo Stadium still had not been given anything to eat after forty-eight hours of confinement. He blamed it on the collapse of the French administration. Rumors were flying, duly recorded by the Fascist correspondent: various political as well as military leaders had been shot, journalists had been shot; generals had committed suicide. Léon Blum, a rumor had it, was in Paris setting up a provisional government that would hand over power to the Germans. Bernacconi thought this last report might be true. Fearing the people's anger, the Italian imagined, Blum would throw himself at the mercy of the Reich to save his skin.

Sergeant Guy Bohn, an attorney in civilian life, now assigned to the legal section of the Engineers, learned that morning that what remained of his corps was to be evacuated by truck convoy to Royan, on the Atlantic coast. Immediately after lunch he was called to the office of the corps commander, Colonel Albert Regimbal, on Rue de Grenelle, steps away from the War Ministry. Regimbal had a job for him: Bohn was to blow up the Eiffel Tower! The structure happened to hold the highest, most powerful antenna in France, a vital asset in military communications. Bohn's first reaction he kept to himself: Why me? By military standards he was an old soldier, having passed his thirty-third birthday. The son of a naval officer, Sergeant Bohn had applied for officers' school when he reached military age, but was deemed unsuitable because he couldn't tell his left hand from his right. That didn't keep him out of the Engineers, where he learned a good deal about explosives. During the phony war he was on the Luxembourg front, but after a lung infection that winter he was brought back to Paris as unfit for active duty, where he was given legal work that made use of his civilian skills.

He told the colonel, calmly and with proper respect for rank, that he was not the right man for the job. It belonged to an officer directly attached to the district Engineers. Regimbal replied that he didn't have a choice, for all the men now under his command were reserve officers, older men from other services who couldn't handle explosives. Bohn was the only noncom with qualifying skills. There had in fact been someone else, but he had been sent to blow up a bridge west of the city, in the path of the German advance.

Still Bohn insisted, respectfully, that he could not do the job—certainly couldn't do it alone, without a team of sappers. Then he'd need the plans of the tower, if only to see whether emplacements for explosives already existed. And even then the job could take a couple of days. Perhaps they could concentrate on the north pillar, the one nearest the Seine, since prevalent winds were south-southwest. If the explosives were powerful enough the tower would be knocked over; otherwise it would only lean, but even in this case the damage would be critical. He compared it to the condition of a car smashed up in a collision. That would end broadcasting from the Eiffel Tower.

When it was built, the Eiffel Tower was the tallest man-made structure in the world, at 984 feet (the Woolworth Building, New York's first skyscraper, stood 792 feet tall). It was also easy to discover that the Eiffel Tower weighed 15.4 million pounds, contained twelve thousand metal parts, rested on four massive concrete blocks, each 280 square feet in surface, plunging up to forty-six feet into the ground. Although the tower hadn't been conceived as a transmitter by its creator, Gustave Eiffel, back in 1889, this utilization occurred to the pioneers of radio in the early twentieth century. In the prewar decade it became the world's highest antenna, one of the world's most powerful transmitters, with a cable measuring the height of the tower plus another 410 feet underground. Even before the First World War the transmitter could reach France's distant colonies and, with a relay network, linked Paris to military installations along the frontier with Germany. Indeed, this newly discovered use for it saved Eiffel's folly from demolition early in the century.

Sergeant Bohn raised another point with the colonel. Paris had been declared an open city, which meant no act of war was allowed. Blowing up the Eiffel Tower would certainly be considered one. Noncom Bohn would himself be held liable, especially because of his detached status.

He could raise technical questions, and legal ones. What Bohn could not do with a colonel, he knew, was to address the other question: How can you blow up the symbol of the City of Light?

The colonel broke the silence. Sergeant Bohn was to remain at headquarters to await further orders. And at three he was called back to the colonel's office. They wouldn't blow up the tower after all, but simply destroy the wireless facilities at the base. But there was something else Bohn could do—something only he could do now. He was to proceed to the fort of Issy-les-Moulineaux, a mile south of Paris, and blow up the military wireless installation there. Its strategic importance was considerable, as the relay to French forces in the Middle East.

Bohn saluted, marched out, and discovered that no transport was available to take him to the fort he had to blow up. So he rode the subway to Place Balard on the city's southern rim, looked for a taxi—vain hope. Desperate, he flagged down an automobile that turned out to be an American Embassy vehicle. The chauffeur was a young woman. "I've got to get to the Fort d'Issy right away to blow it up before the Germans arrive," he explained to this representative of a nation he considered almost an ally. "The Germans are pretty close," the woman agreed. She followed his directions to the fort, which was set on a rise, but stopped at the bottom of the hill, unwilling to go farther because of U.S. neutrality. He climbed the final five hundred yards on foot.

What he found when he got there was a facility consisting of twin steel towers 150 yards apart, each tower 230 feet high and topped with an antenna. He noted that the towers resembled the awesome Eiffel Tower, and each had the same curved legs. So he did what he would have done at the Eiffel Tower: he played the winds, placing explosives—melinite in small sticks—under the pillars opposite the prevailing southwest winds. There would be more melinite for the transmitting equipment. A captain from the general staff of the Engineers showed up, approved Bohn's plan, and drove him back to Paris to report and to collect the required explosives. In a headquarters virtually deserted they found a senior officer attached to the military government who approved the plan and even urged immediate execution, as if that needed to be said. Bohn took the opportunity to comment that it seemed late to be carrying out demolition on such a scale, given Paris's status as an open city. The officer agreed, but added that the strategic importance of the transmitters overruled such reservations.

So the hapless sergeant found himself on the street, again on foot. He walked over to the barracks on Boulevard de Latour-Maubourg to draw the supplies he needed—explosives, cord, fuses—but how to carry them? The man in charge wouldn't give him a truck; they were getting ready to evacuate. Bohn had to threaten to appeal to headquarters before they'd lend him a vehicle. He sat beside the driver, who grumbled all the way about the dangerous material he was being asked to carry. Bohn placed the box of detonators of mercuric fulminate on his lap to isolate them from the explosives in the rear. As they drove out of the city Bohn took a moment to reflect on the absurdity of his position. He was pretty sure that if he carried it off he'd never get official recognition.

It was 7:00 P.M. when they reached the fort. He got to work at once, largely by guesswork, for the manual he had flipped through during a short supper break had been published in 1890. At ten that evening, messages were still coming in from the Eiffel Tower for relay by short wave to Beirut. They were to encode and dispatch all telegrams by 1:00 A.M., after which the transmitters were to be put out of action.

As Bohn began placing his charges he heard distant firing, and wondered whether the local gendarme detachment was already defending the fort. And then at one the operator sent out the last message: it was time to inform French facilities abroad that the station was closing down. "I can't make them understand it's all over," the operator told Bohn. There was no code word for the fall of Paris. That part of the message was sent in clear, by a radio man visibly affected by what he was telling the world.

So was Guy Bohn, now alone in the fort with the radio operator and a handful of soldiers to assist him. They attacked the transmitters with hammers, and ripped out electrical connections. By 2:30 A.M. the first stage of the job was done. In the distance, machine-gun fire broke the night's silence, seemingly closer all the time. Bohn found the kitchen, made himself a snack. There was a cot in the guardhouse, and he snoozed for half an hour.

First light came at four. Bohn used a cigarette to ignite the safety fuse, and, when he was sure it was burning, began to run. He counted off 110 seconds before the blast—a single dry burst, followed by a shower of metallic debris. That for tower one. When the second tower hit the radio room it inflicted further damage to the transmitting facilities—an unexpected dividend. But there was more to do, for the transmitters themselves were dug into the stone bastion. Bohn had his helpers soak the rooms with gasoline; the melinite would do the rest to ensure that abandoned documents were destroyed. When he could, Bohn returned to the compound to inspect the crushed pylons, the demolished buildings, and the gaping hole where the main installation had been.

He was back at the Eiffel Tower at eight-thirty that morning, and was told to stand by as the engineer unit destroyed underground installations, using sledgehammers and not explosive charges, as well as the generators on the lowest platform of the tower itself. Then the antennas were simply cut up.

The officer in charge of the Fort d'Issy eventually wrote out a demolition report citing Sergeant Bohn's courage and initiative. But as he had predicted, he never got a true citation, nor did he tell the story to anyone outside official channels. Later, when he asked for authorization to enter the fort to see what remained of it, permission was denied.

At 6:30 P.M. on June 12, in President Lebrun's chambers at the castle of Cangé, solemnly protected by two ushers who in happier times stood guard at the Palais de l'Elysée, the French cabinet convened in the presence of the general-in-chief. Asked by Lebrun for a report on the situation, Weygand began by recalling his recent memoranda assessing French prospects, warning of the consequences of failure. Things were even worse now than they had been when he submitted those reports, with Paris outflanked, a total absence of reserve troops. Only a cessation of hostilities could save the rest of France from invasion, and keep French forces intact. If the battle continued, he predicted rout and disorder—among civilians as well as soldiers. It was time to sue for peace. "You must feel," he concluded, "how hard it is for me to say something like this. It was I who in Foch's name dictated the armistice terms to the Germans in 1918. I was a victorious general, now I am a vanquished and dishonored general. I have only one desire: that a bomb fall on me so that I exist no longer."

Reynaud didn't like that kind of talk. Weygand may not have succeeded, but he had saved French honor. Pétain, alone among ministers present, agreed with Weygand that it was time for peace terms. Weygand asked to be allowed to withdraw, feeling that some of his listeners were mocking him, but Lebrun assured the general that he had been heard out with respect.

There was no decision that night.

Colonel Jean Perré would later be remembered as anti–de Gaulle, a tactician who saw tanks only as an auxiliary of infantry, not as a decisive element in an offensive. Later Perré was a staunch supporter of Pétain at Vichy, commander of his personal guard.

But now, in June, Colonel Perré was an admired officer. And it was the patriot in him that ordered his command car to stop at the Arch of Triumph on the night of June 11. He got out to pay his respects to the Unknown Soldier under the monument. How could a patriot allow this tomb to fall into enemy hands?

As soon as he reached his new headquarters at Arpajon, below Paris, Perré sent a staff officer back to the city to take up the question with the military government, the prefecture, even with members of the city council remaining in the capital. And that night—the night of June 12—Perré was back, this time with other senior officers including Colonel Adrien Roche, commander of the Second Tank Brigade. Colonel Roche's chauffeur, Eugène Goormachtigh, who was also his colonel's secretary, waited in the staff car as the officers debated at the foot of the monument—alone. For there was no longer any movement on the always-busy square or on the twelve surrounding avenues. A circle of small lanterns surrounding the arch was the only light source, throwing long shadows behind the clustered men, while the flame of remembrance continued to flicker. For Colonel Roche's driver it was a solemn, deeply felt funeral service. Colonel Perré contributed to the solemnity by saying a few words of homage, but his voice broke.

The officers pursued their discussion. They wanted to exhume the Unknown Soldier, and do it while a drum and bugle corps stood by. They had other plans. . . . But soldier Goormachtigh was convinced that nothing would happen that night.

For one thing, even if the authorities remaining in the city approved the plan (and this symbolic defiance might be interpreted as a violation of Paris's status as an open city), the division lacked equipment to lift the sealed marble lid or to raise a heavy coffin; the engineers were already far south of the city. It was nearly 3:00 A.M. when Perré called his officers to attention, asking for a minute of silence. Then the little group returned to the staff cars. As they rode off, Eugène Goormachtigh was thinking: Let the Unknown Soldier continue to mount guard. It was a symbol the enemy dared not touch. The Germans would be awed in its presence.

37

THURSDAY, JUNE 13

When reports began coming in to field commanders, then to headquarters on the Loire, it became even clearer than it had been that
Paris was not all. The enemy hadn't concentrated the flower of its
striking force, its best armored divisions, for quick and brutal seizure
of the capital; for the Germans, the Battle of France was a whole.
Now, for example, the enemy was moving to end even symbolic
resistance of French troops holding the Maginot Line. General Heinz
Guderian's Panzers were driving not through the Ile de France—the
petals protecting the Paris flower—but farther east along the Marne,
the intention being to cut off the retreat of French units moving
toward the so-called French heartland. That retreat became rout. The
armored group commanded by General Paul von Kleist moved due
south along a line stretching from Epernay and Romilly to Auxerre. So
neither von Kleist nor Guderian would enjoy a well-earned triumphal
entry into Paris.

To the northwest, crossing the Seine, the enemy now entered
Evreux, descending along the western flank of the city. French forces
until then positioned north of Paris respected Weygand's order for-
bidding them to cross the city as they retreated. Thus the "position
of Paris," in the military phrase, was abandoned. The city was truly
open now.

The man destined to test Paris's defenses, or absence of defenses, was Georg von Küchler, commander of the German 18th Army, who had already distinguished himself by smashing Dutch resistance. He might have marched into Paris at the head of his troops, almost did it this morning along the main highway from Senlis. He actually drove past the first troops of the advance division, the 87th, in an open staff car, but scattered fire at Saint-Witz, a bare eighteen miles from the capital, changed his mind. Still, Paris was the next stop. "Paris, unrealized dream of the First World War!" meditated one of von Küchler's junior officers. "Starting in midmorning, full of pride and with fast-beating hearts, we could see the city spread out before us—the outline of the delicate Eiffel Tower, the heavy white marble dome of Sacré Coeur, monuments which grew as we advanced mile by mile."

At the village of Louvres they encountered French resistance, quickly came to terms with it. More at Roissy-en-France (not yet the site of a great airport), and at Villepinte. The men of the 87th Infantry Division found that they could all but ignore enemy defenses now. It sufficed to push on without paying attention, then to brandish white handkerchiefs as an indication of what the adversary should be waving. Had they stopped to respond to French shelling they might have found themselves engaged in a firefight, slowing them down and perhaps stiffening enemy resistance.

By six that afternoon advance German units—tanks and reconnaissance troops—joined up on the north bank of the Ourcq Canal near Sevran (today only minutes from Paris by rapid transit). German tanks quickly secured the railway bridge in the center of the village. The bridge over the canal, however, was being doggedly defended by riflemen with artillery support. It took the Germans until eight to take the canal bridge, with the help of tanks from the Ninth Infantry Division, which happened to show up at the right time.

The men of the 87th learned something then. The heaviest fire on the French side hadn't been that at all. It was simply that a French ammunition train, apparently hit by German guns, was exploding in bursts, one carload at a time.

They could also cross the Marne now, continuing their flanking movement around Paris to the east, en route to the Loire and the core of French resistance. But an unexpected order came in from the High Command:

87TH INFANTRY DIVISION OBLIQUE ON 14 JUNE
ON THE OURCQ CANAL AND OCCUPY PARIS.

Some officers would have preferred to pursue the advance toward the Loire battle front rather than serve as an occupation army. But soldiers obey.

The division historian does not mention Vert Galant, near Villepinte, site of another bridge over the Ourcq Canal. There a detachment of the 87th preparing the crossing was pinned down by machine-gun fire from a French infantry battalion. Convinced that villagers had taken part in the resistance, the Germans rounded up fifteen civilians and shot them. One survived to tell; his name didn't have to be engraved on the marble column later put up to mark the tragedy. A dozen other villagers were commandeered to dig graves, under threat of being shot in turn. The rest of the population was kept under guard. Then, as François Maspero heard the story, the German detachment received orders to move on. Surviving villagers were freed.

The 19th Panzer Division, which would also play a part in the occupation of Paris, was then a reserve force. By June 13, however, it was engaged in sweeping the Compiègne forest for remnants of French resistance. Only ten French soldiers and ten black Africans were captured—the Germans choosing to distinguish between Frenchman and *Neger*, especially for purposes of propaganda. Some of the Germans found themselves at the famous Crossroads of the Armistice, where they could peer into Marshal Foch's railway car to see the table on which the Germans signed the armistice on November 11, 1918. Who would have thought then, reflected the division historian, that in 1940 German troops would march by the same forest clearing in victory?

Still another division that would enter Paris, the 30th Infantry, had also been part of the reserve. Its marching log showed no combat along the way. Only one big gun had been fired against the city, the division historian noted.

It happened when the men were advancing in summer heat, passing destroyed vehicles, dead horses, dead enemy soldiers at either side of the road—black Africans among them—and abandoned arms. The advance unit stopped at a French artillery position along the way. The blacks who manned it had been captured, or had fled. Men of the 30th were inspecting the abandoned equipment when they heard a ferocious explosion. A shell screeched as it passed overhead; the men braced themselves for action.

It turned out that one of their group, a motorcycle messenger, had been tinkering with a French cannon. He had pulled something to see what would happen—and the shell went off. It had been aimed in the direction of Paris, but might have killed men of the 30th Infantry Division instead.

The fall of Paris was now inevitable, correspondent Carlo Dall'Ongaro assured readers of *Giornale d'Italia.* The Italian reporter was traveling with German forces marching on Paris. He knew that to take the enemy capital was a politically important act. But from the military point of view it was only an element in a vast maneuver, the German advance along a front running 250 miles from the English Channel to the Rhine River. Stopping the Germans would have taken a miracle; the miracle did not occur. "The flight of the British from the continent, their no less hasty retreat from the last Arctic bases in Norway, but above all the news of the entry into the war of Italy, made the collapse certain."

"Paris is lost. Panic reigns." Jottings of Propaganda Minister Goebbels this day. "Torgler is doing his job," he added, a reference to the former Communist now advising the Nazis on how to win over the French working class. "Paris is on the brink of revolution."

Again: "We are 12 miles northwest of Paris. Such military triumphs cause the heart to beat faster. It is a joy for the entire nation."

Then: "Towards evening things become dramatic in and around Paris. We shall do everything we can to turn things upside down."

Goebbels's men continued to grind out Communist-sounding propaganda, but so did genuine French Communists, despite the ban on both the Party and its press. In an issue of the official Communist Party organ *L'Humanité*, the clandestine apparatus told followers: "The people have had enough of this war." A second article in this issue, dated June 14, probably published on the 13th if not earlier, was headed:

PARIS MUST BE DEFENDED AGAINST FAMINE AND EPIDEMICS

The shortages, asserted *L'Humanité*, were the fault of those who had abandoned the city. "But those who could not leave because they don't have a motorcar or sufficient funds to hire a taxi to take them all the way to the center of France or Brittany, those people didn't hoard sugar, condensed milk, and canned goods the way the rich did. . . ."

At last Parisians were informed officially of the new status of their city:

NOTICE
To Residents of Paris

Paris having been declared an OPEN CITY, the Military Governor urges the population to abstain from all hostile acts and counts on it to maintain the composure and dignity required by these circumstances.

The Governor General of Paris
DENTZ

That morning the indefatigable William Bullitt telephoned the American Embassy in Bern, capital of neutral Switzerland, relaying a message to the German government:

Paris has been declared an open city. General Héring, Military Commander of the Paris District, is withdrawing his army which has been defending Paris. All possible measures are being taken to assure the security of life and property in the city. The gendarmerie and police are remaining and the firemen are also remaining to prevent fire. General Dentz is remaining as Commander of the Paris area but without troops, simply with the gendarmerie and police.

Ambassador Bullitt is remaining in Paris with the gendarmerie, Military and Naval Attachés, the Counselor of Embassy and six Secretaries of Embassy as the representative of the Diplomatic Corps. Mr. Bullitt hopes to be of any assistance possible in seeing to it that the transfer of the government of the city takes place without loss of human lives. This entire communication is made at the personal request of General Dentz.

Bullitt's statement was telephoned from Bern to the American Embassy in Berlin for transmittal to the German Foreign Ministry. The time in Berlin was 2:15 P.M. (or 1:15 French summer time).

"Phone call from Bullitt," Prefect Langeron noted in his diary. "The ambassador, with his habitual warm generosity, expresses his admiration for the behavior and attitude of the police. He knows that nothing means more to me than his confidence."

Seen from the observation post of the Invalides, Paris had indeed been abandoned. So reflected Colonel Georges Groussard, formerly General Héring's chief of staff and now General Dentz's. Personally, Groussard felt "full of rage." Soldiers were supposed to fight, not surrender. He begged Dentz to release him. The general told him that according to international law the Germans should liberate them as soon as they turned over Paris to the occupation authorities; after that, Dentz and Groussard could fight again.

One who studied the exodus later, Jean Vidalenc, found that the announcement that Paris was an open city, thus a city in which no fighting would take place, contributed to a relaxation of tension, a halt to the flight from the city. But this was not to speak for the refugees from everywhere else who continued to cross Paris. Prefect Langeron still had them on his mind. "Will this exodus go on until the very last minute?" he wondered. He found that there were more fugitives now than on previous days. "No other sounds than those of cars, horses. No human being speaks. The atmosphere is heavy."

His duty, he knew, was to the Parisians who stayed, keeping them supplied with what they needed, food first of all. He noted that despite the requisition orders, many food shops were shut.

And French tanks were crossing the city in their retreat, which did seem a violation of the city's status. Meanwhile Langeron was taking phone calls from all over France, from people wanting to know what was happening. He warned the callers that this was the last day such phone conversations would be possible. It was a strange feeling, hearing these far-off voices before the "total encirclement." What would happen to loved ones who had gone? How long would they be separated? In the previous war, the separation between those in enemy territory and the rest of France went on for years.

And who would be in greater danger, he wondered, those in Paris or those outside?

There was a simple answer to the riddle of the smoke, of course; it had been neither a smoke screen nor poison gas. It was an order of the French command that ignited oil reserves which might otherwise have fallen into enemy hands; fires were lit as far north as Port-Jérôme, upriver from Le Havre, as early as June 10. American Embassy Counselor Robert Murphy remembered receiving a phone call from the American manager of the French branch of Standard Oil of New Jersey, who had been asked by the French general staff to destroy the company's large stocks of petroleum in the Paris region. But he wanted to check in with the embassy before blowing up supplies accumulated at great expense over a period of months. Murphy told the man to go ahead, "since everybody agreed that Paris was about to be occupied." The result, observed Murphy, was a "Dante's Inferno."

Stocks of fuel outside Paris may have been the responsibility of the High Command, but Paris remained the jurisdiction of the military government. Here the decision was taken—now, on the afternoon of June 13—to destroy stocks only in depots lying beyond city limits, so as not to give the enemy a chance to say that acts of war had been carried out within the city.

There was also a humane reason for restraint, as Colonel Groussard later explained. Total destruction, at a time when everything was in short supply, would have deprived Parisians of fuel for domestic use and essential transport. So that afternoon the reservoirs at Le Pecq,

Port-Marly, and Colombes were set afire; and that night, only hours before the Germans reached the city's outskirts, those at Vitry, Villeneuve-le-Roi, Villeneuve-Saint-Georges, Juvisy. They were also supposed to blow up bridges, but that would be to cut electric cables and water pipes. What military interest would that serve now?

Michèle Rogivue and her sister Yvette stood on Boulevard Berthier watching some of the last French soldiers filing by. Michèle later imagined that they had been wearing old World War I uniforms, so disparate was their attire. A few neighborhood people took pity and offered the stragglers glasses of wine, but the soldiers protested that they craved plain water. A couple of soldiers walked up to the Rogivue girls to warn them not to stay, for the Germans would rape them. "Follow us," they said. But the girls went home.

But Englishman Peter Fontaine was still trying to get out of the city. He had spent much of the previous day looking for motor transportation; undaunted, he was now looking for a bicycle. Most shops had long since run out, of course, but on Avenue de la Grande-Armée, then and later Paris's bicycle boulevard, he found a store that still had stock. After waiting in line for what seemed hours he was able to purchase one of the last. He had not ridden a bike in a quarter of a century; could he handle it? He found that his machine lacked a bell—but then there wouldn't be any traffic to warn off. Passing the Arch of Triumph—walking his bike around the circle—he felt a pang, reflecting on the German victory march soon to pass this way.

There were no streetlights that evening, no open restaurants. Fontaine heard gunfire, and explosions everybody assumed to be war factories being blown up before the arrival of the enemy. The lone Englishman crossed the street to a small grocery with tables in the back; he could get something to eat there. The shopkeeper and her daughter were in tears—wouldn't the Boches violate women? He did what he could to reassure them; the German army, he said, was the best disciplined in the world. A friend from the prefecture of police walked in, surprised to find Fontaine still in Paris. If he didn't leave quickly he'd find the city surrounded.

The food shop owner refused to take money from him; he'd need it on the road. He prepared his bicycle by candlelight, attached a small hand case to it, and all the personal possessions he could carry. Then he was off, "last to leave Paris," as he would call his diary.

Round trips were still being made. Christian Pineau, who had been taken into the Information Ministry by his stepfather Jean Giraudoux, had evacuated the Hotel Continental with everybody else when the time came. His convoy of automobiles had reached Moulins, 175 miles south of Paris, on the night of June 11; everybody found a place to sleep there. Next day Pineau and his immediate superior, Guillaume de Tarde, in exchanging impressions, suddenly realized that they had forgotten to remove sensitive archives from the ministry. It was a serious oversight, for the files contained names of persons who had sent in information to be used in propaganda, including Dutch and Belgian nationals who had taken refuge in Paris, French Jews, even anti-Hitler Germans.

Pineau and Tarde knew that something had to be done to keep these files from falling into German hands. They called for volunteers. Christian Pineau took command of the task force, which consisted of three muscular clerks. They found a reliable old Citroën, made it back to Paris easily despite the flow of refugees going the other way. Driving through the city was even easier; they were at the door of the Continental early on the morning of the thirteenth. All that day they piled up papers in the hotel's palatial inner court, making no attempt to sort things out; they simply burned everything, taking care not to burn down the hotel (or their Citroën, for they intended to leave it inside the courtyard overnight). Pineau walked home across the Seine to his apartment on Rue de Verneuil; next morning, without any idea where the Germans might be, he walked back to the hotel to join up with his crew. Only two of the three helpers showed up. The third, he was to learn later, had looted the hotel's wine cellar and, after the war, opened a café. Driving proved more difficult this morning, and it took five and a half hours to reach Etampes, thirty miles south of Paris. The next time Christian Pineau went to Paris, it was as head of a resistance movement based in the German-occupied north.

*   *   *

A Parisian, Louise-Hermence Dethomas, who lived on the way to the Porte d'Orléans, observed a curious sight that afternoon: a large truck bearing a distiller, one of those monstrous vehicles that travel from village to village to turn the products of trees and bushes into brandies. Men and women were piled up on the truck, fitted in among the brass valves and switches; lacking baggage, they seemed to be parading on a holiday float. At the rear a man was seated with legs hanging; a red-faced man, looking joyful, stood in top hat and evening clothes. Mademoiselle Dethomas guessed that he was saving what he valued most, his wedding suit.

Edouard Gurevitch was nineteen; he worked daytimes, taking a high school correspondence course at night. He lived in a Jewish neighborhood—along Rue de Tournelle, near the Bastille. His father was dead; his mother had brought up Edouard and three sisters, working as a typist in the Armament Ministry.

The young man was simply too busy to be affected by the transformation of Paris after the launching of the German offensive. A house on his street was requisitioned as a shelter for Belgian refugees. Dirty, unshaven soldiers rode the subways. Policemen bore rifles. But Parisian Jews were unafraid. None thought that what had happened in Germany could happen here, none believed France would be defeated. Some young men of draft age left, but not older people. The Gurevitches didn't even own a radio; few on their street did. But now, on June 13, someone told him that young men were to report to local garrisons. The one he found was deserted.

So he left Paris on foot. He walked as far as Orly, and there hopped a freight train, sitting on the freight. It took him as far as Orléans, where he walked across the Loire bridge before it was blown up to stop the German advance.

Josephte Lesot found that she and her parents were among the four remaining families in their apartment building near the Luxembourg gardens. Her brother Jean, of military age, had gotten on a bicycle to ride out of Paris in search of a regiment that would let him enlist. The Lesots became de facto concierges of their building.

A neighbor living just below kept an aquarium in which she had miniature crocodiles. Josephte worried that she and her parents would be asked to take care of the little creatures when she joined the exodus. But the neighbor had another idea. She simply tossed them through the bars of the iron fence surrounding the garden of the School of Pharmacy, where presumably the crocodiles prospered and multiplied.

"After lunch I go to Paris to do my shopping," noted Paul Léautaud, who saw nothing unusual about returning to a city about to fall in order to purchase food for pets. Columns of refugees on Boulevard Saint-Michel, as always. There was no mail for him at *Mercure de France*; the butcher who sold him tripe was still closed. "My animals are going to begin to feel it."

Today he took a long walk across Paris, north to Rue Blanche and back again. From Place de l'Opéra, looking as far as he could see up and down the boulevard, there was no one. Soot fell, dirtied his face. He was "delighted" to see Paris this way; few Parisians had. Nobody in or around the Louvre; you could set fire to it if you had a mind to. He continued the walk singing to himself—what else could he do?

Back on Boulevard Saint-Michel, in the parade of refugees, he spotted a woman laden with belongings, wearing wooden shoes. A neighborhood concierge told Léautaud, "By the time she gets to the Porte d'Orléans she won't be able to go a step further." Seeing a retreating cavalryman, with a dirty uniform and splendid white horse, Léautaud felt sorry for men and horses both. "The Germans in Paris in a couple of days? What will I feel? How will I behave, what will be my reaction when they knock at my door? And my books, my papers, my pets, surviving?"

He managed to live all right, compromising himself a little, notably with collaborationist writers more ideological than he. He and his pets survived.

American correspondent Virginia Cowles, though based in London, desperately wanted to be in Paris for the end. She had even tried to reach the front, not considered a place for a woman then, but she had been promised at least a visit. Her visa came through on June 10 for the flight to Paris; at that moment Lord Halifax, the foreign secretary, assured her that the French capital would stand firm. Next day she was given twenty minutes' notice to pick up a plane ticket. There were twenty passengers, most of them English, on an Imperial Airways flight to a destination "somewhere in France."

The pilot remained at a low altitude, on a zigzag route. Only when they were on the ground did she learn that they had landed in Tours. There was a half-day wait until a customs officer could be found to clear their entry onto French soil; until then she hadn't even been allowed to use the airport lavatories. Paris? Everybody considered going there too dangerous. But there was actually a train scheduled to make the trip. She rushed to the station to find herself in a mob scene reminding her of India. The train left hours after the scheduled departure time, she in a compartment so packed in it was difficult to breathe. But then everybody got out in a mile or so; the mob was not going to Paris at all, only changing for another train headed south. Only two other persons were traveling with her all the way to Paris, an Egyptian official who had left his young children there, and a Frenchman worried about his store.

They were in Paris at 5:00 A.M. on June 12. By then the Gare d'Austerlitz was deserted; the shouting horde was outside the gates. Policemen had climbed up the railings to shout back at would-be passengers, trying to convince them there would be no more trains. "Open the gates!" came the shouted reply. "If they won't run the trains for us," a man cried, "we'll run them ourselves!"

Suddenly a taxi appeared, carrying no fewer than nine people to the station. Later Cowles was told it was the only taxi still cruising the city. She held on to it. First to the Ritz Hotel, where after a five-minute wait she was told by a porter that the hotel was closed. She tried the nearby Vendôme, to hear the same story; she tried over a dozen hotels in all, getting angry replies, doors slammed in her face, sometimes no reply at all.

Until then Cowles had been led to believe that Paris was going to be fought over. But where were the barricades, the soldiers, the guns? In all she had encountered a dozen concierges, three policemen, a panicked crowd at the station. She began looking for other foreign correspondents, in vain, until she remembered the Hotel Lancaster on Rue de Berri; during the Finnish war, Walter Kerr had told her that reporters used to play poker there. The hotel was functioning, and so was Kerr! "What in heaven's name are you doing here?" was his first question. "Have you come for the occupation?"

She was sure that she was seeing a city no one else had ever seen: the gayest city in the world, now silent and abandoned. When she rode with Kerr up Avenue des Champs-Elysées, theirs was the only automobile in sight. Kerr told her that French leaders had behaved disgracefully, declaring that they would stay in Paris, then fleeing without saying a word. Parisians were told nothing, except that men of military age were advised to leave.

At the Arch of Triumph three solitary policemen were standing guard at the Tomb of the Unknown Soldier; the eternal flame was still burning. They crossed the river. At the Invalides taxis were lined up, apparently waiting for a last-minute evacuation of official papers. Same sight at the Ecole Militaire. Then in less central, less elegant neighborhoods they found the people of Paris at last. "This is a morning we'll never forget," said Kerr. But Virginia Cowles didn't want to remember Paris like this; it was like watching someone you love die. Kerr made her aware that the Germans were going to march in without a fight; right now the enemy was only a twenty-minute drive from the city, and no cannon could be heard. Cowles spent the rest of the day cocking an ear to listen for gunfire; there was none. On Place de la Concorde she saw half a dozen soldiers with grimy faces, clothing caked with mud. Two of them limped, one wore a head bandage. Another walked in his socks, carrying his shoes.

They talked about how she was going to get out of Paris again, how Kerr would get out. There was a garage next to his hotel; she asked the owner if he had any cars for sale or hire. He glared at her angrily as he replied that if there were a single car left in Paris, he'd get it; even if there were a car left to steal, he'd get it. Her last hope was the American Embassy. Outside on the street an elderly man ran up to them to ask their help in leaving. He was a German Jew, head of an anti-Nazi movement; he'd be shot if the Nazis caught him. Cowles explained that she was in the same situation; couldn't the embassy help the man? He shook his head. Kerr told her that the embassy was being besieged by hundreds of such people, and helped them when it could. But this German Jew, with his accent, didn't have much of a chance. No one would give him a lift for fear he would turn out to be a member of the fifth column.

They called on the military attaché, Colonel Fuller. He seemed annoyed at having to deal with a stranded woman journalist. Then they ran into another reporter, Henry Cassidy of the Associated Press, who sent Cowles to see a London *Daily Mirror* correspondent, Tom Healy, who had an automobile. She typed out a story in the *Herald Tribune* office, and Kerr gave her one that he had written, which she promised to send from Tours. All they could find in a bistro was coffee, but Kerr had biscuits—her first solid food in nearly forty-eight hours. She drove off with Healy at five that afternoon. When she picked up her bag at the Lancaster, the porter, looking sad, was almost reproachful. "Your country is our only hope now," he said. "Americans have always loved Paris. Perhaps now they will help us." She felt like telling him that in the past nine months America had watched eight countries being overrun; the land of liberty sent plenty of sympathy but little else.

From London at noon a cable went out, Secret and Personal for the President from Former Naval Person. Code clerks who took it down in Washington at 9:10 A.M. local time were not supposed to know that the signer of this message to Roosevelt was Winston Churchill.

> French have sent for me again, which means that crisis has arrived. Am just off. Anything you can say or do to help them now may make a difference.

The prime minister was accompanied by his foreign secretary, Lord Halifax, by General Ismay, and by Minister for Aircraft Production Lord Beaverbrook. This time, with their escort of Hurricane fighters, they were to make a still wider detour to avoid flying over German-held territory en route to Tours. As they approached the airfield they could see it had been bombed, but Churchill's Lancaster bomber and its escort managed to land between the craters. It was two, well past the Englishman's lunchtime. They hadn't been met, so the British party went off in search of a café, negotiating at length with the owner of a closed establishment until he agreed to serve them. At the Tours prefecture they found Paul Reynaud, who wondered if the British realized how bad things were. Shouldn't France be released from the obligation not to make a separate peace with the Germans?

Churchill's answer was no. He said that the question shouldn't even be discussed until a further appeal was made to Roosevelt. Reynaud felt that he could not ask his people to fight on without hope of ultimate victory.

While they talked, a message from Roosevelt was on its way, a reply to Reynaud's plea of June 10. Roosevelt began by saying that he had been much moved by what Reynaud had to say.

> As I have already stated to you and to Mr. Churchill [Roosevelt added], this Government is doing everything in its power to make available to the Allied Governments the material they so urgently require, and our efforts to do still more are being re-doubled. This is so because of our faith in and our support of the ideals for which the Allies are fighting.

The American people, explained their president, were impressed by Allied resistance. He personally was impressed by Reynaud's pledge to fight on, to fight even in France's overseas territories. And Roosevelt was sure that naval power, which the Allies possessed, would resolve the battle.

Churchill read this message only after returning to London. From there he cabled Roosevelt:

> It seems to me absolutely vital that this message should be pub-lished tomorrow, June 14, in order that it may play the decisive part in turning the course of world history. It will I am sure decide the French to deny Hitler a patched-up peace with France.

But Roosevelt's words had come to Reynaud with a warning. Ambassador Biddle, standing in for Bullitt, handed it to the French premier with Secretary of State Cordell Hull's proviso:

> When this message is delivered it must be made entirely clear that the message is personal and private and not for publication.

Presidential elections were not far off in the United States; as Robert Murphy would say, Roosevelt had every intention of showing American voters that he was the peace president.

Ambassador Joseph Kennedy in London, no friend of the Allies and their war, was all too happy to call on Churchill with the bad news that Roosevelt did not want his message published. He followed up with a telephone conversation in which he explained, at the president's behest, that there was simply no authority in the U.S. government other than the Congress that could commit the nation to war.

Churchill was disappointed (so Kennedy admitted to Roosevelt). He had counted on this message "to put a little stiffening into the French backbone." Churchill feared that if he told the French that Roosevelt didn't want the message published, it would have the effect of dampening "what fires remained."

It becomes clear, reading once-secret dispatches, that Ambassador Kennedy—the isolationist counterpart to interventionist Bullitt— bears considerable responsibility for Roosevelt's decision to keep his message to Reynaud secret. Kennedy advised Roosevelt

The danger of publication of your note to Reynaud as I see it is that Churchill sees in your note an absolute commitment of the United States to the Allies that if France fights on the United States will be in the war to help them if things go bad at some later date.

Roosevelt replied at once—to Kennedy:

My message to Reynaud not to be published in any circumstances. It was in no sense intended to commit and does not commit this Government to the slightest military activities in support of the Allies.

And an embarrassed presidential press secretary in Washington, asked by reporters how Roosevelt was replying to Reynaud, replied that Roosevelt's speech in Charlottesville represented a complete response, even though Roosevelt hadn't had the premier's message in hand when he delivered it. Pure coincidence, explained the press secretary. And it showed how familiar Roosevelt was with French developments.

Reynaud's day was far from over. He drove on to the Cangé castle, where President Lebrun and the cabinet had been waiting—hours— for a meeting. There was disappointment that Reynaud hadn't brought Churchill with him. When Reynaud told the cabinet that he had informed the British that the French government wasn't accepting Weygand's recommendation on an armistice, there was heated discussion; some ministers felt that they hadn't yet had the opportunity to say yes or no. Then Pétain spoke up to support Weygand's call for an armistice. Weygand followed. For him it was the proper time to cease hostilities, while sending the fleet to North Africa, out of enemy reach.

The general-in-chief had an ace up his sleeve. He announced solemnly that advance German units had taken Pantin, the blue-collar district just beyond Paris's northeast gates. Further, there was a report that Communists had staged a coup in Paris, and that Party chief Maurice Thorez had taken power. The Paris police and motorized corps had been disarmed.

Nothing Weygand could have said could have frightened the cabinet more. The general's source was his trusted aide-de-camp, Captain Roger Gasser. Gasser had been on the phone with General Dentz—the source of the report on Pantin—and with an officer of the naval ministry, on the Communist coup d'état.

Interior Minister Georges Mandel asked to be excused, and walked out to the telephone in the antechamber; in an instant he had Prefect Langeron on the phone.

"Nothing new?" he asked the prefect.

"No."

"No incident?"

"None."

"It's that . . ." began Mandel, and he was not a man to hesitate, thought Langeron. Langeron assured his minister that he was "well informed and absolutely master of the situation."

"Well then," pursued Mandel, "here is why I ask. Someone important just told us that the Communists had taken over Paris and that Thorez was at the Elysée."

"Who could have told you that? Whoever it was, I'm willing to believe, is the victim of a plot. You can assure him that Paris is unquiet, but Paris is calm." The police chief went on, "There has been no incident and there will be none. The Communists aren't budging, nobody is budging. . . ." Thorez wasn't even in Paris, and the only sign of life at the Elysée palace was the Garde Républicaine unit placed there by Langeron himself.

But the incident was too important to be forgotten. Weygand himself realized that he stood accused of spreading a false report to sway the resolve of cabinet members. He phoned Dentz for a denial of the reported coup, and relayed the denial to the assembled ministers. Investigators later took the testimony of two naval officers who explained that after discovering that policemen were guarding the naval ministry they had asked Prefect Langeron why, and he had replied that Thorez would soon be at the Elysée. They reported this to Admiral Maurice Le Luc, chief of staff to Admiral Darlan; Le Luc asked that Darlan be informed—and Weygand's Captain Gasser happened to pick up the phone. . . .

After leaving his colleagues at Cangé, Premier Reynaud drove to Tours, broadcasting from there to the nation at ten that night. "At the instant that the outcome of the battle is being decided," he began, "I want to tell the world about the heroism of the French army." The soul of the nation had not been vanquished. France had been fighting for all free people, he said, so a wounded France had the right to turn to the other democracies for assistance. "We know how important ideals are in the life of the great American people. Will it continue to hesitate to declare itself against Nazi Germany?" Roosevelt had always helped France, but now considerably more help was required.

He explained why the government had left Paris. "We had to make sure that Hitler, by doing away with the legal government, would not be able to say to the world that France has no other government than a government of puppets in the service of Germany."

*   *   *

Newsman Quentin Reynolds had arrived in France to cover the war when the war was all but over. He stayed to cover the siege of Paris, but now it was clear there would be no siege. Paris was "a lonely old lady" and therefore not a military priority; she could be "reluctantly abandoned." In any case, even if he had a story he couldn't send it: "A reporter without means of communication is a jockey without a horse."

He solved his problem thanks to incredible good luck. A woman at a café table was telling bystanders how she had driven into Paris in a tiny Baby Austin that morning. She still had the vehicle but intended to stay; further, she didn't have a centime, and hoped to be able to sell her car. Knowing that for weeks people had been combing the city in search of a vehicle, any vehicle, Reynolds bought it from her on the spot, and never mind about transferring ownership. There was a full tank of gas, room for a knapsack, a mattress, a typewriter, a steel helmet. Soon Reynolds had caught up with the column of refugees.

His colleague Walter Kerr continued to wander about the shadow city, a city without newspapers, now also without banks. He learned at the American Embassy that two or three hundred of his countrymen were still in town. The American Hospital was open, with both American churches, American Legion headquarters, and the Paris office of the American Chamber of Commerce.

His wanderings took him to the Invalides compound. There he walked up and down stairs and knocked on doors of empty offices until he ran into a lone officer, a major. Kerr asked whether French armored divisions were concentrated east and south of the city, and the officer stared at him as if Kerr were an idiot. So Kerr asked whether the army would make a stand in the northern outskirts of Paris. The first reply of the officer was, "There is no France." Then he confided that, under orders, he would proceed after midnight to a northern suburb and there surrender the city. So the unidentified major must have been André Devouges, who would indeed meet the Germans to negotiate their entry. Kerr could have had a scoop, had he been able to do anything with it.

That night Ferdinand Dupuy, chief clerk at the sixth *arrondissement* police station, was dining with colleagues at one of the last surviving local bistros when a woman seated alongside him began berating the "bunch of incompetents" who had brought the nation to ruin. Dupuy observed softly that the woman might well save her anger for Hitler, the aggressor; when a bandit holds up a peaceful citizen, you don't blame the victim because he wasn't prepared. After dinner he and some of the other off-duty policemen crossed Paris on foot. He wondered how long it had been since Paris had been this silent, this dark.

They heard barking dogs—certainly dogs that had been left behind. It added an element of desolation to the picture. As they crossed the courtyard of the Louvre, their footsteps echoed "as in an empty village street." On Place de la Concorde they saw a convoy of heavy trucks moving south; along the Champs-Elysées a fleet of automobiles drove past without headlights. Germans? On reflection the policemen knew they were not Germans. Not a soul on the quays. Far off, to the east, there was a sudden explosion. Resistance? But then the gun—if that was what it was—fell silent, adding to the anguish.

Back at the police station Dupuy learned that four police sergeants and ten patrolmen had left that night, against orders. Another man was found dead at home, a suicide.

American Embassy Counselor Robert Murphy decided to take a last walk in the eerie atmosphere of pre-invasion Paris, accompanied by the naval attaché, Commander Roscoe Hillenkoetter. They left the remaining staff inside the embassy—sleeping as best they could in the chancery offices.

Outside the embassy they ran into the Great Rabbi of Paris with his wife and two friends. Although the leader of the city's Jewish community had intended to stay, the government's departure now led him to reconsider; could a place be found for his group in the embassy convoy that was leaving for Bordeaux? Murphy had to tell him that the staff assigned to Bordeaux had already departed, and that in any case Paris was now surrounded by German tanks. To convince him of that, Murphy had an embassy chauffeur drive the rabbi's party to the outskirts of the city. They were turned back.

Murphy and Hillenkoetter met no one else on the street. Not a café was open, no light showed anywhere. They observed occasional flashes of artillery fire that seemed to be coming from the southeast.

* * *

In Tours at seven that evening, Ambassador Biddle scrawled a message to be encoded for Washington:

Bullitt has just telephoned that the German army is inside the gates of Paris. The city was quiet.

At eleven, Bullitt sent his own message to Washington, informing the State Department that he had just destroyed the last two secret codes in his possession, doing so in the presence of two witnesses.

André Wurmser, journalist and critic, then and later a convinced Communist, would soon be handed a letter taken from the desk of his friend Valentine Prager, scholar and heiress, half paralyzed. The enemy would surely be in Paris the next day, she wrote, but she would wait until the following day, Saturday, to kill herself, for she wished to give some personal belongings to her chambermaid. That day, the thirteenth, seemed so strange, with the heavy black clouds, rain falling as "cataracts of soot." Now, at nightfall, there was no electricity. She was writing at her window, where there was still sufficient light now that the "mountain of soot" had shifted to the east; she faced a sunset gray and pink. . . .

I think with horror of the years that you are going to live through, my friends. How long will the triumph of the dictators last? Anything, anything rather than to be present to watch the ugly treason of those who will rally to the new masters. . . . What sinister years are coming now!

It is almost to get inside the minds of senior officers of the German general staff preparing the investment of Paris to read a dramatized account of that moment written by a staff officer shortly after the events. In a propaganda tract written in the form of a novel, Wilhelm Ehmer lets us see his general, who would be Erich Marcks, chief of staff to General Georg von Küchler, commander of the 18th Army, as he contemplates an etching of Notre Dame cathedral hanging in a manor near Chantilly that then served as temporary headquarters. Marcks regrets the need to attack Paris, even to destroy its historic bridges; yet they are an obvious military target, especially if the French are using them to move troops south to new defensive positions.

Just then, General von Küchler enters the room. "Our troops will find it difficult to understand that with the chance of a great battlefield success we hold them back," von Küchler declares. "But the decision to attack Paris depends on the enemy. If he defends the city and makes it a war zone, the situation will resemble that of Rotterdam." Of course Georg von Küchler knew a lot about what had happened at Rotterdam in May. "Warsaw refused to capitulate, Rotterdam ignored our deadline. But both Brussels and Oslo surrendered as we approached, and neither of these cities was touched." Clearly von Küchler was ready to see Paris as another Rotterdam—razed.

Yet at the moment German air reconnaissance showed no French troop movements in Paris, no movement in the direction of German lines, only the disorderly flight of scattered French units southward. Aerial photographs portrayed a Paris without any life at all. Only the legendary monuments were there, monuments of the French and of all mankind. The city was too big to be bypassed; the logical move for the Germans would be to save its bridges so that their troops could continue their progression southward. Not encirclement but frontal attack was called for—unless the French gave in. If the Germans did have to destroy Paris—writer Ehmer puts the words into the mouth of General Marcks's chief of staff—they'd have right on their side, "the implacable law of war."

There could indeed be a destructive battle, ripping through the countryside surrounding Paris and then the northern suburbs, smashing into the City of Light at an inestimable cost. "I can't stop the advance of my troops even if this is bad for Paris," Ehmer quotes von Küchler. "You don't make an omelette without breaking eggs!" He had been ready to move against the city as early as June 12. But his superior, Fedor von Bock, seemed convinced by reports that Paris was an open city. Direction-finding equipment confirmed that no French military units were transmitting north of the city. It was now that von Bock's army group gave von Küchler's 18th the order to move in.

*   *   *

On his own initiative, without referring back to the army group, General von Küchler decided to send an emissary to Paris with precise instructions concerning the transfer of power. This moment has also been recorded by a staff officer who was also a writer, Wilhelm Ritter von Schramm. He had just returned from a tour of the countryside near Chantilly and was getting ready to jot down his impressions of the charm of the Ile de France when a superior, Major Theo Heinrich, asked what he was writing. "Some lines on the Paris region," Schramm told him. "Your pen will soon be able to attack a still more noble theme!" Would von Schramm like to accompany Heinrich on a mission—"to demand that Paris surrender!"

Preparing for the mission, headquarters sent an uncoded radio message to the military governor of Paris to inform him that a German envoy would proceed to the intersection of highways 1 and 16, respectively the Paris-Dunkirk and Paris-Calais roads, just north of the suburb of Saint-Denis at 6:00 P.M. German time (an hour ahead of French summer time). They expected a French negotiating team to meet them there.

The afternoon was drawing on when the German party left the manor in two open vehicles. In the first sat Wilhelm von Schramm, acting as Heinrich's aide-de-camp, with a noncommissioned officer carrying a truce flag. Heinrich followed in the second auto, with a captain who spoke French. They drove off in a rain shower. Von Schramm observed that firing was sporadic as they approached the last German positions before the French lines. At a crossroads they saw antitank guns, and were ordered to stop. Soldiers of this forward regiment warned the truce party that the battle was not quite over. True, French resistance was weak, but shots might come from any village, any patch of woods. The emissaries drove on, and had soon reached the last German outpost, armed with machine guns and antitank weapons. There was a reconnaissance group still farther ahead, but the officer in charge could not say precisely where it was. They could hear artillery fire.

Before entering no-man's-land the German negotiators picked up a bugler from one of the companies they encountered; he was placed in the lead car. Night hadn't fallen, but the storm had darkened the sky;

the poet in von Schramm felt how sinister it all was. The silence was disturbing. Surely not all of the French had vanished; there must be enemy soldiers in some of the houses and gardens along the road. Had the French received their radio message?

Von Schramm kept the white flag ready to use, worrying only that its mast was a bit short. Surely the French were expecting them; that could explain the absence of fire. At his order the lead car accelerated. He nodded to the bugler, who stood up in the vehicle to sound the cease-fire, three times. The warning, or invitation, was met with silence. They could only drive on; that the war hadn't quite ended was made clear by the occasional dull explosion of a shell, the flames pouring from fuel tanks, the falling soot.

Ahead, a barricade was thrown across the road. Von Schramm ordered his bugler to blow as hard as he could. The vehicles slowed to a crawl. He guessed that they were approaching the intersection of the highways. After signaling a halt he descended from the lead car to walk toward the barricade some 150 yards farther on, taking the time to inspect the houses along the side of the road, fronted by small gardens. Suddenly silhouettes appeared alongside the road; shots rang out. Von Schramm grabbed the white flag, shouting "Halt!" as ferociously as he knew how. The firing increased, forcing the Germans to cover. Rifle fire was reinforced by the tick-tack of machine guns.

The French seemed to be firing wildly. But the lead car had been struck by several bullets. The driver of the second car jumped back into his vehicle and sped off as von Schramm and his team took what shelter they could as they retreated. The enemy was only two hundred yards behind them, their own first line two and a half miles north. Should they wait for nightfall to regain their lines, then try again for passage on another road? Major Heinrich assembled his men, six in all including the bugler, behind a garden wall. Each of the three officers had a pistol, each pistol held eight cartridges. The three soldiers were unarmed. Now artillery was being used against them. For Wilhelm von Schramm it seemed a repetition of 1918, when he had dodged between houses and across fields under fire.

As they retreated, still on foot, they could see furtive movements along the sides of the road. At the village of Saint-Brice, when they managed to attain it, a French soldier crossed rapidly in front of them.

The three officers held their pistols in outstretched arms, ready to expend their twenty-four bullets, but targets lacked. Before they had reached the far end of Saint-Brice, German soldiers appeared, part of a patrol sent out to find them when the firing became worrisome.

In the fictional version of the incident, Wilhelm Ehmer explains that the French soldiers at the barricade were *Negern*, Negroes—savages, in Nazi ideology. When the Germans tried to send two white prisoners back to the barricades to explain the peace mission, the Frenchmen refused (said Ehmer), convinced that the Negroes would cut their throats. The question remained, what to make of an attack on the truce mission? Should it be taken as a sign that Paris would continue to resist? Or was it simply an error due to confusion? In Ehmer's dramatic account, General Marcks argues that they may be pushing their concern for the enemy's interests too far. A captain protests that the fate of Paris should not hang on the error of subordinates on the French side. At that moment General von Küchler bursts into the room. He wants his men to attack Paris at daybreak. Imagine, he says, if the situation were reversed; the French would already have bombed Berlin. He carries an order ready for his signature; it calls for an immediate decisive attack, and even then Parisians should consider themselves fortunate that the victorious Germans weren't going to undertake reprisals. The von Küchler portrayed by Wilhelm Ehmer is the von Küchler who in real life, not in fiction, had razed Rotterdam only a month before.

Now it is his chief of staff, General Marcks, who takes the soft approach. "If white Frenchmen had fired on us, that would have been a fault of particular gravity against international law," he says. "But since it was done by Negroes, men lacking military morality, perhaps we can treat the matter differently."

Marcks prevailed; the Germans gave Paris another chance. But Georg von Küchler took out an insurance policy on that. He ordered the massive attack on Paris for nine on the morning of June 14. There would always be time to call it off.

At midday that June 13, General Henri Dentz had looked on as his predecessor, Pierre Héring, drove away from the Invalides to join his troops. Then, under what he thought of as a "sky of disaster," he toured this city whose safety was now in his hands. He spoke briefly with the prefects, Langeron and Villey, to coordinate action that could be taken to prevent looting.

Shortly after five, General Dentz was handed the text of the German radio message inviting him to send a truce team to meet the Germans north of the Saint-Denis suburb. He decided to ignore the message, for as military governor of an open city he had no obligation to enter into contact with the enemy. His mission was to maintain order, nothing more. The Germans would come when they would come, and they'd do with the military governor what they chose to do, but he would send no one to negotiate with them.

To play it safe, however, he made telephone contact with headquarters on the Loire, explaining his position that the commander of an open city is not qualified to entertain a dialogue with the invader, but could only *receive* his communication. General Georges agreed. Then at seven General Weygand put a call through to him, a call that happened to be a source of personal satisfaction to the military governor, who had stayed on in Paris without written orders, stayed on to be made a prisoner. "Are the Germans there?" asked Weygand. "No, General, not yet. But they'll be here tonight or tomorrow. At present they are at Pantin and at Aubervillers. They've asked me to send them negotiators for a truce. I haven't replied."

"You did right," Weygand told him. "No incident in Paris? Is the city calm?"

"Very calm, ominous. I've put guards at the Police Prefecture and the City Hall. I've ordered posters which ask Parisians to show themselves dignified."

Now police monitors picked up a new radio message: The German negotiators had been fired on, and demanded that a French negotiator come to Sarcelles, just north of the earlier meeting point, at five the next morning (German time, of course). If he failed to appear, the offensive against Paris would be launched.

Somehow a police interpreter got a German verb wrong, translating *beschossen*, "fired upon," as "killed." To the end of their lives Dentz and Langeron, not to speak of a number of war historians, remained convinced that the French had killed a German truce envoy. This German message, at least in the erroneous form in which Dentz received it, seemed to call for further reflection; Dentz spent an hour with the text in front of him. In the end he ceded. He could not take responsibility for a German assault on Paris—big guns against the city.

It was now that he ordered one of his remaining staff officers, Major André Devouges, to proceed to the meeting point, taking along a second lieutenant as interpreter. By the time a radio reply was ready for transmission to the Germans it was two in the morning. Dentz informed the Germans that his emissary would appear at five o'clock French summer time—six, German time.

Major Devouges's report to Dentz, discovered by historian Pierre Bourget, underscores the distress of the unlucky French officers left behind in Paris. It was 2:40 A.M. on the night of June 13–14 before the major got under way, after making sure to equip his car with a white flag. He and his interpreter stopped briefly at a garrison on Rue de Babylone to rouse a member of the Garde Républicaine from sleep; he'd be their bugler. They sped up the Champs-Elysées, at the Arch of Triumph turning into Avenue de Wagram and continuing north-ward toward the city's rim. Then they slowed down, white flag flying, in anticipation of an encounter with trigger-happy French troops. At Saint-Ouen they were indeed stopped, warned that they would en-counter the rear guard of an infantry regiment; they did. The officer asked for Devouges's papers, also asked if he was on the way to discuss a cease-fire. The major said no.

The prudent Devouges stopped again, this time of his own volition, at the Saint-Denis barracks, for he wished to be sure it contained no French troops. He also checked to see that there were neither men nor guns at the antitank barrier north of Saint-Denis on the road to Creil. Then, at the intersection of highways 1 and 16, the crossroads to which the Germans had dispatched the first emissaries, he discovered an antitank barrier still in place—mined, and protected by a row of trucks. The Frenchmen reached Sarcelles at 4:45 A.M., Paris time; the Germans were there minutes later. They invited the Devouges party to follow them to Ecouen, a village twelve miles north of Paris.

Meanwhile General von Küchler's staff was distributing orders for the offensive against Paris, set for nine that morning—eight French time. Chief of staff General Marcks had set up a command post at Ecouen, dominating the Paris highway. The old village boasted a splendid Renaissance castle, but Marcks had selected a manor closer to the road; it was "almost a castle," decided Wilhelm von Schramm. The house belonged to a local family (later it became a girls' school, for it was big enough).

The Frenchmen were led into a large drawing room, actually the music room, with its grand piano. Heavy fog kept daylight from penetrating. The Germans lit candles in ornamental holders, von Schramm remembered. In Major Devouges's less sentimental recollection, the candles had simply been fixed to overturned glasses. Only when they looked out the window was the mood spoiled: German tanks were parked on the lawn, camouflaged with branches.

Of course there was no negotiating; the Germans simply read out their terms. As his interpreter translated from the German Devouges wrote them down:

I. So that Paris does not become a combat zone we demand:
   1. That inside Paris and as far as a line running from Saint-Germain, Versailles, Juvisy, Saint-Maur, to Meaux, there be no resistance either by the army or the population.
   2. That inside Paris there be no destruction of bridges or public services (particularly water and electricity), as well as broadcasting facilities. If the governor general cannot guarantee this peaceful solution, the city's resistance will be broken by the most rigorous means both on land and in the air.
      In the interests of maintaining order and public tranquillity it is stipulated:
      1. That the municipal police, maintained on duty, take responsibility for protection against criminals, looters, etc., and prevent sabotage.
      2. That from the moment of entry of German troops into the city, the population remain indoors for 48 hours.
II. The German command recognizes that the governor-general of Paris will be responsible for guaranteeing the above conditions only in the zone indicated on an attached map.

III. The governor-general will attempt to contact the French
high command, to make sure that the French forces remain
below the line indicated in paragraph I section 1.

André Devouges listened to the terms with tight lips, interrupting
only to be sure that he understood his interpreter. At the end of the
reading he raised one objection: In discussing a cease-fire he could
speak only for Paris, which was the responsibility of the military
governor, but not for the whole region extending south of the city to
Meaux. In such a case, retorted the German envoy, there was no point
in pursuing the talks. Either the French obtained a guarantee from the
High Command before nine—or Paris would be bombed. The French
major protested: no reply could be received that soon. But this was a
crucial point for his commanding officer, said the German.

Devouges persisted. There would be no resistance, he promised, not
even in suburbs south of Paris about which they expressed concern. He
also pointed out that to confine Parisians to their homes for forty-eight
hours would create enforcement problems, considering the large number of homeless refugees now in the city, to say nothing of the need to
allow those connected with essential city services the possibility of
moving about. If people could not go out, how would they feed
themselves? To this last point the Germans replied that if notified in
advance, Parisians could lay in sufficient supplies.

The chief German negotiator left the room to phone staff headquarters. Before leaving, as von Schramm remembered it, he delivered
himself of a threat. If he did not return in one hour the talks could be
considered to have failed, in which case German bombers would be
unleashed over Paris, and German guns would begin to shell the city.
The Frenchman said nothing. It was now six-thirty German time, or
just two and a half hours before the attack on Paris was to begin—also
on German time.

After the senior German negotiator left, the others—Germans and
French both—lit cigarettes. There was some small talk, but von
Schramm could see that the two French officers had their eyes glued to
the wall clock. When German tanks outside the window started up
their motors, he saw the Frenchmen jump.

The German negotiator walked back into the room fifty-five minutes after marching out—von Schramm's calculation. The news was good; the matter of the cease-fire line south of the city was not to hold up the triumphant march of the Germans into the enemy capital, capital of a world that was everything they stood against and secretly coveted. There was deathly silence as both sides initialed the protocol. Only the candles, thought von Schramm, seemed alive. "Paris has surrendered!" his orderly shouted, rushing out to the garden, embracing the first tank driver he met. Soon all the tankmen were gathered round; it would not have taken much to set off a cheer.

But just then the front door opened. The two French officers appeared, on the way to their automobile. "Attention!" came the command, and the German soldiers snapped hands to foreheads, saluting the vanquished enemy. Then they broke ranks, to prepare the joyride into Paris.

One German was convinced that he alone had saved part of humanity's heritage from destruction. Indicted in the Nuremberg High Command case with thirteen other high-ranking officers, accused of mistreating civilian and military prisoners during the campaign against the Soviet Union, in 1948 General Georg von Küchler appealed to French military authorities to help him prove that despite the firing at his peace envoys he had saved Paris, sparing blood on both sides, preserving precious cultural values.

No one in liberated France jumped to help. Von Küchler drew a twenty-year (later reduced to twelve years) sentence from a court composed of American judges. In a hagiographic record of his career published in the *Neue Deutsche Biographie*, von Küchler is seen as an anti-Nazi at heart, opposed to SS crimes, seeking to soften the consequences of the Dutch capitulation.

38

FRIDAY, JUNE 14

In his account of the German march into Paris, soldier-author Wilhelm Ehmer accompanies the first German staff officers to reach the vanquished city as they contemplate it at dawn from the heights of Saint-Denis. There the coveted capital "spread itself like a vast field of gray stone under the already hot June sun. To the left they made out the somber dome of the Pantheon; at the right, the Eiffel Tower's sharp needle pierced the blue silk of the sky."

"There it is!" exclaimed the senior officer—General Erich Marcks—stretching his arms to embrace the city. "From here, kings of other times scrutinized the horizon, here Blücher and York, Bismarck and Moltke paused to contemplate." But it was time to move on. The column of command cars soon caught up with a motorcycle company, which served as their escort as they drove into Paris through empty streets.

Not quite empty. For some people stood at the intersections as they sped by. "Parisian workers," noted Ehmer, "their wives and children, astonished and disconcerted, trusted the conquerors"—at least this is the impression they gave the credulous conquerors. There were policemen here and their along their way. "White sticks in hand, they were the last defenders of an order which would soon be in other hands."

General Marcks had his driver take the main avenue leading to the Gare du Nord. "This is where trains coming from Germany arrived!" he exclaimed, wishing to make the ride interesting for his junior officers. Not a soul on Boulevard Sébastopol leading to the dead center of the city, save for another faithful traffic policeman. Empty streets, closed houses and shops . . . The convoy crossed the Seine at the Place du Châtelet, passing the Palace of Justice before screeching to a halt on the second bridge, Pont Saint-Michel, for here they had a close-up view of Notre Dame. The Germans contemplated the old stones above the river—same stones, same waters, as seven centuries past. General Marcks told them it was a beautiful sight, and they would not have disagreed with him.

Then it was time for serious business, getting troops across Paris via Boulevard Saint-Michel and the Porte d'Orléans, en route south to the remaining battlefront. A second column of invaders crossed the city farther to the west, giving them the chance to march over Place de la Concorde. A third column entered Paris still farther west, giving them the Arch of Triumph and the Champs-Elysées. General Marcks was there to inspect them. At the Arch of Triumph he ordered his driver to stop, got out with his chief aides to salute the Unknown Soldier. The eternal flame had been extinguished, so Ehmer remembered. The guardian of the tomb would swear that the flame never ceased to burn.

Soon after that, General von Küchler drove up, accompanying his superior, General Fedor von Bock. "For a short instant," reported Ehmer, "the column halted. Then the troops took parade formation, the music began, and with considerable enthusiasm the march began before the victorious generals, the march toward achievement and crowning of the victory."

Lieutenant General Bogislav von Studnitz, whose 87th Infantry Division would receive the honor of occupying Paris—and not simply marching in and out again—stood on the bridge over the Ourcq Canal at Bondy, less than four miles northeast of the Porte de Pantin, precisely at nine (8:00 A.M. French time). He who had never set foot in Paris assigned specific sectors of the city to different units. He made sure that the regimental bands were brought up to the front of the division, so that each unit would be accompanied by music as it marched into the conquered capital.

The 187th section of tank destroyers, which, during the advance toward Paris, had often served as a forward element, received the distinction of being the first military unit to occupy the principal office buildings. The first thing they did was to wash both their vehicles and themselves in water drawn from the Ourcq, so as to look their best in Paris.

Then the advance through the suburbs of Noisy-le-Sec and Montreuil, in the middle of Friday-morning markets. Unsuspecting shoppers stared at the motorized columns. When they realized whose columns they were looking at, they snatched up children, slammed doors and shutters. But then there were second thoughts. Since nothing terrible seemed to be happening, they opened their doors again, returned to the streets. Place de la Nation, Place de la Bastille . . . On Place de l'Hôtel de Ville, the tank destroyer detachment drew up in close formation. The commander stepped out of his armored car, crossed the pavement to the main entrance of City Hall. Obviously he was expected; ushers in livery threw open the huge doors. "As commander of the first German occupation unit of the city of Paris," the officer declared, "I have the honor, Mr. Prefect, to transmit a message from the commanding general of my division."

That for the form. Then his interpreter stepped forward to explain to Prefect Achille Villey that General von Studnitz wished to see him later that morning at the quarters he was to occupy at the Hotel Crillon. The prefect, whom the Germans found to be slender and distinguished, wore his ceremonial uniform, with a large blood-red sash across his chest. Villey nodded approval, but then asked that the division commander's name be repeated several times before writing it down. Even so, most contemporary historians spell it Stutnitz.

During the prefect's meeting with the German officer, soldiers outside busied themselves with the French flag, lowering it from the mast before raising the swastika emblem. The Germans thought they could hear a collective sigh as it reached the top of the mast, for by now a curious crowd had gathered around City Hall.

*　　*　　*

As he entered his office early that morning, Prefect Langeron wondered how the day would end. He was not just any prefect of police, he was the man who had been the guardian of democratic Paris, investigator of plots against the Republic, and many of these plots involved Nazi sympathizers. He could be arrested at once and shipped to Germany; yet there was still a job to be done.

At 7:45 A.M. he had been informed that four German officers had driven into the courtyard of the prefecture. Minutes later two senior officers were standing before his desk. But not before a polite halt at the door, and a salute that was almost respectful. Speaking French, the Germans requested that the prefect come to the Hotel Crillon at eleven to meet the general commanding the occupation army.

It was close to eight when the first Germans showed up at the office of the military governor. Colonel Groussard had first seen infantry columns marching past the Invalides on their way south, after which German traffic police had begun taking up positions at important intersections. He observed that the German soldier posted at the corner of Rue de Grenelle was soon surrounded by Parisians who tried to engage him in conversation; some even joked with him. It was Groussard's first personal experience of what he considered shocking behavior on the part of many Parisians.

The Germans who entered his office now had a curious mission. They were asking to recover German flags captured by the French in the First World War. It was as if they had been planning this visit for twenty-two years.

General Dentz replied firmly that he had no idea where the German flags could be. And that reply didn't please. Soldiers immediately took up menacing positions in the building. Two helmeted men with submachine guns actually moved into the room where Dentz and Groussard were talking. All the while, out of doors, more soldiers paraded. The sights and sounds reinforced the impression of the two French officers that they had been placed in an impossible situation.

After an hour, Groussard rose to get his cigarette case from his office; he was shouted back to his chair. A lieutenant entered to say that he was supposed to cut the phone lines, but would accept the promise of the Frenchmen not to use the phones. Groussard replied that he would give his word to no one; they could cut the telephone wires if they wished. The lieutenant remained in the room, sending away the soldiers.

The atmosphere changed when General von Studnitz's emissary arrived with an invitation for General Dentz to call on him at the Crillon. As Groussard recorded the moment, Dentz made no objection—but Groussard did. He told Dentz that for his part he would not budge. For if they went to the Crillon in broad daylight they'd be the laughingstock of Paris. "It is humiliating and ridiculous for a French general and colonel to have to walk around in uniform, empty handed and unguarded, in a city occupied by the enemy."

"We'll certainly be accompanied by a German officer," Dentz replied.

"In that case we shall agree to be considered as prisoners of war. But according to international law we should be treated as truce emissaries and not as captives."

The German lieutenant who had been sitting with them now put in a phone call to the Crillon. After talking to someone who might have been von Studnitz himself, he told General Dentz that the German commander agreed to postpone the meeting until ten that night, adding, "You will not be accompanied."

At noon the tank destroyer commander was able to report to General von Studnitz that the occupation of the center of the city had been accomplished. He was in time to watch the march-past of the Ninth Infantry Division, parading on Place de la Concorde before General von Küchler.

Walter Kerr was up at four that morning. He climbed onto his bicycle in front of the Hotel Lancaster on Rue de Berri, to wheel down to Place de la Concorde, where he waited. Other American reporters had joined him before the first Germans appeared. First came two motor-cycle scouts, followed by two command cars racing down the Champs-Elysées, crossing Place de la Concorde to pull up at the venerable Crillon. The Germans hammered at the hotel's heavy entrance door as other German vehicles appeared on the square, some arriving from the Champs-Elysées, others from Rue Royale. By now day was breaking. Then someone turned up to unlock the door of the hotel.

Kerr biked to his office in the *Herald Tribune* building, to type out a story that he hoped he'd find a way to send.

The commotion at City Hall had an official witness in finance director Eugène Depigny. He saw the German antitank batteries speed into the square from Rue du Temple, placing themselves at strategic corners as if City Hall were being defended by hostile forces. Antitank guns were actually brought up to face the two main gates leading into the building, and they remained at the ready while the German officers were inside talking to Prefect Villey. Soon the marching of German troops began, a seemingly unbroken parade along the main north-south avenues. "Green, gray, green, green, always gray, always green, to the point of nausea!" Nearly all the Germans looked fresh, their matériel newly painted, as if it had just come out of a box.

It was clear to city officials, watching this spectacle from front-row seats, that the tired French armies were not going to win back the lost ground. All the more reason to hold on to Paris, as one could, and employees of City Hall were prepared to do that. Only 2 percent of their number had left their jobs. Most of them were women with young children to be evacuated, young girls following their parents, young men approaching draft age.

A French battalion that had committed the imprudence of crossing Paris in its retreat was still moving through the city as the Germans took the gates of Paris, one after another. The battalion commandant was able to get a message to the commissioner in charge of the fourteenth *arrondissement* police headquarters. The commissioner at once made his way to the Porte d'Orléans, found a pretext to distract the German unit he found there, while other police officers guided the hapless French unit out of the city by the less used Porte d'Arcueil.

The mobilized gendarmerie was something of an anomaly now. A police formation, but dependent on the Defense Ministry, the mobile police was virtually a military force in time of war. Based in the north of Paris, unit commander Georges Benoit-Guyod followed developments that morning by telephone. First came the disarming of the Garde Républicaine, then of the city police. A civilian on a bicycle rode up to the gate of his garrison to let the commander know that the Germans were arriving via Boulevard Victor-Hugo in Clichy. Just then, on Avenue des Grésillons, Benoit-Guyod spotted soldiers of a French artillery regiment who seemed lost. They didn't even know that Paris was an open city. He invited them into the garrison for a bite to eat.

The phone rang. Benoit-Guyod's colonel was confirming the entry of the Germans into the city; the military government had ordered that there be no resistance. Nor could there be any patrols that night; his men were to remain inside the building if possible. Even the armed sentinel was to be replaced at the gate by a simple orderly. Two hours later, another order: the gendarmes could resume regular patrols. Thanks to their dark blue uniforms resembling those of the city police, there should be no mistaking them for soldiers. When challenged they were to say—loudly—*"Gendarmerie française!"*

When Benoit-Guyod drove out to place a guard at a gas depot in Saint-Denis, he found himself confronting two Germans armed with submachine guns. So he shouted *"Gendarmerie française!"* and got a friendly nod, even a smile from a noncom.

For Louis Lochner, who had been chief correspondent of the Associated Press assigned to Berlin for a dozen years, and who was now accompanying German troops in their march across Europe, no experience of the ghost towns of Belgium and northern France prepared him for what he was to find in Paris that day. He had known the lively Paris.

You who have been to Paris [he cabled *Life* magazine], just imagine this picture: at the Place de la Concorde no such merry-go-round of honking autos, screaming news vendors, gesticulating cops, gaily chatting pedestrians as usually characterizes this magnificent square. Instead, depressing silence broken only now and then by the purr of some German officer's motor as it made its way to the Hotel Crillon, headquarters of the hastily set up local German commandery. On the hotel's flagstaff, the swastika fluttered in the breeze where once the Stars and Stripes had been in the days of 1919 when Wilson received the cheers of French crowds from the balcony.

The scenes of desolation were repeated wherever Lochner turned. "Boulevards normally teeming with life . . . were ghost streets." Only one café was open on the Champs-Elysées. Lochner's colleague William Shirer, also in from Berlin, summed it up in his diary: "I have a feeling that what we're seeing in Paris is the complete breakdown of French society—a collapse of the army, of government, of the morale of the people. It is almost too tremendous to believe."

There was a swastika flag atop the Eiffel Tower, noted Lochner (who was of course used to seeing Nazi symbols back in Berlin), another over the Ministry of Foreign Affairs on the Quai d'Orsay, and—"most grotesque of all"—another on the Arch of Triumph. Lochner was one of nine foreign correspondents who had come to Paris at noon on June 14, accompanied by representatives of the German army, Propaganda Ministry, and Foreign Office. At first they were turned down when they asked for rooms at the Hotel Scribe, a favorite of foreign journalists, for it had been taken over by the German occupation authorities. But the lieutenant colonel in charge of the correspondents ordered the hotel manager to make rooms available.

One of the things Lochner and his colleagues did not report that day—for they were subject to military censorship—was that they and other reporters from nonbelligerant nations were warned by their German escorts not to visit their respective embassies. When one of the visiting newsmen, Fred Oechsner of United Press, returned to Berlin he carried with him fourteen stories written by Walter Kerr, which the *Herald Tribune* correspondent hadn't been able to send from Paris. Only one of them passed the Berlin censor.

Eleven-year-old Claude Poirey had come to Paris from Dieppe with his aunt and grandfather when they decided that a Channel port was not the place to be just then. A relative offered them an empty apartment on Rue Blanche. They watched as Parisians fled the city; they had already done their exodus.

At dawn this day they were awakened by strange sounds, a sort of uninterrupted rumble, like boots on pavement. Claude's aunt took him out to see what was going on. When they reached Place Blanche they saw the soldiers in tight rows, an endless column, a serpentine formation coming from Place Pigalle, heading toward Place de Clichy.

A Parisian standing nearby had it all wrong. "We're saved!" he cried out. "Paris will be defended! Here's the British army!" Claude's aunt cut him off: "The British don't dress that way." She, who had seen lots of them in Dieppe, knew that. To settle the argument they approached a policeman, who confirmed that they were seeing the first German soldiers in Paris. The man who thought he was looking at British saviors broke into sobs.

After breakfast Claude and his aunt were out on the street again. This time, on their narrow Rue Blanche, they ran into French soldiers on a motorcycle and sidecar—riding in the direction of the square. Claude's aunt hailed them to a stop, to warn them away from the parade route; they turned around to head south.

Erna Friedlander, the anti-Nazi refugee from Germany who had tried so hard to be locked up as an enemy alien so as not to be alone, had spent a fortnight in her benefactor's apartment, not going out at all. In the last days she didn't even undress at night, keeping a packed suitcase close at hand. Then at last she decided that she needed a real night's sleep; she undressed. Her hostess had to shake her awake at ten the next morning, then drew her over to the window, which looked out on a corner café. At an outdoor table Germans in uniform were singing a song she knew well, "Blue is My Flower." Erna turned from the window and sat down to cry.

The Rogivues had White Russian friends who lived on the Champs-Elysées just above the Ermitage cinema theater. Michèle Rogivue's parents worried that their friends might be feeling lonely, with all the Parisians gone. Early that morning it was decided that the whole family, the three Rogivue daughters and their small son, with mother and father, would walk all the way from their apartment house on Rue Albert-Samain in northwest Paris to the Champs-Elysées to comfort their friends. They were stopped on Avenue Hoche, close to the Arch of Triumph, by a motorcycle detachment speeding past—Germans! The streets were all but deserted, windows shuttered, but there was a military band on the avenue, and more soldiers. Michèle found the invaders tall and good-looking, and very much cut of the same cloth; certainly Hitler had sent his best troops to Paris. As she turned away she noticed that a woman who had been watching the march-past was weeping. A man nearby cautioned Michèle not to move away, for she could get into trouble by an obvious gesture of hostility to the invaders. Michèle's father, knowing his impetuous daughter, held her hand tightly. So the family didn't budge. And still the soldiers all looked alike. The crazy idea came to the Rogivues that the soldiers were marching around the neighborhood in circles to fool the Parisians who watched them.

Chief clerk Ferdinand Dupuy perceived no sign of movement of any kind as he made his way to his office in the Place Saint-Sulpice police station at eight that morning. But at the corner of Rues Madame and Vaugirard he couldn't help hearing the talk outside the bakery shop. "They are all over the place," said one shopper. "I come from the Boulevard Montparnasse, and found myself stumbling into one of them. . . ."

Dupuy received confirmation of the expected event at his office. The Germans were indeed everywhere, but they were not aggressive. Parisians were reacting with "consternation," he noted, to which was added "a kind of fearful curiosity." It was not until eleven that he himself saw his first enemy soldiers outside the police station. Two men in a field-green vehicle stopped in front of the district hall to deliver a message by loudspeaker: German troops had occupied Paris, French authorities had requested that the population remain calm, and that request must be obeyed. The German High Command would tolerate no act of hostility. Aggression or sabotage would be punished by death. Arms must be turned in. The population was to stay indoors for forty-eight hours.

Fearful curiosity: chief clerk Dupuy's description can be applied to many of the day's encounters. Initial alarm, then relief when the Germans showed themselves to be without hostility. The observations of a German war correspondent quoted by historian Henri Amouroux do not contradict what many Parisians saw for themselves. French civilians coming into contact with the invaders seemed resigned, reported journalist Leo Leixner. They looked for signs, on the faces of these strangers, of what was in store for them. German smiles even brought responses. "How happy I am that the first German soldier I meet is so friendly," a woman of the suburbs exclaimed. A German officer, during a halt, purchased bananas from a street vendor as mothers hid children behind their skirts. Noticing this, the officer returned to the shop to purchase chocolate to give to the children. Leixner thought he could hear the sighs of relief. A woman wept, "My poor France! The misfortune isn't our fault." Cohabitation became easier when Parisians realized that Germans were not as bad as the papers said they were (said German correspondent Leo Leixner).

General Dentz's deputy, Colonel Groussard, took an early opportunity to inspect occupied Paris, curious to know how Parisians were receiving the invaders. Often enough he found the behavior of fellow Frenchmen lamentable. In lower-class neighborhoods as in upper- and middle-class ones, Germans were constantly being approached by Parisians who laughed along with the enemy, offering to be helpful.

Groussard was a patriot in a difficult position; perhaps he was fated to overreact. He noted that despite the French major's objection at Ecouen to a forty-eight-hour curfew, the Germans were announcing it by loudspeaker truck. By evening, however, the order was rescinded. "Really," thought Groussard, "they had nothing to fear from that huge amorphous mass sometimes lacking the most elementary instincts of dignity."

As the Germans marched along Boulevard Saint-Germain that day, Amalia Mangin noticed that some Parisians were applauding. A few shouted "Bravo!"

Max Taumann was coming out of the subway at the Poissonnière station when he saw the first German columns. A young woman next to him murmured, "They have lovely eyes." She turned to find an Indochinese standing nearby, and snapped at him, "Go back to your own country—what are you doing here!"

Taumann watched as a German soldier broke ranks to buy bananas from a street stall. The vendor wouldn't accept German money. A French policeman stepped up to pay for the bananas, accepting the German bill in exchange.

* * *

Some of the "bravos" that greeted the Germans had Italian accents, certainly. Correspondent Walter Kerr spotted Italians just released from internment as enemy aliens, bouncing along beside the German military bands. "They are in civilian clothes," he noted, "and so proudly happy one would think they captured Paris single-handed."

"People are made to understand each other," a letter to the collaborationist *La Gerbe* declared (the letter was ostensibly from a reader of the pro-German paper, which began to publish shortly after the Nazi occupation began). "On June 14 the profiteers had skipped town, the people remained behind. At noon that day the people were fraternizing with the Fritzes." The letter-writer admitted that some Frenchmen and women overdid their welcome. During a German march-past on Rue Lafayette "a fat little lady couldn't hold still. She couldn't stop saying how handsome the Germans were, how fine their horses were." The letter-writer reminded the fat lady that Frenchmen had died in battle.

Another reader told *La Gerbe* how impressed he was with German equipment (field-green jackets of pure wool, for example), with the way the soldiers looked—freshly shaved, in contrast to the bearded French stragglers who had so recently crossed the city. The newcomers were polite, asking for what they wanted, and paying for it (with marks, it was true, and since no one was sure what marks were worth, they gave the merchandise away without payment). The letter-writer concluded with the thought that if Parisians were angry, it was with their own government, which had sold them out.

Colonel Hans Speidel was sent into the city that day by General Fedor von Bock to set up the military government. He had soon decided that Parisians were relieved to see the Germans, for their presence signified that the city would not be destroyed. Another man on the headquarters staff, economist Herbert Eckelmann, told historian David Pryce-Jones how helpful the French had been; all they wanted was a return to normality. Once they realized that the Germans were paying, shopkeepers were grateful to have them as customers. What reticence there was came from the oldest generation of Parisians.

* * *

Youki Desnos, woman of Montparnasse, companion of poets and painters, was present that morning when the swastika rose over Place de la Concorde. The sight of it made her dizzy; to recover she found a table outdoors at Chez Maxim's, around the corner. A German naval officer joined her at the table, ordered champagne, and began telling her his troubles. He was delighted to be in Paris, he said, but he had been ordered to report to Rouen. Would he find women there? he wondered. Or would *she* be willing to accompany him? (She was then thirty-seven years old.) He had caviar and champagne in his car, he said. What was she doing at wicked Maxim's if she was not the kind of woman ready to drive to Rouen with this debonair officer?

Pietro Solari, longtime correspondent of Italy's *Corriere della Sera* in Berlin, arrived with the first German divisions. He watched German officers place wreaths on the Tomb of the Unknown Soldier, on a square all but deserted. He did notice some women bystanders, most dressed in black, praying, making the sign of the cross, weeping. The Germans behaved differently, said the Fascist journalist—but they were no less moved for that. A German major confided that he had been on the Marne in the earlier war, this time fought on the Seine; the moment would not be forgotten. "A blind governmental policy is responsible for all this," concluded the German. "It's true, it's true," Solari hears the women onlookers reply.

The Italian journalist was another observer who couldn't help noticing the contrast between the deserted center of the city and the lively blue-collar neighborhoods to the north. He counted only ten people up and down the Avenue des Champs-Elysées. At Notre Dame cathedral he discovered a French light armored vehicle half turned over, a couple of policemen, some forgotten ambulances. German troops were visible only on bridges and crossroads. Some buildings were guarded, but neither the Quai d'Orsay nor the Chamber of Deputies was among them—perhaps, said the Italian correspondent, "because the evil that could come from these sinister buildings was henceforth and forever extinguished."

Frenchmen on the street, Solari decided, seemed annoyed to have to admit that the Germans were behaving properly, even generously.

*   *   *

A quiet evening had surprised artist Hélène Azenor, then a quiet morning: where had the war gone? She left her studio on Rue Campagne-Première for a bicycle ride to the right bank to see her mother. She wheeled past the deserted Tuileries gardens, turning right on Place de la Concorde. This was where she saw them. She was so surprised that she braked sharply, nearly falling over the handle-bars. A German soldier barred the way; she was not allowed to cross the square. She could see why, with the swarming mass of German soldiers busy with their trucks, tanks, motorcycles. It took some detouring to reach her mother's flat on Rue de Miromesnil. And she managed to return to Montparnasse without seeing another German; back on Rue Campagne-Première no one would believe that she had even seen one. There were a few French stragglers in uniform wandering on Boulevard du Montparnasse; they didn't believe her either.

By afternoon there were field-green troops at the sidewalk tables of the celebrated cafés of Montparnasse—Dôme, Rotonde, Coupole. Other soldiers, in formation, marched south toward the roads that would take them to the new battle lines. "They were big and blond," Azenor remembered, and their uniforms were "impeccable." That night the efficient enemy arrived in trucks at the shelter at the corner of Raspail and Campagne-Première to load up the refugees still living there. They were to be sent back to northeast France and Belgium.

As the first German units fanned out over the city, one prominent Parisian set in motion a long-deliberated plan. He had made it clear to friends that he would not see Germans in his beloved city—but neither would he join the exodus. Thierry de Martel, son of Count de Martel de Janville and a famous woman writer who signed her novels "Gyp," had made his own name as a skilled brain surgeon. The declaration of war had found him as chief of the surgical service in the prestigious American Hospital in Paris. When wounded soldiers began to arrive, Dr. Martel took the difficult cases, such as removing shrapnel from head wounds. Hospital records show the sixty-four-year-old surgeon manning his station for nearly twenty-four hours at a time.

He was also a very sociable person, this great-nephew of the Count de Mirabeau, an imposing figure of the French Revolution. One of his friends was William Bullitt, who, as ambassador, was honorary president of the American Hospital. Martel had called on Bullitt at the embassy on June 12 to explain that he could not live in a Paris overrun by Germans; he wished the ambassador's permission to leave. Bullitt, or so the legend has it, asked Martel to remain at his post. There is other evidence of Thierry de Martel's growing apprehension as the Germans approached. Writer André Maurois, his friend, heard him say that as soon as the Germans entered the city he'd kill himself. He explained that most people did not know how to go about committing suicide, but a surgeon could handle a revolver as easily as a scalpel. He even offered to help Maurois, should he too wish to avoid seeing the Germans.

On May 23 Dr. Martel wrote himself a prescription for two boxes of phenobarbital in the form of injectable doses. He had already sent his wife to Bordeaux, put his staff on holiday. He dispatched his chief assistant to Angoulême, where the American Hospital had its rear base. Then on June 13, alone in his town house at 18 Rue Weber, Thierry de Martel sat down to his final letters. To Bullitt:

I promised you that I would not leave Paris, but I didn't say whether I would stay in Paris dead or alive. In remaining alive I'd be giving a blank check to my adversary. If I remain in Paris dead, it's a check with no cash to back it up. Adieu.

A copy of Victor Hugo's *Hernani* was found near his body, open to an underlined phrase: "Since one must be grand to face death, I rise."

In a note to his secretary this devout Christian expressed the hope that he would receive a religious burial. It would be useless to attempt to revive him. "I prepare what I do better than our politicians do." He made it as easy as he could for those who would discover his body as day broke on June 14. He shaved a last time, tied a mortuary band around his chin. At 8:25 A.M. his cook found him on the floor of his operating room, detected a faint odor of gas. The police inspector who made an official report found a disconnected pipe from a small gas stove, as well as a large injection needle. The coroner attributed death to phenobarbital and cooking gas.

It was hard, all the same, to accomplish an exemplary, useful death that day, with no press or radio to spread the news, no friends within hundreds of miles. The prefect of police heard about Dr. Martel, of course; his suicide happened to be one of more than a dozen reported that day. Another who didn't stay around for the Germans was the watchman of the Pasteur Institute, who had been the first child saved from rabies.

Even a history of the American Hospital of Paris in the Second World War, published later in the year, described Dr. Martel's heroic work at the operating table, but not his death. The little book was published in German-occupied Paris and bore the endorsement of the Minister of War in Marshal Pétain's Vichy government.

At three that afternoon, as writer Marcel Jouhandeau stood outside the neighborhood grocery store waiting for it to open, a woman alongside him suddenly burst into tears. She was Dr. Martel's servant. "For sixteen years, sir, I served a just man. He didn't want to see what we see, and I have to see what he refused to see, but I can't see *him* anymore."

The archives of the public prosecutor concerning deaths reported by the police become more readable when placed in the context of the German invasion. Suicides of Jewish refugees, for example. "He was suffering from neurasthenia," another refugee told the police about one such case (the dead man was a Russian émigré who had jumped from a roof). "He was no longer able to sleep or eat and acted extremely nervous and depressed." Another refugee, a Czech, killed himself with a razor. A woman of sixty-one with a son at the front posted a letter on June 13 to the commissioner of the fifteenth *arrondissement:* "Not wishing to see the arrival of the Germans in Paris, I am going to kill myself. I give you this warning . . . so that there is no explosion."

As soon as her letter was opened, the commissioner sent a patrolman to her apartment. He did indeed smell gas as he opened the door, before discovering the body.

Most suicide victims were not foreigners or refugees or Jews, but the anguish and depression brought on by France's defeat was a constant refrain in the postmortem investigations.

*   *   *

Preparing her own suicide, André Wurmser's handicapped friend Valentine Prager continued to put her papers in order, hampered by an electricity cut that had begun at four that morning and lasted until eight-thirty. She took up the unfinished letter of adieu to Wurmser. Friends, she said, were telling her what Paris had begun to look like, with the swastika over the Arch of Triumph. She listened to a neighbor's shortwave radio, heard Reynaud's speech a total of four times. She thought that he could simply have said that Paris had been abandoned to save it from destruction.

The silence was astonishing, she told Wurmser. "One can hear a woman walking in the street. And, farther off, a drum. Apparently they are parading without a stop."

The parading is what Parisians remember best about that day. The interminable parading. Police clerk Ferdinand Dupuy heard an account of the doings at the Arch of Triumph from the official guardian of the Eternal Light. German sentinels with submachine guns were posted all around the monument, with an armored car actually parked beneath the arch. Cannon had been positioned at the entrance to each of the principal avenues leading to the arch, with machine guns atop a government building located on the corner of Avenues Wagram and Mac-Mahon. All this, it seemed, in preparation for the visit of Generals von Bock and von Küchler. Dupuy saw irony in this German homage to an Unknown Soldier whose tomb was being profaned by the swastika hoisted above the arch. He noted with satisfaction that after protests the swastika disappeared from the monument, never to return.

After the generals had paid their respects the parade got under way, with troops arriving at the monument from Avenues de Wagram and Friedland, moving on to Avenues de la Grande-Armée and Kléber. All that day, all night, the troops paraded to military music. Presumably this tour of the arch was an obligatory maneuver for the best-dressed regiments in Paris that day, on the way to the final battles of the Battle of France.

With their flair for pictorial propaganda, the Germans were soon ready with films and photographs of the marching men. The illustrated propaganda weekly *Signal,* published in English as well as

French, would be available on all newsstands in Paris. In an early issue, a photograph of German troops at the Arch of Triumph was reproduced alongside another showing a triumphant French army led by Marshal Joffre at the same site in 1919, and on the following page an illustration showed German soldiers passing under the arch on the first of March 1871. *Signal* showed the French their gas reservoirs on fire, but also let them see fellow Parisians seated on the Champs-Elysées as German military trucks rolled by. Or a sidewalk café, with Parisians sipping aperitifs alongside uniformed Germans. "Just as in peacetime," the caption reads, "Parisians are seated at outdoor cafés on the Champs-Elysées. . . ."

Newsreels made by and for the Germans show their soldiers walking up the steps of the Eiffel Tower to hang the swastika flag, and parading on the Champs-Elysées, black smoke in the western sky. French civilians seen in these newsreels seem curious to find out what is going on around them, but they do not smile. The cameraman clearly has trouble finding happy faces, until he catches the smiles of two young ladies who do not bear the world on their shoulders.

HOLIDAY IN REICH
MARKS PARIS FALL

———

Hitler Orders 3-Day Festival
As Exultant Crowds Sing
"Deutschland Ueber Alles"

This from the *New York Times*, with a report that Hitler ordered church bells rung to commemorate the victory. In Berlin bands played and crowds cheered, and the State Opera gave a special performance of one of Hitler's favorites, *Die Meistersinger*. The entire cast came to the front of the stage to raise arms in the Nazi salute, with a response in kind from the audience (except, the *Times* was careful to note, in the box of U.S. chargé d'affaires Alexander C. Kirk, whose American guests only stood, presumably not joining in the singing of the Nazi anthem *Horst Wessel Lied* or *Deutschland Über Alles*).

Hitler's own newspaper said the three-day flag display celebrated not only the fall of Paris but victory in Norway. The loss of the industrial capacity of Paris, explained *Völkischer Beobachter,* considerably weakened French military and economic potential—half the production of plane motors and equipment, of armored vehicles and machine tools, with much of the country's chemical output and manufacturing of arms and munitions, optical equipment, and ball bearings.

In his diary Joseph Goebbels added to that: "Panic and disintegration have demoralized the entire city."

Headquarters of General Bogislav von Studnitz at the Crillon Hotel happened to be steps away—across narrow Rue Boissy d'Anglas—from the American Embassy. As soon as it was clear who his new neighbor was—as soon as the swastika was raised over the hotel—Ambassador Bullitt sent his chief aides over to meet the German commander. The point was to find out what was happening, to ascertain German attitudes toward the civilian population, and to see how the Americans could be helpful to Parisians under occupation.

A narrow street separated embassy and hotel, but it was a busy one. As Bullitt's emissaries—Counselor Robert Murphy, Colonel Horace Fuller, Commander Roscoe H. Hillenkoetter—stood on the sidewalk waiting for a military convoy to go by, a German vehicle drew up in front of them and an officer stepped out and said in English, "You are Americans, aren't you?" The officer had lived in the United States for some years. "Can you tell us where we might find a suitable hotel here?"

The question was so unexpected, so incongruous, as Murphy later recalled the moment, that the Americans burst out laughing. One of them—Hillenkoetter or Fuller—replied to the German, "The whole city seems to be in your possession. It has hundreds of empty hotels. Take your pick."

In the lobby of the Crillon, the Americans ran into a police commissioner they knew. He told them how he had been ordered to open the Crillon and raise the swastika in place of the French flag. When he could find no way to get into the locked and shuttered establishment, a German colonel warned him, "If the hotel is not open in fifteen minutes and the French flag is not down, we will shoot it down and shoot you, too!" A locksmith was quickly located. "I perspired," the police officer added. Now this grand hotel, whose guests had included kings and chiefs of state, could be the home of the conquerors. The building had been designed by architect Jacques-Ange Gabriel in the reign of Louis XVI to serve as the home of ambassadors and distinguished foreign guests. . . .

Murphy and the attachés went up to the Prince of Wales suite. There Murphy found a colonel who remembered him from Munich fifteen years earlier. He was now von Studnitz's aide-de-camp, so from then on the Americans were treated as old friends. The general ordered up champagne from the hotel's cellar, the best in the house, he said. (It didn't make much of an impression, for Hillenkoetter remembered that they drank brandy.) The attachés got a chance to question the general about the military situation, and his answers seemed frank enough. He expected mopping-up operations in France to take another ten days, after which preparations would begin for the invasion of Britain.

Ambassador Bullitt had wished no contact with the occupation forces. But when his chief assistants told him that von Studnitz was offering to come over to see him to reciprocate for the courtesy visit, and that the general was talking freely about German military strategy, the ambassador changed his mind. Murphy was to find the German commander cooperative in other ways, notably in granting exit visas to Americans and even to some French and British nationals. This suggested that the Germans were confident that the war would soon be over.

At eleven that morning the two senior civil authorities remaining in Paris, Seine Prefect Achille Villey and Police Prefect Roger Langeron, filed into the Hotel Crillon together. Langeron noted that General von Studnitz wore a monocle. That and the little mustache, and the somewhat passé allure of a cavalry officer, prompted Langeron to wonder: Was the Nazi army so much like the Kaiser's? Studnitz was accompanied by Colonel Hans Speidel, then and later the good German. The commander led off with a question: "Do you guarantee order?" Langeron replied for the French side, "I guarantee it if I'm left to work in peace." The general paused, then declared, "If order is kept, if I can count on the security of my troops, you won't be hearing from me."

Fair enough; the rest was detail. The Germans were prepared to rescind the forty-eight-hour curfew, but there would have to be a nightly curfew at nine (and since Paris was switching to German time, that meant eight o'clock to Frenchmen).

At one-thirty that afternoon it was the turn of General von Studnitz to leave the Crillon and cross the narrow street to call on William Bullitt. He promised the ambassador that American property would be respected, and that the German military administration would be cooperative.

That morning, during the meeting of Robert Murphy and the military attachés with the German commander, von Studnitz had invited his visitors to attend the parade of his former division, the 185th Infantry Division, known as the Green Heart; they were to march across Place de la Concorde at three-thirty that afternoon. The Americans accepted. When they walked to the center of the square at the appointed time, von Studnitz invited them to join him on the reviewing stand. That would not look good in newsreels, the Americans decided, and so they replied that it was the general's division, and his glory. And then, in Murphy's recollection, they beat a hasty retreat toward the crowd of ordinary Parisians gathered to watch the goings-on.

But correspondent Walter Kerr was also there, and to his astonishment he spied Robert Murphy walking from the embassy to the reviewing platform to take his place alongside von Studnitz. The band struck up a military march, troops began to pour in from Rue Royale. And there, in front of this unhappy newsman, was a representative of his government standing alongside a Nazi officer while German army cameramen recorded every instant of the scene for the newsreels. Later, walking back to the embassy with Murphy, Kerr asked why he had allowed that to happen. Murphy said the answer was simple: "The general wanted the ambassador, and the ambassador told me to take his place." Clearly the Counselor of Embassy was as unhappy about the matter as Kerr was, and preferred to say nothing more.

The American Hospital had discharged its duty to French soldiers by June 13, when French military authorities requested that all soldiers who could sit up be evacuated; they were taken by ambulance to railway stations, where special trains waited to remove them from the battle zone. Now, on the first day of the occupation, hospital authorities discovered that some eight hundred French soldiers, many of them wounded, were being held in the presidential Elysée palace. Two American volunteer ambulance drivers, Mrs. Laurens Hamilton and Miss Charlotte Moulton, sped off to the Rue du Faubourg Saint-Honoré and talked their way into the Elysée prisoner camp. Finding that a number of the interned soldiers were badly wounded, they managed to persuade their German guardians to allow the evacuation of twenty of the most desperate cases; they were taken to a hospital near the Gare d'Austerlitz. Then the women returned to the American Hospital to tell the officer in charge, managing governor Edward B. Close, what they had discovered, especially that many more soldiers detained at the Elysée were in immediate need of help. Although it was then ten-thirty at night, Close and Mrs. Hamilton, with a doctor and a nurse, drove back to the presidential palace with medical supplies, got German approval to administer first aid. Next morning the team returned to pursue the treatment, taking along a supply of bread. On that and the following days they were able to evacuate more soldiers to Paris hospitals.

PEOPLE OF PARIS

German troops have occupied Paris.

The city is placed under Military Government.

The Military Governor of the Region of Paris will take necessary measures for the security of troops and the preservation of order.

The orders of the Military Authorities must be obeyed without conditions.

Avoid any irresponsible action.

Any act of sabotage, active or passive, will be severely punished.

It is up to the prudence and intelligence of the population of Paris for the city to benefit from the advantages due to an open city.

German troops have received the order to respect the population and its property, on condition that the population remain calm.

Everyone must remain in his home or place of work and resume his activity.

> This is the best way for each person
> to serve the city, the population,
> and himself.
>> The Commander-in-chief
>> of the Army Group

Few who read this wall poster could know that the general who signed it was German general Fedor von Bock, whose divisions had not been responsible for the sickle-cut operation and Sedan, but had spearheaded the drive south, east, and west of Paris, and then straight through.

Before the day was over, Germans in loudspeaker trucks became a familiar sight—and sound. Even at City Hall two German officers were seen descending from an open staff car to harangue the crowd, and in excellent French. Their message: If the French signed a peace agreement with Germany, the Germans would take care of Britain in a fortnight.

Prefect Villey put final touches to the issue of the *Bulletin Municipal* to be distributed next morning—a shorter-than-usual issue, printed on two sides of a single sheet. His declaration assumed all the more importance in it:

It is possible to carry out one's responsibilities because, following orders of the Government, all necessary measures concerning security, hygiene, food, and fuel supply, administrative matters, have been taken to allow normal activity to continue.

The population will show dignity by maintaining order, discipline, and harmony.

Among the institutions that worked that day was the municipal subway system, the Métropolitain, now in fact the only means of public transport. But it carried only 300,000 passengers a day now, the lowest number since 1903, at which time only two lines functioned. There didn't happen to be many Parisians around to travel by subway or any other means, and those who were there didn't have many places to go. By the end of the year, with restrictions still in place on surface travel, the subway was carrying 2.8 million persons daily.

Late in the afternoon a young black man who worked for the Paris *Herald Tribune* walked into the office of Walter Kerr, to confess that he was afraid: could Kerr help him find a bicycle so that he could get out of Paris? "But you're an American," Kerr replied. "You have nothing to worry about." "Yes, I do. I was born in Georgia, but they didn't keep records of colored people then. My father took me to Jamaica when I was a boy, and I have a British passport." That was indeed a problem, for everyone expected that British subjects remaining in Paris would be rounded up any day. "Besides," the man added, "the Germans think I'm Senegalese, and you know what they do to Senegalese." He drew his finger across his throat. Kerr went out to talk with Edward Haffel, city editor of the closed *Tribune*. Haffel mentioned an extra bicycle stashed in the basement. The safest place for the Georgia-born Jamaican, in fact, would be the island of Batz, off the Brittany coast. Haffel's wife and children were there, so the would-be fugitive was given a letter for Haffel's wife. He set off after dark.

Marcel Jouhandeau's first encounter with the enemy took place as early as six that morning, when, as he crossed Avenue Malakoff, he found himself face to face with two German noncoms taking tourist snapshots of the Luna Park amusement grounds. Then from his window he watched as the conquering troops followed the same route the refugees and stragglers had used on their north-south trek. Watching the endless procession, Jouhandeau saw it as a bronze fresco. "From a distance the faces appear to be of the same metal as the helmets and the vehicles; they seem unaffected by their surroundings."

In the desert island his neighborhood had become, the still-open pharmacy became a kind of clubhouse. "One laments, one hopes together."

When Paul Léautaud was shaved and ready to take the suburban line into town at noon, he knew that he would find Germans there, for a family that passed through Fontenay-aux-Roses that morning with a pushcart for their belongings had seen them. Léautaud put on his sturdiest shoes before leaving—should he have to come home on foot. On his way to the station he met the mayor's wife, who had heard on the radio that Paris was under the protection of the American Embassy. "We're in great shape," he grumbled. "The American embassy versus the German army. That's what will stop us from having our throats cut. The American ambassador arrives: 'Well, he's dead!' " As always, Léautaud acted out the part, and made the mayor's wife and her children laugh.

He followed his usual route inside Paris, walking up Boulevard Saint-Michel from the Luxembourg station; he was to see his first German now. Then over to Rue de Condé: nobody in at *Mercure de France*. On to his bakery at Carrefour de l'Odéon: no bread. To a second bakery on Rue de l'Ancienne-Comédie: a queue. He did find food for lunch and, just to be sure, some butter, as well as bananas for his little monkey.

Friends tell him that German loudspeaker trucks announce that Parisians are to stay indoors for two full days, while looters are threatened with death. The friends turn on their radio and Léautaud hears "a deep voice, melodramatic, full of tremolos." He begs them, "Oh no, turn that off. Who is this ham?" They tell him the speaker is Paul Reynaud. He finds that hard to believe. "Such a small man to have a voice like that." He decides that Reynaud is an imbecile.

Wakened by the sun, Maurice Kahane looked out over Boulevard Saint-Germain to see the silhouette of a soldier dressed in a long gray-green leather coat, "helmeted to the eyebrows" and directing traffic in a relaxed manner. The oddness of his situation struck him: his only identity document was a British passport; he had a Jewish name. He thought that his career as a publisher was behind him.

In fact he would soon assume his mother's maiden name, Girodias, and under that name become one of the most enterprising publishers in German Paris, even publishing some of his books in German.

As the day drew on, Prefect Langeron decided to make another tour of the city, especially of local police stations, so that his officers could feel that he cared. Everything, everybody was calm. But on his return he learned that his chief deputy, Jacques Jacques-Simon, who also had the rank of prefect as director of police intelligence, had been called in by the Germans and asked to turn over his precious files concerning political activities. In fact the most sensitive documents had already been removed by river barge, then the barge was sunk far from Paris; other files had been burned in Paris. Now Prefect Jacques-Simon was also accused of violating the open-city agreement, which did not permit such destruction.

Langeron ordered his driver to take him to the American Embassy, where he told Ambassador Bullitt that he could not accept this violation of the assurances that had been given him that morning. Bullitt sent Robert Murphy across the street to warn that in these circumstances no one would take responsibility for the security of the city. Jacques-Simon was soon released; he'd later say that Robert Murphy saved his life.

Police clerk Ferdinand Dupuy decided to take a closer look at those famous German soldiers: were they actually bigger and better than Frenchmen? The encounter took place at the corner of Boulevard Raspail and Rue de Sèvres, near the Hotel Lutétia, requisitioned by the Germans. He found the soldiers blond enough, closely shaven, windburned, all in green. They seemed tired, somewhat indifferent to their surroundings, but courteous. Later that evening curiosity drew Dupuy to Montparnasse, where only a couple of cafés were open, though curtained. At the Dôme he found German officers standing at the bar alongside elegantly dressed women wearing swastika armbands; the women seemed to be German too. At another café the women were unmistakably professionals, waiting for German officers to walk in and take them away.

On the first day of their occupation the Germans were deferential, concluded the police clerk. Whether they were going to stay that way remained to be seen. That morning the police had been instructed to turn in their weapons, so they spent the day unarmed, a gesture smacking of a defeated soldiery. By evening a counterorder got them their pistols back, even their carbines, with the suggestion that these arms never be brandished against German soldiers. Civilian Parisians also had to give up their weapons, and soon pistols and hunting rifles and even swords were piling up at neighborhood police stations, for carting away by the Germans to unknown destinations.

At ten that night, General von Studnitz sent a staff car to the Invalides to pick up General Dentz and Colonel Groussard. It was dark, the curfew was on, so no Parisian was likely to see the military governor or be in a position to call him a traitor, as the historians of the von Studnitz division were to say with a touch of irony. The German commander greeted the callers with a stiff bow. Groussard sized up von Studnitz as one of your standard Germans, born in uniform. He had a brick-red complexion set off by small blue eyes; his color got even redder when he was angry.

Dentz told von Studnitz that if he was still in Paris it was by order, a disagreeable order for him to obey. When asked how many men he had at his disposal, he replied that had had some supply and medical corpsmen, a few platoons of gendarmes. "Your goals?" "We no longer have any. We were to preserve order in Paris and provide for food supplies as well as the evacuation of essential state services, but it goes without saying that your arrival has released us of all obligations." Georges Groussard, who was not always to admire Henri Dentz, admired him then. He remembered this instant when Dentz was found guilty of treason.

The tension mounted all the same. Von Studnitz blamed Dentz for the destruction of fuel depots, a violation of the conventions of war. He said that both Dentz and Groussard would be tried for that. Meanwhile they were prisoners. Dentz replied that he had ordered the depots destroyed the previous day, when he had every right to do so. Groussard broke in to say that their presence in the city on French orders did not allow von Studnitz to take them prisoner; they had the right to a safe-conduct back to their own lines. He would take the protest to neutral nations. . . . The German commander was suddenly less angry. He said that the fate of the French officers would be decided by the High Command.

That morning in Tours, Premier Reynaud wrote out a new message for President Roosevelt, and when Ambassador Biddle called on him, the premier asked that it be sent to Washington. It was a confidential document, Reynaud added, but if Roosevelt found it useful he could divulge it to secret sessions of the U.S. Senate and House of Representatives. Four days of bloody fighting had occurred since Reynaud last wrote Roosevelt, his message began. Now France had to choose between more sacrifice, a government in exile continuing the war—or armistice.

The French could elect resistance "only if a chance of victory appears in the distance," explained Reynaud—in the language in which Biddle transmitted the statement to Washington. "The only chance of saving the French nation, vanguard of democracies, and through her to save England, by whose side France could then remain with her powerful Navy, is to throw into the balance this very day, the weight of American power." Even if this did not entirely depend on Roosevelt, concluded Reynaud, if the president could not promise that his country would soon join the war the fate of the world would be different. "Then you will see France go under like a drowning man and disappear, after having cast a last look towards the land of liberty from which she awaited salvation."

In relaying these strong and pathetic words, Biddle added observations of his own. "Reynaud was in a state of profound depression and anxiety." But there was no quibbling with the content of the message: Without action on the part of the United States in the next forty-eight hours, France would have to surrender.

Before the Reynaud plea was on his desk, Roosevelt had sent his own conclusions to the Former Naval Person—Churchill, of course. He assured the allies of his support, but he hadn't committed and couldn't commit the United States to war. Only Congress could do that, and as a first step he was asking the two houses to appropriate fifty million dollars for food and clothing for civilian refugees in France.

Roosevelt added that he hoped France would keep its fleet out of the terms of an armistice.

As supreme commander of the Wehrmacht, the German army, guide of the nation, Adolf Hitler issued a directive from his field headquarters near the Franco-Belgian frontier. The French had not only evacuated the Paris region but had begun to withdraw from the fortified triangle of Epinal-Metz-Verdun behind the Maginot Line, and a fallback below the Loire River was not excluded. It was now possible to prevent the enemy retreating below Paris from establishing a new defense line, and to destroy French forces to the east. Hitler ordered that the offensive be pursued with vigor, supported by Hermann Goering's Luftwaffe. An escape by sea would be rendered impossible by the destruction of harbors and shipping.

That evening one of the best German experts on France, Otto Abetz, who had spent a considerable part of the Hitler era establishing political and cultural ties with Frenchmen willing to listen to what the Nazis had to say, was called to the phone by Foreign Minister Joachim von Ribbentrop, ordered to fly to Hitler's headquarters. It was a Paris mission—this was all von Ribbentrop would say. Hitler was more forthcoming: Abetz was to move to the German Embassy in Paris to represent the Foreign Ministry in its dealings with military occupation authorities.

Abetz was ready for that. In fact he had been flown to Belgium with some of Germany's best French specialists, such as Friedrich Sieburg, author and propagandist; Karl Epting, formerly head of the German University Agency in France; Rudolf Schleier, an official of the German-French Friendship Society. Soon, when Abetz was formally appointed German ambassador to France, these men would prove themselves redoubtable advocates of Nazi doctrine, doctrine not always administered in benign doses.

One of the first jobs Hitler and von Ribbentrop assigned to Abetz was the surveillance of works of art in occupied France. Collections belonging to Jews, for example.

Goebbels could now beam his transmitters away from Paris, to the French heartland. The theme of the pirate radios now became: "It is senseless to die for France at the last hour; it is much more important to live for France."

In New York the publisher of the weekly *New Leader,* Sol Levitas, clipped the day's headline from the front page of the *World Telegram:*

PARIS HAS FALLEN

His young son Mitchel asked why he had done that. "Because I want to frame it with another headline: 'Paris Liberated.' " And when it happened, he did frame the two headlines together.

French counterespionage officer
Col. Paul Paillole.
(*Courtesy Paul Paillole*)

Sgt. Guy Bohn and his wife in
February 1940.
(*Courtesy John Bohn*)

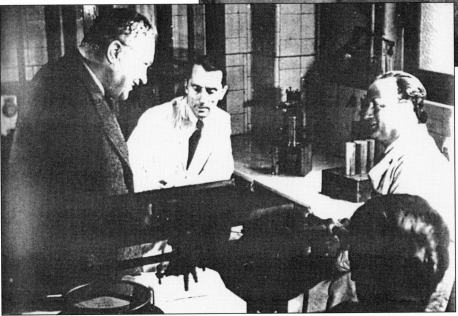

The atomic scientists at the Collège de France. *Left to right*: Lew Kowarski,
Frédéric Joliot, Hans Halban. (*Courtesy Peter Halban*)

German bicycle troops shortly after their arrival in the French capital.
(*UPI/Bettmann*)

German warplanes over Paris.
(*Roger-Viollet*)

The site of French-German discussions in Ecouen on the night of June 13–14.
(*Jérémie Véron*)

German troops file past Arch of
Triumph as they enter central
Paris.
(*Bibliothèque de Documentation
Internationale Contemporaine
{BDIC}*)

Germans parade as they enter the
Place de la Concorde on June 14.
(*BDIC*)

Paris policemen received
rifles on May 17, 1940.
(*Keystone*)

Hitler's *Völkischer Beobachter* headlines the fall of Paris.

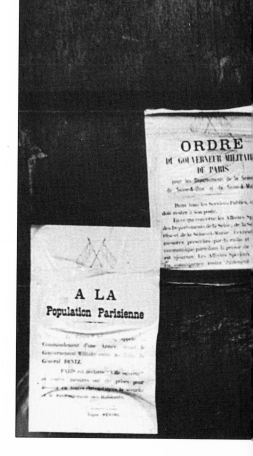

Wall posters on the last day of free Paris: The one on the right announces that Paris is an open city. (*BDIC*)

French officials enter the armistice train in the Compiègne forest. (*BDIC*)

A German armored vehicle drives past the closed Gare Saint-Lazare. (*BDIC*)

Religious procession outside Notre Dame cathedral. (*BDIC*)

Hitler and his staff in Montmartre, on the terrace below
Sacré-Coeur church. (*BDIC*)

U.S. war correspondent Virginia Cowles. (*UPI/Bettmann*)

Paul Reynaud (*right*) the new premier of France, and his predecessor, Edouard Daladier, leaving the Elysée Palace. (*UPI/Bettmann*)

Maurice Chevalier performing in Paris before the German invasion.
(*UPI/Bettmann*)

Ambassador Bullitt, *second from left*, leaving Notre Dame with French political leaders after a service for the victory of Allied forces in May 1940.
(*AP/Wide World*)

Reynaud, *third from left*, poses with his new cabinet, including Charles de Gaulle, in early June 1940. (*Photofest*)

U.S. Ambassador William C. Bullitt
holds a press conference on his return
from Europe to New York in July 1940.
(*UPI/Bettmann*)

German occupation troops visit Notre Dame. (*Sygma*)

Left to right; General Maxime Weygand, Allied commander in chief; Reynaud's deputy Paul Baudouin; Premier Paul Reynaud; and Marshal Philippe Pétain, the new vice-premier; en route to a conference with President Albert Lebrun, May 20, 1940. (*Sygma*)

Civilian refugees heading south to escape the
German army leave Paris with their belongings.
(*La Documentation Française*)

Winston Churchill, General John Dill, Paul Baudouin, Sir Ronald Campbell, Major Clement Attlee, and Premier Paul Reynaud after a war conference in Paris on May 31. (*Sygma*)

39

AFTER JUNE 14

The rest is history. It is recorded in remarkably candid photography taken by or for the Germans, above all in indelible memories, and of course in the transcripts of war crimes and treason trials. The occupation army lost no time in beginning to exercise the victor's prerogatives. General Dentz and Colonel Groussard bore three days of gentlemanly confinement in their headquarters at the Hôtel des Invalides, then were released—with Ambassador Bullitt's help—on the signing of the French-German armistice agreement on June 22.

German officials were soon looking over the shoulders of French officials in every governmental and municipal office. All the details of their occupation had been worked out in advance, printed up in manuals; occupation officers received special training. Places to go, things to do there, had been assigned in advance. Thus a detachment of the German military intelligence corps, the Abwehr, marched into the Left Bank's most spacious hotel, the Lutétia on Boulevard Raspail, to inform management that it had twenty-four hours to vacate all its rooms. Some fifty Abwehr officers took up quarters there immediately.

At the Hôtel du Louvre, across the square from the Comédie Française, one of the new guests was Helmut Knochen, who held a doctorate in philosophy from the University of Göttingen. An SS officer, he was in charge of a small unit of Reinhard Heydrich's Sicher-heitsdienst (security service), responsible for tracking down anti-Nazis, especially Jews. He began at the most obvious source of information, the Prefecture of Police, demanding the files of German political refugees, French anti-Nazi activists, leaders of the French Jewish community.

There were some lucky finds. An Abwehr unit discovered intact files at the headquarters of the security police in the Rue des Saussaies wing of the Interior Ministry, a service responsible for domestic intelligence and counterintelligence. Before long the Gestapo was pouring over captured files in an attempt to discover who on the German side had been leaking sensitive military information. As soon as they could, the Germans carried out house searches at the homes of leading French personalities such as Georges Mandel, Edouard Daladier, and Paul Reynaud, as well as Léon Blum and his air minister, Pierre Cot, and trade union chief Léon Jouhaux. Nor did they miss the headquarters of Masonic institutions.

On June 20 the Hotel Lutétia received a new client in the person of Major Oscar Reile, in charge of counterespionage for the army. As he recalled that instant, he arrived in Paris with a certain trepidation; he had never set foot in the city before. But he had been working against France since 1935, knew the country as well as a student of its language and its culture could from afar, and he commanded thirty agents who spoke French well. Reile got along with the chief of Abwehr operations in Paris, Colonel Friedrich Rudolph, who warned him that if they did not do the job of protecting German forces against espionage and sabotage, the feared Gestapo would be called in—and it would do a rougher job.

Reile was informed of another bit of luck. When German troops reached La Charité-sur-Loire they discovered sealed railway cars containing top secret archives, including those of French military intelligence. What Reile didn't know, of course, was that the French had managed to hide the two most vital of their secrets, the identity of the spy known as H.E., and the codebreaking operation against Enigma.

Now Parisians began to come home. The Germans helped them, offering truck transport when necessary, distributing gasoline to fugitives with motor vehicles in working order. Neighborhood statistics suggest that poorer people returned faster than richer ones.

Jews, even foreign Jews who had taken refuge in France during the Hitler era, returned to Paris. Thus Edouard Gurevitch, the correspondence-course student of nineteen who had walked out of the city on foot while his mother and sister stayed. He had his high school exams to pass, and where could he do that if not in Paris? On the day of his return he discovered that he had arrived just in time for the exam for the next-to-last year of secondary school, held at the Sorbonne. He walked in and passed it, and even had time to complete the high school program before going underground.

The Gurewicz family (no relation), which had never left Paris, suddenly found that their friends—like themselves, Jews of foreign origin—were returning to the German-occupied capital from temporary refuge in the provinces. Paris was their home, and their source of livelihood. Mirra Gurewicz escaped the roundup of foreign Jews in July 1942 by sleeping over at a friend's. Her parents stayed home since they had understood that only young people were to be taken away (for forced labor). The Germans didn't take her father because he was over sixty; her mother, under fifty-five, was arrested and never heard from again.

German refugee Erna Friedlander, who with the friend who had taken her in when her request for internment had been refused hadn't left home all during the tense days of June, finally decided that she could safely venture out into the streets of German Paris. Erna's friend said that for her part she couldn't spend another day without going to her hairdresser.

They walked. They got as far as the Parc Monceau, the largest park in northwest Paris. There the two women found freshly painted signs in German: RASEN NICHT TRETEN—Keep Off the Grass. Erna began to laugh uncontrollably. It was so typical of Germans!

Police clerk Ferdinand Dupuy was now collecting stories from returning Parisians. He learned how one family, which fled Paris on June 12—husband, wife, two daughters—managed to do only eighteen miles in thirty-seven hours. Forced to abandon their car under German air attack, they returned to find it had been burned to cinders, along with their clothing and cash. When the Germans caught up with them they proved to be gentle, sent them walking back to Paris, a four-day trip, since they avoided highways and walked across fields, with nights spent in barns, daytime forays into roadside orchards. Another family of five had a breakdown on the road to Orléans. The Germans found them a car in working order and gave them the gas they needed to get back to Paris.

Soon the Paris police had a new assignment: to keep the parade of returning Parisians, their misery showing, away from Place de la Concorde, seat of the High Command.

Stadtkommissar Helmut Rademacher, a senior official in the Reich Finance Ministry, had been given a crash course in occupation duties; yet he found running an occupied city a very big job. By the time the Germans marched in, the food chain had come to a total standstill. In the first days of the occupation, the only available stocks were of perishable foods, discovered in the storerooms of the city's railroad stations. These were hauled out, along with refrigerated stocks of butter, eggs, cheese, frozen fish, and meat.

Gradually, often with the encouragement or material assistance of the authorities, the market gardeners of the countryside surrounding Paris began showing up on the traditional market square in central Paris with their crops; neighborhood street markets also began to receive fresh food again. Prices moved, but the police were even swifter. On June 22 a decree reduced maximum prices of essential foods to levels in effect at the beginning of the month. Starting on June 17, Parisians were restricted to 350 grams a day of ordinary bread, although at the insistence of the gluttonous Germans, pastry shops were authorized to concoct their traditional delicacies. To believe city official Eugène Depigny, in the first days the Germans concentrated their purchases on field glasses, cameras, road maps, comfortable shoes. Later, senior officers would go for antiques. Coal was reserved for bakers, laundries, restaurants, or homemakers using it for cooking; milk was for infants under eighteen months, then for children up to five, the ill, and the elderly.

Supplies came closer to normal, of course, when the trains were running again. Meat production at the Villette slaughterhouse was back to normal within a month of the invasion.

When Prefect Langeron discovered that pharmacies which remained open sometimes lacked basic ingredients to fill subscriptions, he ordered that stocks be taken from those pharmacies that had been abandoned by their owners or managers. An emergency medical service was set up. And there was still the problem of stray dogs; there were quite a lot of them now, and the danger of rabies was never absent.

Near the Saint-Odile church in her northwest Paris neighborhood, Michèle Rogivue watched as German soldiers set up outdoor tables and then put a tent roof over them. Bread and cheese were spread out on the tables, while loudspeakers announced that the food was free: "All French people can serve themselves. . . ." But "all French people" turned their backs on the tent, at least at first. Michèle stayed around long enough to see hunger win out over principle, especially after dark, when there were fewer people to watch. "It's our cheese, after all," murmured the Parisians who accepted it. The Rogivues did not approach the tables, but their faithful concierge did, and distributed what she took away generously. "It will be that much less for them," she explained.

When Germany's ambassador-to-be Otto Abetz strolled the streets of Paris in the first days, he saw gratifying examples of what he considered to be fraternization, above all in working-class districts. Thus he came upon a happy member of the occupation army at a café table on the boulevard not far from the Opéra. Speaking with the accent of a dockworker, the soldier was displaying his biceps, explaining in broken French, "Gold *kaput,* work gold—look at my gold." Abetz remembered seeing French bystanders applauding this elementary demonstration of economic philosophy.

Claude Poirey, the eleven-year-old who lived down the street from Place Blanche, was walking past the garish Moulin Rouge cabaret when an open German car pulled up. The driver sat at the wheel while his officer stood to take tourist snapshots. While looking for suitable subjects, the officer spotted a familiar face, a famous music hall singer.

"Fréhel," he called out to her, "a photo!" Turning to see who was addressing her, the singer caught sight of the uniform, then showed her back again, jabbing at her posterior. "Here she is, Fréhel!" she snapped. She happened to be an amply endowed Breton woman. The German took it with a laugh; little Claude stood openmouthed at her daring. (If only this chanteuse had continued to show only her backside. Soon she was performing in Nazi Germany, an act not forgotten at the liberation.)

The would-be Fascist Pierre Drieu La Rochelle, who had been hiding out in the last days of free Paris, worried about "the Jews and Anglophiles" who might have done him harm, knew that with the Germans in charge the literary scene was bound to change—even his favorite publishing house of Gallimard and its *Nouvelle Revue française,* so he confided to his diary. It would "crawl at my feet. This heap of Jews, pederasts, and weak-livered Surrealists is going to bow its head now." Drieu's vision proved accurate. With German support he became master of the *Nouvelle Revue française,* which no longer had room for Jews, nor for many pederasts or weak-livered Surrealists either.

The Germans did get the trains moving. Gradually the subway returned to prewar standards. What lacked were the buses, which were often stuck in the provinces, and in any case there would have been no fuel to run them. Suburban commuters used railway lines or bicycles, or walked to the nearest subway. Telephone service was limited to Paris, but letters could be sent anywhere within the zone occupied by the German army; service to Vichy and the south would come later.

Banks reopened, although reduced personnel and monetary restrictions kept activity at a minimum. Thus individual depositors were able to withdraw a maximum of five hundred francs each fortnight from the national savings bank, the Caisse d'Epargne. Those banks that had transferred their activities to safer quarters in the south now found work to do in the Vichy zone.

Maurice Zuber, a young employee of the Comptoir d'Escompte de Paris (nucleus of what would become the Banque Nationale de Paris), had been evacuated from the capital on June 9, to wind up in the watering town of Châtel-Guyon in the Auvergne hills. The Hotel

Splendid there had been requisitioned for his bank, while other Parisian banks were housed in other resort hotels around town. He was soon to learn that one could phone only to Vichy (some thirty miles away) or to the regional capital, Clermont-Ferrand, and to do this one waited five or six hours (or tried one's luck at night). One day Zuber was called to the phone to speak to the stationmaster of nearby Riom, who said he'd been keeping a heap of burlap bags in a storeroom, each bearing the stencil of the Bank of France: what was he supposed to do with them? Young Zuber biked over to Riom, dutifully poked around. What he found in the burlap bags were gold bars meant for the various Parisian banks now scattered around the Auvergne landscape.

When it was possible to do so, Zuber's bank sent its people back to Paris. But some were put to work in the Vichy zone. Maurice Zuber was assigned to the branch in Lyon, which had soon become the metropolis of Pétain's France.

Back in Paris, schools reopened. Teachers who hadn't gone too far away were back on duty by June 17. On July 10 the authorities counted 346 elementary schools in operation, with 38,000 pupils, five junior high schools, ten high schools, fifteen professional and technical schools. The postponed high school graduation exams were scheduled for July 28 and 29.

But many of the factories that had made Paris the industrial center it was remained closed, even if the workers were back (or had never left). The Germans knew what to do with closed factories: they requisitioned them, filled them with skilled workers, gave them orders for war matériel. Renault was one of the big companies soon operating under German authority, with its directors on the premises.

With the French government far from Paris—shifted from the Tours region to still more remote Bordeaux—and a deputy ambassador substituting for stay-behind Bullitt, communications between Washington and the French went through U.S. Consul Henry S. Waterman in Bordeaux. This was how Roosevelt's reply to Reynaud reached the French premier on June 15. Americans admired and supported France, Roosevelt insisted, and they would continue to send materials required for the French war effort. "I know that you will understand," added

Roosevelt to a Reynaud who of course could not understand, "that these statements carry with them no implication of military commitments. Only the Congress can make such commitments."

Churchill tried from his side, cabling Roosevelt that night: "A declaration that the United States will, if necessary, enter the war might save France. Failing that, in a few days French resistance may have crumbled and we shall be left alone." Churchill went further, letting the American president see the possibility that his war cabinet might be overthrown by a pro-German majority, and a new government that would place His Majesty's navy alongside that of Germany, Japan, France, and Italy, a coalition stronger than the United States.

That day William Bullitt, as dean of the diplomatic corps—indeed, as just about the only senior diplomat left in Paris—paid a courtesy call at the Hotel Crillon, a visit not recorded in the annals of the U.S. State Department. But a member of General von Studnitz's staff who would become his division's historian was present. "What could have been the feelings of Bullitt," wondered he, "in this Hotel Crillon which, 20 years earlier—*tempora mutantur*—after the German defeat in the first World War, had served as President Wilson's residence and where Wilson had his first talks—which eventually turned out so badly— about the creation of the League of Nations? And especially Bullitt who was known as one of the most vehement defenders of the 'anti-Fascist' policies of his President Roosevelt, and a determined opponent of appeasement?"

Whatever he may have felt, Bullitt remembered why he was there. He politely but firmly asked the protection of the German command for foreign missions in Paris, empty or occupied.

Later that day, for a less momentous request, Bullitt sent naval attaché Roscoe Hillenkoetter across the street. Bullitt wished to drive up to Chantilly to see how his house had survived the battle. The question seemed to unsettle General von Studnitz; then he said, "Of course," but could the ambassador wait a day? Since there had been heavy fighting up there—which of course Bullitt knew—he wished to have the house looked over first.

That same night German soldiers climbed to the roof of the American Embassy to string telegraph and telephone lines for the communications center being set up at the Crillon across the way. Bullitt rushed another emissary to the hotel to warn that if the lines were not removed within the hour, he would consider it a violation of American soil and personally would shoot at any German still on the premises. And the ambassador actually posted himself and his chief aides at windows, each with a revolver in hand. They were loaded, six bullets for each weapon.

The Germans began to remove the lines at once.

Next day General von Studnitz was as good as his word, assigning the American ambassador and his group a motorcycle platoon for the ride up to Chantilly. On inspection, Bullitt found that the house had suffered only minor damage (a shell had knocked off a piece of an upper corner). There had been no break-in, no looting.

So Bullitt remained in Paris longer than he had originally intended, because, in the words of Robert Murphy, the Germans were "so unexpectedly communicative about their accomplishments and intentions." The information couldn't be sent home, so it was stored up, reported to Washington a bit later.

Murphy remembered another detail. When a consignment of food and cigarettes for the embassy was held up at customs, the problem turned out to be a German officer who, when told where the shipment was to go, said, "So these are Bullitt's cigarettes! Well, he won't get them. I used to live in Philadelphia and I never did like Bullitt."

On occasions when the ambassador really did need to get word to Washington, he would say what he had to say to Ernst Achenbach, the official in charge of reopening the German Embassy; Achenbach would relay the message to the German Foreign Ministry in Berlin, which would pass it on to the American Embassy there. Bullitt never knew whether a message had actually been received by Washington.

Two of the legislators who had stayed in Paris, Jean Chiappe and Noël Pinelli, made their way through barricades and artillery positions to call on Bullitt, and found that he had switched from his customary joviality to "somber pessimism," in Pinelli's phrase. The visitors asked if the ambassador could help protect civilian property, and heard him reply that he was not going to stay around much longer. They resisted the temptation to remind Bullitt of earlier promises to stay. And they remembered being shocked by his disabused comment, "The way they're going, they'll be at the White House by Christmas."

In truth, Bullitt could only preside over a house of asylum now. The ambassador's residence was open to any embassy official who wished to live there. Of the approximately 500 American citizens who stayed on in Paris, 266 had registered with the embassy. And while some of those who had joined the exodus returned, about half of the total American population wished to leave. With valid passports they could travel to the Vichy zone, but getting motor fuel proved an insurmountable obstacle for most, and with the suspension of bank operations the financial situation of many had become desperate. Some Americans moved into the Hotel Bristol on Rue du Faubourg Saint-Honoré, an easy walk from the embassy; the hotel was placed under American protection. In all, the embassy issued some seven hundred certificates for posting on business and residential properties, attesting to their American ownership; all seemed to be respected. The American Hospital, the American Red Cross, and even some businesses continued to function. Bullitt and his staff enjoyed freedom of movement.

British official buildings were sealed, and about one thousand British subjects required protection. Some of them also needed cash, and a voluntary British Colony Committee helped provide it. The official premises of Canada, South Africa, and Egypt were also sealed under American authority. Bullitt tried to do the same for Belgium, but the Germans refused to accept that. All bank accounts were blocked; there was no foreign exchange, although the Germans were buying French francs with their marks.

On Sunday, June 16, the war still raged, with French divisions retreating under fire to the Loire valley; they continued to hold Orléans and Gien, while the Germans advanced along their flanks. General Georges held ground where he could, identifying strong points that could block or at least slow down the enemy advance. But, as he now informed General Weygand, it was no longer possible to do what he had been doing. Weygand arrived in Bordeaux at noon that day with this bad news. The French army needed an armistice, but would not capitulate. The distinction was important to Maxime Weygand; capitulation signified dishonor, armistice an honorable peace.

Parisians could not know these things, of course, no more than they knew what their government was deciding in Bordeaux. At that morning's cabinet meeting Reynaud had to confess that Roosevelt was offering nothing more than material aid, while the British were reminding the French that they had an engagement not to make a separate peace. Because the government was still unready to sue for peace, Pétain announced his resignation. "Oh no, you can't do that to us, not now!" exclaimed President Lebrun. The meeting took a decision all the same: Reynaud would fly to Nantes in southern Brittany to meet Churchill, whom he had warned that if Reynaud himself wasn't allowed to ask for an armistice, a new French premier who was ready to agree to whatever Hitler desired would replace him.

Churchill didn't fly to France this time. He informed Reynaud by cable that Britain was holding France to its agreement not to sign a separate peace. But if France would sail its fleet to British ports, His Majesty's Government could let France talk to the Germans. On the other hand, Britain was also prepared to merge with France in a permanent union, with combined defense, political and financial institutions. . . .

We are asked to believe that Hélène de Portes, still at Reynaud's side, slipped him a note. "I hope that you will not be an Isabelle of Bavaria," she wrote, referring to the French queen who recognized an English king, her son-in-law, as successor to the throne of France.

It was too late, of course, even for an Isabelle. That night a Reynaud who would not surrender yielded his chair to a Pétain who would.

Bullitt waited until June 30 to leave Paris. Then he organized a veritable caravan including Robert Murphy, his military and naval attachés, and Third Secretary Carmel Offie. There was even a stowaway in the person of Dudley Gilroy, a retired English major who managed a racing stable near Bullitt's home in Chantilly; he was accompanied by his American-born wife. Bullitt gave Gilroy an American passport and told him not to open his mouth when they passed German control points. The weather was superb. They made good time on the way to

La Bourboule, another spa in the Auvergne hills with an abundance of hotels, stopping for a picnic on the way. At La Bourboule, and when he reached Madrid a week later on his way back to America, Bullitt composed lengthy cables based on talks with Pétainists and anti-Pétainists in Vichy. He was to return to a Washington not quite ready to employ his energies; eventually he would turn to the Free French for suitable work.

Before anybody back home knew what had become of William Bullitt, the American Embassy in Berlin dispatched a first secretary, young but seasoned diplomat George Frost Kennan, to find out what was happening in Paris. He drove there from Brussels on July 2 in a borrowed Chevrolet with an American ambulance driver as companion. They passed scenes of devastation, for they necessarily followed the invasion route, and didn't fail to meet the flow of weary refugees returning to their homes. Paris seemed deserted, and even the German officers sitting outdoors at the Café de la Paix appeared lonely. The American Embassy, noted Kennan, had lost its flag and its shield, and the high iron gates were closed. In the absence of Bullitt, Kennan talked to Maynard Barnes, the press attaché, who told him how exasperated the ambassador had become over the inability to send or receive messages. Kennan promised to persuade Washington to make things just as difficult for the German Embassy there.

He spent the night at the Hotel Bristol. "Much of the hotel personnel was missing," he noted; "the whole place had a make-shift atmosphere; but the Americans had succeeded in keeping the Germans out and were pleased enough with the arrangement."

Next day he tried to find friends; nobody home. Noticing Germans in restaurants "trying so desperately to be genteel when there was nobody to be genteel before," he looked for a metaphor to sum up what he was seeing. "Could one not say to the Germans that the spirit of Paris had been too delicate and shy a thing to stand their domination and had melted away before them just as they thought to have it in their grasp?"

Leaving southern France for Spain, William Bullitt and his party ran into trouble at the border, where a Spanish immigration inspector questioned the identity of ex-Major Gilroy and his wife. Bullitt was passing them off as his butler and maid, but Frances Gilroy, a Philadelphia lady from Bullitt's society days, was anything but a maid in bearing. It took Third Secretary Carmel Offie to solve the matter. Taking the Spanish officer aside, he whispered, "Don't you understand that the ambassador has a mistress?"

For Paris-American Florence Gilliam, it was like the song Americans would soon be singing about the French capital, "No matter how they change her, I'll remember her that way." The city's essential beauty had been preserved. Indeed, with sandbags and other protective structures removed, Paris looked better than it had for many months. She found it possible to get around without running into signs in German, or German sentinels or vehicles. One could even see the blackout as "at once fearsome and beautiful." Of course there were inconveniences, such as the ban on private automobiles. That meant a lot of walking, a lot of subways, and because the underground was now the principal means of getting around for German soldiers as well as Parisians, the trains were crowded. And better not miss the last subway, even if one had permission to be out late, for then there would be a long walk home or an expensive ride in a horse-drawn buggy or bicycle taxi. More evenings were spent at home.

In the early days of the occupation, Sylvia Beach kept her Shakespeare & Company bookshop open on Rue de l'Odéon. Business was good, with French customers avid for reading matter in English. Eventually she got a helper, a young French Jewish woman excluded from her Sorbonne studies under Nazi regulations. Miss Beach decided to share her new friend's fate, which meant staying out of public places. Soon Jews could not even sit on benches in the park. Shakespeare & Company survived as long as American neutrality did.

By the time the Germans marched in, the American Church on the Quai d'Orsay was filling up with members of the choir, of the congregation, anyone belonging to the church who felt safer within its walls than outside. The church obviously benefited from an American Embassy certification that both the religious edifice and the adjoining service facilities were its property, a notice put up personally by U.S. Vice-Consul John R. Wood.

Organist Edmund Pendleton conducted what he called "talks" every Sunday morning. His congregation was reduced to an ever smaller group of regulars, mostly women; the number declined further when the embassy urged citizens to leave Paris in the spring of 1941, and when the United States actually joined the war that December, and Americans were interned, only a few elderly ladies continued to show up for services conducted by French Protestant ministers. By then the Germans had begun to take over the commodious church installations, starting with the gym.

The last days of the Paris *Herald Tribune* center on its principal hold-out, sports columnist W. H. Robertson, the diminutive eccentric known as the Sparrow. He and Laurence Hills, director of the Paris edition, had refused to leave. Hills was to succumb to fatal illness within months, leaving the plant in the hands of the paper's French manager. Meanwhile, so his biographer tells us, the Sparrow would not admit that anything had changed. He continued to go to the office each day and even wrote his column and kept his room at the Hotel Lotti on Rue Castiglione, although all the other rooms were occupied by German officers. According to Walter Kerr, on the very first night of the occupation the Sparrow was stopped by a guard as he left his hotel, for the curfew was in effect. Drawing himself up to his full four-feet-eight, he roared, "Where do you get that *stuff?*" The officer who was called down to arbitrate happened to have met the Sparrow at the Berlin Olympics in 1936. The American got out of his hotel, and the officer went with him.

As for Kerr, he kept fighting for the right to send news stories to his New York paper, without success. At the Paris *Tribune* office, where there was nothing to do, he had a surprise one day when the paper's black employee who had left on a bicycle for the Brittany coast turned up, exhausted but happy to be back. He had gotten as far as Roscoff, but never made it to the island elected as sanctuary; local inhabitants felt they had just enough food for themselves. On his way back to Paris he was picked up by the Germans in Le Mans, and they were convinced that he was a colonial soldier; he was placed in a prisoner-of-war compound. But he carried a letter Kerr had given him, attesting to his American citizenship, on assignment for an American newspaper; that won him his freedom. Now he sat down to remove a shoe and sock, brandished a piece of grimy paper. It contained the names of fourteen British soldiers in the camp who wanted their families to know where they were. Kerr told the black American, who was really a British subject, that if the Germans had found the list on him he would have been shot. "I know it, but they were nice fellows, and they had to do all the dirty work in the camp."

Kerr's own war with the Third Reich was entering a decisive phase. It was made clear that he would *never* get permission to send stories from Paris. Nor could he go to Berlin; his paper's bureau there had been closed by the Germans. He had a visa for Portugal, but to reach there would have to cross Spain, and his Spanish visa had expired. So he got himself some red ink and changed the date on it, and traveled through Spain to Portugal without a hitch. In Lisbon he ran into the Duke of Windsor at the bar of his hotel. "I am being sent as governor of the Bahamas," the duke explained with an obvious lack of joy. Kerr told him he understood it was a nice place to be. "Yes?" replied the Duke of Windsor. "Well, name more than one town there." Kerr could not. He returned to his room to write the first of a series of articles on occupied Paris. Then home. His next war would begin in June 1941 in the USSR.

While studying at the Sorbonne, Max Imhoff, Jr., worked as a copy editor on the Paris *Tribune* (where Walter Kerr remembered him as a tall, thin young man with thick eyeglasses). Although born in Clinton, New Jersey, he had a Swiss father and a French mother, so he felt much at home in Europe. When Americans began to leave Paris, he stayed on. There was still work to be done at the *Tribune* office, cleaning up, storing things away for the day the paper could publish again. There was so much to do that one day he was still in the office at curfew time. When he began walking back to his room near the Sorbonne he realized that he had left his glasses in the office, so he returned to retrieve them.

On his way home again he was stopped by German plainclothes

police. He was somewhat casual with his interrogators, making up a
story about taking his girl home. But then he had no name for her. He
was taken to a more serious place of detention and this time he told his
interrogators, in fluent German, the real story about forgetting his
spectacles. They didn't believe that story either, and broke the glasses
to see whether he really needed them. He was escorted home at 3:00
A.M. with a severe warning. Next day there was another round of
questioning, and he was told not to return to the *Tribune*. But he did
get in touch with American correspondent Eric Sevareid, who helped
him get to Spain. From there he walked and hitched rides on peasant
carts all the way to Portugal, where he hired on as a ship's steward to
get across the Atlantic, and home.

Russian writer Ilya Ehrenburg stayed on and on as a guest of the Soviet
Embassy, walking the streets of German Paris in the paradoxical position of an ally of the Nazis who was a Russian Jew and notorious
anti-Fascist intellectual. For this man of Montparnasse it was a dead
city now; in his novel on the fall of Paris, a character refers to it as
Pompeii. Among rare passersby were the physically handicapped, old
women knitting on public benches. All this, mused Ehrenburg, came
as a shock to Germans expecting Sin City. They dined studiously in
open restaurants and photographed each other in front of Notre Dame
and the Eiffel Tower. They purchased souvenirs, obscene postcards,
pocket dictionaries. Prostitutes entreated them. Then the signs began
to appear: ARYAN FIRM. ENTRANCE FORBIDDEN TO JEWS. Occupation
authorities protected their own soldiers with signs like the one posted
at the Dôme café: FORBIDDEN TO GERMANS.

Everything was still in place, decided Ehrenburg, the monuments,
the cafés. Only one thing was missing, and that was Paris.

In his Saint-Sulpice police station, chief clerk Ferdinand Dupuy found
that the German regulations were piling up. In July there would be
some good news for a change: the curfew was put back to 10:00 P.M.,
giving Parisians an extra hour out of doors. Restaurants, cafés, and
other public places had to close at 9:30 P.M., the subway shut down
at 9:45. Between ten at night and five the next morning all movement, by wheel or foot, was *verboten*.

* * *

After driving out of Paris with his precious cargo of heavy water to be used to split the atom, physicist Hans Halban had found temporary quarters for himself, his wife and child, and a laboratory assistant—*and* his precious notes—in a villa outside Clermont-Ferrand. Early in June his colleague Lew Kowarski joined him, bringing equipment from their Paris laboratory transported in military trucks. Frédéric Joliot-Curie stayed on in Paris until June 10 to make certain that everything that could be carried was removed from the Collège de France. He burned the papers he couldn't carry. Then he and wife Irène moved in with the research team in Clermont-Ferrand, only to be ordered by Armament Minister Raoul Dautry on June 16 to proceed to Bordeaux, and then to go abroad, taking the heavy water with them.

The Halbans and Kowarskis drove together to Bordeaux, using roads reserved for the military but open to them thanks to their priority; it was during a lunch stop that Marshal Pétain's appeal for an armistice reached them on a radio in a café. Halban said nothing, but went off to buy poison to use in the event they were intercepted. Unaware of his intention, Kowarski's wife commented, "That's Hans, always shopping." They had their big old Peugeot, the trunk filled with jerry cans of heavy water. Halban's wife, by now aware of their significance, realized that she and Mrs. Kowarski and their two young children were seated just above them in the rear seat.

At the last minute, Joliot decided to stay behind. There were a number of reasons for that, the most important being Irène's health; she was under treatment for chronic tuberculosis, and their children had already been sent to shelter in Brittany. But his teammates and their families sailed to the United Kingdom aboard a small British coal ship, armed with orders "to pursue in Britain research undertaken at the Collège de France, concerning which there must be absolute secrecy." In the judgment of a historian of French atomic research, the hastily scribbled mandate, dated June 16, just before the resignation of the Reynaud cabinet, served to maintain a French presence in wartime nuclear research, while paving the way for the ambitious postwar atomic energy projects that produced both French bombs and French electricity.

The Halbans and Kowarskis spent a dangerous day on the docks at Bordeaux waiting for Joliot, and while they waited a ship moored alongside theirs blew up and sank, victim of a floating mine. On the first day at sea, Halban, with a Belgian diamond dealer also on board, built a raft to preserve their valuable baggage—heavy water and diamonds—in the event of submarine attack.

They made it to Britain, and so did the heavy water. Or, as Joliot-Curie explained it in a note to a colleague: "H. and K. have gotten to England with the gurgle." In the absence of competent French authorities they placed themselves under the British, although their research had gone beyond what their hosts were doing (for the British were busy perfecting radar for war use, leaving atom research to Jewish refugees kept at a distance from military projects). In 1942 Churchill sent the Halban group to Canada to facilitate access to American activities in the field.

The Joliot-Curie team was not to receive credit for its pioneering work for nearly a quarter of a century after the liberation of Paris. When they did, it took the form of a citation and a symbolic payment "in recognition," declared U.S. Atomic Energy Commission director Glenn Seaborg, "of their entitlements for inventions and discoveries under the Atomic Energy Act."

One of the first tasks of the newly installed Gestapo, as monitored by Police Prefect Roger Langeron, was to hunt for Herschel Grynszpan. In November 1938, Grynszpan, then seventeen years old, had shot and killed a German embassy official in Paris, his way of avenging the Nazi deportation of his father and thousands of other Polish Jews (he had really wanted to assassinate the German ambassador). The Paris murder served as the pretext for anti-Jewish rioting in Germany that resulted in the killing of Jews and the looting and destruction of their homes and synagogues—the so-called Crystal Night. Grynszpan was arrested by French police, tried and sentenced. By the time the Germans reached Paris in June 1940 he was in relative safety in Orléans, and Langeron guessed that he had since been taken farther south. When at last he was found—for the disorganized prison system in defeated France could no longer hide him—he was taken away, and never heard from again.

When they weren't looking for Grynszpan, the Germans were reviewing the cases of prisoners in French jails who had been accused of defeatism or worse—and freeing them.

Langeron was now virtually a prisoner himself, dependent on those who could move around, with little opportunity to verify what he heard. This explains his erroneous diary entry of June 18, which he still believed when he published it after the liberation of Paris. "Hitler has been here, on a rapid visit," he wrote. "He went directly to the Arch of Triumph, and reviewed his troops. . . ." When Langeron's men were seeing Hitler in Paris, the Führer was in fact in Munich conferring with Mussolini about peace terms. Hitler had decided to deal softly with the French, both to keep in power a French government the Germans could talk to, and to prevent the French from trying to send their fleet to British ports. In a word, Hitler had conceived Pétain's Vichy regime, which would keep France quiet so that Germany might pursue the war against Britain.

In Bordeaux on June 18 the new Pétain government, which had replaced Reynaud's, put an end to the debate about whether to continue the war or to sue for peace. President Lebrun, with the presidents of the Senate and Chamber, favored pursuing the war from North Africa. Pétain, in the driver's seat now, said it was his duty to stay in France with the French people.

Reynaud could leave if he wished to; Pétain was ready to send him to Washington as ambassador. Reynaud did not go to the United States, or anywhere else he could have been of use; henceforth nothing would go right for the scrappy little ex-premier. Even the woman who encouraged him or (depending on one's viewpoint) sapped his courage would be absent in his travails, for Hélène de Portes was to die in a car accident in which Reynaud was seriously injured, on the way to her home in southern France. He was arrested and put on trial by Vichy, kept in custody by Pétain and his vindictive advisers until the war ended. He had been right about the war, and about the appeasers, but never had a chance to prove it. He was France's least-loved hero.

If they listened to London radio that evening, Parisians would hear the first radio address by that singular junior general, Reynaud's protégé Charles de Gaulle.

France is not alone! She is not alone! She has a vast empire behind her. She can join up with the British empire which controls the seas and continues the war. She can, as Britain does, make use of the vast industrial plant of the United States.

He solemnly invited French officers and men then in Britain, as well as engineers and skilled arms workers, to contact him in London.

Later on, nearly everybody who wished to be somebody remembered hearing Charles de Gaulle's June 18 appeal. Few really did, and it was never recorded or repeated. Listening to London radio had not yet become the habit it was to be in occupied France. By then Radio Paris was silent, but soon there was a new Radio Paris under German sponsorship, just as there were enough newspapers supported by the occupation authorities to make newsstands—to make Paris itself—seem normal again. Some of the dailies bore familiar titles, but there was a flock of new ones, many published by French Fascist movements. Thus a former leader of a movement called the Anti-Jewish Movement of France launched a newspaper whose title translates as "To the Pillory," devoted to denouncing Jews and Freemasons to the Gestapo and to public opprobrium.

One of the surprising political revivals was that of the Communist Party. Acting for party leaders then in hiding, junior officials applied to the German *Kommandantur* for permission to publish *L'Humanité.* The paradox is that the Germans, still allied to the Soviet Union, were ready to say yes; it was the French police who forced a veto. When the French arrested Communists who had come out of hiding to publish *L'Humanité,* the Germans released them.

The police could also say, on July 16, that in the first month of occupation there had not been a single incident between the people of Paris and the occupation forces. Criminality, which had all but disappeared in June, had not reappeared.

Hitler's surprise—he had kept it secret even from Mussolini—was the site of the armistice talks: the Compiègne forest in which the railway car was kept that had served negotiators of Germany's surrender on November 11, 1918. William Shirer was there, reporting for the Columbia Broadcasting System in New York, telling Americans that

Adolf Hitler was at that moment in the chair in which Marshal Foch had sat a war earlier. Inside the car, out of sight and out of hearing of even William Shirer, the Germans made it clear that their peace terms could not be altered. What came out of Compiègne was a France Hitler could live with.

40

SUNDAY, JUNE 23

The unbelievable: Adolf Hitler, incarnation of evil, visiting Paris as a tourist. It is the stuff of fantasy. Even Police Prefect Roger Langeron, we have seen, was ready to believe that it had happened (five days before it actually did); inevitably the tale reported to Langeron, repeated by him, became a source for historians. In his own wartime reminiscences, Pierre Mendès France portrays a Hitler in Paris even earlier (on June 15, the day after the Germans marched in), laying a wreath at the Tomb of the Unknown Soldier. It should be sufficient that Hitler did tour the city he conquered nine days afterward, and a day after signing the armistice.

Thanks chiefly to the revelations of Hitler's preferred architect, Albert Speer, it is known that the Führer was an amateur town planner, like other emperors anxious to transform his capital. "Look at Paris, the most beautiful city in the world," the German dictator told his architect. "Or even Vienna. Those are cities with grand style." For years Hitler had thought of monumental Paris as a model for Berlin. He had in mind the Avenue des Champs-Elysées and the Arch of Triumph; he'd have a taller and broader arch, and in Unter den Linden an avenue even wider than the Champs-Elysées.

* * *

If Hitler had an official sculptor it was Arno Breker, exponent of heroic statuary of the kind both Nazis and Fascists admired. The forty-year-old artist showed German muscle the way the new Germans liked to see it. He was in Berlin on June 22, in his studio home near Grunewald, the woods within the city; it all spelled peace. But shortly after seven that morning there was a sharp rap at his door—the Gestapo. He was asked, politely, to pack for a brief trip; he would be picked up in an hour.

Breker wasn't told more; his wife was upset. And in precisely one hour two junior SS officers were at his door; they had nothing to say either. They drove him through the woods to a small airstrip where there waited a JU-52, the ubiquitous Junkers three-engine military transport. Soldiers were loading it up with crates and baskets of vegetables, bottles of fruit juice—strange war cargo. After three hours of flight the plane landed in unfamiliar country; it was only when he got out of an automobile inside a temporary camp that he found familiar faces, Albert Speer, Hermann Giesler (another of Hitler's preferred architects)—and they were all smiling. Breker learned that he was at Hitler's field headquarters in Bruly-de-Pesche, south of Charleroi, just inside the frontier Belgium shared with France.

Hitler wore a simple uniform, without decorations, a cap pushed down on his head (Breker thought he looked very much like any other soldier). "I intend to discover Paris with you, Speer, and Giesler," the Führer told the artist. "Knowing you to be an old Parisian, I wanted you to set up an itinerary with the most important sights both for architectural significance and picturesqueness." Breker did indeed know Paris. Like so many other foreign artists before him, he had worked there (as early as 1925), and had come to know its cafés and studios (as well as its monuments).

"Paris has always fascinated me," Hitler told him now. For years he had been wanting to go there. But his political activity, starting in 1918, and events since then had made such a visit unlikely. "Now the city gates are open to me!" He wished to enter the world's art capital with artists at his side.

Hitler confided that he might well have marched in Paris, at the head of his troops, even paraded beneath the Arch of Triumph. "But

I just don't want to inflict such a thing on the French after their defeat." Breker's Hitler is not a bad man. But one of Hitler's generals was to say that the Führer had given up the idea of a parade on the advice of Luftwaffe Marshal Goering, who feared a British air attack.

The night at Hitler's headquarters was a short one. Breker remembered rising for breakfast not long after midnight, and the convoy of military vehicles left the base at three for the airstrip. The four-engine Focke-Wulf 200, the famous Condor, had Hitler's regular pilot, Captain Hans Baür, at the controls. At Le Bourget airport, outside Paris, another suite of cars—large Mercedes sedans, Speer remembered—was waiting. Hitler sat next to the driver in the first open vehicle, with Breker, Speer, and Giesler behind. The civilians wore field-gray uniforms so that they did not attract attention. The motorcade—which also included Hitler's deputy, Martin Bormann, and his doctor, Karl Brandt—sped into Paris through deserted northern suburbs, then Porte de la Villette, Rue de Flandre, Rue Lafayette—which gave the party its first sight, the dome of Charles Garnier's ornate Opéra. Still not a soul on the streets, so Breker later remembered, although Hitler's pilot saw concierges on their doorsteps, morning workers, and even thought some of them recognized the Führer in his open car. Certainly policemen spotted him, immediately alerting Prefect Langeron, who, "rather imprudently," so he admitted, had the Reichsführer followed. (For "we're athletic types" at the prefecture, joked its chief.)

> At six a.m. he enters the Opéra [read the report to Langeron]. He visits everything, from top to bottom. He spends a long time on the stage and in the dressing rooms.

No one on the street recognized Hitler, asserted the police report, adding that there were very very few people on the street anyway. No one in Hitler's group, recollecting the visit, mentioned the flock of photographers—still and motion picture—who covered his every gesture during the tour.

His leader, as Arno Breker observed him in the leather coat that fell almost to his ankles, seemed affected by the lifelessness of this city usually so vibrant; he himself remained silent, sullen even. When the convoy reached the monumental entrance to the Opéra theater, Colonel Hans Speidel was on the steps to welcome Hitler officially on behalf of the occupation government. Only then did the visitor come awake. He strode about the theater, obviously familiar with Garnier's design, commenting on the successful marrying of architecture and ornamental sculpture. Inside the theater, Breker noted that a uniformed guardian, recognizing who the intruders were, turned abruptly away—the sculptor's first experience, he said, of the stone face of occupied Paris. They walked into the orchestra—"the world's most beautiful theater!" Breker hears Hitler exclaim.

Outside, they followed Boulevard des Capucines, which itself seemed a stage set without people or cars. When they reached the Madeleine church, Hitler explained its origin as a lay temple to the glory of Napoleon's army. They drove on to Place de la Concorde, where the Führer clearly admired the proportions of Gabriel's twin palaces, but also the square's statues, the marble horses guarding the Champs-Elysées. At Hitler's request they drove slowly up that avenue, for now they were examining the prototype for the future Berlin. At the Arch of Triumph, Breker remembered that Hitler's arch in Berlin was to be so big that the Paris monument could fit beneath it. Speer was designing it; Breker would do the bas-reliefs.

At Place du Trocadéro they left the cars to walk to the esplanade for the spectacular view of the city—Hitler's first. He liked the French sense of *mesure*, the facility with which styles and eras mixed, the marriage of art and technique displayed in the Eiffel Tower.

Across the river, outside Napoleon's tomb, Hitler couldn't help seeing the statue of General Charles Mangin, responsible for the occupation of the Ruhr after the First World War; the reminder of that humiliation clearly disturbed him. "We should no longer burden the future with memories of that kind!" he snapped. He was soon drawn to the superb façade of the Invalides chapel, designed by Hardouin-Mansart. Inside, they were all affected by the solemnity of the atmosphere. The artist in Breker wondered whether it was the effect of volume or of light. At the ramp surrounding Napoleon's tomb, Hitler held his cap to his chest, inclined his head in silence.

They finished their tour of the Invalides with a look at the façade on the Seine, drove past the Foreign Ministry and Chamber of Deputies to the German Embassy on nearby Rue de Lille, followed Boulevard Saint-Germain past the War Ministry, turning on Rue Bonaparte to Place Saint-Sulpice, then the Luxembourg palace, Rue Soufflot, the Panthéon.

The police were there ahead of him. Clerk Ferdinand Dupuy got the news from colleagues in the fifth *arrondissement:* how the Panthéon's guardian had been roused from sleep by German soldiers, ordered to have the main gate of the mausoleum dedicated to France's great men open at seven sharp. Half an hour after that a dozen vehicles appeared before the monument, which by then was protected by soldiers with submachine guns. (In his recollection, Breker marvels at the total absence of protection of the Hitler party.) Hitler admired the proportions of the lay temple, although according to Breker he remained unmoved by the interior. Suppose, he said to his favorite sculptor, we go to see your Montparnasse. So they did; it wasn't far from where they were standing. First, there was the famous Closerie des Lilas café, the adjacent statue of Marshal Ney by Rude, on the site of his execution, then the superb fountain across the square with its horses and its turtles, its Carpeaux topping. They were walking now.

Breker later told David Pryce-Jones that Hitler would have liked to visit the studio in which the sculptor had worked in his Montparnasse years. They were close enough—at one point only five minutes on foot—but time was running out. Legend has it that Hitler and Breker did stand before the house where Breker had his studio, but when they rang to be let in, the concierge opened to Hitler's face, shrieked, and slammed the heavy door shut again.

Now they drove north on Boulevard Saint-Michel. In Breker's recollection, here they saw their first traffic policeman wearing the traditional cape. The policeman saluted the convoy; Hitler responded. At Notre Dame cathedral, Hitler delivered the judgment that France's eternal classicism pervaded the Gothic. For his part, Speer said later—after the defeat of Nazism—that Hitler had been indifferent to some of the most beautiful of the city's architectural works, such as the Place des Vosges, the Louvre, the Justice Palace, and Sainte-Chapelle.

The central markets were all but empty, save for a newspaper vendor crying *"Le Matin,"* whose voice choked when he realized to whom he was trying to sell a paper. Then the fabled market women—the stoutest of the stout pointed to the Führer, exclaiming, "It's him! It's him!" These women, the paper vendor, the guard who took them around the Opéra, were the only contacts with people Hitler was to have.

Passing the Opéra again, the motorcade moved more swiftly toward Place Clichy, to wind its way up the Montmartre hill to Sacré Coeur church, the final stop. They left their cars to stare out at Paris from the terrace below the basilica. Hitler's zenith, thought Breker. But nobody in the group really liked Sacré Coeur. Hitler would tell his generals who stayed behind that he found it "appalling."

Breker remembered that Hitler said now, "At the outset of hostilities I gave the order to circumvent Paris and to avoid all combat in the vicinity." If he did say that to Breker, and did think he had given such an order, the commanders of the army group sent into Paris on the night of June 13–14 were never informed.

Hitler took leave of Colonel Speidel at 8:15 A.M. Then the race to Le Bourget, where Captain Baür's Condor had its motors roaring. Hitler asked his pilot to fly low over the French capital before turning north. "It was the dream of my life to be permitted to see Paris," he told Speer, who felt "something like pity" for this man who had only three hours in Paris the one and only time he was to see it. The question of a triumphal parade was discussed. Now Hitler gave a new reason. "I am not in the mood for a victory parade. We aren't at the end yet."

But that night at Hitler's quarters they celebrated the victorious conclusion of the Battle of France all the same. Later that evening architect Speer found himself alone with Hitler in the farmer's cottage that had been chosen as the Führer's humble headquarters. "Draw up a decree in my name ordering full-scale resumption of work on the Berlin buildings," Hitler declared. "Wasn't Paris beautiful? But Berlin must be considered far more beautiful. In the past I often considered whether we would not have to destroy Paris. But when we are finished in Berlin, Paris will only be a shadow. So why should we destroy it?"

CBS correspondent William Shirer woke that Sunday to the news that he'd had a scoop on the signing of the armistice (Walter Kerr found that out by turning the short-wave dial to an American station). He had such a scoop, this Berlin correspondent who was in Paris with a German escort, that he had slept through Hitler's visit. He breakfasted at noon with Kerr and another colleague in the sun outside the Café de la Paix. Later, in trafficless Paris, he walked through Place Vendôme to the Tuileries, rejoicing at the sight of children on seesaws and the merry-go-round (until an irate policeman, perhaps to curry favor with the Germans, ordered it shut down). On the Seine, fishermen dangled lines as they always did on Sundays; they'd be doing it until the end of time. At Notre Dame the sandbags had been removed from the central portal (possibly, although Shirer couldn't know this, in anticipation of the dawn visit by Hitler). Inside the cathedral the faithful heard a message from Cardinal Suhard, recommending calm, work, prayer.

Unknowingly, Shirer followed Hitler's itinerary for a time, along Boulevard Saint-Michel to the Panthéon, on to Montparnasse, whose cafés were "as jammed with crackpots as ever." There were also some proper ladies of the bourgeoisie, inveighing against younger Parisian women who were flirting with German soldiers.

EPILOGUE

The armistice signed by the victorious Germans and defeated French in the forest of Compiègne on June 22, with the second agreement signed by the French and Italians on June 24, called for an end to hostilities shortly after midnight, German time, on June 25. "What our relations will be with the Bordeaux government I cannot tell," Winston Churchill confessed to the House of Commons that day. "They have delivered themselves over to the enemy, and lie wholly in his power." Henceforth the British would have to look to their own salvation and defense, added Churchill, "upon which not only British, but French, European and world-wide fortunes depend."

In his diary, Goebbels reported a phone call from Hitler. "He is quite boisterously happy. . . . Does not yet know for certain whether he will proceed against England. . . . But if England will have it no other way, then she must be beaten to her knees."

In the evening, Philippe Pétain made a speech to all France by radio from Bordeaux. For the new chief of government, as for Maxime Weygand, honor was safe, and France could begin to think about the future. "A new order begins," Pétain announced. Life would be hard, but he would not hide the truth. "Our defeat was born of our laxity. The spirit of pleasure destroys what the spirit of sacrifice has edified."

Later Emmanuel Berl, eclectic editor, a French Jew who was accepted by some of the most extreme of right-wing polemicists, admitted that he had written this and other speeches of the first days of the Pétain government.

Shortly after Hitler looked at it in anger, the statue of General Mangin, the World War I general whom the Führer took to be an architect of German humiliation, was removed from its pedestal across the way from Napoleon's shrine, removed and pitilessly destroyed. It may have been the first act of revenge since the Germans took Paris. No Parisian knew what Hitler had felt or said during his dawn visit, of course, and no one could know why the demolition of this particular statue had so high a priority. Certainly Prefect Roger Langeron must have wondered, for he marveled at the perseverance displayed by the wreckers. First, holes were drilled into the bronze to gauge its thickness; a group of officers stood around to watch. Then some thirty laborers were assigned to knock the statue down and chop it up with a cutting torch. After that the inscription was smashed to bits with sledgehammers. Finally explosives were employed to unearth the stone base. "How much care was taken, and what a homage!" thought Langeron.

This painstaking destruction of a statue, the attempt to obliterate a moment of French history, was only a presage of what was to come: the dismantling of French politics and culture and social life. For this the Germans in Paris found allies in Vichy.

One of the good Germans, who happened to be an anti-Nazi from a family of anti-Nazis (and he and his would be punished for it), was a nineteen-year-old Luftwaffe corporal named Bernt Engelmann. Stationed outside Rouen, he was sent into Paris late in June on a mission to buy some Parisian trifles for his major's wife. He discovered that the French he met were not hostile—at most reserved, but quite friendly when they were dealt with politely. Perhaps it helped that he spoke French, was unarmed, wasn't even wearing boots—and that he showed the sympathy he really felt. Fraternization was at the time "quite frequent" and even "normal," he remembered, especially in the working class; the middle and upper classes were more distant. German soldiers had a reputation for being "correct" and well-behaved, "and in fact they were," added Bernt Engelmann. "There was actually a certain respect for each other at that time."

That time would end with the brutality of a thunderclap; the German occupation of Paris would become Inferno. Soon the Gestapo would begin its ravages, assisted by French mercenaries, volunteers from the ranks of prewar Fascist movements. Often the French auxiliaries were allowed to keep part of the loot taken from arrested resistance activists, Jews, and simple patriots who rejected the new order. Collaborators gradually filled all the influential jobs in German Paris. They often went further in their publishing, broadcasting, and speechmaking propaganda than the Germans asked or expected them to.

In their pillaging of France—its manufacturing potential, its agricultural and natural resources—the Germans left Paris hungry and cold, without fuel or even simple materials for clothing. Black markets flourished, and a new class of Parisians that thrived on betrayals and profiteering ruled side by side with the Nazi civil and military administrators. The City of Light would become a dark and evil place for four long years. Nobody has been found to speak well of it.

Acknowledgments

Contemporary history depends so much on surviving witnesses, or, in their absence, on those who have preserved precious records to make them available to researchers. Specific contributions to this book are acknowledged in the Sources. But this is the place to express gratitude to those who helped the author in his search for witnesses, or who placed private or public documents at his disposal, as well as to the institutions that opened their doors to him.

A special word to friends who volunteered translations, notably (from the German) the indefatigable Michel Hourst, and Mrs. Renette van Wessem. To the editors of *The New York Times Book Review,* who published my request for testimony (bringing responses from Britain and France as well as from the United States!), to *Historama* in France and *Alte Kamaraden* in Germany for publishing similar queries.

In the United States I received a cordial and attentive reception at the National Archives and the Library of Congress in Washington, and spent useful hours at the old reliable New York Public Library on Forty-second Street. In Paris my indispensable resource was the Institut d'Histoire du Temps Présent, my best helper its librarian Jean Astruc. I am also grateful to those who administer the archives of the Préfecture de Police, the Ministry of Foreign Affairs, the Service Historique de l'Armée de Terre in Vincennes, the Archives de la Ville de Paris, the Météorologie Nationale. I was given encouragement and advice by Emmanuel Le Roy Ladurie at the Bibliothèque Nationale, Chantal de Tourtier-Bonazzi at the Archives de France. May I also mention the Commissariat à l'Energie Atomique, the Association du Musée de la Résistance Nationale (and Isabelle Widloecher), the Institut de Recherches Marxistes (and Roger Bourderon). Among German institutions that offered generous help and advice, the Militärchiv of the Bundesarchiv in Freiburg-im-Breisgau deserves special thanks. I am also grateful to the Institut für Zeitgeschichte in Munich and to the Bildarchiv Preussischer Kulturbesitz in Berlin.

And then to Dr. François Bernard, Gilbert Bloch, Max Brusset, Hans Buchholz, Maurice Darbellay, Joann Davis, Elaine Felsher, Eugénie Gemähling, Beverly Gordey, Edward Grecki, Richard Greeman, Renato Grispo, Anne M. Imhoff, Walter Kerr (of Santa Fe, New Mexico), Vlady Kibalchich, David Koblick, Mitchel Levitas, Nancy Macdonald, Russell Porter, Melsene Timsit, Jérémie Véron, Henri de Wailly.

Sources

Prologue

Pierre Lazareff, *De Munich à Vichy* (New York: Brentano's, 1944); Paul Reynaud, *Mémoires*, vol. 2, *Envers et contre tous* (Paris: Flammarion, 1963); Pierre Rocolle, *La Guerre de 1940*, vol. 1 (Paris: A. Colin, 1990); Maxime Weygand, *Mémoires*, vol. 3, *Rappelé au service* (Paris: Flammarion, 1950).

1. Prelude to the First Day

From conversations with Max Brusset.

Bulletin Municipal de la Ville de Paris, vol. 59, March 1–7, 15–21, 22–28, April 19–25, 1940; *Cahiers d'histoire de l'Institut de recherches marxistes* (Paris) 14 (1983); *Le Figaro*, February 28, March 1, 2, 12, April 28, May 10, 12, 1940.

Yvon Bizardel, *Sous l'occupation* (Paris: Calmann-Lévy, 1964); Stéphane Courtois, *Le PCF dans la guerre* (Paris: Ramsay, 1980); Georges Bernstein Gruber and Gilbert Maurin, *Bernstein le magnifique* (Paris: Lattès, 1988); Alistair Horne, *To Lose a Battle: France 1940* (London: Macmillan, 1969); Philippe Richer, *La drôle de guerre* (Paris: Orban, 1990); Jean Touchard, *La gauche en France depuis 1900* (Paris: Seuil, 1977); Rose Valland, *Le Front de l'art (1939–1945)* (Paris: Plon, 1961).

2. Thursday, May 9

Jacques Bardoux, *Journal d'un témoin de la Troisième* (Paris: Fayard, 1957); Charles de Gaulle, *Lettres, notes et carnets (1919–Juin 1940)* (Paris:

Plon, 1980); Dominique Leca, *La Rupture de 1940* (Paris: Fayard, 1978); Météorologie Nationale, *Résumé mensuel du temps en France, Années 1940 à 1944* (Paris: Météorologie Nationale, 1951); Anatole de Monzie, *Ci-devant* (Paris: Flammarion, 1941); Robert Murphy, *Diplomat Among War-riors* (New York: Doubleday, 1964); Reynaud, *Mémoires*, vol. 2; Robert de Saint Jean, *Démocratie, beurre et canons* (New York: Maison Française, 1941).

3. Friday, May 10

From conversations with Fernande Alphandery, Walter Kerr (Santa Fe, New Mexico).

Archives of Ministère des Affaires Etrangères, Papiers 1940 Charles-Roux, vol. 14, Papiers Maurice Dejean PAAP 288, vol. 4; U.S. National Archives, 740.0011/280, 851.00/2017.

Janet Flanner, "Mr. Ambassador," *The New Yorker*, December 10, 24, 1938; Martin Gilbert, "A Lion at Number 10," *The Jerusalem Post International Edition* (Jerusalem), May 19, 1990; A. J. Liebling, "Letter from Paris," *The New Yorker*, May 18, 1940; Robert Scheer, "The Diplomat as Dandy and Cad," *Los Angeles Times*, June 26, 1988; Gordon Wright, "Ambassador Bullitt and the Fall of France," *World Politics* (Princeton) 10, 1 (October 1957).

Bardoux, *Journal*; Simone de Beauvoir, *La Force de l'âge* (Paris: Galli-mard, 1960); Orville H. Bullitt, ed., *For the President: Personal and Secret* (Boston: Houghton Mifflin, 1972); J. R. M. Butler, *History of the Second World War*, vol. 2 (London: Her Majesty's Stationery Office, 1957); Maurice Chevalier, *Ma route et mes chansons*, vol. 2, *Tempes grises* (Paris, Julliard, 1948); De Gaulle, *Lettres (1919–Juin 1940); Foreign Relations of the United States, Diplomatic Papers (1940)*, vol. 1 (Washington: Govern-ment Printing Office, 1959); Adolphe Goutard, *1940: La Guerre des occasions perdues* (Paris: Hachette, 1956); Marie-Thérèse Guichard, *Les égéries de la République* (Paris, Payot, 1991); Gen. Louis Koeltz, *Comment s'est joué notre destin* (Paris: Hachette, 1957); Jean Lacouture, *De Gaulle*, vol. 1 (Paris: Seuil, 1984); Alain Laubreaux, *Ecrit pendant la guerre* (Paris: Inter-France, 1944); Albert Lebrun, *Témoignage* (Paris: Plon, 1945); Leca, *La Rupture*; B. H. Liddell Hart, *The Other Side of the Hill* (London: Cassell, 1951); Pierre Mendès France, *Liberté, liberté cherie* (Paris: Fayard, 1977); Monzie, *Ci-devant*; Murphy, *Diplomat*; Pertinax, *The Gravediggers of France* (New York: Doubleday, 1944); Reynaud, *Mémoires*, vol. 2; Rocolle, *La Guerre*, vol. 1; Saint Jean, *Démocratie*; Paul de Villelume, *Journal d'une défaite* (Paris: Fayard, 1976).

4. SATURDAY, MAY 11

From talk with Christian Pineau.

Archives, Service Historique de l'Armée de Terre, 31 N 36 Région de Paris.

Antoine Lefebvre, "Le Rôle et l'influence politique de la radio en France pendant la Seconde Guerre Mondiale," mémoire de maîtrise, Université de Paris I, Année 1971–72.

Louis De Jong, "Les Pays-Bas dans la Seconde Guerre Mondiale," *Revue d'Histoire de la Deuxieme Guerre Mondiale* (Paris) 50 (April 1963); Karl Drechsler, "Les 'Emetteurs clandestins français' de Goebbeles en mai-juin 1940," *Recherches internationales à la lumière de Marxisme* (Paris) 1961, 23–24; A. J. Liebling, "Paris Postscript," *The New Yorker*, August 3, 10, 1940; *Le Figaro*, May 12, 1940.

Goutard, 1940; Reynaud, *Mémoires*, vol. 2; Quentin Reynolds, *The Wounded Don't Cry* (New York: Dutton, 1941).

5. SUNDAY, MAY 12

Le Matin (Paris), May 13, 1940.

Clare Boothe, *Europe in the Spring* (New York: Knopf, 1940); Louis De Jong, *The German Fifth Column in the Second World War* (London: Routledge & Kegan Paul, 1956); *La Fin des Illusions: l'An 1940* [Brussels, 1940]; Michael R. Marrus and Robert O. Paxton, *Vichy et les juifs* (Paris: Calmann-Lévy, 1981); Jean Vidalenc, *L'Exode de mai-juin 1940* (Paris, Presses Universitaires de France, 1957).

6. MONDAY, MAY 13

Bardoux, *Journal*; Butler, *History*; Winston S. Churchill, *Blood, Sweat and Tears* (New York: Putnam, 1941); Goutard, *1940*; General Heinz Guderian, *Souvenirs d'un soldat* (Paris: Plon, 1954); Horne, *To Lose a Battle*; Eberhard Jäckel, *La France dans l'Europe d'Hitler* (Paris: Fayard, 1968); Koeltz, *Comment s'est joué*; Liddell Hart, *The Other Side*; Gen. Erich von Manstein, *Victoires perdues* (Paris: Plon, 1958); *Le Procès du Maréchal Pétain*, vol. 1 (Paris: Albin Michel, 1945); Paul Paillole, *Notre espion chez Hitler* (Paris: Laffont, 1985).

7. TUESDAY, MAY 14

Archives, Ministère des Affaires Etrangères, Papiers 1940 Dejean, vol. 5.

De Jong, "Les Pays-Bas"; Louis Gabriel-Robinet, "Le Rassemblement au Stade Buffalo," *Le Figaro*, May 15, 1940; *Le Matin*, May 13–15, 1940.

Bullitt, *For the President*; Butler, *History*; Jean Chauvel, *Commentaire*, vol. 1 (Paris: Fayard, 1971); Virginia Cowles, *Looking for Trouble* (New York: Harper, 1941); De Jong, *The German Fifth Column; La Fin des Illusions; Foreign Relations*; Raffaele Guariglia, *Ricordi* (Naples: Edizioni Scientifiche Italiane, 1949); Leca, *La Rupture*; Saint Jean, *Démocratie*.

8. WEDNESDAY, MAY 15

From talk with Erna Friedlander.

Archives Ministère des Affaires Etrangères, Papiers Maurice Dejean PAAP 288, vols. 6, 8; Archives, Service Historique de l'Armée de Terre, 31 N 36 Région de Paris.

Wright, "Ambassador Bullitt"; *Le Matin*, May 24, 1940.

Actes et Documents du Saint-Siège relatifs à la Seconde Guerre Mondiale, vol. 1, *Le Saint-Siège et la Guerre en Europe* (Città del Vaticano: Libreria Editrice Vaticana, 1970); *Les Barbelés de l'exil* (Grenoble: Presses Universitaires, 1979); Boothe, *Europe*; Bullitt, *For the President*; Charles de Gaulle, *Mémoires de guerre*, vol. 1 (Paris: Plon, 1954); Jacques Fauvet, *Histoire du Parti Communiste français,* vol. 2 (Paris: Fayard, 1965); Lisa Fittko, *Escape Through the Pyrenees* (Evanston, Ill.: Northwestern University Press, 1991); *Foreign Relations*; Goutard, 1940; Roger Langeron, *Paris Juin 40* (Paris: Flammarion, 1946); Leca, *La Rupture*; Manstein, *Victoires perdues;* Douglas Porch, *The French Foreign Legion* (New York: HarperCollins, 1991); Reynaud, *Mémoires,* vol. 2; Saint Jean, *Démocratie*.

9. THURSDAY, MAY 16

From conversations with Max Brusset, Mrs. Els Placzek (formerly Mrs. Hans Halban), Peter Halban, Bertrand Goldschmidt.

Archives, Ministère des Affaires Etrangères, Papiers Maurice Dejean PAAP 288, vol. 8; Papiers 1940 Dejean, vol. 6; Papiers 1940 Rochat, vol. 44; U.S. National Archives, 740.0011-3115, 3115 2/8.

Liebling, "Paris Postscript"; *Le Figaro*, May 17, 1940.

Pierre Andreu and Frédéric Grover, *Drieu La Rochelle* (Paris: Hachette, 1979); Bardoux, *Journal*; Bullitt, *For the President*; Chauvel, *Commentaire*, vol. 1; Winston S. Churchill, *The Second World War*, vol. 2, *Their Finest Hour* (London: Cassell, 1949); Ronald W. Clark, *Einstein* (New York: World Publishing Co., 1971); Courtois, *Le PCF*; De Jong, *The Fifth Column*; Gen. Maurice Gamelin, *Servir*, vol. 3, *La Guerre* (Paris: Plon,

1947); Bertrand Goldschmidt, *Pionniers de l'atome* (Paris: Stock, 1987); Jules Jeanneney, *Journal politique* (Paris: A. Colin, 1972); Laubreaux, *Ecrit pendant la guerre*; Lazareff, *De Munich à Vichy*; Paul Léautaud, *Journal littéraire*, vol. 13 (Paris: Mercure de France, 1962); Leca, *La Rupture*; Mendès France, *Liberté*; Jacques Minart, *P.C. Vincennes, Secteur 4*, vol. 2 (Paris: Berger-Levrault, 1945); Monzie, *Ci-devant*; Murphy, *Diplomat*; Pertinax, *Gravediggers*; Reynaud, *Mémoires*, vol. 2; Saint Jean, *Démocratie*; François Seydoux, *Mémoires d'Outre-Rhin* (Paris: Grasset, 1975); Spencer Weart, *Scientists in Power* (Cambridge, Mass.: Harvard University Press, 1979).

10. FRIDAY, MAY 17

Archives, Service Historique de l'Armée de Terre, 31 N 2 Région de Paris.

Bulletin Municipale 59, 36 (May 18, 1940); Drechsler, "Les 'Emetteurs Clandestins français' "; A. J. Liebling, "Letter from Paris," *The New Yorker*, May 25, 1940; *Le Figaro*, May 18, 1940; *Le Matin*, June 9, 1940.

Bardoux, *Journal*; Léon Blum, *Mémoires (1940–1945)* (Paris: Albin Michel, 1955); Courtois, *Le PCF*; De Gaulle, *Mémoires*, vol. 1; *Foreign Relations*; Jeanneney, *Journal politique*; Lacouture, *De Gaulle*, vol. 1; Laubreaux, *Ecrit pendant la guerre*; Léautaud, *Journal littéraire*; Leca, *La Rupture*; Claude Paillat, *Le Désastre de 1940*, vol. 3 (Paris: Laffont, 1985); Reynaud, *Mémoires*, vol. 2; Weygand, *Mémoires*, vol. 3.

11. SATURDAY, MAY 18

From talk with Max Brusset.

U.S. National Archives, 740.0011/3139.

Liebling, "Letter from Paris," May 25, 1940; ———, "Paris Postscript."

Boothe, *Europe*; Bullitt, *For the President*; De Gaulle, *Mémoires*, vol. 1; *Foreign Relations*; Joseph Goebbels, *Die Tagebücher*, vol. 1, 4 (Munich: K. G. Saur, 1987); Jeanneney, *Journal politique*; Laubreaux, *Ecrit pendant la guerre*; Gen. Emile Laure, *Pétain* (Paris: Berger-Levrault, 1941); Herbert R. Lottman, *Pétain* (New York: Morrow, 1985); Minart, *P.C. Vincennes*; Monzie, *Ci-devant*.

12. SUNDAY, MAY 19

From Dr. Pierre Daunois.

Archives, Ministère des Affaires Etrangères, Papiers Maurice Dejean PAAP 288, vol. 6.

Drechsler, "Les 'Emetteurs clandestins français' "; *L'Action Française* (Paris), May 19, 1940; *Le Figaro*, May 20, 1940.

Bardoux, *Journal*; Paul Baudouin, *Neuf mois au gouvernment* (Paris: Table Ronde, 1948); Churchill, *Blood, Sweat and Tears*; Ilya Ehrenbourg, *La Chute de Paris* (Paris: Hier et Aujourd'hui, 1944); ———, *La Nuit tombe* (Paris: Gallimard, 1966); Gamelin, *Servir,* vol. 3, Goebbels, *Tagebücher*, vol. 1, 4; Léautaud, *Journal littéraire*; Paul Reynaud, *La France a sauvé l'Europe*, vol. 2 (Paris: Flammarion, 1947); Weygand, *Mémoires*, vol. 3.

13. MONDAY, MAY 20

From Fernande Alphandery.

Archives Nationales, W-III 278, 523 Mi-3; Archives, Service Historique de l'Armée de Terre, 31 N 36 Région de Paris; U.S. National Archives, 740.0011 2855 1/28.

Drechsler, "Les 'Emetteurs clandestins français' "; *Le Figaro*, May 20, 1940. Henri Amouroux, *Pétain avant Vichy* (Paris: Fayard, 1967); Arved Arenstam, *Tapestry of a Debacle* (London: Constable, 1942); Baudouin, *Neuf mois*; Bullitt, *For the President*; Chevalier, *Ma route*, vol. 3; De Jong, *The German Fifth Column*; Fauvet, *Histoire du Parti communiste*, vol. 2; Gamelin, *Servir*, vol. 3; Ugoberto Alfassio Grimaldi and Gherardo Bozzetti, *Dieci Giugno 1940: Il Giorno della Follia* (Bari: Laterza, 1974); Guariglia, *Ricordi*; Laubreaux, *Ecrit pendant la guerre*; Léautaud, *Journal littéraire*; Monzie, *Ci-devant*; Reynaud, *Mémoires*, vol. 2; Alexander Werth, *The Last Days of Paris* (London: Hamish Hamilton, 1940); Weygand, *Mémoires*, vol. 3.

14. TUESDAY, MAY 21

Roger Bourderon, "Mai-septembre 1940: l'activité de direction du PCF," *Cahiers d'histoire de l'Institut de Recherches Marxistes* (Paris) 42 (1990); Drechsler, "Les 'Emetteurs clandestins français' "; Liebling, "Paris Postscript"; *Le Figaro*, May 20, 22, 1940.

François Charles-Roux, *Cinq mois tragiques aux affaires étrangères* (Paris: Plon, 1949); Chauvel, *Commentaire*, vol. 1; De Gaulle, *Lettres (1919–Juin 1940)*; Goebbels, *Tagebücher*, vol. 1, 4; Léautaud, *Journal littéraire*; Leca, *La Rupture*; Werth, *The Last Days*.

15. WEDNESDAY, MAY 22

From Walter Kerr, Jeanine LeCocq (née Huzard). From the diary of Jean Lescure, with the author's permission.

Archives, Ministère des Affaires Etrangères, Papiers Maurice Dejean PAAP 288, vol. 8; Archives, Service Historique de l'Armée de Terre, 31 N 2 Région de Paris.

La Croix (Paris), May 24, 1940; *Le Figaro*, May 22, 1940.

Andreu and Grover, *Drieu*; Beauvoir, *La Force de l'âge*; Charles-Roux, *Cinq mois; Foreign Relations*; Goebbels, *Tagebücher*, vol. 1, 4; Saint Jean, *Démocratie*; Weygand, *Mémoires*, vol. 3.

16. THURSDAY, MAY 23
Archives, Service Historique de l'Armée de Terre, 31 N 2 Région de Paris.

Drechsler, "Les 'Emetteurs clandestins français' "; *Le Matin*, May 24, 1940. Andreu and Grover, *Drieu*; Baudouin, *Neuf mois*; Marcel Jouhandeau, *Journal sous l'occupation* (Paris: Gallimard, 1980); ———, *Le Peril juif* (Paris: Sorlot, 1939); Laubreaux, *Ecrit pendant la guerre*; Louis Noguères, *Le Véritable procès du Maréchal Pétain* (Paris: Fayard, 1955); Werth, *The Last Days*.

17. FRIDAY, MAY 24
Archives, Ministère des Affaires Etrangères, Papiers 1940 Dejean, vol. 5; Papiers Reynaud, vol. 5.

Drechsler, "Les 'Emetteurs clandestins français' "; *Le Matin*, May 24, 1940.

Baudouin, *Neuf mois*; Courtois, *Le PCF*; De Gaulle, *Lettres (1919–Juin 1940)*; Jacques Duclos, *Mémoires*, vol. 3 (Paris: Fayard, 1970); Ehrenbourg, *La Chute de Paris*; ———, *La Nuit tombe*; Fauvet, *Histoire du Parti communiste*, vol. 2; Horne, *To Lose a Battle*; Laubreaux, *Ecrit pendant la guerre*; Ministero degli Affari Esteri, *I Documenti Diplomatici Italiani, Nona Serie (1939–1943)*, vol. 4 (Rome: Istituto Poligrafico dello Stato, 1960); Villelume, *Journal*; Weygand, *Mémoires*, vol. 3; André Wurmser, *Fidèlement vôtre* (Paris: Grasset, 1979).

18. SATURDAY, MAY 25
Archives, Ministère des Affaires Etrangères, Papiers 1940 Reynaud, vols. 5, 6; Archives Nationales, W-II 10.

Geoffrey Cox, "Paris Moved Out When the Germans Moved In," *The Independent* (London), June 5, 1940; *Le Figaro*, May 25, 1940.

Bardoux, *Journal*; Baudouin, *Neuf mois*; *Documents on German Foreign Policy (1918–1945), Series D*, vol. 9 (Washington: Government Printing

Office, 1956); Jeanneney, *Journal politique*; Lebrun, *Témoignage*; Leca, *La Rupture; Procès de Pétain*, vol. 1; Reynaud, *La France*, vol. 2; Edward L. Spears, *Assignment to Catastrophe*, vol. 1 (London: Heinemann, 1954); Weygand, *Mémoires*, vol. 3.

19. Sunday, May 26

Liebling, "Paris Postscript"; *La Croix*, May 28, 1940; *Le Figaro*, May 26, 1940.

Bardoux, *Journal*; Gen. André Beaufre, *Mémoires* (Paris: Presses de la Cité, 1965); Bullitt, *For the President*; Charles-Roux, *Cinq mois*; Chauvel, *Commentaire*, vol. 1; *Foreign Relations*; Maurice Girodias, *J'arrive!* (Paris: Stock, 1977); Reynaud, *La France*, vol. 2; ———, *Mémoires*, vol. 2; Reynolds, *The Wounded*; Franklin D. Roosevelt, *Selected Speeches, Messages, Press Conferences, and Letters* (New York: Holt, Rinehart & Winston, 1964); Spears, *Assignment*, vol. 1; Sir Llewellyn Woodward, *British Foreign Policy in the Second World War*, vol. 1 (London: Her Majesty's Stationery Office, 1970).

20. Monday, May 27

Archives, Ministères des Affaires Etrangères, Papiers 1940 Reynaud, vol. 5; Archives, Service Historique de l'Armée de Terre, 31 N 2 Région de Paris.

Bullitt, *For the President*; Charles-Roux, *Cinq mois; Foreign Relations*; Lazareff, *De Munich à Vichy*; Reynaud, *Memoires*, vol. 2; Weygand, *Mémoires*, vol. 3.

21. Tuesday, May 28

From Walter Kerr; talk with Annette Sireix.

Archives, Ministère des Affaires Etrangères, Papiers 1940 Reynaud, vol. 6. Drechsler, "Les 'Emetteurs clandestins français' "; Liebling, "Paris Postscript"; *Le Figaro*, May 28, 1940; *Le Matin*, May 29, 1940.

Boothe, *Europe*; Bullitt, *For the President*; Jean-Baptiste Duroselle, *L'Abîme* (1939–1945) (Paris: Imprimerie Nationale, 1982); *Foreign Relations*; Lacouture, *De Gaulle*.

22. Wednesday, May 29

From Hélène Gibert (née Rogivue), Julian Green, Michèle Miller (née Rogivue), Annette Sireix, Wilebaldo Solano, Julius P. Winter.

Le Figaro, May 31, 1940; *Le Matin*, May 24–31, 1940.

"The American Hospital of Paris in the Second World War" [Paris] 1940; Eugène Depigny, "Juin 1940 à l'Hôtel de Ville de Paris" [Paris, 1945].

Actes et Documents du Saint-Siège, vol. 1; Hélène Azenor, *Vivre tout haut* (Paris: Les Octaviennes, 1989); Emmanuel Berl, *La Fin de la IIIe République* (Paris: Gallimard, 1968); Boothe, *Europe*; Grimaldi, *Dieci Giugno*; Edouard Herriot, *Episodes (1940–1944)* (Paris; Flammarion, 1950); Leca, *La Rupture*; Jacques-Henri Lefebvre, *1939–1940: Le Suicide* (Paris: Durassié, 1942); Ministero degli Affari Esteri, *Documenti*, vol. 4; Nicole Ollier, *L'Exode* (Paris: Laffont, 1969); Weygand, *Mémoires*, vol. 3.

23. THURSDAY, MAY 30
Archives, Service Historique de l'Armée de Terre, 31 N 36 Région de Paris.

Le Figaro, May 31, 1940.

Bullitt, *For the President; Foreign Relations*; Grimaldi, *Dieci Giugno*; Guariglia, *Ricordi*; Leca, *La Rupture*; Franklin D. Roosevelt, *Complete Presidential Press Conferences* (New York: Da Capo, 1972).

24. FRIDAY, MAY 31
Clare Boothe, "Paris Whispers," *Life*, June 10, 1940; *Le Figaro*, May 31, 1940.

Actes et Documents du Saint-Siège, vol. 1; *Archives secrètes de la Wilhelmstrasse*, vol. 9, 2 (Paris: Plon, 1961); Assemblée Nationale, *Les événements survenus en France de 1933 à 1945, Témoignages*, vol. 7 (Paris: Presses Universitaires de France, 1951); Bardoux, *Journal*; Boothe, *Europe*; Bullitt, *For the President*; Charles-Roux, *Cinq mois; Foreign Relations*, vol. 2; Ministero degli Affari Esteri, *Documenti*, vol. 4; Weygand, *Mémoires*, vol. 3.

25. SATURDAY, JUNE 1
From talk with General Paul Nérot.

Archives, Service Historique de l'Armée de Terre, 31 N 36 Région de Paris.

Baudouin, *Neuf mois*; Charles-Roux, *Cinq mois*; De Gaulle, *Lettres (1919–Juin 1940)*; ———, *Mémoires*, vol. 1; *Foreign Relations*; Guariglia, *Ricordi*; Leca, *La Rupture*; Roger Peyrefitte, *La fin des ambassades* (Paris: Flammarion, 1953); Henri de Wailly, *De Gaulle sous le casque: Abbeville 1940* (Paris: Perrin, 1990).

26. SUNDAY, JUNE 2

Archives, Service Historique de l'Armée de Terre, 31 N 36 Région de Paris; Archives Nationales, W-III 280.

Drechsler, "Les 'Emetteurs clandestins français' "; Lefebvre, "Le Rôle de la radio"; Liebling, "Paris Postscript"; *Le Figaro*, June 2, 3, 1940.

Assemblée Nationale, *Evénements survenus*, vol. 7; Chauvel, *Commentaire*, vol. 1; De Gaulle, *Lettres (1919–Juin 1940)*; Peter Fontaine, *Last to Leave Paris* (London: Chaterson, 1941); Goebbels, *Tagebücher*, vol. 1, 4; Grimaldi, *Dieci Giugno*; Météorologie Nationale, *Résumé Mensuel*; Reynaud, *Mémoires*, vol. 2; Edward L. Spears, *Assignment to Catastrophe*, vol. 2 (London: Heinemann, 1954).

27. MONDAY, JUNE 3

From conversations with Fernande Alphandery, Dr. Pierre Daunois, Raymond Martin, Henri Quéffelec.

Archives, Ministère des Affaires Etrangères, Papiers Maurice Dejean PAAP 288, vol. 8; Papiers 1940 Dejean, vol. 5; Archives Nationales, W-III 280; Archives, Service Historique de l'Armée de Terre, 31 N 36 Région de Paris; U.S. National Archives, 740.0011/3468 1/2.

Cox, "Paris Moved Out"; Nicolas Weill, "Je Suis Partout reparaît," *Le Monde*, February 10–11, 1991; *Le Temps*, June 4, 11, 1940.

Assemblée Nationale, *Evénements survenus*, vol. 7; Sylvia Beach, *Shakespeare & Company* (New York: Harcourt, Brace, 1959); Emmanuel Beau de Loménie, *La Mort de la Troisième République* (Paris: Conquistador, 1951); Beauvoir, *La Force de l'âge*; Bullitt, *For the President*; Chauvel, *Commentaire*, vol. 1; De Gaulle, *Lettres (1919–Juin 1940)*; Depigny, "Juin 1940"; *Documents on German Foreign Policy*, vol. 9; Marcel Duhamel, *Raconte pas ta vie* (Paris: Mercure de France, 1972); Paul Durand, *La SNCF pendant la guerre* (Paris: Presses Universitaires de France, 1968); Ehrenbourg, *La Nuit tombe*; Fontaine, *Last to Leave Paris*; Georges Friedmann, *Journal de guerre* (Paris: Gallimard, 1987); Goebbels, *Tagebücher*, vol. 1, 4; Arthur Koestler, *The Invisible Writing* (London: Collins–Hamish Hamilton, 1954); André Laffargue, *Le Général Dentz* (Paris: Iles d'Or, 1954); Lazareff, *De Munich à Vichy*; Léautaud, *Journal littéraire*; Leca, *La Rupture*; Geo London, *L'amiral Estéva et le général Dentz devant la Haute Cour de Justice* (Lyon: Bonneron, 1945); André Maurois, *La Bataille de France*, in Louis L. Snyder, *Guerre sur tous les fronts* (Paris: Calmann-Lévy, 1965); Pietro Nenni, *Vingt ans de fascismes* (Paris: Maspero, 1960); Ollier, *L'Exode*; Paul Paillole, *Notre espion*; ———, *Services spéciaux (1939–1945)* (Paris: Laffont, 1975); Reynaud, *Mémoires*, vol. 2; Jean Robert, *Notre*

Métro (Paris: Régie Autonome de Transports Parisiens, 1967); Victor Serge, *Mémoires d'un révolutionnaire* (Paris: Seuil, 1978); Spears, *Assignment*, vol. 2; Vidalenc, *L'Exode*; Werth, *The Last Days*.

28. TUESDAY, JUNE 4
Archives, Service Historique de l'Armée de Terre, 31 N 2, 8 Région de Paris.
Le Figaro, June 7, 1940; *Le Matin*, June 4, 5, 1940.
Amouroux, *Pétain avant Vichy*; Churchill, *Blood, Sweat and Tears*; Robert Debré, *L'Honneur de vivre* (Paris: Stock-Hermann, 1974); Fontaine, *Last to Leave Paris*; Girodias, *J'arrive!*; Goebbels, *Tagebücher*, vol. 1, 4; William L. Langer, *Le Jeu américain à Vichy* (Paris: Plon, 1948); Leca, *La Rupture*; Roosevelt, *Press Conferences*; Werth, *The Last Days*.

29. WEDNESDAY, JUNE 5
Archives, Service Historique de l'Armée de Terre, 31 N 6 Région de Paris.
Le Figaro, June 7, 1940; *Le Matin*, June 5, 1940; *Le Temps*, June 6, 1940.
Baudouin, *Neuf mois*; Beau de Loménie, *La Mort*; Pierre Bourget and Charles Lacretelle, *Sur les murs de Paris (1940–1944)* (Paris: Hachette, 1959); Bullitt, *For the President*; Butler, *History*, vol. 2; Churchill, *Second World War*, vol. 2; De Gaulle, *Mémoires*, vol. 1; *Documents on German Foreign Policy*, vol. 9; *Foreign Relations*; Girodias, *J'arrive!*; Col. Georges Groussard, *Chemins secrets* (Paris: Bader-Dufor, 1948); Leca, *La Rupture*; Pierre Lyet, *La Bataille de France* (Paris: Payot, 1947); Noguères, *Le Véritable procès*; Reynaud, *La France*, vol. 2; ———, *Mémoires*, vol. 2; Weygand, *Mémoires*, vol. 2; Woodward, *British Foreign Policy*.

30. THURSDAY, JUNE 6
From conversations with Walter Kerr.
L'Action Française (Paris), June 7, 1940; *Le Figaro*, June 7, 1940; *Le Matin*, June 6, 1940; *Le Temps*, June 6, 8, 1940.
Lefebvre, "Le rôle de la radio."
Baudouin, *Neuf mois*; Beau de Loménie, *La Mort*; Beaufre, *Mémoires*; Bullitt, *For the President*; Jérôme Carcopino, *Souvenirs de sept ans (1937–1944)* (Paris: Flammarion, 1953); Charles-Roux, *Cinq mois*; Chauvel, *Commentaire*, vol. 1; Evelyne Demey, *Paul Reynaud, mon père* (Paris: Plon, 1980); Fontaine, *Last to Leave Paris; Foreign Relations*; Pertinax, *Gravedig-*

gers; Saint Jean, *Démocratie*; Spears, *Assignment*, vol. 2; Vidalenc, *L'Exode*; Villelume, *Journal*; Weygand, *Mémoires*, vol. 3.

31. Friday, June 7
From talks with Walter Kerr.
Le Figaro, June 7, 1940.
Baudouin, *Neuf mois*; Bullitt, *For the President*, Friedmann, *Journal*; Leca, *La Rupture*; Villelume, *Journal*.

32. Saturday, June 8
From talk with Perla Epstein; correspondence with Raymond Martin.
Archives, Ministère des Affaires Etrangères, Papiers 1940 Reynaud, vol. 5.
Archives, Préfecture de Police: "La Situation à Paris depuis le 14 Juin 1940," Renseignements Généraux, July 16, 1940.
Cox, "Paris Moved Out"; *L'Action Française*, June 8, 1940; *Le Figaro*, June 8, 9, 1940; *Le Matin*, June 8, 9, 1940.
Assemblée Nationale, *Evénements survenus*, vol. 7; Baudouin, *Neuf mois*; Beauvoir, *La Force de l'âge*; Blum, *Mémoires*; Bullitt, *For the President*; De Gaulle, *Mémoires*, vol. 1; Fernand Gregh, *L'Age de fer* (Paris: Grasset, 1956); Alfred Fabre-Luce, *Journal de la France (Mars 1939–Juillet 1940)* (Ain: Imprimerie de Trévoux, 1940); Fontaine, *Last to Leave Paris*; Jouhandeau, *Journal*; Leca, *La Rupture*; Ministero degli Affari Esteri, *Documenti*, vol. 4; Reynaud, *Mémoires*, vol. 2; Saint Jean, *Démocratie*; Vidalenc, *L'Exode*; Villelume, *Journal*; Werth, *The Last Days*; Weygand, *Mémoires*, vol. 3.

33. Sunday, June 9
From talk with Marguerite Monino.
Correspondence of Victor Serge, with permission of Vlady Kibalchich, courtesy of Richard Greeman.
Archives Nationales, W-III 279; Archives, Service Historique de l'Armée de Terre, 31 N 6, 36 Région de Paris; Observatoire Municipal (Paris), "Observations faites à Montsouris," June 9, 1940, courtesy of Météorologie Nationale.
Sergio Bernacconi, "Le ultime ore della Francia democratica," *Il Giornale d'Italia* (Rome), June 19, 1940; Cox, "Paris Moved Out"; Liebling, "Paris Postscript"; Pierre Lyet, "Paris 'Ville Ouverte'?" *Revue Historique de l'Armée* (Paris), June 1948; Wilhelm Ritter von Schramm, "Paris se rend:

Notes d'un officier d'ordonnance qui assista à l'événement," *Signal* (Berlin), July 25, 1940; *Le Figaro*, June 10, 1940; *Le Jour-Echo de Paris* (Paris), June 9, 1940; *Le Matin*, June 9, 10, 1940; *Le Petit Journal* (Paris), June 10, 1940; *Le Temps*, June 10, 11, 1940.

Pierre Audiat, *Paris pendant la guerre* (Paris: Hachette, 1946); Assemblée Nationale, *Evénements survenus*, vol. 7; Bardoux, *Journal*; Baudouin, *Neuf mois*; Beau de Loménie, *La Mort*; Beauvoir, *La Force de l'âge*; Blum, *Mémoires*; Bullitt, *For the President*; Carcopino, *Souvenirs*; Robert Cardinne-Petit, *Les Secrets de la Comédie Française* (Paris: Nouvelles Editions Latines, 1958); Chauvel, *Commentaire*, vol. 1; Ehrenbourg, *La Chute de Paris*; ———, *La Nuit tombe*; Fontaine, *Last to Leave Paris*; Georges A. Groussard, *Service secret (1940–1945)* (Paris: Table Ronde, 1964); Guariglia, *Ricordi*; Herriot, *Episodes*; Jeanneney, *Journal politique*; Pierre Lazareff, *Dernière édition* (New York: Brentano's, [1942]); Léautaud, *Journal littéraire*; Lebrun, *Témoignage*; Leca, *La Rupture*; Maurice Martin du Gard, *La Chronique de Vichy (1940–1944)* (Paris: Flammarion, 1975); Maurois, *Bataille de France*; Nenni, *Vingt ans*; Louis Noguères, *La dernière étape: Sigmaringen* (Paris: Fayard, 1956); Peyrefitte, *La fin des ambassades;* Reynaud, *Mémoires*, vol. 2; Saint Jean, *Démocratie*; Roger Stéphane, *Toutes choses ont leur saison* (Paris: Fayard, 1979); Vidalenc, *L'Exode*; Werth, *The Last Days*; Weygand, *Mémoires*, vol. 3.

34. Monday, June 10

From talks with Fernande Alphandery, Gilbert Bloch, Marguerite Bouchardeau, Walter Kerr, Mirra Lustig (née Gurewicz), Paul Paillole, Denise Schorr (née Khaitman).

Archives, Ministère des Affaires Etrangères, Papiers Maurice Dejean.

Bernacconi, "Le ultime ore"; Liebling, "Paris Postscript"; Lyet, "Paris 'Ville ouverte'?"; *Le Figaro*, June 10, 11, 1940; *Le Matin*, June 10, 1940; *Paris-Soir*, June 11, 1940; *Le Temps*, June 10–13, 1940.

Actes et documents du Saint-Siège, vol. 4; Andreu and Grover, *Drieu*; Arenstam, *Tapestry*; Assemblée Nationale, *Evénements survenus*, vol. 7; Audiat, *Paris*; Raymond Barillon, *Le Cas Paris-Soir* (Paris: A. Colin, 1959); Baudouin, *Neuf mois*; Beau de Loménie, *La Mort*; Beauvoir, *La Force de l'âge*; Gustave Bertrand, *Enigma* (Paris: Plon, 1973); Gilbert Bloch, *Enigma avant Ultra* (privately published, 1988); Bullitt, *For the President*; Cardinne-Petit, *Les Secrets*; De Gaulle, *Mémoires*, vol. 1; Ferdinand Dupuy, *Quand les allemands entrèrent à Paris* (privately published, 1947); Ehrenbourg, *La Nuit tombe*; Fontaine, *Last to Leave Paris; Foreign Relations*, vol. 2; Józef Garlínski, *Intercept: The Enigma War* (London:

Dent, 1979); Guariglia, *Ricordi; Histoire générale de la presse française*, vol. 3 (Paris: Presses Universitaires de France, 1972); Anne Jacques, *Pitié pour les hommes* (Paris: Seuil, 1943); Jouhandeau, *Journal*; Langeron, *Paris Juin 40*; Lazareff, *Dernière édition*; Leca, *La Rupture*; Lefebvre, *1939–1940*; Herbert R. Lottman, *Albert Camus* (New York: Doubleday, 1979); Maurois, *Bataille de France*; Monzie, *Ci-devant*; Murphy, *Diplomat*; Nenni, *Vingt ans*; Paillole, *Notre espion*; ———, *Services spéciaux*; Noël Pinelli, *Les journées de juin 1940 à Paris* (Paris: Centre d'Etudes des Questions Actuelles, 1951); Vidalenc, *L'Exode*; Villelume, *Journal*; Weygand, *Mémoires*, vol. 3; Col. Frederick Winterbotham, *The Ultra Secret* (New York: Harper & Row, 1974).

35. TUESDAY, JUNE 11

From conversations with Odette Daviet, Ruth Dixon, Walter Kerr, Henry Lemarié, Henri Quéffelec, Henri de Wailly.

Correspondence of Victor Serge, with permission of Vlady Kibalchich, courtesy of Richard Greeman.

U.S. National Archives, 124.516/277.

Bernacconi, "Le ultime ore"; Drechsler, "Les 'Emetteurs clandestins français' "; Gen. Pierre Héring, "Pourquoi n'a-t-on pas défendu Paris?" *Ecrits de Paris* (Paris), July 1947; Lyet, "Paris 'Ville ouverte'?"; Wright, "Ambassador Bullitt"; *New York Herald Tribune*, June 13, 1940; *Le Temps* (Angers), June 15, 1940.

Kazar Nergararian, "The American Church in Paris during German Occupation and After Liberation," 1945, courtesy American Church in Paris.

Assemblée Nationale, *Evénements survenus*; Emmanuel d'Astier, *Sept fois sept jours* (Paris: Minuit, 1947); Audiat, *Paris*; Azenor, *Vivre tout haut*; Jean-Louis Barrault, *Souvenirs pour demain* (Paris: Seuil, 1972); Georges Benoit-Guyod, *L'Invasion de Paris* (Paris: Scorpion, 1962); Bizardel, *Sous l'occupation*; Blum, *Mémoires*; Bullitt, *For the President*; Guy Chapman, *Why France Collapsed* (London: Cassell, 1968); Churchill, *Second World War*, vol. 2; Winston S. Churchill and Franklin D. Roosevelt, *The Complete Correspondence*, vol. 1 (Princeton: Princeton University Press, 1984); Depigny, "Juin 1940"; De Gaulle, *Mémoires*, vol. 1; Ehrenbourg, *La Nuit tombe*; Fontaine, *Last to Leave Paris*; Florence Gilliam, *France: A Tribute by an American Woman* (New York: Dutton, 1945); Goutard, *1940*; Guariglia, *Ricordi*; Peggy Guggenheim, *Ma Vie et mes folies* (Paris: Plon, 1987); Jeanneney, *Journal politique*; Jouhandeau, *Journal*; Richard Kluger, *The Paper: The Life and Death of the New York Herald Tribune* (New

York; Knopf, 1986); Langeron, *Paris Juin 40*; Lazareff, *Dernière édition*; Léautaud, *Journal littéraire*; Lebrun, *Témoignage*; Leca, *La Rupture*; Lefebvre, *1939–1940*; London, *L'amiral Estéva*; Mendès France, *Liberté*; Pinelli, *Les journées de juin*; République Française, Haute Cour de Justice, *Procès du Maréchal Pétain* (Paris: Imprimerie des Journaux Officiels, 1945); Reynaud, *La France*, vol. 2; ————, *Mémoires*, vol. 2; Reynolds, *The Wounded*; Charles R. Robertson, *The International Herald Tribune: The First Hundred Years* (New York: Columbia University Press, 1987); Serge, *Mémoires*; Spears, *Assignment*, vol. 2; Gen. Maxime Weygand, *En lisant les Mémoires de guerre du Général de Gaulle* (Paris: Flammarion, 1955); ————, *Mémoires*, vol. 3

36. WEDNESDAY, JUNE 12

From talks with Guy Bohn, Odette Daviet, Eugène Goormachtigh, Walter Kerr, Gen. Paul Nérot, Bertha Pons, Henri de Wailly.

Archives Nationales, 72 AJ 271: "Destruction de la Station Radio-télégraphique Militaire du Fort d'Issy-les-Moulineaux"; Archives, Préfecture de Police: "La Situation à Paris"; Archives, Service Historique de l'Armée de Terre, 31 N 2 Région de Paris.

Bernacconi, "Le ultime ore"; Drechsler, "Les 'Emetteurs clandestins français' "; Héring, "Pourquoi"; Lyet, "Paris 'Ville ouverte'?"; Schramm, "Paris se rend"; *Edition Parisienne de Guerre* (Paris), June 12, 1940; *La Gerbe* (Paris), July 11, 1940; *New York Herald Tribune*, June 13, 1940; *New York Times*, June 12, 1940; *Le Temps*, June 12, 1940.

Audiat, *Paris*; Baudouin, *Neuf mois*; Pierre Bourget, *Paris 1940–1944* (Paris: Plon, 1979); Bullitt, *For the President*; Butler, *History*, vol. 2; Churchill, *Second World War*, vol. 2; Churchill and Roosevelt, *Complete Correspondence*, vol. 1; Edmond Dubois, *Paris sans lumières*, in Gérard Walter, *La Vie à Paris sous l'occupation* (Paris: A. Collin, 1960); Anthony Eden, *The Eden Memoirs: The Reckoning* (London: Cassell, 1965); Fontaine, *Last to Leave Paris; Foreign Relations*, vol. 1; Gilliam, *France*; Goutard, *1940*; Groussard, *Chemins secrets*; Jouhandeau, *Journal*; Lacouture, *De Gaulle*, vol. 1; Laffargue, *Le Général Dentz*; Al Laney, *Paris Herald: The Incredible Newspaper* (New York: Appleton-Century, 1947); Langeron, *Paris Juin 40*; Léautaud, *Journal littéraire*; Lebrun, *Témoignage*; London, *L'amiral Estéva*; Nenni, *Vingt ans;* Nougères, *Dernière étape*; ————, *Le Véritable procès*; Pinelli, *Les journées de juin; Procès de Pétain*; Reynaud, *La France*, vol. 2; Bruce Singer, *100 Years of the Paris Trib* (New York: Abrams, 1987); Wailly, *De Gaulle*; Weygand, *Mémoires*, vol. 3.

37. THURSDAY, JUNE 13

From conversations with Rabbi Edouard Gurevitch, Walter Kerr, Jean Lesot, Michèle Miller (née Rogivue), Christian Pineau.

Archives, Ministère des Affaires Etrangères, Papiers 1940 Dejean, vol. 5; Archives, Préfecture de Police: "La Situation à Paris"; Archives, Service Historique de l'Armée de Terre, 31 N 2 Région de Paris; U.S. National Archives, 740.0011/3763, 124.516/287.

René Bluet transcript, trial of Gen. Henri Dentz, Archives Nationales 334 AP 31.

Bourderon, "Mai-septembre 1940"; Louis-Hermence Dethomas, "Porte d'Orléans," *Journal de la France* (Paris: Tallandier), April 12, 1971; Lyet, "Paris 'Ville ouverte'?"; Carlo Dall'Ongaro, "L'avanzata germanica," *Il Giornale d'Italia* (Rome), June 14, 1940; Schramm, "Paris se rend"; *La Croix* (Bordeaux), June 15, 1940; *Le Temps* (Angers), June 13–15, 1940.

Baudouin, *Neuf mois*; Pierre Bourget, *Histoires secrètes de l'occupation de Paris*, vol. 1 (Paris: Hachette, 1970); Hans Breithaupt, *Die Geschichte der 30. Infanterie-Division (1939–1945)* (Bad Neuheim: Podzun, 1955); Bullitt, *For the President*; Churchill, *Second World War*; Churchill and Roosevelt, *Complete Correspondence*, vol. 1; Cowles, *Looking for Trouble*; Dupuy, *Quand les allemands*; Wilhelm Ehmer, *La Nuit devant Paris* (Paris: Trois Epis, 1943); Fontaine, *Last to Leave Paris; Foreign Relations*, vol. 1; Goebbels, *Tagebücher*, vol. 1, 4; Goutard, *1940*; Groussard, *Chemins secrets*; ———, *Service secret*; Otto von Knobelsdorff, *Geschichte der Niedersächsischen Panzer-Division* (Bad Neuheim: Podzun, 1958); Laffargue, *Le Général Dentz*; Langeron, *Paris Juin 40*; Léautaud, *Journal littéraire*; Lebrun, *Témoignage*; Leca, *La Rupture*; Lefebvre, *1939–1940*; François Maspero, *Les Passagers du Roissy-Express* (Paris: Seuil, 1990); Murphy, *Diplomat*; Heinrich Oehmichen and Martin Mann, *Die Weg der 87. Infanterie-Division* (Eschwege: Traditionsgemeinschaft der 87. I.D., 1969); Paillat, *Le Désastre*, vol. 3; *Procès de Pétain*; Reynolds, *The Wounded*; Pierre Rocolle, *La Guerre de 1940*, vol. 2 (Paris: A. Colin, 1990); Norman E. Turorow, *War Crimes, War Criminals and War Crimes Trials* (New York: Greenwood Press, 1986); Vidalenc, *L'Exode*; Weygand, *Mémoires*, vol. 3; Wurmser, *Fidèlement vôtre*.

38. FRIDAY, JUNE 14

From talks with Erna Friedlander, Walter Kerr, Mitchel Levitas, Liliane Lévy-Osbert, Amalia Mangin, Michèle Miller (née Rogivue), Claude

Poirey. On Dr. Thierry de Martel: Otto Gresser, Dr. Alain Pierandrei, American Hospital of Paris.

Archives Nationales, W-III 279–280; Archives, Ville de Paris, 222/74/1, Parquet du Tribunal de Grande Instance: Morts sans suite; U.S. National Archives, 124.516/290.

Lefebvre, "Le rôle de la radio"; Isabelle Maheo de la Tocnaye, "Thierry de Martel," thesis, Université de Rennes (1979). Jean Lefranc, in *Journal de la France* 104 (April 19, 1971); Louis P. Lochner, "Germans Marched into a Dead Paris," *Life*, July 8, 1940; Yvette Ouvriez, in *Journal de la France* 104, April 19, 1971; Renée Parizot, in *Journal de la France* 104, April 19, 1971; Pietro Solari, "A Parigi con le truppe del Reich," *Corriere della Sera* (Milan), June 17, 1940; Max Taumann, in *Journal de la France* 104, April 19, 1971; *Bulletin Municipal Officiel de la Ville de Paris*, June 15, 1940; *Corriere della Sera* (Milan), June 16, 1940; *New York Times*, June 15, 1940; *Signal* (Berlin), July 7, 15, 1940; *Völkischer Beobachter*, June 15, 1940.

Otto Abetz, *Histoire d'une politique franco-allemande* (Paris: Stock, 1953); "The American Hospital"; Henri Amouroux, *La Vie des français sous l'occupation* (Paris: Fayard, 1961); Azenor, *Vivre tout haut; Archives secrètes de la Wilhelmstrasse*; Benoit-Guyod, *L'Invasion*; Gruber and Maurin, *Bernstein*; Bullitt, *For the President*; Churchill and Roosevelt, *Complete Correspondence*, vol. 1; Charles de Gaulle, *Lettres, Notes et Carnets* (Juin 1940–Juillet 1941) (Paris: Plon, 1981); ———, *Mémoires*, vol. 1; Depigny, "Juin 1940"; Youki Desnos, *Les Confidences de Youki* (Paris: Fayard, 1957); Dupuy, *Quand les allemands*; Ehmer, *La Nuit; Foreign Relations*, vol. 1; Girodias, *J'arrive!*; Goebbels, *Tagebücher*, vol. 1, 4; Groussard, *Service secret*; Jouhandeau, *Journal*; Langeron, *Paris Juin 40*; Léautaud, *Journal littéraire*; London, *L'amiral Estéva*; André Maurois, *Destins exemplaires* (Paris: Plon, 1952); ———, *Mémoires* (Paris: Flammarion, 1970); Murphy, *Diplomat*; Oehmichen and Mann, *Der Weg*; David Pryce-Jones, *Paris in the Third Reich* (New York: Holt, Rinehart & Winston, 1981); Robert, *Notre Métro*; William Shirer, *Berlin Diary* (New York: Grosset & Dunlap, 1943); Walter, *La Vie à Paris*; Wurmser, *Fidèlement vôtre*.

39. AFTER JUNE 14

From talks with Odette Daviet, Bertrand Goldschmidt, Rabbi Edouard Gurevitch, Peter Halban, Anne M. Imhoff, Walter Kerr, Mirra Lustig (née Gurewicz), Michèle Miller (née Rogivue), Els Placzek (formerly Mrs. Hans Halban), Claude Poirey, Maurice Zuber. With the cooperation of the Collège de France and Jacques Bounolleau, chargé d'archives at the Commissariat à l'Energie Atomique in Paris. Archives, Préfecture de Police: "La Situation à Paris"; U.S. National Archives, 124.513, 124.516, 124.51 series.

Raymond Dallidet, "Eté 40 à Paris," *Cahiers d'Histoire de l'Institut de Recherches Marxistes* (Paris) 42 (1990); Depigny, "Juin 40"; G. Gilguy, "L'histoire des brevets de base de l'équipe Joliot," *Bull. d'Informations Scientifiques et Techniques* (Paris, Commissariat à l'Energie Atomique) 71, April 1973; Wright, "Ambassador Bullitt."

Abetz, *Histoire*; Henri Amouroux, *Le 18 Juin 1940* (Paris: Fayard, 1964); Baudouin, *Neuf mois*; Beach, *Shakespeare & Co.*; Philippe Bourdrel, *Histoire des juifs de France* (Paris: Albin Michel, 1974); Will Brownell and Richard N. Billings, *So Close to Greatness: A Biography of William C. Bullitt* (New York: Macmillan, 1987); Bullitt, *For the President*; Churchill and Roosevelt, *Complete Correspondence*, vol. 1; Courtois, *Le PCF*; Jean-Louis Crémieux-Brilhac and Hélène Eck, "France," in *La Guerre des ondes* (Paris: A. Colin, 1985); Dupuy, *Quand les allemands*; Ehrenbourg, *La Chute de Paris*; ———, *La Nuit tombe; Foreign Relations*, vol. 1; Gilliam, *France*; Anatol Goldberg, *Ilya Ehrenburg* (New York: Viking, 1984); Bertrand Goldschmidt, *Le Complex atomique* (Paris: Fayard, 1980); ———, *Pionniers*; Jäckel, *La France*; George F. Kennan, *Sketches from a Life* (New York: Pantheon, 1989); Laffargue, *Le Gen. Dentz*; Laney, *Paris Herald*; Langeron, *Paris Juin 40*; Lebrun, *Témoignage*; Leca, *La Rupture*; Lefebvre, *1939–1940*; Noëlle Loriot, *Irène Joliot-Curie* (Paris: Presses de la Renaissance, 1991); Henri Michel, *Paris allemand* (Paris: Albin Michel, 1981); Ministère des Affaires Etrangères, *Inventaire de la Collection des Papiers 1940* (Paris: Imprimerie Nationale, 1990); Murphy, *Diplomat*; Oehmichen, *Die Weg*; Paillole, *Notre espion*; Pryce-Jones, *Paris*; Oskar Reile, *Treff Lutetia Paris* (Munich: Welsermühl, 1973); Reynaud, *La France*, vol. 2; Snyder, *Guerre sur tous les fronts*; Walter, *La Vie à Paris*; Weart, *Scientists in Power*; Weygand, *Mémoires*, vol. 3.

40. Sunday, June 23

"L'Armistice vu par un officier allemand," *Le Monde*, July 1–2, 1940.

Abetz, *Histoire*; Gen. Hans Baür, *J'étais le pilote d'Hitler* (Paris: France Empire, 1957); Arno Breker, *Paris, Hitler et moi* (Paris: Presses de la Cité, 1970); Alan Bullock, *Hitler: A Study in Tyranny* (New York: Harper & Row, 1962); Adolf Hitler, *Libres propos sur la guerre et la paix* (Paris: Flammarion, 1952); Jäckel, *La France*; Langeron, *Paris Juin 40*; Mendès France, *Liberté*; Pryce-Jones, *Paris*; Shirer, *Berlin Diary*; Albert Speer,

Inside the Third Reich (New York: Macmillan, 1970); Walter Warlimont, *Inside Hitler's Headquarters* (New York: Praeger, 1964).

EPILOGUE

From conversations with Bernt Engelmann.

Emmanuel Berl, *Interrogatoire par Patrick Modiano* (Paris: Gallimard, 1976); Churchill, *Blood, Sweat and Tears*; Bernt Engelmann, *In Hitler's Germany* (London: Methuen, 1988); Joseph Goebbels, *The Goebbels Diaries (1939–1941)* (London: Hamish Hamilton, 1982); Langeron, *Paris Juin 40*.

INDEX

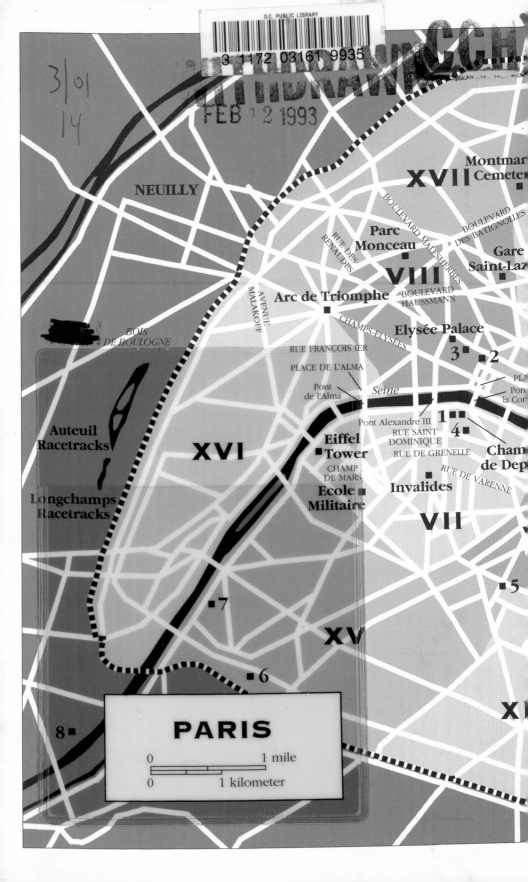

3/01
14

NEUILLY

XVII Montmar Cemeter

BOULEVARD MALESHERBES

BOULEVARD DES BATIGNOLLES

Parc Monceau

RUE DES RENAUDES

VIII

Gare Saint-Laz

Arc de Triomphe

BOULEVARD HAUSSMANN

CHAMPS-ELYSÉES

Elysée Palace

AVENUE MALAKOFF

BOIS DE BOULOGNE

RUE FRANÇOIS IER

PLACE DE L'ALMA

Pont de l'Alma

Seine

3 ■ ■ 2

PLA
Pon
la Cor

Pont Alexandre III

Auteuil Racetracks

XVI

Eiffel Tower ■

RUE SAINT DOMINIQUE

1 ■ ■

■ 4

Cham
de Dep

CHAMP DE MARS

RUE DE GRENELLE

Longchamps Racetracks

Ecole Militaire ■

■ **Invalides**

RUE DE VARENNE

VII

■ 5

■ 7

XV

■ 6

XI

8 ■

PARIS

0   1 mile

0   1 kilometer